Small Business Management in Cross-Cultural Environments

Products and services created by small and medium-sized organizations account for the vast majority of economic activity across the globe. These organizations will prove vitally important to the emerging and developing economies that will shape future decades.

Small Business Management in Cross-Cultural Environments is one of very few books to take the cross-cultural context as an opportunity to analyse and discuss the key concepts of small firm management in different parts of the world. This textbook covers important topics, such as:

- the global economic development process;
- entrepreneurship;
- the role of government; and
- SME growth and collaborations in a global context.

By explaining how culture shapes and conditions the reality of small businesses and how organizational theories and models fail as management tools, this book fills an important gap. Supplemented by a compendium of compelling case studies drawn from across the world, and based upon 25 years of international research by the author, *Small Business Management in Cross-Cultural Environments* is a useful guide for students and practitioners of SME and International Management.

Per Lind is Professor of Industrial Development at Gotland University, Sweden. He has published several books, and made contributions to many others, on management and developing countries. He is married and has two sons and a daughter.

Small Business Management in Cross-Cultural Environments

Per Lind

Routledge
Taylor & Francis Group

LONDON AND NEW YORK

First published 2012
by Routledge
2 Park Square, Milton Park, Abingdon, Oxon OX14 4RN

Simultaneously published in the USA and Canada
by Routledge
711 Third Avenue, New York, NY 10017

Routledge is an imprint of the Taylor & Francis Group, an informa business

British Library Cataloguing in Publication Data
A catalogue record for this book is available from the British Library

Library of Congress Cataloging in Publication Data
Lind, Per, 1940–
Small business management in cross-cultural environments / Per Lind.
p. cm.
Includes bibliographical references and index.
1. Small business—Developing countries. 2. Small business—Cross-cultural studies.
3. Small business—Developing countries—Case studies. 4. Small business—Cross-
cultural studies—Case studies. I. Title.
HD2346.5.L558 2011
658.02′2091724—dc23
2011021921

ISBN 978-0-415-59252-9 (hbk)
ISBN 978-0-415-67818-6 (pbk)
ISBN 978-0-203-15546-2 (ebk)

Typeset in Times New Roman
by Book Now Ltd, London

Printed and bound in Great Britain by
TJ International Ltd, Padstow, Cornwall

Contents

Tables

Figures

Boxes

Preface

Small and medium enterprises (SMEs) have emerged from a rather peripheral role in earlier business literature to the central focus that the sector occupies today in government policies, in academic research and among international organizations such as the World Bank and the United Nations. In high-income countries as well as in the poorer parts of the world, the expectations that small businesses will create jobs and that these jobs will eventually lead to the alleviation of poverty are as high today as they have been for many years past. It is true that small firms – in particular very small firms with no or only few employees – account for the vast majority of all jobs. But it is also true that very small firms hardly grow to create more jobs – something that also applies to somewhat larger firms. The situation, therefore, is that the growth of the small business sector lags behind the growth of the population seeking jobs.

Some of the difficulties encountered when trying to understand and explain what hampers the growth of the small business sector are related to the sheer complexity of the small firm community. The heterogeneity of SMEs can create insurmountable problems for academics and policy-makers seeking universal explanations for SME growth, success and competitiveness. Small firms are usually locally-based and therefore subject to local conditions: these conditions may be characterized by cultural norms and behaviour which are not reflected in general theories and models. By responding to signals from the local market, firms may exploit niches that lead to a successful business but not necessarily to growth.

Globalization and the global economy have been regarded by many as providing small business with potential for growth, and a few small firms in the developed countries have been able to exploit this opportunity and find new markets for their products and services. However, a majority of small firms in low- and middle-income countries are becoming increasingly challenged, as many of them have yet to find any meaningful market access opportunities for their products. Empirical evidence shows that globalization has contributed to further marginalisation of a large number of countries, in particular, small and vulnerable economies and the least developed countries.

In the short term, business opportunities in a majority of developing countries may come from various forms of partnerships between local and foreign enterprises, facilitated by the levelling of the playing field in world economic relations. However, a necessary precondition for such partnerships to be of mutual interest is that the local partner in the developing country learns to operate in accordance with modern management principles, emphasizing a well structured business strategy, serviceability to clients and efficient costing and pricing functions. The competitive strength of the local partner is its familiarity with and knowledge of local market behaviour and values. Local managers therefore need to integrate modern management principles, adapting them to local practices and norms.

Despite this, the predominant management, organization and economic principles and models are still characterized by views, norms and values having deep roots in Western culture. Models imported into other cultural settings without being integrated into the cultural context remain alien and do not contribute to the development of indigenous and more appropriate management concepts and theories. Although there is a growing awareness and understanding of management theory and techniques as being deeply culture-bound, management education at the academic level in developing countries is treated as largely context-free. Indigenously-developed models and theories are largely non-existent, whereas Western theories are readily accepted.

The challenges to Western management models are central to the current debate on management and culture, in which two opposite standpoints define the spectrum of discourse. One standpoint claims that the non-cultural factors (which act in the same direction upon management in all cultures) are getting stronger; the other standpoint has it that, while some features of particular 'recipes' may be readily transferred between contexts, others require substantial modification or translation. Cultural differences have a major impact on how organizations function. Since national cultures change slowly, transfer of technology, knowledge and skills will always be reinterpreted by the receiving culture, and this will set firm limits on the tendencies to managerial convergence. Any conclusion on this issue must necessarily be a tentative one. It is within this context that this book has been written.

The book has two perspectives, each perspective making up a part of the book. Part 1 is descriptive and assumes that small firms are subject to – rather than lead – changes in the world economy and the economic development process. Whereas large firms – in particular, multi-national companies – are active players on the world stage where they can to some extent set their own rules, small firms are compelled to act in accordance with local rules and regulations. Due to the large number of small and medium firms, their accumulated contribution to economic growth at the national level is significant, even if the individual contribution per firm is rather limited. For an understanding of the varying conditions for the small business sector in both time and space, it has been considered relevant and necessary to include cross-cultural outlines and their characteristics as described in Part 1.

Part 2 is the normative part, posing the question: what is needed for SMEs to contribute to economic development? Keeping in mind the fact that small firms are local and do not fit easily into pre-constructed moulds, the focus of this part is on management and the importance of creating awareness about business realities defined, not by general theories and models, but by the cultural environment where the firms operate. This cannot exclude the fact that small firms need to comply with international rules aimed at removing hazardous products from domestic and international trade.

This book is the result of many years of research in developing countries, where small and medium enterprises have been the focus most of the time. Ten years of consultation for international organizations in around twenty countries in Africa, Asia and Latin America and academic research on SME related issues have provided the background for the following pages. This was complemented by several visits as guest lecturer at various universities in Europe, Africa, Asia and Latin America, which offered many opportunities to study local enterprises and to participate in valuable projects and discussions.

Many people have contributed to developing my understanding and knowledge of SMEs and SME management in different parts of the world, and I wish to place on record my thanks to the following colleagues: Heinz Erbe (Technical University Berlin), Edmundo Sepulveda (Universidad Tecnica Federico Santa Maria, Valparaiso), Ivan Zambrano (Escuela Politecnica Nacional, Quito), Raul Dichiara (Universidad del Sur, Bahia-Blanca), Kobus Visser

(University of the Western Cape, Cape Town), Eslyn Isaacs (University of the Western Cape, Cape Town), Julian Nananyakkara (Kelaniya University, Colombo), among many others.

I am most indebted to Richard Koehler (Gotland University) and Bengt Sandkull (former Linköping University) for their valuable support and comments during the preparation of this book.

For the text in the following pages and for any misconceptions, obscurities and doubtful conclusions, I carry full responsibility!

Part 1

The cross-cultural SME environment

Cross-cultural studies seek to describe and compare phenomena in different cultural, social and economic environments. Cross-cultural studies focusing on small businesses are based on different kinds of data, from official statistics to research reports, and the rich literature of cross-cultural studies which encompasses a wide variety of perspectives and aspects. An individual author's own background, based on knowledge and experience gained in different cultural settings, makes any book a personal document and more or less different from other similar publications.

Official statistics are available from international organizations and statistical offices of individual countries. However, formal faults and shortcomings reduce the usefulness of such statistical information. These arise from inappropriate data collection mechanisms, inconsistency in definitions and uncertainty about original data accuracy. A considerable amount of research and literature about small and medium enterprises in international contexts makes reference to such statistics without mentioning or even being aware of its potential lack of reliability.

The study of facts and phenomena in other cultures requires that activities and events are understood and can be accounted for. Language is important not only as a means of communication but also in defining the names of subjects and activities. As the following extract demonstrates, local names which are deeply culturally-rooted cannot always be translated into another language while keeping their original meaning: distortion of words and meanings becomes a complication in cross-cultural studies. The extract goes on to consider African traditional political thought using terms not of African origin but that come from foreign countries, particularly from Europe: the problem arises from having to formulate concepts through translations.

> In religion, for instance the Christian missionaries with the assistance of their few African proselytes translated "God" into all sorts of words. In Acholiland, God was translated as Jok, although, as we have been told, the term Jok does not mean the "High God" which the white missionaries had in mind. The term normally means the God of a particular Acholi chiefdom so that the Jok of an Acholi clan or Chiefdom A is not necessarily the Jok of the Acholi clan or Chiefdom B. For instance, the Jok of the Koch Chiefdom, one of the largest chiefdoms in Acholi, is Lebeja; whereas the Jok of Padibe Chiefdom is Lan'gol. To make it even more complicated, we find that the Payira Chiefdom has seven clans and each of these clans has got its own Jok. The seven Jogi of the Payira people, representing the seven clans of Paiyira are Jok Kalawinya, Jok Kilegaber, Jok Byeyo, Jok Ona, Jok Lwamwoci, Jok Ang'weya, and Jok Goma. In other words there is no one Jok for all the Acholi clans; and, consequently, Jok cannot be said to represent the Christian High God who is supposed to be the God of all men, including, of course, the Acholi in northern Uganda.
>
> So it is with the African traditional political thought. We are faced with the problem of having to apply European terms to explain concepts which are uniquely African; we

have to formulate concepts of African experiences and thought-systems in terms of European languages and philosophy. The result of this is that while we may be able to conceive and appreciate African ideas on politics, economics, religion or culture, we may be unable, because of our inadequacy in the English or French language, to express these ideas articulately and meaningfully. When this happens, we may then conclude that the African ideas are inadequate, poor or even barbarian. On the other hand, while we recognise the problems involved in the use of European languages in explaining African concepts, we cannot all the same avoid using these languages in discussing African political thought because in Africa we do not have one single language in which all Africans can exchange their own ideas and their own experiences in their own language or thought-system. That is why, while a Muganda can sincerely enjoy a joke with an Englishman, he may not be able to enjoy the same joke if it is presented by a Matabele with whom he shares the African continent. (Mutibwa 1977)

This rather long quotation from *African Heritage and the New Africa* by Phares Mukasa Mutibwa of Makerere University in Uganda spells out a picture of African culture at a detailed level that is unusual in general descriptions. Similarly-detailed levels are, of course, not necessary every time a cultural phenomenon is to be described. The dilemma is, however, that we cannot know how much detailed understanding is necessary to fully grasp a cultural phenomenon. It is possible that cultures are incommensurable and it is therefore not possible to fully understand unless one is part of that particular culture.

Chapters 1 to 5 are characterized by a macro perspective which assumes enterprises are parts of a development process taking place in their operating environment. Since a process requires a structure that is fixed during the time frame of interest, this structure is primarily defined by the legal system, the political system and traditions and values from the culture. Within this structure different processes take place, one such process being the development of the small business sector. The parameters that may vary in this process include management styles, employee attitudes and the strategies of the firms, all being subject to the structure that provides the limits within which the process parameters may vary. The picture of structures given in this first part is intended to provide the background for Part 2.

Chapter 1 presents a picture of small business in different parts of the world in terms of definitions, demography and various statistical data. Growth of the SME sector is discussed and the small business sector of four is scrutinised in some detail.

Chapter 2 gives an overview of economic development, and includes a discussion about different measures of development. After an initial discussion of SMEs and economic development (expanded in the next chapter) a number of influential development researchers are profiled.

In Chapter 3, the question is raised as to the extent small firms contribute to economic development. The concept of added value is introduced as an important parameter for the discussion of small business growth.

Chapter 4 discusses entrepreneurship and asks if the entrepreneur and the small business manager play the same roles. The motives for starting up a small business in different cultures are discussed, as well as the nature of entrepreneurship in cross-cultural environments.

Chapter 5 considers whether Government is facilitator or 'trouble-maker' for SME growth. What are the roles of Government in supporting the SME sector, and why is it that otherwise laudable interventions can have counterproductive effects?

Reference

Mutibwa, P. M. (1977) *African Heritage and the New Africa*. Nairobi: East African Literature Bureau.

1   Small business in the world

Introduction

'Small business' is not a homogenous concept and cannot be treated as such. In many countries, small business is all business, whereas in others the small business sector is distinct from large firms. Given the ambition of this book to give an overview of small firms, their operational environments and their management in a cross-cultural context, the choice of aspects and perspectives become critical. The external perspective dominates in the first part of the book, where small firms are seen in their respective contexts characterized by political systems, economic sectors and competence levels. The role of governments and public administration differ widely between regions and countries in respect of industry support. While insufficient access to risk capital, hindering bureaucracy, bribery and corruption and inefficient legal and infrastructure systems form part of the business reality for many small firms in many countries, the corresponding situations for small business in Europe, North America and Japan are both different and more supportive. It is inevitable that the conditions for efficient management depend crucially on the influence of different factors prevailing in different parts of the world.

The dominance of the service sector as contributor to the national economy in high-income countries[1] creates business opportunities and has been important for entrepreneurship and small business growth. In low- and middle-income countries, where the agriculture and manufacturing sectors are significant for the domestic economy, the production of goods is important, and many small firms belong to the manufacturing sector. Although in discussing small business this book does not distinguish between different industry sectors, examples and case studies are drawn from many different sectors. However, the variety and types of firms are such that it is impossible to include all of them in one book. In the manufacturing sector, firms range from those of low technological level relying on manual labour, to highly advanced firms with fully automated production processes. Although different types of firm in different environments have different needs in respect of management theories and tools, a more generic set of business theories is also useful in widely different cultural contexts.

Questions and aspects related to the growth of the small business sector is a dominant theme throughout Part 1, as well as in Part 2. The focus is motivated not only by the significant interest that has been placed on small firms for their expected contribution to job creation and economic growth, but also by the disappointment and growing mistrust in small firms as engines of growth in the economy. This view requires a shift in perspective from the external macroeconomic perspective, where small firms can be assessed in their contribution to society growth, to the internal perspective, where performance and management of individual firms are viewed based on their own individual conditions.

'Small business' is an ill-defined concept, not least because 'small' is a relative term. A small business in a Western country may be regarded as a medium-size or even a big business in a developing country. A small business can be anything from a one person bicycle repair shop in a street in Hanoi to a high-tech manufacturing company in Stockholm with around 50 employees. It can be officially registered or not, it can be an entrepreneurial activity that has just started or it can be a stable business that has been operating in the market for many years. The European Union (EU) has adopted a standard definition that classifies small and medium firms into three categories according to number of employees and annual turnover. Firms with less than ten employees are thus classified as 'micro enterprises', firms with between ten and 50 employees are referred to as small and those with between 50 and 250 employees as medium-sized enterprises; firms with more than 250 employees are large enterprises. Table 1.1 summarises the EU definition, also used by the World Bank and United Nations.

Referring to small and medium enterprises (SMEs) as a group can give the impression that firms have essential features in common. In fact, many medium-size firms have more in common with the lower end of large enterprises than with small firms. Above a certain size, firms tend to develop organizational structures and hierarchies that are characteristic of larger firms. There is no definite measure when this happens, but at around 20–25 employees administration begins to need a more diversified organizational structure. The differences in administrative structure between the smallest and largest firms are so great that in many ways it is hard to see that the two species belong to the same genus (Penrose 2009).

Not only do definitions of SMEs vary between countries, they can also vary within the same country. Different industry sectors may have their own classifications for micro, small and medium-sized firms. Moreover, in a broader international context, reference to SMEs as something well-defined is not always very meaningful, since in many countries virtually all businesses are SMEs. The label may therefore not be significantly different from speaking of the full and diverse set of domestic enterprises.

The heterogeneity of the SME business sector thus creates difficulties when seeking universal explanations for SME-related issues, such as growth and competitiveness (Tilley and Tonge 2003). The absence of a uniform definition also makes statistical analysis hazardous when we move outside the EU where the definition shown in Table 1.1 no longer applies. Although the World Bank and the United Nations follow the same definition, the composition of the SME sector can differ between countries. For example, agriculture firms in the United States are generally not represented in SME statistics, likewise small businesses in Japan owned by large firms are not separately classified as SMEs. Comparing SME-related statistics on macro levels between countries can therefore be hazardous and yield misleading results. Below, the definitions of the small business sector used in a selection of

Table 1.1 Definition of small and medium enterprises in the European Union

Criterion	Micro firm	Small firm	Medium firm
Maximum number of employees	9	49	249
Maximum annual turnover (millions USD)	–	5	31
Maximum annual balance sheet (millions USD)	–	4	21

countries are compared. However, we begin by noting that definitions may vary even within the same country.

Variety in SME definitions – an example

The following example from Sri Lanka shows how different organizations within the same country define a SME, depending on the aspects of a company of primary interest to the organization.

The official definition of SMEs in Sri Lanka is based on assets (fixed and current), but excludes land and buildings, and leads to the following four categories of firms:

Very small/micro enterprise:	Assets below 10,000 USD
Small enterprise:	Assets between 10, 000 and 200,000 USD
Medium enterprise:	Assets between 200,000 and 500,000 USD
Large enterprise:	Assets above 500,000 USD

In addition to this official definition, different organizations apply their own definitions, making statistical analysis of the SME sector complicated. Some examples are given in Table 1.2.

Comparison between selected countries

The variables normally used to define SMEs are employment, annual sales revenue and annual balance of assets. Employment figures dominate in European countries whereas in other parts of the world the value of assets together with revenue figures is more common. Annual assets can include or exclude land and buildings, and employment can be permanent, permanent *and* part time or converted to full time equivalents. As in the example of Sri Lanka above, different organizations can use different definitions. Likewise, different industry sectors have their own definitions as to the number of employees in a small and medium business.

Table 1.2 Official SME definitions in Sri Lanka

Organization	SME definition
Department of Census and Statistics	No capital limits. Less than 25 employees.
Industrial Development Board	Characterized by fixed assets (excluding land and buildings) and with permanent working capital not exceeding 35,000 USD. Less than 50 employees.
Department of Small Industries	A firm with initial capital not exceeding 35,000 USD. No employment limit.
Ministry of Rural Industrial Development	Value of machinery and buildings not exceeding 35,000 USD. No more than 50 employees.
Central Bank and National Development Bank	A firm, the value of whose fixed assets (excluding land and buildings) does not exceed 45,000 USD. Electricity usage must be less than 50 kilowatt hours. No employment limit.
Small & Medium Scale Industrialists Association[a]	A firm with net assets (excluding lands and buildings) not exceeding 140,000 USD.

Note
a Based on the policy adopted by the Asian Development Bank.

Table 1.3 SME definitions in selected countries, measured by employment

Country	Organization/sector	Micro	Small	Medium
China	Industry, construction, transport			< 2000
	Retail			< 500
	Wholesale			< 200
Colombia		1–10	11–50	51–200
Egypt		< 5	5–14	15–49
Indonesia	Department of Trade and Industry		< 19	20–99
	Centre for SME Development		< 49	50–99
Japan	Industry, construction, transport			< 300
	Service			< 100
Malaysia	Manufacturing, agriculture-based	< 5	5–50	51–150
	Service, information technology	< 5	5–19	20–50
Pakistan		1–9	10–35	36–99
Peru		1–10	11–100	
Tanzania		1–4	5–49	50–99
Ukraine		0–10	11–50	51–250

For a variety of reasons, comparison between countries using data from Table 1.3 (or any similar table) is hazardous because the variables may have very different meanings in different contexts. For example, fixed assets in one country can be the value of advanced technology and tools, whereas in another less-developed country fixed assets can be based on recycled second hand material or tools, the value of which is difficult to assess in economic terms. The Peruvian economist Hernando De Soto[2] has discussed alternative approaches to land and assets valuations among the poor (De Soto 2000). His research is focused on the informal economy and whether property rights could make homeowners out of the world's poor squatters.

The table shows that the upper limits of the three categories vary substantially, from 15 to 100 employees for small firms and from 50 to 2,000 for middle-sized firms. In the following section, the SME sectors in different countries are compared using some of the common measures, such as number of SMEs per 1,000 population. Due to the variation in SME definitions, it goes without saying that the data have a high degree of uncertainty!

Comparing the SME sector in different countries

Due to the great variety in the way the SME sector is defined in different countries, various benchmarks are used to enable comparisons to be made.

Box 1.1 Mini-encyclopaedia: benchmarking

The term benchmarking was first used by cobblers to measure people's feet for shoes. They would place someone's foot on a 'bench' and mark it out to make the pattern for the shoes. Benchmarking is most often used to measure performance using a specific indicator (such as cost per unit measure, productivity per unit measure, cycle time of something per unit measure or defects per unit measure) resulting in a performance metric that can be used to make comparisons.

Also referred to as 'best practice benchmarking' or 'process benchmarking', it is a process used in management and particularly strategic management, in which organizations evaluate various aspects of their processes in relation to best practice companies' processes, usually within a peer group defined for the purposes of comparison. This then allows organizations to develop plans on how to make improvements or adapt specific best practices, usually with the aim of increasing some aspect of performance. Benchmarking may be a one-off event, but is often treated as a continuous process in which organizations continually seek to improve their practices.

Source: Wikipedia.

Table 1.4 gives the values of two macro benchmarks for the agriculture, manufacturing and service sub-sectors of the overall SME sector of various countries. One benchmark is the number of SMEs per 1,000 population, the other gross national income (GNI) per capita expressed as purchase power parity (PPP) in USD.

Figure 1.1 attempts to show from a macro perspective how, on average, the number of SMEs per 1,000 population varies with increasing wealth, measured by GNI. The diagram reflects the data presented in Table 1.4, but it is obvious that not all countries fit with the diagram. For example, Italy and the United States are both high-income countries with 72 and 20 SMEs per 1,000 population respectively, far above and below the 50 mark level in the diagram. The lack of a uniform SME definition system makes statistical analysis of SMEs uncertain.

According to Bannock (2005) the numerical (size and volume) importance of small firms changes in character as countries move through different stages of economic development. There is evidence that across a large number of countries the share of SMEs in output and employment tends to decline with economic development, and the average size of SMEs tend to increase. For reasons already stated, statistical data from the SME sector must, however, be handled with care!

Table 1.4 Data from selected countries showing number of SMEs per 1,000 population and GNI per capita, measured by PPP in USD

Country	SMEs per 1,000	GNI per capita
Algeria	18.8	8,130
Brazil	27.4	10,260
Britain	73.8	36,240
China	6.3	6,710
Egypt	26.8	5,470
France	43.3	35,020
Germany	42.0	36,960
Italy	72.0	31,330
Jordan	26.8	5,840
Lebanon	47.2	13,230
Morocco	15.2	4,450
Romania	14.0	14,460
Sweden	58.0	38,560
USA	20.0	46,790

Source: OECD and United Nations Development Programme (2001).

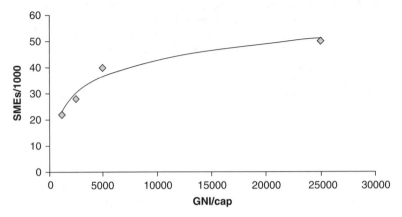

Figure 1.1 Number of SMEs per 1,000 population.
Source: International Finance Corporation, Washington, DC, 2006.

SME statistics

The discussion above shows the difficulties that arise when analysing and comparing SME-related issues using statistical data. This also applies to determining the number of SMEs in a country. Based on official data from the national statistics board in Sweden the number of SMEs in Sweden in 2003 was 854,742. According to Eurostat (the statistical unit of the EU), the number of SMEs in Sweden in the same year was 485,000, a ratio of nearly 2:1. A variety of reasons explain the discrepancy, for example, agriculture and some other sectors were included in one type of data but excluded in others. In certain countries, one-person firms (zero employees) are not included in the formal SME statistics.

Statistical data on business activities are mostly based on formally-registered firms and often, but not always, on estimations of businesses in the informal sector. Informal sectors exist in developed as well as in developing countries, although their share of total economic activity is smaller in countries with high levels of GDP. Taking Egypt as an example, informal firms constitute around 85 per cent of all SMEs in the country.

The foregoing suggests that statistics on SME are highly unreliable and any conclusions must be drawn with great caution. Elaborate statistical analysis of SMEs in a cross-cultural context therefore has limited value to due to the lack of reliable definitions and statistical data. This makes it all the more remarkable that much of the literature related to development theory in general – and SME sector development in particular – is founded on various types of statistical analysis models (economic, industry) *as if* the data were mostly relevant and accurate. Many of these models emanate from Western countries where more reliable data can (but far from always!) be found.

The increasing need for reliable data creates challenges for statistical offices in many countries around the world, many of which are already weak and lacking in capacity. Reliable and accurate statistical data are therefore almost non-existent. The lack of uniform principles to define, collect and aggregate data makes comparison between countries hazardous. The majority of statistical data available on many countries in Africa, Asia and Latin America is therefore not suitable for comparative analysis. The systems of data gathering do not comply with the same standards (methodology, definition and mode of calculation of indicators or of economic aggregates). Use of faulty statistical data for economic analyses and private sector development can lead to inappropriate policy recommendations or strategies.

SME sector growth

Small business has always been a significant component of society. Small firms were always present in various forms, as shopkeepers and artisans, as carpenters and blacksmiths and as plumbers and repair shops. Small-scale business activities have always contributed to GNI and created work opportunities for people. But small business was never considered anything other than a peripheral part of the economy when compared with large enterprises, which were seen as the drivers of economic growth. Alfred Chandler, one of the more influential American management scholars and known for his support of large firms, suggested that the big industrial company has been the engine of economic growth for the past 100 years, and will continue to be so for the next 100 (Chandler 1977). Chandler argued that 'the economies of scale and scope bestowed by size had been grossly undervalued by the 'small is beautiful' brigade' (*The Economist* 1990). Also development economists such as Raúl Prebish insisted that new and dynamic industries in Latin America required economies of scale for attracting investments, new technology and high productivity to soak up an expanding labour force (Dosman 2008). However, towards the end of the 1960s and during the 1970s, it became professionally respectable to suggest that reversal – or at least a weakening – of the trend towards ever-larger organizational size had occurred (Piore and Sabel 1984). In spite of this, large firms are still the major contributors to economic growth, and from a decade-long experience it is clear that the SME sector is not sufficient by itself to create successful economic growth (McIntyre 2003).

The arguments in favour of scale are to a great extent based on more efficient utilization of resources, such as capital and labour. The productivity of large enterprises, measured as added value production per employee, has been steadily increasing for many years, which means that the net demand for more employment has declined. Labour-intensive production has been replaced by more capital-intensive production requiring a skilled workforce and investments in new technology. The productivity of large firms has increased to the extent that production output can be increased substantially without a corresponding increase in employment. At the beginning of the 1970s it was realised that large enterprises will not contribute significantly to new job creation. As a consequence, the remaining potential for job creation was expected to lie in the small business sector.

The creation of jobs is therefore a central theme in the economic agenda of practically all governments today, at the same time as more people add to the potential work force from population growth in primarily low-and middle-income countries. *Global Employment Trends* published by the International Labour Organization (ILO) reports that the global youth unemployment rate reached 13.4 per cent in 2009, an increase of 1.6 per cent relative to 2007. This represents the largest increase since at least 1991, the earliest year for which global estimates are available (International Labour Organization 2010). The unemployment rate in the developed economies and the EU jumped to 8.4 per cent in 2009, up from 6.0 per cent in 2008 and 5.7 per cent in 2007. The number of unemployed in the region is estimated to have surged by more than 13.7 million between 2007 and 2009, with an increase of nearly 12 million unemployed in 2009 alone. Employment in the industrial sectors has suffered more than employment in agriculture or services (ibid.). In Latin America and the

Caribbean, the unemployment rate is estimated to have risen from 7 per cent in 2008 to 8.2 per cent in 2009, amounting to 4 million additional jobless in 2009. Current estimates also indicate that the proportion of workers in extreme poverty ranged from 7.0 to 9.9 per cent in 2009, an increase of up to 3.3 per cent from 2008 (ibid.). If small and medium firms are to accommodate even a fraction of these jobless people, significant initiatives by governments and others are needed to promote growth of small firms. The creation of new one-person firms which do not grow and which are more than likely to disappear within a three-year period does not represent the optimal solution (though it has to be said that a one-person business is far better than one jobless person).

Aspects of growth

Assessing the growth and importance of the SME sector requires the number of firms and employment to be quantified, and three types of measures are used. Growth is measured in terms of number of firms, in the size of firms and as contribution to GNI. In the political rhetoric of governments, there is a tendency to focus on the entrepreneurial aspect of creating new firms, disregarding the fact that the survival of new firms beyond three years is rather low in many countries, falling below 50 per cent in some countries. The approach of high-lighting the number of firms has taken many governments needs to be combined with a quali-tative approach which focuses on firms with the ability to grow and to survive. Rather than prioritizing the setting up of new firms, existing firms that have proved their ability to survive should be the primary group to be supported by government initiatives. For the economy as a whole, the average productivity of newly-established firms, measured as the ability to produce efficiently, is low compared to older firms. From a statistical point of view, newly-established firms can even reduce economic growth (Institutet för TillväxtPolitiska Studier 2007).[3]

A firm's contribution to the country's GNI is measured by the amount of value that is cre-ated. Added value per employee gives an indication of the effectiveness of internal processes in terms of cost reduction to develop and introduce new or improved products (Jones 2003). Small firms' ability to produce added value is, however, generally lower than for large firms, not only in absolute terms (which would be obvious) but also relatively, as added value in relation to revenue or sales.

Newly-created firms grow slowly and are therefore a doubtful measure of expansionist economic policies. From a national perspective, the creation of new firms is of limited value, partly due to a relatively high proportion of new-born firms disappearing within three years and partly because those that survive remain very small in the medium term. From an indi-vidual perspective, there may be a number of reasons to start a firm, and public support in this endeavour is highly appreciated by prospective entrepreneurs. In political rhetoric, it is thus attractive to refer to the number of new-born small firms as a simple and easily under-stood measure of a government's efficiency. Alternative aspects such as productivity and competitiveness are not as easily measured due to definition problems, time frames and measurability, and hence less attractive to politicians.

Contribution to gross national income

Industrial activities in a country contribute to the national economy, measured by gross domestic product (GDP) and gross national income (GNI). (For more detailed discussion and definitions of these measures see chapters 2 and 3.) Contribution from the SME sector as a share of total industry contribution varies between countries. A review of 76 countries

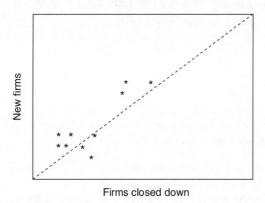

Figure 1.2 New firms versus closed down firms in various sectors.

showed that the contribution made by SMEs in low-income countries was 16 per cent of GDP, in medium-income countries 39 per cent and in high-income countries 51 per cent (Ayyagari *et al.* 2003). Remarks above about inaccurate statistical data motivate careful interpretation of these figures, particularly for low-income countries where agriculture represents a significant part of the contribution. The inclusion of agriculture data in the official statistics is very uncertain.

Births and deaths

A significant number of small businesses (one-person firms, entrepreneurships) cease to exist within a three-year period after start-up. In cross-country comparisons, this three-year period has become standard for calculating the company 'birth-to-death' ratio. The variations between countries are large: while data for Sweden shows that on average 30 to 50 per cent of all start-ups disappear within three years, the corresponding number for South Africa is around 80 per cent. Even in the absence of figures for the number of entrepreneurs starting new businesses after previous failures, it can be assumed that the short life of many ventures is not enough to produce sustainable growth.

Figure 1.2 gives a overview of birth and death among SMEs (more correctly known as *new firm formations and terminations*). It shows how different sectors are placed in relation to the diagonal where new formations and terminations are equal. While service-oriented sectors, such as business services, personal services and information technology, tend to make a net contribution to the number of firms, other sectors, such as agriculture firms in the more developed countries, are in decline. This picture varies considerably between countries and economic levels.

Since it is impossible to cover all countries within one book, the following section examines the SME sector and SME development in four selected countries.

Overview of the SME sector in four countries

Each of the four countries selected is situated on a different continent, but can by no means claim to be representative of that continent. Variations in the availability and accuracy of statistical data, industry structures, government incentives and the ease of establishing new businesses mean that no single small business can be chosen as representative of a region, let alone a whole continent.

Chile – Latin America

Box 1.2 Mini-encyclopaedia: Chile

Chile is a country in Latin America occupying a long, narrow coastal strip between the Andes mountains to the east and the Pacific Ocean to the west. It borders Peru to the north, Bolivia to the northeast and Argentina to the east.

The shape of Chile is a distinctive ribbon of land 4,300 kilometres long and on average 175 kilometres wide. Its climate varies, ranging from the world's driest desert – the Atacama – in the north, through a Mediterranean climate in the centre, to a rainy temperate climate in the south. The northern desert contains great mineral wealth, principally copper. The relatively small central area dominates in terms of population and agricultural resources, and is the cultural and political centre from which Chile expanded in the late nineteenth century when it incorporated its northern and southern regions. Southern Chile is rich in forests and grazing lands and features a string of volcanoes and lakes. The southern coast is a labyrinth of fjords, inlets, canals, sinuous peninsulas and islands.

Today, Chile is one of South America's most stable and prosperous nations. It leads Latin American nations in human development, competitiveness, quality of life, political stability, globalization, economic freedom, low perception of corruption and comparatively low poverty rates. It also ranks high regionally in press freedom and democratic development. However, as measured by the Gini coefficient, income inequality is high. In May 2010 Chile became the first South American country to join the OECD. Chile is also a founding member of both the United Nations and the Union of South American Nations.

Data (2006):
Population: 16.7 millions
Capital: Santiago
GNI per capita (PPP): 14,700 USD
Labour force: 7.4 millions (agriculture 13.2 per cent, industry 23 per cent, service 63.9 per cent)

Chile experienced high economic growth for a number of years until the very end of the 1990s when the East Asian economic crisis brought a temporary halt to growth. In the 1990s Chile was the focus of outsiders' praise as a model, not only in Latin America but also in countries in Africa and Asia (*La Presse* 1997). In recent years the Chilean economy (measured as GPD per capita) has taken the lead in Latin America.

However, two factors should be noted regarding growth. First, Chile is still a major exporter of low added-value goods such as copper and agriculture products. Second, economic growth has not resulted in a major increase in investment in added-value industries such as metal manufacturing. Although Chile has experienced a notable increase in added-value manufacturing during this period, only modest growth has been recorded in high added-value industry. This should be a warning signal, since high added-value in the metalworking sector is closely linked to the use of new technologies, to the demand for a skilled workforce and to improvements in organizational efficiency. These, in turn, are driving factors towards economic development.

The growth of the manufacturing sector in Chile follows closely the overall industry growth of the country, and has surpassed mining both in production value and in export earnings. However, if the food industry (a low added-value sector) is excluded from manufacturing growth, then copper mining is still by far the dominant industry sector. A characteristic dilemma of Chilean industry is therefore the absence of high added-value production in the sub-sectors generally considered significant for development, as they bring in new technologies and organizational structures to a country (Katz 1996).

The government's industry programme emphasizes the importance of increased added-value production, competitiveness and higher productivity. However, two factors counteract the effects of this strategy. The first is the traditional focus on the primary sector (copper, fruit) that still has a deep influence on industrial development, directing and attracting capital investments to that sector and thereby constraining the development of the high added-value manufacturing sub-sectors. The second factor is the obvious difficulty that the new global changes in management practices, such as serviceability and empowerment, have in securing a foothold in Chilean business, particularly among small and medium enterprises.

The SME sector is divided into five categories, ranging from the very small (*Pequeñas-Pequeñas*) to medium-to-large (*Medianas-Grandes*). Category is determined according to annual turnover measured in an accounting unit called the *Unidad de Fomento* (UF). The exchange rate between the UF and the Chilean peso is constantly adjusted for inflation so that the UF value remains constant. Converting the UF to USD at the 2010 rate of 1 USD = 502 Chilean pesos, the SME definition used in Chile is as follows:

Very small firms:	0.1–0.4 million USD
Small firms:	0.4–1.0 million USD
Medium to small firms:	1.0–2.1 million USD
Medium firms:	2.1–3.2 million USD
Medium to large firms:	3.2–4.2 million USD

Table 1.5 provides an alternative definition corresponding to the four-category international classification, in which the number of employees is not a criterion that is used.

Using official data to describe the SME sector in Chile is subject to similar difficulties as discussed above regarding structure of data, accuracy and reliability. The following attempt to give an account of the number of enterprises in the different-sized groups should be treated with caution. Table 1.5 is based on taxation data, while Table 1.6 is based on number of employees. Table 1.5 counts formally-registered firms paying value-added tax; the firms represented in Table 1.6 are a mix of formal and informal firms. The difference between these two methods of counting firms is substantial. For the year 2003, the number of formally-registered firms was reported as 697,513, with the number of mixed formal and informal firms being put at 1,445,921, a ratio of more than 1:2 (Government of Chile 2005).

Figure 1.3 shows the relative number of firms and employees from Table 1.6 as a percentage of the total. It is obvious that micro and small firms dominate both in categories.

Table 1.5 Classification of firms in Chile

	Micro	Small	Medium	Large
Employees	–	–	–	–
Turnover (000s USD)	< 75	75–750	750–3,000	> 3,000

Source: El Institutio Nacional de Estadísticas INE, 2008.

Table 1.6 Number of enterprises in the formal category of firms in Chile (2003)

Category	Number of firms	Employees	Average employees per firm
Micro	570,544	992,022	1.7
Small	15,524	822,745	7.8
Medium	14,577	600,787	41.2
Large	6,868	933,858	136
Total	607,513	3,349,412	

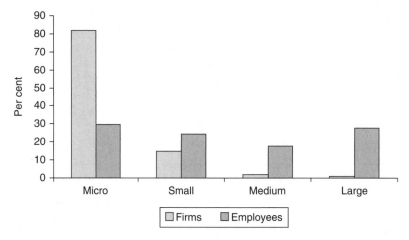

Figure 1.3 Relative percentage of firms and employees in Chile, 2003.

The industry structure of Chile, dominated by copper mining and with a relatively low proportion of added-value industry, has led to a somewhat different employment structure compared to many other countries. While large firms account for close to 80 per cent of the total sales, they employ only around 28 per cent of the Chilean workforce. The micro and small firms account for 54 per cent of the workforce, but only 13 per cent of annual sales. The comparison is illustrated in Figure 1.4.

South Africa – Africa

Box 1.3 Mini-encyclopaedia: South Africa

The Republic of South Africa is located at the southern tip of Africa, with a 2,798 kilometre coastline to the Atlantic and Indian Oceans. To the north lie Namibia, Botswana and Zimbabwe; to the east are Mozambique and Swaziland, while Lesotho is an independent country wholly surrounded by South African territory.

South Africa is known for its diversity of cultures and languages. Eleven official languages are recognized in the constitution. Two of these languages are of European origin: Afrikaans, a language which originated mainly from Dutch that is spoken by the majority of white and coloured South Africans, and South African English. Though English has a large role in public and commercial life, it is nevertheless only the fifth most-spoken home language.

South Africa is ethnically diverse. About 79.5 per cent of the South African population is of black African ancestry, divided among a variety of ethnic groups speaking different Bantu languages, nine of which have official status. South Africa also contains the largest European, Indian and racially mixed communities in Africa.

South Africa is a constitutional democracy in the form of a parliamentary republic with a parliamentary-dependent head of state. It is one of the founding members of the African Union, and has the largest economy of all the members. South Africa is a member of the Commonwealth of Nations, Antarctic Treaty System, Group of 77, South Atlantic Peace and Cooperation Zone, Southern African Customs Union, World Trade Organization, International Monetary Fund and G20.

Data (2009):

Population: 49.1 millions

Capital: Pretoria

GNI per capita (PPP): 10,100 USD

Labour force: 17.4 millions (agriculture 9 per cent, industry 26 per cent, service 65 per cent)

Official estimates of the number of SMEs in South Africa carry the same reservations as for many other countries, particularly regarding the lower (micro) end of the sector. An official report from 2002[4] states that accurate information is far from being available in South Africa, especially on the informal sector, which apparently represents at least two-thirds of the SMME (small, micro and medium enterprises) population.

Different sources give highly different figures for the number of SMMEs, and it should be noted that the official sources (Ntsika[5] and Statistics South Africa) suggest much lower totals than private research groups. The best estimate of SMEEs in South Africa is therefore between 1.6 and 3 million! A data and methodology problem is encountered in the consideration of size categories. Although the Government's Small Business Act has provided an official definition of four size categories (micro, very small, small and medium), this is not followed by the official state agencies, in that they either add new categories (for example, 'survivalist' enterprises[6]) or ignore some very small firms without explanation. Private

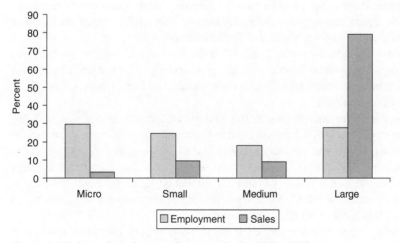

Figure 1.4 Sales and employment for enterprises in Chile, 2003.

Table 1.7 Number of firms and employment in South Africa (2000)

	Firms		Employees		
	Number	*Percentage*	*Number*	*Percentage*	*Average per firm*
Survival + micro	1,138,854	70.0	2,705,000	26.1	2.4
Very small	330,271	20.2	1,332,003	12.8	4.0
Small	94,804	5.8	1,252,298	12.1	13.2
Medium	52,620	3.2	1,591,046	15.3	30.2
Large	12,249	0.8	3,488,653	33.6	286.0
Total	1,628,797	100	10,369,000	100	

Sources: number of firms: University of Cape Town; number of employees: Ntsika, Statistics South Africa.

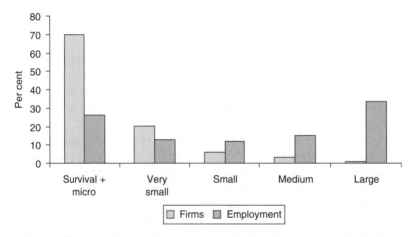

Figure 1.5 Relative percentage of firms and employment in South Africa, 2000.

studies are probably even less disciplined as far as their definition of size categories is concerned, sometimes combining a legal criterion (formality) with a size criterion (micro-enterprises), which makes comparisons rather hazardous. Table 1.7 is based on the most reliable official data available from Ntsika and Statistics South Africa.

Figure 1.5 presents the information in Table 1.7 in the form of a histogram. South Africa is no exception from the general U-shape found in practically all countries where large enterprises are also present: small firms dominate in number of firms whereas large firms dominate in number of employees.

The small business sector contribution to the country's GDP was 33 per cent in 1999, increasing to 35 per cent in 2008, a relatively modest increase. Small businesses are predominant in community, social and personal services and the finance, real estate, wholesale and agriculture sectors. The mining, electricity and water sectors are dominated by large enterprises. Based on the data in Table 1.7 and the population figure for South Africa, the SMME density is estimated at 33 SMMEs per 1,000 population, though, being based on unreliable statistics, this number is highly uncertain.

Table 1.8 presents the contribution to GDP as added-value per enterprise size group (millions of Rand).

Table 1.8 Contribution to GDP by firm size (2000)

Very small	Small	Medium	Large	Total
47,027	112,314	121,607	527,070	808,017
6%	14%	15%	65%	100%

Source: Ntsika.

The failure rate of new firms in South Africa is high, and fewer than 20 per cent survive beyond two years.

Vietnam – Asia

Box 1.4 Mini-encyclopaedia: Vietnam

Vietnam is the eastern-most country on the Indochina Peninsula in Southeast Asia and the thirteenth most highly populated country in the world. It is bordered by China to the north, Laos to the northwest and Cambodia to the southwest; the South China Sea is to the east. The northern and southern regions are low-lying areas with a flat delta, while the far north and northwest are mountainous and the central region is a highland. Vietnam is rich in natural resources such as phosphates, coal, manganese, chromate, offshore oil, forests, hydropower and bauxite.

A developing country, Vietnam had to recover from the ravages of war, loss of economic support from the Soviet Bloc and the inflexibility of a centrally planned economy. In 1986, the government instituted economic and political reforms with the result that the country shifted from a centrally-planned, bureaucratic and subsidised economy to a market economy and started on a path towards international reintegration (*doi moi*). By 2000, it had established diplomatic relations with most nations. Its economic growth has been among the highest in the world in the past decade. These efforts resulted in Vietnam joining the World Trade Organization in 2007. In 2001, the country reaffirmed its commitment to financial liberalisation and international integration. In the years since, Vietnam has implemented structural reforms for modernizing the economy and generating competitive export-driven industries.

Data (2009):

Population: 89.6 million

Capital: Hanoi

GNI per capita (PPP): 2,800 USD

Labour force: 47.4 millions (agriculture 56 per cent, industry 19 per cent, service sector 25 per cent)

When referring to the SME sector in Vietnam, the launch of the market-oriented economic development strategy in 1986 (*doi moi*) must be taken as starting point, as it marks the transition from a centrally-planned to a market-oriented economy. The privatization of state-owned enterprises (SOEs) and the opening of private enterprises followed in its wake. Small businesses have proliferated throughout the country, both in urban and rural settings, and the Government has put great emphasis on nurturing and supporting vulnerable SMEs with varied privileged policies (Taussig 2005).

Effective 2009, a new definition of the small business sector applies, where SMEs are grouped into micro enterprises, small enterprises and medium enterprises (Table 1.9).

Table 1.9 New definitions of SMEs in Vietnam (2009)

Criterion	Valid	Micro	Small[a]	Medium[b]	Large
Total capital (millions USD)	Throughout	–	< 1.2	1.2–6	> 6
Employees	Pre 2009	< 10	10–49	50–249	250 +
	After 2009	< 10	10–200	200–300	300 +

Notes
a In trading and service the definitions are: capital less than 0.6 million USD, employees 10–50.
b In trading and service the definitions are: capital 1.2–3 million USD, employees 50-100.

Table 1.10 Number of firms by group size (2002)

	Firms		Employees		
	Number	Percentage	Number	Percentage	Average per firm
Micro	2,660,000	97.8	4,375,000	52.1	1.6
Small	46,700	1.7	887,000	10.5	19
Medium	11,000	0.4	1,221,000	14.5	111
Large	2,500	0.1	1,909,000	22.7	764
Total	2,720,200	100	8,392,000	100	

Source: Ministry of Planning and Investment.

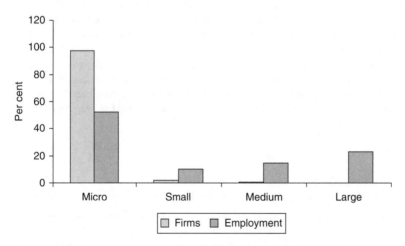

Figure 1.6 Relative percentages of firms and employees in Vietnam, 2002.

Vietnam likewise follows the general U-shape form for number of firms and employment that applies to other countries, with the exception that large firms do not dominate in terms of employment (Figure 1.6).

While some state-owned SMEs have been shut down as part of state sector reforms, new start-ups in the domestic private sector have more than compensated for such losses, resulting in the growth of the SME sector. Small private Vietnamese businesses now employ at

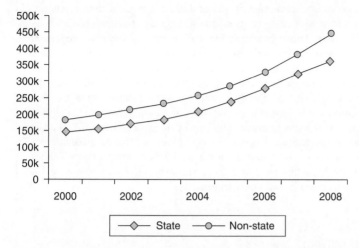

Figure 1.7 Gross domestic product at current prices by ownership and by kind of economic activity in 2005.

Source: Statistical Office, Vietnam.

least twice as many people as the state and foreign sectors combined. Employment in the narrower category of private companies has also surpassed that of state-owned firms. This growth in importance of more formal kinds of enterprise is significant, as companies are subject to stricter regulation of their impact on public goods, such as health and labour conditions, than are, for example, household businesses. Reflecting their dynamic and labour-intensive nature, these formal firms are now the country's most prolific sources of much-needed non-farm employment creation, and in some provinces (especially in the south) have even surpassed their larger state-owned counterparts in terms of contributions to industrial output and exports (Taussig 2005).

Figure 1.7 shows the GDP contribution by the non-state sector in comparison with state owned enterprises.

Sweden – Europe

Box 1.5 Mini-encyclopaedia: Sweden

Sweden is the third largest country in Western Europe extending 1,574 kilometres north to south. A military power during the 17th century, Sweden has not participated in any war for almost two centuries. Armed neutrality was preserved in both World Wars. Sweden's long-successful economic formula of a capitalist system leavened with substantial welfare elements was challenged in the 1990s by high unemployment and in 2000–2002 and 2009 by the global economic downturns, but fiscal discipline over recent years has enabled the country to weather the economic storms. Sweden joined the EU in 1995, but the public rejected the introduction of the euro in a 2003 referendum.

The engineering industry made its breakthrough at the end of the nineteenth century around innovations with high market potential, for example the ship's propeller, the ball-bearing, the safety match, dynamite, the pace-maker and, more recently, the computer mouse. The developing industrial base could take advantage of one of Sweden's major natural resources: hydroelectric power. Thanks to an abundance of rivers and waterfalls in the north of the country, electricity was relatively cheap. This substantially lowered the costs of industrial production which, in turn, raised the demand for Swedish products on the international market.

The Swedish labour market saw a major change in the 1960s. While the number of people employed in the service sector increased, there was a drop in the number of industrial workers, especially in the textile and leather sectors. The 1970s brought many changes in international trading conditions which turned out to have a negative effect on Sweden. Since the country's domestic market is relatively small, many industries rely heavily on exports. The 1973 oil crisis and the subsequent decline in international business activity therefore affected Sweden more severely than many other countries. The political answer to this was government subsidies to sectors like steel and shipbuilding that were in distress. However, these measures were not altogether successful, maintaining employment only temporarily.

Data (2008):

Population: 9.1 million

Capital: Stockholm

GNI per capita (PPP): 36,800 USD

Labour force: 4.9 million (agriculture 1.1 per cent, industry 28.2 per cent, service sector 70.7 per cent)

The small business sector in Sweden has been stable over the last ten years as shown in Table 1.11.

Figure 1.8 shows the distribution of firms in different size groups.

In addition to the number of firms, Figure 1.9 shows employees by size group in 2008. Again, the typical U-shapes can be discerned, number of firms dominating for the smallest firms and number of employees dominating for the large firms.

Table 1.12 shows the number of firms and employees for the year 2008. Note that one-person firms (zero employees) are a major part of the micro group. One-person firms number 720,733, representing nearly 74 per cent of all firms in Sweden in that year.

Table 1.11 Change in number of SMEs, employment and average size in the period 2000–2008

Measure	Size category	Year			
		2000	*2002*	*2005*	*2008*
Firms (% of total)	One-person	73.8	74.6	75.1	73.8
	1–9	22.0	21.3	20.9	22.0
	10–49	3.4	3.4	3.2	3.3
	50–200	0.5	0.4	0.5	0.5
	Large	0.2	0.2	0.2	0.2
Average employees per firm	1–9	2.7	2.7	2.7	2.6
	10–49	19.4	19.5	19.4	19.4
	50–200	91.4	91.0	90.6	90.2
	Large	1242	1242	1242	1242
Proportion employed (%)	SMEs	48	49	49	50
	Large	52	51	51	50

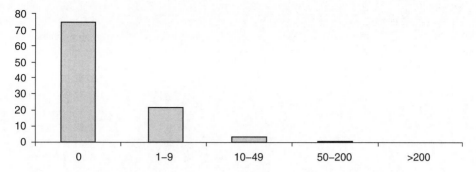

Figure 1.8 Relative distributions of firms in different size groups in Sweden in 2008.

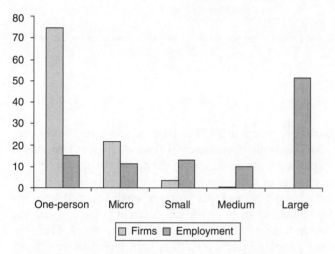

Figure 1.9 Number of firms and employees by firm size in 2006.

Table 1.12 Number of firms, employees and contribution to gross national income (GNI) in Sweden (2008)

	Firms		Employees			Contribution to GNI	
	Number	Per cent	Number	Per cent	Average/firm	000s	Per cent
Micro	936,372	95.8	1,281,394	26.5	2.6	436,090	24
Small	33,265	3.5	645,341	13.3	19.4	339,268	18
Medium	5309	0.5	478,872	9.9	90.2	315,874	17
Large	1844	0.2	2,435,924	50.3	1321	784,219	41
Total	976,790	100	4,841,531	100		1,839,452	100

Source: Author.

The data in Table 1.11 shows that the average employees per firm has been very stable for small firms during the period covered, varying somewhat (but not much) for middle- and large-size firms. The average annual increase in number of firms is about 2 per cent,

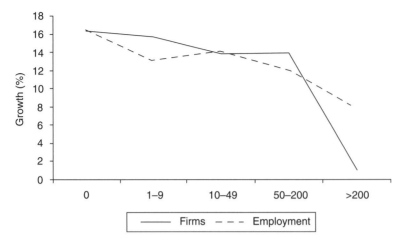

Figure 1.10 Total growth in number of firms and employment by firm size in Sweden for the period
2000–2009.

Source: Author.

but also the total number of employees is increasing. The increase seen over the ten year
period 2000–2009 is, however, not evenly distributed over all firms. As Figure 1.10 shows,
the number of firms and total employment has grown during the period but growth has slowed. The average growth in the number of micro firms with ten employees or less was 16
per cent for the whole period, or around 2 per cent per year. For small and medium firms
the figure shows that growth in the number of firms and employment is more or less the
same, which means that firm size in these two categories has been quite stable. This is in
contrast to the large firms, where growth in employment has been higher (around 8 per
cent) compared to growth in the number of firms (less than 2 per cent). In other words, if
we define growth as growth in average number of employees per firm, only the large firms
would have grown during the this period.

Growth in average number of employees is thus lower than the average growth in the
number of small firms, while the opposite happened for large firms with more than 200
employees. It is of course desirable that the number of employees should grow faster among
small businesses, which would mean that new jobs are being created. It is noteworthy that
Figure 1.10 contradicts much of what has been the fundamental idea behind the strategy of
furthering SME sector growth, i.e. to reach higher average employment in small firms in
order to compensate for declining average employment in larger firms. At least for the
period under consideration, the Swedish example shows a different pattern.

In recent years, the official strategy in Sweden – with its focus on entrepreneurship and
small firms – has favoured the creation of new firms. However, this strategy has been criticised for a number of reasons. One argument is that the need for firms which are growing
should have a higher priority than starting up new firms, since experience shows that at
least one third will disappear within a three-year period. It is further argued that new firms
have a lower average productivity compared with older, established firms (Institutet för
TillväxtPolitiska Studier 2007).

The four country comparison

From the comparison of the four countries in the previous section it is obvious that small firms are facing many similar situations, despite different cultural and social–economic contexts. For example, the U-shaped form of the firm size and employee histograms is common to SMEs in all the four countries, i.e. the very small firms dominate in numbers but as firms grow in size in terms of employment they tend to contribute more to the gross national income (GNI) of the country. Tables 1.13 and 1.14 summarise the comparison.

A striking observation from the comparison is that the micro firms, which dominate in numbers, are of similar size measured by average employment per firm. Further, it has been shown in various other studies that a significant percentage of the micro firms are owner-manager firms with no employees. Even a very modest growth of employment in this category would have a significant impact on the job creation situation.

The fact that there are relatively more large firms in Chile and South Africa compared with the other two countries is due to the mining industry which is less labour intensive, as can be seen from the average employment figures. Sweden, in contrast, has a relatively large manufacturing industry that is more labour intensive. Vietnam also has labour-intensive industries, such as the paper industry.

Small business research

One of the pioneers of research on small businesses was Joseph Schumpeter, whose original interest focused on the dynamism of a changing economy and the opportunities created for entrepreneurs and small firms. Very early Schumpeter placed technological change as the driving force behind competitive industry in a capitalist society. This fits today's information society and the introduction of computers, semi-conductors and telecommunications, which, together with takeovers and mergers, are creating change through *creative destruction* – an expression coined by Schumpeter. Creative destruction refers to the breaking old traditions and the creation of new ones by identifying and understanding how new structures

Table 1.13 Number of firms as percentage of total for the four countries

Country	Micro	Small	Medium	Large
Chile	94	2.6	2.4	1
South Africa	90	6	3	1
Vietnam	98	1.5	< 0.5	0.1
Sweden	95.8	3.3	0.5	0.2

Table 1.14 Average employees per firm for the four countries

Country	Micro	Small	Medium	Large
Chile	2.7	7.8	41.2	136
South Africa	2.7	13.2	30.2	286
Vietnam	1.6	19	111	764
Sweden	2.6	19.4	90.2	1,321

and functions can be combined. The question of whether new jobs are created when old ones are made redundant was faced by Schumpeter and answered in the affirmative for capitalist societies. Both the innovator and the entrepreneur were central.

The idea of the entrepreneur came to be central for the Austrian School of Economics, to which Schumpeter and other prominent researchers such as Ludwig von Mises and Carl Menger belonged. Although Menger was the first to give a theoretical appreciation of the nature of the entrepreneur in economic life by emphasising the role of ignorance, error and uncertainty in human affairs, it was Schumpeter whose name became permanently linked to the idea of entrepreneurship and the word 'entrepreneur'. According to Schumpeter, it was the repetition of the processes of creative destruction that raised mankind to ever higher levels of welfare. The entrepreneur was therefore a kind of social leader, almost replacing the aristocracy whose social function was primarily a military one (Leube 1996). In Schumpeter's world, uncertainty is a driving force for the entrepreneur who needs imagination, problem-solving capacity and in readiness for anything to happen!

By 'development', therefore, we mean only such changes in economic life as are not forced upon it from without but arise by its own initiative, from within. Should it turn out that there are no such changes arising in the economic sphere itself, and that the phenomenon we call economic development is in practice simply founded upon the fact that as the data change so the economy continuously adapts itself to them, then we should say that there is *no* economic development (Schumpeter 1934).

For Schumpeter, the entrepreneur has specific knowledge and skills that constitute the special production units of the firm. The entrepreneur or the manager is thus crucial in Schumpeter's view. For Edith Penrose, however, it is the organizational form of the firm rather than the entrepreneur which is the decisive factor behind growth and development of the firm: the organization is not only a response to the market but in the first instance the result of decisions taken by the manager. The firm is not, in a rational way, reduced to a production function but is seen as a collection of different resources that can be mobilized in more or less efficient ways. Like in Schumpeter's theory Penrose also focuses on knowledge and skills, but not only regarding the manager but collectively in the firm. The skills that are specific and unique to the firm and are difficult to copy, and make the firm competitive. In the *resource-based approach*, it is the management of resources and the growth of knowledge within the firm rather than the growth of knowledge within the market that are important. The *Penrose Effect* describes how the traditional and unreflective utilization of resources in a firm hampers growth and development. The release and development of potential and sleeping resources provides the opportunity to diversify production, products and services by utilizing the firm's collection of competences and capacities.

The assumption that small and medium firms are different from large enterprises is the basic notion of the *bottom-up approach*, claiming that theories developed for large firms are not applicable to small businesses. Small firms, according to this approach, are specific in the sense that they seldom have an abundance of financial resources, have a mostly short-term perspective and are generally not in the position to spend large amounts of time and money on training and consulting. Analytical tools that are common for analysing mainstream organizational and management situations are less common, or even useful in the small business field, mostly because of the assumptions that small business are unique and difficult to fit into more common moulds. That the unique aspects of small firms, such as the centrality of the owner-manager, the limitation of time and resources and a vulnerability to the environment, do make a difference to the way small firms develop their strategies is in no doubt, even if questions have been raised about how significant these differences are (Marsden and Forbes 2003).

A very different view is presented in the *top-down approach* that states that small and medium firms are no different from large enterprises! Models and theories developed for large firms (mainstream organization and management theories) are therefore also applicable to small businesses. This approach has its roots in the field of strategic management, where a set of guidelines describe how to achieve a position for the firm that optimizes the possibility of reaching business goals. Although this approach looks at business as a general concept without specific consideration of firm size, it does look at some specific features of small firms in particular market situations. For example, when new technologies emerge they create business opportunities where large firms might hesitate due to uncertainty and strategic considerations. Since small businesses may be more prone to risk-taking and since competition may be limited at the beginning, the entry barriers are lower. It seems that today the 'positioning' approach of the top-down view is losing ground in favour of the resource-based approach.

Finally, the *personality-based approach* is a set of disparate models having in common the view that small businesses are special and therefore require special theories and models that take into account the manager's role. Different characteristics of the person behind the manager are scrutinised, such as age, gender, family and social background, educational attainment, etc. In various research efforts attempts have been made to identify the typical (and successful) entrepreneurial and managerial type for small firms. However, research results have failed to demonstrate that there is something like the typical entrepreneur type.

Summary and conclusion

Summary

The definition of small and medium firms varies from country to country, which creates huge difficulties when making comparison between countries as to the number of small firms and number of employees. The EU together with other major international organizations (e.g. Word Bank, United Nations) has contributed to reducing the difficulties by suggesting a definition of small and medium-sized firms that is primarily based on employment. However, most countries outside the EU have their own and local SME definitions, which may vary within the same country, even being different for different sectors. Statistical comparison of the small business sector in international contexts is therefore highly uncertain, yielding results that are mostly inaccurate and often come with so many question marks that interpretation becomes hazardous.

Conclusion

Even if the small business sector has many similarities in terms of statistical characteristics in different countries, because of its limitations in size and resources, the small firm is predominantly local. General theories and models developed for organization and management behaviour do not automatically fit with the small firm. Large enterprises can benefit by general management and organization theories as they have the potential to influence and manipulate markets due to their size and potential for sustainability. Small firms, on the other hand, must adapt to the local market and seldom have the luxury of implementing new strategies and waiting for them to become efficient. Variations in local consumer behaviour must be met with corresponding variations in small firms' strategies and operations. General theories and models are not always of any use here since they are too general.

Notes

1 Low-, middle- and high-income countries are defined in Chapter 2.
2 Born in 1941, De Soto is currently head of The Institute for Liberty and Democracy in Lima, Peru.
3 Since 2009, the Swedish Agency for Economic and Regional Growth.
4 Trade and Industrial Policy Strategies, December 2002.
5 Ntsika Enterprises Promotions Agency belongs to the Department of Trade and Industry.
6 A 'survivalist' enterprise is a business in which the income generated is less than the minimum income standard, an amount that varies in different years. In 1999 the amount was 12,000 South African rands.

References

Ayyagari, M., Beck, T. and Demirgüç-Kunt, A. (2003) *Small and Medium Enterprises Across the Globe: A New Database*. Washington, DC: World Bank. Policy Research Working Paper 3127.
Bannock, G. (2005) *The Economics and Management of Small Business*. London: Routledge.
Chandler, A. (1977) *The Visible Hand: The Managerial Revolution in American Business*. Cambridge, MA: Harvard University Press.
De Soto, H. (2000) *The Mystery of Capital: Why Capitalism Triumphs in the West and Fails Everywhere Else*. London: Basic Books.
Dosman, E. (2008) *The Life and Times of Raúl Prebish*. Toronto: McGill-Queen's University Press.
The Economist (1990) 'Why Big Might Remain Beautiful'. No. 24.
Government of Chile (2005) *La Situación de la Micro y Pequeña Empresa*. December.
Institutet för TillväxtPolitiska Studier (2007) *Swedish Agency for Growth Policy Analysis*. Östersund.
International Labour Organization (2010) *Global Employment Trends*. Geneva: ILO.
Jones, O. (2003) 'Competitive Advantage in SMEs: Towards a Conceptual Framework', in Jones, O. and Tilley, F. (eds) *Competitive Advantage in SMEs*. London: John Wiley.
Katz, J. (1996) *Establización Macroeconómica. Reforma Estructural y Comportamiento Industrial*. Buenos Aires: Alianza Editorial S.S.
La Presse (1997) (Tunisia) 'Les expériences du Chili, de l'Irlande et de la Malaisie'. December 19.
Leube, K. (1996) *Krise und Exodus: Österreichische Sozialwissenschaften in Mitteleuropa*. Vienna: WUV–Universitätsverlag.
McIntyre, R. (2003) 'Small Enterprises in Transition Economies: Casual Puzzles and Policy-Relevant Research', in McIntyre, R. and Dallago, B. (eds) *Small and Medium Enterprises in Transitional Economies*. London: Palgrave.
Marsden, A. and Forbes, C. (2003) 'Strategic Management for SMEs', in Jones, O. and Tilley, F. (eds) *Competitive Advantage in SMEs*. London: John Wiley.
Penrose, E. (2009) *The Theory of the Growth of the Firm*. Oxford: Oxford University Press.
Piore, M. and Sabel, C. (1984) *The Second Industrial Divide: Possibilities for Prosperity*. New York: Basic Books.
Schumpeter, J. (1934) *The Theory of Economic Development*. London: Oxford University Press.
Taussig, M. (2005) *Domestic Companies in Vietnam: Challenges for Development of Vietnam's Most Important SMEs*. Ann Arbor, MI: University of Michigan Press. Policy Brief #34.
Tilley, F. and Tonge, J. (2003) 'Introduction', in Jones, O. and Tilley, F. (eds) *Competitive Advantage in SMEs*. London: John Wiley.
United Nations Development Programme (2001) *Human Development Report*. Washington, DC: World Bank.

2 The economic development process as a framework for small business

Introduction

Ever since attitudes began to change in the 1960s and 70s about the performance limits of large scale firms, the privatization of state-owned enterprises and the small business as necessary for the creation of new jobs, small and medium enterprises (SMEs) have become increasingly central to government growth strategies. Since large firms could benefit from new technology and increase productivity many times over, it soon became obvious they would neither be able – nor would it be in their interests – to create jobs for the growing number of job seekers. For governments, there was only one way out of the emerging unemployment dilemma: the SME sector. It was not long before the rhetoric concerning the importance of this sector in the economic development process began.

Since the 1980s, there have been three main areas where SMEs have been expected to contribute: creating jobs, promoting economic growth and reducing poverty in poor countries. Jobs have been created despite the vast majority of SME firms sector being one-person operations that seldom grow. But they create jobs, even if only for the owner. The expectation that small business growth would lead to economic growth was taken as an obvious truth and became part of the growing SME rhetoric, repeated over and over by academics as well as by policy-makers. This rhetoric won support as economic growth was statistically correlated with the growth in number of SMEs, and it was generally assumed that SME sector growth was driving economic growth; the debate did not consider that things might be the other way around: that economic growth facilitates small business growth! Only recently has it been suggested that an effective and supportive business environment might facilitate growth and development for both small and large firms (Beck and Demirgüç-Kunt 2004).

Development levels and development periods influence societies differently, and thereby also business environments like property rights, access to finance, effective enforcements of business deals and contracts, in addition to other preconditions for business such as political and financial stability. This chapter therefore looks at the many different development views, models and theories that have been current since the Second World War, coinciding with the beginning of the postcolonial era in Africa and Asia. Some of the periods discussed below were characterized by the underlying theories or model that dominated thinking about development at the time. Thus we have periods that we refer to as the *import substitution approach*, or the *basic needs approach* etc. In each of these periods, small businesses in the new emerging countries either benefited or suffered. For example, the import substitution approach created opportunities for local small firms to develop, but when trade was opened up in the 1960s, local small business experienced growing competition from Western exporters. Many small firms view the present attempts by the World Trade Organization to reduce and eliminate hazardous products by imposing trade barriers with equal trepidation. On the other hand, the privatization period that began when big state-owned enterprises were privatized created opportunities for small business to thrive and develop. Small and medium firms have therefore been deeply affected by the different phases of economic development.

Development periods – a brief overview

The term 'economic development' denoting a process that societies undergo was hardly used before the Second World War (Arndt 1989). Before the war, many of today's poorer countries were still colonies and did not attract much interest in the field of economic research. Post war, prominent scholars like Gunnar Myrdal, Raúl Prebish, Arthur Lewis and Dudley Seers played an important role in formulating tentative goals for economic development and contributing towards setting an agenda for development.

In attempting to separate post-war economic development into periods, one runs the risk of simplifying and highlighting certain aspects that we retrospectively identify as particularly significant. By regarding the different periods as tokens of specific development models, the post-war development process seems very rational and straight-forward. In reality, the different periods overlapped and models were applied in various forms in different parts of the world.

Development as growth

Development became the main focus after the Second World War and remained so into the 1950s when economic development became practically synonymous with economic growth. While economic growth was a term primarily reserved for the more developed countries (Europe, United States), economic development was mostly used to refer to developing countries. As Arndt points out:

> In Western countries, the tendency to think about economic development mainly as economic growth was undoubtedly strengthened by the fact that in the post-war decade economic growth became a major objective of economic policy in the developed countries and a major interest of economic theory. (Arndt 1984)
>
> There was therefore a tendency to approach the study of problems of economic development with the toolkit designed by economists for the analysis of economic growth in advanced countries. The very fact that economists had a theory, or theories, of economic growth seemed to give them a head start over other social scientists as experts on economic development. (Arndt 1989)

'Modernization' was an important concept in this period where traditional societies were regarded by many as backward and inferior to the more industrialized countries of the West. Gunnar Myrdal, one of many influential international economists after the Second World War, stated that the objective of economic growth was much more than higher material standards: it was 'new men, modern men' (Myrdal 1968). Myrdal also quoted Nehru, then prime minister of India:

> But we have to deal with age-old practices, ways of thought, and ways of action. We have got to get out of many of these traditional ways of production, traditional ways of distribution and traditional ways of consumption. We have got to get out of all that into

what might be called more modern ways of doing so. What is society in the so-called advanced countries like today? It is a scientific and technological society. It employs new techniques, whether it is in the farm or in the factory or in transport. The test of a country's advance is how far it is utilising modern techniques. Modern technique is not a matter of just getting a tool and using it. Modern technique follows modern thinking. You can't get hold of a modern tool and have an ancient mind. It won't work.

(Cited in Myrdal ibid.)

This view of Nehru – prominent in the post-colonial era after the Second World War and an influential spokesman for the emerging liberated countries about to win their freedom after colonialism – illustrates the high expectations from, and strong belief in, technological development as a sacred tool for the new emerging nations. Modern science and technology as a driving force for development, promising wealth and happiness, has been a heritage of Western civilisation thinking from the Renaissance and onwards. This view may still prevail in most parts of the world, even if some ambivalence can be noted in most advanced societies about the limitations of technological systems being implemented on a large scale. Frustrations with this 'myth of modernity' (that the promises of wealth and happiness for all did not come true) has undermined the belief in progress based on technology and science, previously so held enthusiastically (Lyon 1994). The interpretation of this emerging view has been translated into the concept of Postmodernity (Lyotard 1979).

Previously, it was common to regard poor countries as recipients of technology developed by rich countries, in which technological innovations took place and in which new products were designed and manufactured. In recent years, however, this distinction has been fading, as industrializing countries like South Korea, Taiwan, India and Brazil catch up with the more advanced countries in the design and production of new products (Forbes and Wield 2002). In spite of this, the new technologies and techniques that are being developed are closely related to the development level and economic environment for which they are developed. For example, innovations are mostly responses to needs and demands originating in the advanced countries rather than the poorer countries. In the poorer countries of the world – characterized by different economic and social conditions – new technologies therefore do not drive economic development in the same way (Stewart 1978; Lind 1991).

After the Second World War, gross national product (GNP) – total added value produced by a country – was introduced as a measure of economic growth. The measure gives sole emphasis to the economic dimension of development and gives no room for other variables of a social or cultural nature. The underlying assumption among economists of the time was that a sufficiently-high economic growth rate would lead to broader development, such as a better redistribution of wealth, increased income, and hence welfare for all.

One of the essential ideas during the economic growth period was capital formation as a key factor for industrialization. Industrialization of the developing countries was seen as a desirable way of catching up with the more advanced countries and, with a strong industry sector, countries would strive towards self-sufficiency in the production of goods and in the creation of jobs. The mechanism for creating jobs was also a focus of Keynes's model (introduced in the 1930s but revived as a relevant model in post-war economic discussions). According to Keynes, the reason for unemployment was the imbalance between supply and demand in the work place, an imbalance that could be adjusted through intervention by the state. The model thus recommended increased state involvement.

Traditional economic theory explained that unemployment during the great depression in the 1930s was caused by too high wage rates. Figure 2.1 illustrates how the traditional

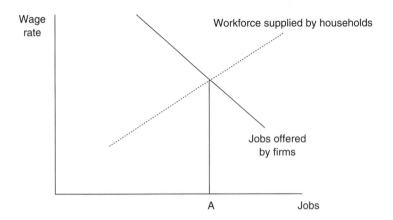

Figure 2.1 Optimal salary level (A) according to traditional economists in the 1930s.

economists of the 1930s claimed there to be precisely one wage rate at which the amount of manpower households are prepared to offer for jobs balances the job openings firms are willing to create. If wage rates increase as a result of trade union demands (according to the economists of the time), the supply of those looking for jobs will increase whereas job openings will decrease. Conversely, if wage levels decrease, the jobs offered would increase while the demand for jobs would decrease. It could therefore be assumed that there exists a stable point where the demand and provision of jobs coincide. This stable point is denoted by A in the diagram.

Keynes's contribution was to show that if the state can create new jobs there would be an increase in job opportunities that pushes the balance point A to the right and creates an increase in job demand. The state can thus regulate the unemployment situation through appropriate interventions in the creation of new job opportunities through, for example, infrastructure projects such as road construction: investments that can be partly financed through the state by controlling the interest rate. What Keynes showed was that there is not, as the classicists held, a single unique equilibrium at the level of full employment, but that there are an infinite number of equilibia related to different savings and investment plans. That Keynesianism worked was evident from the lessons of the post-war success of industrial economies in avoiding the horrors of mass unemployment and extreme business fluctuations (Donaldson 1973). Sweden and New Zealand were among the first countries to adopt the Keynes model successfully in their economic policies.

The human aspects approach

The period that followed began as a reaction to the one-sided focus on economic growth and capital formation as the determining factors for development, and marked a growing emphasis on human capital in addition to physical capital. The proportion of the increase in GDP that could be attributed to measurable inputs of capital and labour was much smaller than had been expected. If the contribution of inputs of capital and labour accounted for only 10 to 20 per cent of secular growth of total output, the explanation of economic growth – and of differences in the rate of economic growth among different countries – had to be sought in the residual factor, which tended to be equated with technical progress or, more generally, advances in knowledge, including those resulting from education (Arndt 1984).

The trade approach

The 1960s saw an increasing focus on trade as an engine of growth in the world economy, although it was obvious that developing countries would find it increasingly difficult to compete with manufactured goods from the more advanced nations. The *import substitution model* was thus expected to protect and stimulate the infant industries of developing countries through penalty schemes for imported goods, such as high customs tariffs and other import costs. The import substitution model turned out to be a disappointment, as the industries protected used skilled labour to produce expensive goods that could have been imported at a lower cost. The skilled labour, which was mostly in scarce supply, had to be transferred from key industries that might have been successfully exporting traditional products and commodities, such as textiles and garments. The import substitution industries mostly produced goods for a limited social group (the middle class) and could therefore not reach the necessary output volumes required for cost reduction through mass production.

The following example from Egyptian industry illustrates effects that could follow adoption of the import substitution strategy.

Box 2.1 Mini-case: El Mehalla el Kobra

El Mehalla el Kobra was the number one textile exporter in Egypt in the 1980s. As the development of the vehicle industry became a State prestigious project with the establishment of El Nasco motor company in 1960, the need for skilled workers could not be supplied from the labour market but had to be recruited from state-owned firms with efficient production. Hence El Mehalla el Kobra was partly drained of its most competent workers who were transferred to El Nasco. The government's strategy was to substitute the import of vehicles by domestic production. The production never reached a volume that created any significant advantages of scale. The end effect was, therefore, that both industries suffered from the Government's import substitution policy (Lind 1991).

The strategic failure illustrated by the case of El Mehalla el Kobra can be explained by Verdoorn's Law relating growth of output and growth of productivity.[1] The successful export of the company had created specialization in the production of the exported products which increased the productivity level and further increased the level of skills. From a national perspective this should have led to a reallocation of resources from the less efficient non-export sectors to the productive export firm. Instead, by adopting import substitution principles, Egypt followed the opposite strategy.

The dependency approach

Classic macro theory maintained that trade between two countries would be favourable for both if they focused on goods for which they both had special comparative advantages, for example unique skills, compatible salary levels or abundance of certain commodities. With examples taken from the commercial links between Argentina and Britain, Raúl Prebish, an Argentinean economist, showed that, in the long run, commerce between the two countries would result in increasing imbalance between the two. Britain, the rich European country with its highly-efficient industry, would continue being in the centre, while agrarian Argentina would continue in her peripheral position. Countries at the periphery will always be dependent on the countries at the centre.

Andre Gunder Frank, a Marxist-influenced development economist, was of the opinion that many underdeveloped countries continued to specialize in raw materials that are increasingly essential for industrial development in the *imperialist metropolis* (Frank 1978). Frank also noted that development in Latin America gave rise to a quantitative decrease in manufacturing and a quantitative increase in the export of raw materials. In a similar way, Chile was engaged in a type of exchange that forced it to export mineral and agricultural products and to import manufactured products. Trade thus generated direct or indirect mechanisms of control in the Chilean and Latin American economies (García 1989).

The dependency approach resulted in the so called Singer-Prebish thesis. This was based on the observation that countries at the periphery produce primary goods such as agriculture products to export to the centre, while the centre produces secondary goods such as machinery for export to the periphery. With technological innovations primarily taking place in the industrialized world, the centre is in a position to retain the savings made and can afford further innovations and technological development, resulting in higher productivity. In addition, workers' unions in the centre are strong and can negotiate higher salaries that contribute to the growing economy. At the periphery, companies are generally less productive and workers are weaker; companies have to pass on technical savings to their customers in the form of lower prices. Hence this vicious circle makes rich countries richer and poor countries poorer.

The basic needs approach

The period of *social objectives* dominated the 1960s and 70s as it became obvious that the so-called *trickle-down* effect – the wide dissemination of increasing prosperity throughout society as a result of economic growth – did not happen. Thus, towards the 1970s, the *content* rather than the rate increase of the GNP became a major theme, and with it a focus on employment, equality and the covering of basic needs.

To meet the basic needs of a nation and its people, the focus of the 1970s and 80s was on *basic need* defined as the minimum standard of living for the poorest groups of society. The standard was intended to cover the minimum requirements of a family, such as food, shelter and clothing, likewise sufficient access to drinking water and sanitation, health and education. The criticism levelled at the basic needs approach at the beginning of the 1990s came primarily from the developing countries, who viewed the basic needs strategy as opposed to modernization and economic growth. A common criticism towards the end of the period was that basic needs as a strategy could appear hypocritical and sour relations between the Third World and the Western industrial powers if taken as a substitute for the broad process of modernization which had brought wealth and power to the West (cited in Arndt 1989).

The New International Economic Order

The dissatisfaction of developing countries with the liberal international economic order surfaced in the 1950s with demands for reform of international trade and calls for increased economic aid (O'Brian and Williams 2004). The North–South conflict was given increased prominence in the 1970s with the debate over a *New International*

Economic Order (NIEO), which dominated the North–South discussion for most of that decade. At the centre of discussions were issues pertaining to international commodity markets. Developing countries argued that international organizations, such as the International Monetary Fund (IMF) and the World Bank, were controlled by the advanced industrial countries and failed to support the interests of developing countries.

The NIEO concept reflected a new optimism after the uncertainty of the 1960s, not least in the developing countries. OPEC (the Organization of Petroleum Exporting Countries) decided to increase its financial support to low-income countries, indirectly increasing oil prices. Part of the financial inflow was recycled back to the developing countries, where it became an important means of financing new, often grandiose, development projects. However, just as often, it resulted in conspicuous consumption, contributing to a debt crisis which overwhelmed many less-developed countries in the 1980s (Cypher and Dietz 2009). Following this, and subject to increasing attacks from the developed nations fearing a destabilization of raw material export prices, the New International Economic Order period ended in failure.

While most developing countries advocated modernization as an alternative to basic needs, *privatization* of state-owned assets and the growing faith in the workings of the market economy dominated the international scene from the beginning of the 1990s. Donor countries were urged to assist poor developing countries to meet the preconditions for the development of a private sector. Among the requirements were the abolition of government monopolies, strengthening of competition, creation of an appropriate regulatory environment and efficient banking, transport and communication facilities (Kingsbury *et al.* 2004).

The privatization approach

To overcome the legacy of underdevelopment, on achieving independence after the Second World War, many Third World countries had embarked on large development projects in agriculture, industry and infrastructure. Due to a lack of skills and capital, local entrepreneurs could not handle many of the projects and, having just emerged from colonialism, there was strong resistance to involving foreign capital. The governments in developing countries therefore took the initiative of establishing a state-owned company sector, and the publicly-owned enterprises were expected to provide economies of scale and the necessary financial means to help build the industries in the national development plans. In addition, the public enterprises were supposed to set examples in corporate behaviour, and to raise the technological base of the country via training and learning-by-doing. Public enterprises were also expected to generate tax incomes for the government and to contribute to regional development as tools in long-term government development plans.

The strategies and goals of the state-owned enterprises were often vague and contradictory, and the performance of the sector became a source of disillusionment. Governments' goals of revenue maximization were contradicted by expansion of producer subsidies. Soft budget constraints encouraged waste and tied-up social capital. A major problem, moreover, was the lack of effective ways of disciplining state-owned enterprises for poor performance.

Some of the strategic goals of privatization have been to improve the efficiency of resource use through increased competition to: increase the tax base of governments as firms and transactions multiply; broaden the commercialization of nations as firms find new business segments and niches; increase investments in infrastructure; expand the export sector; and widen the ownership of key industries. The privatization approach was that any economic activity that can be carried out in a market environment is more efficient if operated on a profit basis. However, since this presupposed the existence of buying power among potential consumers and a flow of money circulating in the country, results have been variable. Economic crises in the 1990s and in the first decade of the twenty-first century, such as the Asian crisis, the Mexican crisis and the global depression in 2008–2010, have shown how vulnerable many developing countries and the less affluent developed countries are. More recently, the neoliberal economic approach, emphasizing market mechanisms as guidelines for healthy development, has been modified towards a *sustainable development* approach.

The Rio conference in 1992 officially declared sustainable development as the new approach to development. Sustainable development is defined as development that meets the needs of the present generation without jeopardising the resources available to future generations. Efforts to make sustainability an operational strategy for adoption in business have met with some difficulties, not least in small businesses.

The Rostow doctrine

One of the early and more influential thinkers on economic development was the American economist W. W. Rostow. He likened the economic development process to a moving staircase on which countries found themselves at different levels. Since the staircase was moving, all countries would move upwards, imitating those countries above and gradually catching up with the more developed and advanced countries. In the eyes of Rostow, therefore, economic development was a linear process, from less to more developed, where the goal of the country should be to 'take-off into self-sustained growth' (Rostow 1960). Rostow adopted an evolutionary view of economic development and argued that the underdeveloped societies at the time were at an earlier stage of development than the advanced industrialized countries. The poor countries could develop if they adopted attitudes and social structures similar to those of the developed world. However, this prescription did come under attack from different directions even before the end of the 1960s, as the trickledown effect from richer to poorer countries was seen not to happen. Instead, the very process of global change that gave rise to prosperity in the North resulted in simultaneous impoverishment of the countries in the South (McKay 2004).

The Rostow doctrine was further criticized on the grounds that, while the linear development process he assumed might have applied to European and Western development, it hardly served as a descriptive model for developing countries, as the following example of Latin America illustrates (cited from Arndt 1989).

Through most of the nineteenth century, the countries of Latin America were much more like the non-European countries of what is now the First rather than the Third World; countries like Australia, New Zealand and Canada. They had neither colonial status nor external threats to react to. Their economies developed as part of the liberal international economic order. Their traditional systems of mining and agriculture were sufficient to supply a growing international market with the primary commodities and agricultural products that Latin America appeared to produce almost effortlessly.

Over the next 50 years, the economic development of Latin American countries fell behind Australia, New Zealand and Canada. By 1945, Latin America had become economically – and even more emotionally and ideologically – part of the Third World. In spite of this, countries like Chile have seen remarkable growth in recent years, which has led to speculation as to whether Chile should strive towards the economic development models of Australia, New Zealand and other East Asian countries, rather than trying to emulate Brazil or Argentina. Such speculations must be questioned for at least two reasons. First, economic development in the past 15 years has not been a linear process but rather fluctuating. For example, in 1970, the GDP per head in Chile was 19 per cent of the average for OECD countries, whereas in 1988 it was only 15 per cent. Second, cultural and other factors mark a significant difference from that of East Asia, as noted by Ching-yuan Lin (1993).

Many different factors have contributed to the divergence in development that has occurred between Latin America and East Asia since the Second World War. Several political and historical factors behind the different development models have been emphasized by researchers. East Asia's strong traditions of authoritarian, closed and technocratically-oriented regimes contrasts with the more open, socially-politicized regimes of Latin America. In comparison, Latin American regimes have greater elements of conflict and open contradictions, but also more insight and participation by various groups.

Value systems in East Asian countries tend to tolerate repression, but generally encourage thriftiness and social and economic realignment. In Latin America, on the other hand, there is a clearly-marked tendency toward opposition and democracy, as well as freedom of speech. However, phenomena such as clientelism, corruption and extravagant spending tend to be tolerated concurrently. Such differences must be assumed to have had great consequences for economic and social progress (Ching-yuan Lin ibid.).

Critics of the 'Western' development model

There is no formally-defined development model that can be referred to as specifically Western, but what most Western countries involved in providing development aid have in common is a belief in democracy and human rights as a precondition for development. Economic development is here considered one among many factors necessary in this development process. In recent years, this view on development has been partly challenged by others, for example in the economic assistance provided by the Chinese government to countries in Africa and Latin America. With the advent of competing alternatives for aid, the Western development model has been criticized as being too soft on the one hand and too demanding on the other towards recipients in complying with Western norms and values. However, criticism and the diversity of views regarding Western development assistance is not new but has been debated for a long time!

Some critics have focused on industrialization in general as a token of Westernisation and a destruction of traditional structures – economic, social and mental (e.g. Latouche 1996). Others (e.g. Mishan 1967) focus on the mechanisms of economic growth, where figures and indices become the tools of our economic planning processes, even if the reality behind the figures is sometimes uncertain, sometimes even obscure. More recently, the flow of aid from developed countries to developing countries in (primarily) Africa has been criticized for being inefficient, misdirected and demanding too little responsibility of the recipients. Moyo (2009) even claims the most important challenge we face today is that of destroying the myth that aid actually works.

Other critics argue alternatives to the development models favoured by Western countries – including the World Bank, the IMF and other international institutions – should be developed, not based solely on economic growth. Within the OECD countries, the idea of economic growth as the only development measure began to give way to a Physical Quality of Life Index (PQLI) in the 1970s (Kingsbury *et al.* 2004), and more recently the government of Bhutan proclaimed the introduction of Gross National Happiness (GNH) as an official alternative to the more conventional GNP (Sen 2009). With the introduction of *sustainability* as a new approach to development, *life quality* is becoming an integrated part of development measures.

The question of *ethnocentricity* comes up when the Western approach to development is discussed. The notion of *the other* (the non-Westerner) as a fundamental idea has influenced and determined the Western world-view both historically and politically. It has been asked if development is really based on transfer of knowledge or rather values and constructs (see, for example, McKay 2004). The Western concern, according to these authors, has been to win markets, gain access to raw materials and avoid being swamped by a massive increase in the populations of impoverished countries. The West, with its blind faith in technology and the effectiveness of planning, has treated the Third World as a child in great need of guidance.

An ideological argument raised by Kabou (1991) regarding economic and social development in Africa is that the very notion of development is considered by many Africans, in particular the African urban elite, as a task or responsibility of the former colonial powers. Kabou argues that Africans look upon themselves as eternal victims of colonization, unwilling or unable to take development of the continent into their own hands without relying on foreign aid.

Development measures

GDP, GNP, GNI and PPP

The most commonly-used measures of development are *gross domestic product* (GDP), *gross national income* (GNI), and formerly *gross national product* (GNP). Data is given as an accumulated value for a nation, or related to the population of the nation as the accumulated value divided by the size of the population, *per capita*. GDP per capita is thus GDP divided by the mid-year population. GDP measures the total final output of goods and services produced by a country, that is, by residents and non-residents, regardless of allocation to domestic and foreign claims. GDP is considered a broad measure of the growth of an economy and is estimated by measuring the total quantity of goods and services produced in a period, valuing them by their *added value* (a term used to denote the net output of an industry after adding up all outputs and subtracting intermediate inputs).

GNI is the broadest measure and measures total value added from domestic and foreign sources claimed by residents. GNI comprises GDP plus net receipts of primary income from foreign sources. Data are converted from national currency to current USD values using the World Bank Atlas method. This involves using a three-year average of exchange rates to smooth the effects of transitory fluctuations. For countries with a high share of remittances from citizens working abroad (e.g. Sri Lanka), GNI and GDP measures may differ, whereas in most cases the two are close.

GDP (or GNI) per capita is a practical measure of development and can be used to compare the development levels of countries; it is a quantitative measure and is therefore useful for analytical purposes. In spite of, this GDP is problematic. First, it relies on statistical data which is a problem in itself, since the availability, accuracy and reliability of data is highly uncertain in many cases. Second, many transactions outside the formal economy are not part of the statistics, or they are included but based on uncertain estimates. Third, the GDP data may be valued at different prices, such as market price for a specific year, or at current

Table 2.1 GNI level in 2008 for selected countries, at current exchange rate and at PPP in USD per capita

Country	GNI per capita		Official (a) versus PPP (b) rates: a/b
	Official rate (a)	PPP rate (b)	
Argentina	7,190	14,000	1.95
Bangladesh	520	1,450	2.8
Chile	9,370	13,250	1.41
Cuba	4,920	9,700	2.0
Ecuador	3,690	7,780	2.1
Egypt	1,800	5,470	3.0
Finland	47,600	35,940	0.75
Great Britain	46,040	36,240	0.8
Guatemala	2,680	4,690	1.75
India	1,040	2,930	2.8
Indonesia	1,880	3,600	1.9
Kenya	730	1,560	2.14
Kuwait	43,930	53,480	1.24
New Zeeland	27,830	25,200	0.9
Poland	11,730	16,710	1.42
Russia	9,660	15,460	1.6
Senegal	980	1,780	1.8
South Africa	5,820	9,780	1.7
Spain	31,930	30,830	0.96
Sri Lanka	1,780	4,460	2.5
Tanzania	440	1,260	2.86
Tunisia	3,480	7,460	2.1
USA	47,930	46,790	0.98
Vietnam	890	2,700	3.0

Source: World Development Report 2010. The World Bank.

price. In countries with price instability due to high inflation or where exchange rates vary, the different values for GDP may be significant.

Since nominal exchange rates do not always reflect the actual buying power between different countries and differences in relative prices, an alternative to measuring GNI in USD, and based on official exchange rates, is to use a conversion factor called *purchase power parity* (PPP). GNI at PPP means that the GNI is modified to reflect the local purchasing power. At the PPP rate, one USD has the same purchasing power over domestic GNI that the USD has over GNI in the United States. By comparing GNI at current price (*a*) and GNI at PPP (*b*) one gets an indication of the value of the local currency in international comparison: if the ratio *b/a* is greater than one, the local currency is said to be under-valued. Table 2.1 shows for some selected countries the difference between GNI measured by the official exchange rate, and by the actual purchasing power in the country.

To illustrate the practical implications of the difference between GNI per capita measured by official exchange rates and at PPP, we take the example of Indonesia.

Referring to Table 2.1, GNI per capita shows how much value each citizen in Indonesia has 'produced' (on average) during the year 2008, expressed in USD. The value 1,880 USD has been calculated from the official exchange rate. However, this amount of money would buy much less in the United States compared to Indonesia, in other words, 1,880 USD has a significantly higher purchasing value in Indonesia than the same amount would have in the

United States. This actual purchase value (PPP) is 3,600 USD. The ratio of 1:9 shows that, in reality, the purchase value of the Indonesian currency in Indonesia is almost twice as much as we would expect from the official exchange rate. Or, phrased differently, things bought in Indonesia for 1,880 USD would cost 3,600 USD in the United States, i.e. 1.9 times more! This also means that the Indonesian currency is *undervalued* in international (USD) comparisons. An undervalued currency may attract tourists but it makes travelling abroad expensive for its citizens; it may be beneficial to the export industry but detrimental to those firms importing components, materials and spare parts.

According to the notion of PPP as one of the oldest concepts of international economics, exchange rates should in the long run move towards the rate that equalizes the price of identical bundles of traded goods and services in each country. Sooner or later, a US dollar should thus buy the same amount anywhere. As an argument against this traditional assumption, the UK-based financial journal *The Economist* suggested in the 1980s a 'Big Mac Index', also referred to as *Burgernomics*, where the bundle is a MacDonald's Big Mac hamburger, since it is produced to more or less the same recipe in about 120 countries. Recently other semi-humorous alternatives have been suggested, such as the Billy bookshelf, produced in many countries by the Swedish furniture company IKEA.

How to calculate the Big Mac Index (BMI)? The price of a Big Mac hamburger in local currency is divided by the price for a Big Mac in New York. This implied purchase power of the USD gives an informal exchange rate that can be compared with the formal exchange rate between the USD and the local currency. Taking Indonesia as an example, the local price for a Big Mac in 2008 was 18,700 Rupiah (local currency) to be compared with the local price for a Big Mac in New York at the same time of 3.57 USD. The implied purchase power of one USD in Indonesia is thus 5,238 Rupiah which is compared with the official exchange rate at the same time of 9,152 Rupiah to the USD. In other words, since the informal exchange rate based on an identical product (the Big Mac) is 43 per cent lower than the official exchange rate, the *Burgernomics* model suggests that the Indonesian currency is undervalued by 43 per cent (a ratio of 1:75)!

Alternative development measures

The idea of per capita GDP as the primary measure of development began to give way to alternative measures and resulted, for instance, in the Physical Quality of Life Index (PQLI), developed in the 1970s. The PQLI emphasized development results rather than capacity for consumption; it also measured infant mortality, life expectancy and adult literacy. In recent years a variety of alternative measures have been suggested, addressing priority areas such as environment, energy, democracy etc. One such measure devised in the 1990s, and which has supplanted the PQLI, is the Human Development Index (HDI): this combines life expectancy, per capita income and a mix of educational measures (Kingsbury *et. al.* 2004). Besides traditional GNI, international reports and statistics tend to use HDI and another measure known as the Gini coefficient, both of which are discussed below.

Human Development Index

The Human Development Index (HDI) was developed as a complement to GDP per capita with the intention of creating a broader measure not solely focused on economic growth. Income per capita was considered by many an insufficient target for ultimately achieving society's broader development goals, and the HDI enables international comparisons to be made in a simplified form by combining the achievement of a number of different variables into a single number. HDI thus measures not only economic level but also non-economic factors such as life expectancy at birth, literacy, access to healthcare and education, access to water, adults living with HIV/AIDS or, in other words, standard of living. The value of the HDI index can vary between 0 and 1, with low values indicating greater distance from the maximum to be achieved on the aggregate of the factors making up the HDI, whereas high values indicate greater achievement relative to the maximum attainable and thus a higher level of human development.

The HDI can be interpreted as a measure of 'relative deprivation', that is, how far a country is from reaching, on average, the maximum value of the components that make up the HDI. Roughly speaking, since this is a deprivation index, one can interpret an HDI of 0.66 to mean that an economy has, on average, attained 66 per cent of what is possible (Cypher and Dietz 2009). The HDI is a weighted average of the three variables: life expectancy at birth, educational attainment and standard of living. The formula for calculating each of these is

$$I = (actual - minimum)/(maximum - minimum)$$

where the *actual* value is derived from national statistics and the *maximum* and *minimum* values are set as follows:

Variable	Minimum	Maximum
Life expectancy at birth (LEI)	25 years	85 years
Educational attainment	0%	100%
Standard of living	100 USD	40,000 USD

The actual life expectancy in India is 63.7 years. Hence the LEI factor for India (63.7 − 25)/(85 − 25) = 0.64. The Human Development Index for a selection of countries is presented in Table 2.2 below.

The Gini coefficient

An alternative method by which social scientists have measured income equity levels is by the construction of a Lorenz Curve and the calculation of what is known as the Gini coefficient.[2] The Lorenz Curve is a straight line when a certain percentage of national income goes to the same percentage of households, no matter what level of income one considers. But this is hardly ever the case: the Lorenz Curve traces the actual relationship between these two percentages. The more the Lorenz Curve bends away from the diagonal, the greater the inequality in distribution of income. If the Lorenz Curve lies on the diagonal, the Gini coefficient equals zero, indicating zero inequality in income distribution. The closer the Gini coefficient gets to unity, the greater the inequality in distribution of income across households (Thirlwall 2003). A value of 0.7 on the *x*-axis and 0.3 on the *y*-axis means that the bottom 70 per cent of the population owns 30 per cent of the total wealth in the country. The Gini coefficient is measured as the ratio between the two areas A and A + B in Figure 2.2. The Gini coefficient for a selection of countries in 2007 is presented along with their figure for GDP per capita and HDI are shown in Table 2.2.

The last column in Table 2.2 has the following meaning. The 182 countries listed in tables in the World Bank annual reports appear on different levels in the tables, depending

Table 2.2 Gini, GDP, HDI and GDP–HDI ranks for selected countries in 2007

Country	Gini	GDP per capita (PPP)	HDI	GDP rank–HDI rank
Argentina	0.46	13,238	0.87	+13
Bangladesh	0.33	1,241	0.54	+9
Chile	0.55	13,880	0.88	+15
Cuba	n.a.	6,876	0.86	+44
Ecuador	0.48	7,449	0.81	+11
Egypt	0.34	5,349	0.70	−20
Finland	0.30	34,526	0.96	+11
Guatemala	0.55	4,562	0.70	−11
India	0.37	2,753	0.61	−6
Indonesia	0.39	3,712	0.73	+10
Kenya	0.43	1,542	0.54	+2
Kuwait	n.a.	47,812	0.92	−23
New Zeeland	0.36	27,336	0.95	+12
Poland	0.35	15,987	0.88	+12
Russia	0.42	14,690	0.82	−16
Senegal	0.41	1,666	0.46	−19
South Africa	0.65	9,757	0.68	−51
Spain	0.32	31,560	0.96	+12
Sri Lanka	0.49	4,243	0.76	+14
Tanzania	0.35	1,208	0.53	+6
Tunisia	0.40	7,520	0.77	−8
United Kingdom	0.34	35,130	0.96	−1
USA	0.45	45,592	0.96	−4
Vietnam	0.37	2,600	0.73	+13

Source: Human Development Index. World Bank 2009.

on what data is shown. For example, Finland had a GDP per capita of 34,526 USD measured by purchase power parity (PPP), ranking Finland 23rd out of the 182 countries in the World Bank GDP table. Finland's HDI of 0.96 ranks it 12th out of the same 182 countries. This means that Finland 'scores' higher for HDI than it does for GDP per capita. Subtracting its HDI ranking (23) from its GDP ranking (12) gives a difference of +11, the figure given in the table. Positive results are taken to indicate that factors such as health, literacy and standard of living have at least as high importance as the economic growth factors. From a general point of view, one could expect that high GDP figures would also lead to high HDI values. This is also true if judged from the relatively high statistical correlation between the two parameters (0.7 to 0.8). There is, however, no obvious systematization of the values in this column of the table.

Cypher and Dietz (2009) ask if the HDI provides different information about the development level of a country than can be obtained from GDP or GNI per capita figures. Is it reasonable to use real GNI or GDP per capita as a proxy for the level of development rather than the admittedly more-difficult-to-estimate HDI? They refer to comments made by the UNDP (United Nations Development Programme):

> Rankings by HDI and by GDP per capita can be quite different, showing that countries do not have to wait for economic prosperity to make progress in human development. Costa Rica and Korea have both made impressive human development gains, reflected in HDIs of more than 0.80, but Costa Rica has achieved this human outcome with only half the

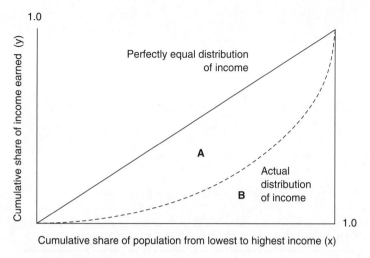

Figure 2.2 The Lorenz curve.

income of Korea. Pakistan and Viet Nam have similar incomes, but Viet Nam has done much more in translating that income into human development. So, with the right policies, countries can advance faster in human development than in economic growth.

(United Nations Development Programme 2001)

Correlation between measures

Applying statistical correlation analysis to the data in Table 2.2, it can be shown that:

*   There is very strong correlation between GDP per capita and HDI.
*   The is very weak correlation between Gini and GDP per capita.
*   There is no correlation between Gini and HDI.

Despite the seemingly weak relationship between Gini and GDP per capita, a study by Simon Kuznet (cited in Cypher and Dietz ibid.) suggests there is a minimum level of income a country must achieve before greater equity and higher levels of development can be attained. The so-called Kuznet curve is shown in Figure 2.3. (Note that a lower Gini coefficient means less inequity.) Once that threshold level of income is reached, further increases in income contribute to greater equity. That threshold level is approximately 1,000 USD per person.

Sectored distribution of GDP

It has been a tradition in economic theory to distinguish between the three economic sectors, namely primary (agriculture, cattle, fishing and forestry), secondary (industry) and tertiary (services and trade). Fischer used this classification to support his theory about the successive transfer of the demand of goods and services from the primary sector to the secondary and thence to the tertiary as income levels increase (Fischer, 1935). The International Standard Industrial Classification (ISIC) uses a more fine-grained classification of the sectors. The agriculture sector corresponds to ISIC divisions 1 through 5, and includes forestry and fishing.

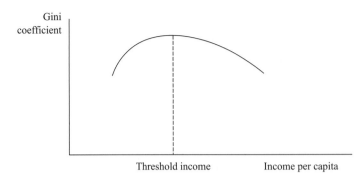

Figure 2.3 The Kuznet curve. Note that a lower Gini coefficient means less inequity.

Table 2.3 Distribution of GDP between the three economic sectors in selected countries, as percentage of added value of GDP in 2008

Country	Agriculture	Industry	Service
Argentina	9	34	57
Bangladesh	19	29	52
Chile	4	47	59
Cuba	4	22	74
Ecuador	7	36	57
Egypt	14	36	50
Finland	3	32	65
Guatemala	11	28	62
India	18	29	53
Indonesia	14	48	37
Kenya	21	13	65
Kuwait	0	48	52
New Zeeland	4	24	72
Poland	4	30	65
Russia	5	38	57
Senegal	15	23	62
South Africa	3	33	66
Spain	3	30	67
Sri Lanka	13	29	57
Tanzania	45	17	37
Tunisia	10	28	62
United Kingdom	1	23	76
USA	1	22	77
Vietnam	20	42	38

Source: World Development Report (2010).

Industry comprises mining, manufacturing, construction, electricity, water and gas (ISIC divisions 10 through 45). The service sector corresponds to ISIC divisions 50 through 99.

Table 2.3 illustrates how the contribution from agriculture is relatively stronger for countries with lower GDP per capita (poorer countries), where a significant portion of the population is still active in agriculture. With economic development the agricultural sector shrinks, whereas industry becomes stronger. For the most-developed countries, the contribution to

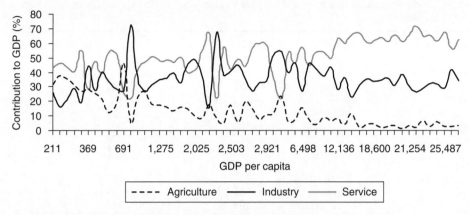

Figure 2.4 Contribution to GNP from the three economic sectors.

Source: Compiled by author from World Development Report 2005.

GDP from the industry sector tends to be lower as a majority of economic and commercial activities belong to the service sector.

Figure 2.4 shows the relative contribution to GDP from the three main economic sectors of agriculture, industry and service from 135 countries. The diagram reveals that a certain pattern tends to develop in countries with a GDP per capita level around 7,000 USD. Above that level, the three sectors start to stabilize, with agriculture at the bottom, service at the top and industry in between.

The relative contribution to GDP within one country shows a similar pattern as illustrated in the following diagram from Sweden between 1900 and 2000 (Figure 2.5). The contribution

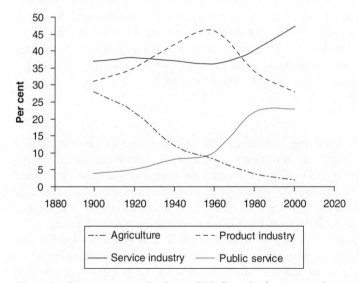

Figure 2.5 Percentage contribution to GDP from the four economic sectors in Sweden 1900–2000.

Source: Statistical Yearbook of Sweden 2008.

Table 2.4 Economic contribution measured by added value in some German provinces and selected countries

German province	Country	GDP (billions USD)	% of German province
Nordrhein-Westfalen		699	
	Turkey	593	85
Bavaria		576	
	Indonesia	515	89
Baden-Württemberg		460	
	Taiwan	357	78
	Argentina	301	65
Hessen		290	
	South Africa	277	95
	Egypt	188	65
	New Zeeland	109	37
	Vietnam	92	32
	Sri Lanka	41	14
	Kenya	30	10

Source: Author.

from the service industry grew from 29 to 39 per cent while the contribution from product industry declined from 31 to 28 per cent after a peak in 1960 of 46 per cent, i.e. almost half of the total contribution came from a strong industry sector. The public service sector – a factor making an insignificant contribution to GDP at the beginning of the century – became increasingly important, growing from 4 to 23 per cent. This sector includes, *inter alia*, social services and medical services, which increase in volume and costs with aging population – a situation that applies to a growing number of high-income countries.

By way of illustrating the imbalance in the world economy, Table 2.4 compares GDP data for some German provinces with data from some middle-income countries in 2009. For example, the table shows that the total GDP in Indonesia, i.e. the total value of all economic activities in the country, was somewhat higher than that of Baden-Württemberg, but 10 per cent lower than in Bavaria and significantly lower than Nordrhein-Westfalen, the richest province in Germany that year. Total value of all economic activities in Egypt was 25 per cent of the economic production value in Nordrhein-Westfalen.

Industry

Industrialization has long been equated with development both in developed and developing countries, and according to the dominant ideology no economic development would be possible without industrialization (Garcia 1989). Germany – the largest economy in Europe and number four in the world – has historically developed a strong manufacturing sector. As early as 1740 King Frederic II set up a department for manufacturing and commerce with the aim of improving production and setting up new manufacturing units (Henning 1977).

Development theory and ideology in general acknowledges the importance of industrialization for economic development, where the industry sector comprises mining, manufacturing, construction, electricity, water and gas. Fischer (1935) and Clark (1940) were among the first to specifically identify the role of manufacturing in industrial development. This

Table 2.5 Estimation of GDP per capita (PPP) in the world from year 1 through 2003, in 1990 international dollars[a]

Country/region	1	1000	1500	1600	1700	1820	1870	1913	1950	1973	2003
Western Europe[b]	576	427	771	889	997	1,202	1,960	3,457	4,578	11,417	19,912
Eastern Europe	412	400	496	548	606	683	937	1,695	2,111	4,988	6,476
Former USSR	400	400	499	552	610	688	943	1,488	2,841	6,059	5,397
USA	400	400	400	400	527	1,257	2,445	5,301	9,561	16,689	29,037
Latin America[b]	400	400	416	438	527	691	676	1,493	2,503	4,513	5,786
Japan	400	425	500	520	570	669	737	1,387	1,921	11,434	21,218
China	450	450	600	600	600	600	530	552	448	838	4,803
India	450	450	550	550	550	533	533	673	619	853	2,160
Other East Asia	425	425	554	564	561	568	594	842	771	1,485	3,854
Africa	472	425	414	422	421	420	500	637	890	1,410	1,549
World	467	450	566	596	616	667	873	1,526	2,113	4,091	6,516

Source: Maddison, 2003.

Notes
a To convert international dollars to local currency units, multiply the international dollar figure by the PPP exchange rate.
b Average.

has been further underlined by observations that countries with a well-developed manufacturing sector have reached a high standard of living (e.g. Bairoch 1975). Development theorists – both capitalist and Marxist – have endorsed the development of manufacturing. The importance of the manufacturing sector as a driver for economic development stems from its integration with other economic activities, generating up-stream as well as down-stream development in other sectors. Manufacturing as the major contributor of added value to gross production requires technology and innovations as well as skills and knowledge. High added-value production therefore requires that basic infrastructure facilities in society, such as education, financial and legal and transport systems, have developed and work properly. The proportion of high technology content in manufacturing can therefore be seen as a measure of development, which becomes apparent when studying the development of GDP around the world from an historical perspective.

How has GDP per capita developed through the years?

In recent years, attempts have been made to construct historic productivity data for the world in the form of GDP per capita, in which a country's accounts have been projected back several decades at a time, all the way to the first year of the Christian calendar. Table 2.5 shows an estimation of GDP per capita for selected regions for the last 2,000 years, based on the pioneering work by Angus Maddison and others (Maddison 2003).[3] Over the past millennium, world population rose 22-fold, per capita income increased 13-fold and world GDP nearly 300-fold. This contrasts sharply with the preceding millennium, when world population grew by only a sixth, and there was no advance in per capita income. From the year 1000 to 1820, the advance in per capita income was a slow crawl – the world average rose about 50 per cent. Most of the growth went to accommodate a fourfold increase in population. Since 1820, world development has been much more dynamic. Per capita income rose more than eightfold, population more than fivefold (Maddison 2002).

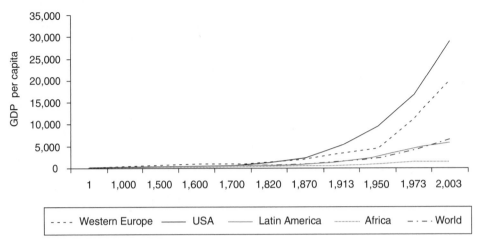

Figure 2.6 GDP growth for selected countries from Table 2.5.

The assumptions about world GDP growth shown in Table 2.5 have been both criticized and supported by academics. For reasons discussed in Chapter 1, even today, statistical data are often uncertain, sometimes inaccurate or misleading, due to inappropriate analysis models or data acquisition methods. Statistical data from historic times have, in addition to these problems, a variety of other shortcomings, such as finding the proper sources of data. Some critics thus claim that figures on India and Pakistan use dubious comparative data; Asian GDP per capita, especially that of China, exceeded and at least equalled that of the West until 1800, which would give a much higher GDP level. Others put China's GDP per capita at a higher level than the West until the nineteenth century (e.g. Bairoch 1975).

Figure 2.6 plots some of the data from Table 2.5. A striking fact is the slow GDP growth for almost 2,000 years when the regions in the world faced very similar development problems. The divergence began with the so-called Industrial Revolution in some European countries towards the middle of the nineteenth century. Since then, financial wealth has accelerated in most regions, even if the difference between countries is significant, and the GDP development of the world as a whole has been significantly slower than in the most affluent regions.

What has contributed to the growth in GDP, seen over a longer time period? It is beyond the scope of this book to discuss this question in detail. However, a few vital background aspects can be mentioned, such as production techniques and the traditional production factors of labour, capital and land. As new and improved techniques came into use and were applied in different countries, agricultural productivity and output increased enabling more people to be fed than before. In Germany, for example, the size of the working population increased from an estimated 0.6 million in the year 800 to 5 million in 1800 (Henning 1977).

Economic development and the SME Sector

Encouraging the growth of the SME sector is an important plank of industrial policy in most countries because of the anticipated contribution of the sector to economic growth and job creation. In the wake of the increased focus on the small business sector, considerable research has been undertaken to understand the nature of entrepreneurship and, in particular, what makes SMEs growth-oriented and competitive. The current research ambition regarding SMEs has thus both descriptive and normative aspects, in which the complexity of the task of formulating a general recipe of competitiveness has yet to be overcome. Although a multitude of factors are hypothesized as impacting on business outcomes, there is no consistent pattern as to the characteristics that contribute to small business competitiveness, success and growth (Ray 1993; Gibb 1996).

Ever since the Bolton Report (discussed in Chapter 5) was published in the early 1970s, the emphasis has been on small business for its potential to create new jobs. The growth expectations of the small business sector became a political objective of many governments as large firms seemed unable to generate all the new job opportunities required. The new technology developed to increase productivity in administration and production required massive capital investments that small firms could not afford. Instead the small businesses – earlier regarded by governments as peripheral actors in the economy – were now expected to shoulder the task of growing and creating jobs. Government logic has been based on the assumption that by introducing incentive schemes for the small business sector, small firms would grow and thereby create new jobs. In reality, however, government initiatives have mostly resulted in a significant increase in the number of micro firms which mostly fail to grow.

Not only national government programmes but also international programmes of development assistance encompass support for the small business sector as part of their overall support for economic development. For example, the World Bank approved programmes worth more than 10 billion USD in support of SMEs in the five years to 2004 (Beck and Demirgüç-Kunt 2004). Many of these programmes are based on the commonly-held belief that, relative to large firms, SMEs:

- increase competition and thereby generate efficient market mechanisms;
- are generally more productive on a per-firm basis; and
- are more labour intensive and therefore more effectively address the pressing need for new sources of stable employment for the poor.

While anecdotal proof abounds, targeted economic research simply does not support any of these arguments (Taussig 2005). Testing all three of the above justifications of pro-SME policy, Beck *et al.* (2005) could not find any causal relationship between SME development and economic growth and poverty alleviation. The Global Entrepreneurship Monitor report (2009) shows either no or only limited expectations of job creation, and the expectation of high-growth entrepreneurial activity varies widely between countries.

Small business in international contexts

Small firms have limited resources (finance and know-how) to venture into international business and, in spite of new techniques for communication across borders, personal contacts are still important. Lack of language skills is therefore a limiting factor for such contacts, in particular, for discussing and negotiating innovations and high-tech issues. The traditional view has therefore been that those small businesses venturing into neighbouring regions and countries do so where cultural and language differences are minimal. Since the end of the 1990s, however, a new trend has been observed in developed countries where newly-established small firms are international from the start – the so-called 'born globals'.

Common factors for many of these firms are either previous international business experience of the owners/managers or already-established business relations with potential international customers.

As formal trade barriers between countries come down, the present world trade environment provides opportunities for developing countries to derive tangible benefits if they produce competitive value-added manufactured goods for the global market. Nevertheless, most developing countries remain marginalized in spite of initiatives to create change, for example, the 'Doha Development Agenda' which aimed at assisting developing countries in becoming more effective partners in the global trading environment. However, the lack of production capacity to supply international customers' demand for high-quality products and services, and the lack of compliance with technical market specifications, such as standards and environmental regulations, continue to be difficult obstacles for developing countries, preventing them from entering international markets.

A characteristic of today's international trade is that only goods of sufficient quality and cost will be able to find customers and secure access to large, stable markets. This phenomenon is a severe disadvantage to local SMEs, since many lack the requisite economies of scale and scope. Lack of macroeconomic stability, adequate logistics infrastructure and sound and fair competition between firms contribute to the disadvantages. International trade is thus discussed and assessed in qualitative and quantitative terms.

International trade has become complex and highly demanding. Continuous improvement and innovation in quality, price and services have pushed competition to levels unreachable by many small firms in developing countries. Stricter regulations and product-specific clauses are being added to global as well as regional trading regimes. Barriers to trade between countries and within regions due to inadequate, toxic or dangerous material are what lie behind the WTO initiative to regulate access to export markets by countries. Implementing the rules of the WTO Agreement on Technical Barriers to Trade (TBT) and the Agreement on Sanitary and Phyto-Sanitary Measures (SPS)[4] on the company site will facilitate access to the international market. Success and survival of SMEs in international trade therefore calls for preparations that are far more comprehensive than ever before. This is discussed further in Chapter 11.

SMEs use relatively less capital to create jobs compared with larger enterprises. This is a salient feature, especially for developing economies with abundant labour but scarce capital. According to various authors, SMEs are supposed to be the main potential source of economic growth and innovation as they are an important source of export revenue in many of the lowest income countries, given their mostly overvalued currencies, lower cost of production and government incentives. However, it has been suggested by Thirlwall (1979) that a country's growth is limited by the balance of payment equilibrium. *Thirlwall's Law* can be interpreted as follows: growth in exports leads to growth in earnings which in turn contributes to economic growth. But what happens if import growth is higher? If economic growth leads to higher salaries, then how this increase in personal income is spent becomes crucial. While the value of the additional imports remains lower than the value of the increased salaries, part of the export income will remain in the country; if not, it will all be exported to the supplier nations. In countries with a limited or non-existent consumer products industry, it is the latter scenario that dominates, reducing the country's potential for benefitting from international trade.

This divide becomes more apparent with globalization, as the competitive advantage of SMEs in developing countries is weakened. The globalization of economic activity affects the development of SMEs in three main ways. For a small proportion of SMEs, globalization opens up new opportunities for export expansion and growth, and such SMEs are already active in overseas markets. For a greater proportion of SMEs, inward globalization poses new competitive challenges and threats from abroad, and SMEs from different industries are likely to be affected in different ways. The SMEs that are potentially competitive (with manufacturing infrastructure close to global standards) are likely to be pushed into export production and upgrading their manufacturing capabilities. Those less likely or unable to adapt are at risk from the competition induced by globalization, and may not survive without significant upgrading to improve output quality, cost competitiveness and management practices. The remaining SMEs are largely insulated from the effects of globalization and are hence likely to have limited capabilities. These SMEs tend to be relatively small, localized service providers.

Development researchers

After the Second World War, and particularly after the rapid success of the US-financed Marshall Plan to help rebuild the European economies, several economists directly involved in the Marshall Plan, or with institutions such as the United Nations and the World Bank, turned their attention to the economic development of less-developed countries (Cypher and Dietz 2009).

Of the many researchers who have influenced and contributed to our understanding of the process of economic and social development, a few are profiled below. They have been chosen for the lead they took in making development research an academic discipline. We look at Gunnar Myrdal, Raúl Prebisch, Arthur Lewis, Dudley Sears, Amartya Sen and Hans Singer.

Box 2.2

Gunnar Myrdal (1898–1987)

Gunnar Myrdal was a Swedish economist with a sociological focus that also included non-economic aspects. He was one of the leading institutionalists defending the view that economy and society must be viewed as a whole, whose separate parts cannot be understood and analysed independently of the whole. Myrdal became famous for his work on the Black poor population in the southern United States (*An American Dilemma*), as well as his research on rich and poor countries. In his later work, his ambition was to shed light on the roots of poverty, and his research findings were published in *Asian Drama*, where he helped demonstrate the differences between the industrial world and the underdeveloped one.

Raúl Prebisch (1901–1986)

Born in Argentina, Raúl Prebisch was the most influential of Latin American economists. He was deeply involved in international debates on economic development. Prebisch was more of a policy-maker than a theorist and is best known for his ideas on international trade. In the 1930s he acted as Argentina's leading trade diplomat when his country's prosperity was threatened by the problems of Britain – Argentina's main market for its meat and grains. He concluded that the price of primary products tended to decline relative to those of manufactured goods (which embodied higher productivity), and thus that industrialized countries derived more benefit from trade than developing ones. The answer was to promote structural change and industrialization in Latin America.

Arthur Lewis (1915–1991)

Arthur Lewis was born in St. Lucia in the Caribbean and is primarily known for his work on *Unlimited Supplies of Labour*. Lewis' idea was that surplus labour in agriculture should be regarded as a hidden reserve that could be tapped for industrialization. Lewis therefore presumed that the typical less-developed nation was dualistic, in the sense that the two sectors, agriculture and industry, had little interconnection. There was a traditional, low-productivity rural and predominantly agricultural sector, where most people worked and consumed what was produced. But there was also a modern capitalist sector, that either existed or could be created, that was more technologically-driven and in which, therefore, worker productivity was higher than in the traditional sector.

Dudley Seers (1920–1983)

Dudley Seers was a British economist who specialized in development economics. He became famous for replacing the 'growth fetishism' of the early post-war period with a greater concern for social development. Seers played a pioneering role in suggesting an alternative approach to the traditional definition of development, which was too restrictive and failed to address its multi-faceted nature. He insisted that development should include social objectives such as employment, health and shelter. The modified view of development suggested by Seers (as a process that could not only be measured by gross national product) prepared the ground for the introduction of the Human Development Index. Seers was highly critical of using indexes such as unemployment and inflation when referring to Third World countries, possibly because the statistics we have from these countries are too unreliable for us to be able to make judgments concerning their economies.

Amartya Sen (b. 1933)

Born in India, Amartyra Sen has made a huge contribution to development economy by bringing clarity to the problem of whether developing countries should use more labour-intensive methods of production than would be profitable at the market wage rate. In many developing countries, labour for production is abundant, whilst capital is very scarce. It is tempting therefore to suggest that labour-intensive production is the most productive. This thinking ignores the fact that savings rates may well be lower if more money is paid out in low wages, thus creating a vicious circle where capital remains scarce. One of Sen's contributions was to create a clear analytical framework in which these issues could be discussed; another has been to legitimize the investigation of topics like famine, which previously were considered outside the scope of economics.

Before presenting Hans Singer, our final economist, we make a few comments on the *Singer–Prebisch Hypothesis* – one of many influential approaches to the development process. Both Prebisch and Singer had independently noted that gains in productivity were greater in industrial than in primary-goods nations. This factor in turn was aggravated by an international trade cycle in which the agricultural countries were more vulnerable than the core economies during recessions, because organized labour in Europe and North America was strong enough to prevent an equivalent collapse of prices. The result of both factors – a secular decline in terms of trade and business cycle vulnerability – explained the fundamental flaw of neoclassical trade theory, which assumed equal benefits for industrial and agricultural exporters and which was assumed to have the same validity in Latin America as in the United States or Britain (Dosman 2008).[5]

Box 2.3 Hans Singer (1910–2006)

A German-born economist, Singer had noted that historical statistics demonstrated a decline in the terms of trade of developing countries. Singer was an outspoken advocate of foreign aid and maintained that aid could take many forms, such as financial assistance to compensate for falling prices of exported primary products, and soft loans below market interest rates to the poorest countries to help them build infrastructure systems or long-term social investments. Singer was also a strong supporter of industrialization in developing countries, since it generated, according to Singer, strong technological externalities and other indirect benefits, such as its effect on education, skill levels, inventiveness and creation of new demand.

Summary and conclusion

Summary

From an early stage both the discipline of development studies and governments of developing countries used economic measures to measure development. Although some researchers argued that broader measures should be used to measure development, it took until the 1970s before HDI and the Gini coefficient were introduced as complementary measures to GDP. Extended study of development resulted in different models that dominated development theories in the period after the Second World War. Some models had contradictory effects and rather created new types of problems. Social aspects have tended to come more and more to the fore.

Conclusion

Small firms are by their nature local rather than international, and therefore closely dependent on conditions in their local environments.

The alleviation of poverty has a high priority in international aid programmes, and various economic theories and models with their focus on poverty reduction have been suggested and tried. The assumption that dominates in most of the theories is that economic growth leads to poverty alleviation, and it is therefore of primary interest of this book to assess and evaluate how much small firms contribute to economic growth.

In high-income countries, political and economic stability are important and often necessary conditions for the establishment and successful running of a business. In these countries, the contribution to economic growth from the small business sector is significant, and even in periods of financial turbulence small firms are only marginally affected. In low-income countries, on the other hand, political and economic uncertainty severely limits the scope of small firms to contribute to the economic growth process.

Notes

1   After Johannes Verdoorn, a Dutch economist.
2   Named after the Italian scientist Corrado Gini (1884–1965).
3   Angus Maddison (1926–2010), British economist.
4   An agreement on how governments can apply food safety and animal and plant health measures.
5   The neoclassical trade theory based on highly rational assumptions was developed in Britain by, among others, David Ricardo (1772–1823).

References

Arndt, A. W. (1984) *The Rise and Fall of Economic Growth*. London: University of Chicago Press.
Arndt, A. W. (1989) *Economic Development: The History of an Idea*. London: University of Chicago Press.
Bairoch, P. (1975) *The Economic Development of the Third World Since 1900*. London: Methuen & Co.
Beck, T. and Demirgüç-Kunt, A. (2004) *Do Pro-SME Policies Work?* Washington, DC: World Bank. Private Sector Note 268.
Beck, T., Demirgüç-Kunt, A. and Levine (2005) *SMEs, Growth and Poverty*. Washington, DC: National Bureau of Economic Research. Working Paper No. 11224.
Ching-yuan Lin (1993) *East Asia and Latin America as Contrasting Models*. Chicago, IL: University of Chicago Press.
Clark, C. (1940) *The Conditions of Economic Progress*. London: Macmillan.
Cypher, J. and Dietz, J. (2009) *The Process of Economic Development*. London: Routledge.
Donaldson, P. (1973) *Economics of the Real World*. London: Penguin Books.
Dosman, E. (2008) *The Life and Times of Raúl Prebisch*. Montreal: McGill-Queen's University Press.
Fischer, A. G. (1935) *The Clash of Progress and Scarcity*. London: Macmillan.
Forbes, N. and Wield, D. (2002) *From Followers to Leaders: Managing Technology and Innovation*. London: Routledge.
Frank, A. G. (1978) *Dependent Accumulation and Underdevelopment*. London: Macmillan.
Garcia, R. (1989) *Incipient Industrialisation in an 'Underdeveloped' Country: The Case of Chile, 1845–1879*. Stockholm: Institute of Latin American Studies. Monograph No. 17.
Gibb, A. A. (1996) 'Entrepreneurship and Small Business Management: Can we Afford to Neglect them in the 21st-Century Business School?'. *British Academy of Management*, 7: 309–321.
Global Entrepreneurship Monitor (2009) *Report*. London: Global Entrepreneurship Research Association.
Henning, F. (1977) *Das vorindustrielle Deutschland, 800 bis 1800*. Paderborn: UTB Schöningh.
Kabou, A. (1991) *Et si l'Afrique Refusai le Développement?* Paris: L'Harmattan.
Kingsbury, D., Remenyi, J., McKay, J. and Hunt, J. (2004) *Key Issues in Development*. London: Palgrave.
Latouche, S. (1996) *The Westernization of the World*. Oxford: Blackwell.
Lind, P. (1991) *Computerisation in Developing Countries: Model and Reality*. London: Routledge.
Lyon, D. (1994) *Post Modernity*. London: Open University Press.
Lyotard, J.-F. (1979) *La Condition Postmoderne: Rapport sur le Savoir*. Paris: Les Editions de Minuit.
McKay, J. (2004) 'Reassessing Development Theory: Modernization and Beyond', in Kingsbury, D., Remenyi, J., McKay, J. and Hunt, J. (eds) *Key Issues in Development*. London: Palgrave.
Maddison, A. (2002) *The World Economy: A Millennial Perspective*. Paris: OECD.
Maddison, A. (2003) *The World Economy: Historical Statistics*. Paris: OECD.
Mishan, E. J. (1967) *The Cost of Economic Growth*. Harmondsworth: Penguin Books.
Moyo, D. (2009) *Dead Aid*. London: Penguin Books.
Myrdal, G. (1968) *Asian Drama*. New York: Random House.
O'Brien, R. and Williams, M. (2004) *Global Political Economy – Evolution and Dynamics*. Basingstoke, Hampshire: Palgrave Macmillan.
Ray, D. M. (1993) 'Understanding the Entrepreneur: Entrepreneurial Attributes, Experiences and Skills'. *Entrepreneurship and Regional Development*, 5: 345–357.
Rostow, W. W. (1960) *Stages of Economic Growth*. Cambridge: Cambridge University Press.
Sen, A. (2009) *The Idea of Justice*. Cambridge, MA: Harvard University Press.

Stewart, F. (1978) *Technology and Underdevelopment*. London: Macmillan.

Taussig, M. (2005): *Domestic Companies in Vietnam: Challenges for Development of Vietnam's Most Important SMEs*. Ann Arbour, MI: University of Michigan Press. Policy Brief #34.

Thirlwall, A. P. (1979) 'The Balance of Payments Constraint as an Explanation of International Growth Rate Differences'. *Banca Nazionale del Lavoro Quarterly Review*, March.

Thirlwall, A. P. (2003) *Growth and Development*. London: Palgrave.

United Nations Development Programme (2001) *Human Development Report*. Washington, DC: World Bank.

3 The contribution of small firms to economic development

Introduction

Gross domestic product (GDP) is a monetary term describing the accumulated value being produced in a country and has several sources of input. Input comes from the four main sectors of agriculture, industrial production, industrial service and public service. Small and medium enterprises are represented in all four sectors and hence contribute to a country's economic development. The direct contribution to GDP comes from the accumulated net value produced by each individual firm and organization. Net value or added value is the value at market price of output produced, where the costs of the inputs required in doing so has been deducted. But small and medium firms also contribute indirectly by offering job opportunities whose salaries contribute to consumption and thereby to the demand for these same products and services.

Official figures show that the small business sector accounts for almost half of total employment in developed countries; significantly more than half in less developed countries. This is of importance from both social and economic standpoints. International aid organizations along with international donors usually claim that small and medium enterprises (SMEs) in the private sector are important actors in the economic growth process because they make investments and adopt technology that leads to an increase productivity and employment (World Bank 2004). Others claim that it is essential to strengthen SMEs in poor countries to reduce poverty (International Labour Organization 2006; Mukras 2003). In contrast, another World Bank study of the relationship between the size of the SME sector, economic growth and poverty could not confirm that small firms either foster economic growth or reduce poverty (Beck and Demirgüç-Kunt 2004). Another decade-long study of SMEs in transitional economies concluded that the SME sector by itself is enough to create successful economic growth (McIntyre 2003).

It is natural to question the SME sector's contribution to economic development, but the answer is uncertain and the supposed contribution seems difficult to verify. In general, opinions originating in academic circles tend to be more sceptical and uncertain, particularly regarding its capacity to create jobs (Bannock 2005). Also scholars with long experience of research into the small business sector tend to be less inclined to take firm positions in this context (e.g. Storey 1997). There are of course others who hold the view that SMEs do contribute to the generation of jobs and economic development (Harvie and Lee 2005), whereas others go so far as to argue that 'SMEs make a significant difference and can lead to economic growth' (Schramm 2004) and

> History demonstrates that a flourishing, responsible private sector, built on a broad base of enterprise, including small and medium-sized enterprises and well-regulated foreign

direct investment, has been key to delivering the sort of economic growth in developing countries that we know pulls poor people out of poverty.

(Hoffman 2005)

Economic growth and a rising standard of living is the result of many contributing factors interacting in a complex pattern. One such factor is the capacity of a nation's firms to achieve high levels of productivity, and to increase productivity over time. SMEs in developing countries have, however, significantly lower productivity (measured by added value per employee) in comparison with developed countries. Several studies of the small sector contribution to economic development have been carried out for limited numbers of countries which reveal low contribution from small and medium-sized firms in low-income countries (around 16 per cent) and high contribution in high-income countries (around 50 per cent).

GDP as measure of development

GDP per capita as a measure of development has been challenged as it gives no indication of how national income is distributed among citizens. It was argued that the income per capita criterion is too simplistic to give a balanced view of the level of progress achieved by many countries, and it is insufficient as a target for achieving society's broader development goals (Cypher and Dietz 2009).

With the introduction of the Human Development Index (HDI), which involves welfare parameters in addition to the pure economic parameters, it could be shown that there is a strong correlation between GDP per capita and HDI. This indicates that GDP per capita is also relevant to the social development of a country, which was further underlined with the observation that GDP per capita is strongly correlated with life expectancy (Sen 1999). The Preston Curve (named after Samuel Preston, an American professor of demography and based on empirical studies) shows that individuals born in richer countries can on average expect to live longer than those born in poor countries. This link between income and life expectancy tends to flatten out at high levels of income, indicating that increased income has little effect on life expectancy. However, at low levels of per capita income increases in income are associated with large gains (Schultz 2008).

Figure 3.1 shows the Preston curve with life expectancy as a variable related to national income as measured by GDP per capita. The curve is an approximation to the empirical data from various countries.

GDP aggregates value of goods and services produced in a country by individual firms and institutions. Value can be produced within one firm but may also be produced in subsequent steps by a chain of firms, where the output of one is the input to another. A supplier–customer relationship is a simple example of a link in such a chain. Value chain analysis (Porter 1985) shows that the total value produced by a chain of firms may be higher than the sum of value produced by each individual firm in the chain. This sum of value is referred to as *added value*, which is defined as the amount by which the income of a business exceeds the cost of its inputs, i.e. materials plus the cost of bringing the material into the company. The total added value produced by a firm not only gives an indication of its contribution to GDP but it also measures the competitiveness of the firm. According to Jones and Tilley (2003), 'Added value is a better measure of competitive advantage for SMEs than profit, return on investment or market share'. Added value is therefore an adequate measure of how much value is added to the material by labour and capital (machinery and other assets) in

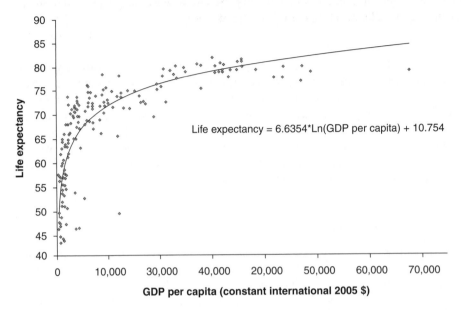

Figure 3.1 The Preston curve with data from 2005.

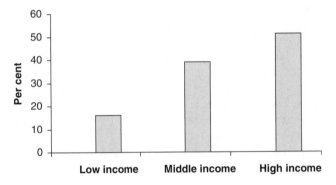

Figure 3.2 SME contribution to GDP for low-, middle- and high-income countries.

order to produce the final product or service. Moreover, added value is also a suitable measure of *productivity*: how much added value can be produced with available resources such
as labour capacity. Arthur Lewis noted (1954) that economic development consists of
changes in the quantity and character of economic value added.

The SME contribution to GDP

The contribution to GDP by a country's SMEs depends both on their number and their productivity. Figure 3.2 shows SME contribution based on GDP per capita level.

The designation of a country as low-, middle- or high-income countries is a World Bank
classification that is modified annually to reflect changes in individual countries' GNI.

According to 2009 GNI per capita data (calculated in national currency and converted to USD at official exchange rates), the classification is:

Low income	995 USD or less
Lower-middle income	996 to 3,945 USD
Upper-middle income	3,946 to 12,195 USD
High income	12,196 USD or more

Income classifications are set each year on 1 July. These official analytical classifications are constant during the World Bank's fiscal year (ending on 30 June), thus countries remain in the categories to which they are assigned irrespective of any revisions to their per capita income data. Taiwan and China are members of the high-income group.

Table 3.1 gives some specific examples to illustrate Figure 3.2.

The numbers for GDP contribution in the table only partly correspond with the diagram in Figure 3.2. Only India, Malaysia and South Africa fall in the range suggested by Figure 3.2, whereas in all other countries except for Namibia the SME contribution is higher in comparison with their GNI levels. This rather wide variation can be explained by high numbers of SMEs (for example, Pakistan) or by high productivity (for example, Sweden). Unreliable statistics can also be a reason in some cases!

SME productivity in cross-cultural environments

Small and medium enterprises in less developed countries (low and middle income) contribute less to gross domestic production compared to the high-income countries. Figure 3.4 (discussed under *The concept of added value*, below) shows that the average added value per employee in developed countries is about five times higher than in developing countries. In this section, we compare the contribution of SMEs to gross domestic production in developing and developed countries and identify a few vital factors that affect this contribution.

SME contribution in high-income countries

In most high-income countries (industrialized countries, developed countries etc.) the contribution to GDP from the small business sector is comparable to large firms. In a typical high-income country with average annual GDP growth of around 2 per cent, the main

Table 3.1 SME contribution to GDP for selected countries

Country	GNI per capita (USD)	Category	Contribution (%)
Bangladesh	520	Low	30
Bulgaria	5,490	Middle	51
India	1,040	Low	17
Indonesia	1,880	Middle	51
Malaysia	7,250	Middle	37
Namibia	4,210	Middle	9
Pakistan	950	Low	30
South Africa	5,820	Middle	35
Sweden	50,950	High	59

Source: Author.

contribution to GDP comes from the industry and service sectors, smaller contribution from the public sector and a diminishing contribution from the agriculture sector. We may thus conclude that the contributions from small and large firms increase by roughly the same amount. However, since the number of large firms increases slowly the accumulated added value per large firm must be growing. This is explained by higher organizational efficiency, the use of more advanced technologies and more capital-intensive production. The number of small and medium firms does grow, but this is mainly due to the increase in micro firms with zero or a few employees. The growth rate of added value per small firm is therefore lower.

In high-income countries, the GDP contribution from SMEs is higher compared with lower income countries, in spite of the slow employment growth rate. While large enterprises strive towards producing high added-value products at less cost (which is possible through more advanced technology and a lower labour content in products), small firms need to grow by increasing revenue from sales. This will lead to higher production volumes and more employees, since small firms are generally unable to afford the kind investment in advanced technology undertaken by large firms. Instead, the small business sector has to rely on more labour-intensive production until increased added-value production and sales has provided a financial surplus that can be used for labour-saving investments. In the global economic situation following the crisis of 2009 and 2010, the economies of rich countries are growing (GDP) while unemployment numbers are reaching record heights. Large firms are the primary contributors to this economic growth.

The structure of the SME sector that is characterized by many small firms with small growth rates means that the contribution to GDP so necessary from a job creation and economic growth point of view is, in reality, limited. Small firms with no or only few employees generally generate little added value since added value per employee tends to increase with firm size (Bannock 2005). When regarded from this standpoint, the support schemes being launched by many governments to promote small business development by fostering the creation of new firms is doubtful. In political rhetoric, it may be tempting to demonstrate how many new firms have been created as numbers can be counted and shown as tangible results of political efficiency. From an economic growth perspective – and with the aim of creating more jobs – the focus should rather be on already-existing firms with growth potential and a proven record of survival, rather the formation of new firms of which 30 and 50 per cent will fail within a three year period. Economic growth and increased employment requires government facilitation programmes that encourage growth of small firms.

SME contribution in lower income countries

The small firms of low-income countries contribute less to GDP than those of middle-income countries, whose contribution is in turn lower than those of high-income countries. In some of the lowest income countries the agriculture sector is the major contributor to GDP. In Tanzania, for example, agriculture contributes 45 per cent to GDP. Total contribution is closely related to productivity by labour and/or capital employed. By productivity we thus refer both to labour and capital productivity, where the former refers to the value of goods and services produced per work hours, or labour salaries paid or per number of employees. Increases in labour productivity may be driven by technological change, but also by better organization of work and improvements in the quality of labour. An increase in capital productivity may be driven by better utilisation of existing equipment through scheduled maintenance schemes and a sufficient supply of proper spare parts. With reference to the previous discussion, in low- and middle-income countries, there is a need to increase the productivity of small and medium firms in terms of both labour and capital. From here on, we use the term *productivity* to mean labour productivity unless otherwise stated.

If labour is more abundant and capital is scarcer in developing countries than in developed countries, we might expect more labour-intensive production techniques in the industrial sector of developing countries, reflecting a lower price of labour relative to capital. In practice, however, it is often the case that for the same outputs produced, the capital intensity of the techniques applied is not very different between developing and developed countries, and that the capital/labour ratio differs between developed and less-developed countries in the aggregate only to the extent that the composition of output differs;[1] that is, because there are large sectors in developing countries' economies where very little capital is employed at all, for example in subsistence farming and micro business activities. In the modern sectors of developing countries, however, techniques are much more capital-intensive than would be predicted on the basis of knowledge of the various factors involved. Given the supply of labour available, and given the rate of investment, the more capital-intensive the technique the less employment and the more unemployment there will be (Thirlwall 2003).

For production systems in low- and middle-income countries, we can expect labour-intensive production to dominate and therefore these countries should have the greatest potential for improvement. However, the utilization of capital in the form of machinery and equipment is more limited due to factors external to the firm, such as unreliable power supply systems, shortage of convertible currency for the import of machinery and spare parts, and lack of information about technology that could be obtained. This is partly due to the uncertainty that business managers are facing in many low- and middle-income countries: uncertainty that jeopardises business planning and hampers the formulation of growth strategies. But internal factors, such as varying quality in products and service, aging machinery, insufficient preventive maintenance and inadequate supply of spare parts, also hamper more efficient utilization of installed capital.

The following brief discussion highlights some of the vital factors limiting efficiency and productivity in small businesses in developing countries. In Part 2 of this book we will return to these same factors and the related problems of how they can be improved.

Maintenance

A vital objective of Total Quality Management (TQM) is the prevention of failures in both production and administration, since these have a high potential for making savings. Maintenance in an enterprise is therefore generally more effective if preventive maintenance and planned repair exceeds (in hours and costs) emergency repair. In developing countries with a high share of externally-caused production interruptions, disturbances cannot always be controlled within the enterprise itself and the share of externally-caused failures is therefore significantly higher in comparison with more developed countries where internally-caused failures account for most of the total quality costs. As a proportion of externally- and internally-caused failures, the latter are relatively fewer in developing countries.

Uncertainty

For a small business manager to plan business activities, create a business plan or to invest for higher production volumes a clear view of the future is crucial. The more uncertainty there is about the future the more difficult it is to plan. All business involves risk taking and exposure to uncertainty, and differences between countries and regions make planning for the future seem either more or less certain. The following attempt at identifying uncertainty levels with respect to business planning and forecasting impact on managers' willingness to take business risks.

- Uncertainty Level One: The future is clear enough for the manager to predict with reasonably high confidence what will happen in the near term. Enough information can be obtained to create a business plan with a high degree of confidence. This may be the case at a local bakery where customers arrive regularly every morning to buy their bread.
- Uncertainty Level Two: The future is one of two alternatives and the possible outcomes are discrete and clear. Knowledge about the two alternatives makes business decisions easier, although, unlike Level One, the risk cannot be eliminated, since the manager's strategy depends on competitors' strategies. This may happen in a situation where local competitors may decide to join in a network or not.
- Uncertainty Level Three: The future is not two but a range of possibilities, where the possible outcome lies anywhere within the range. An example is prior to the opening of a new department store where the selection of products is not yet known and therefore has an unknown effect on local shop keepers.
- Uncertainty Level Four: The most serious level of uncertainty where the future is highly ambiguous, and multiple dimensions of uncertainty interact to create a truly unpredictable environment. This may happen in unstable political situations, in volatile financial markets or in situations where potentially damaging rumours circulate.

Among the four levels the first three are the most likely to occur in countries with relatively stable political systems, established legal business structures and reliable infrastructure. Level four is more likely to happen in countries with high levels of corruption and crime, and with political and financial instability. Various international statistical databases on corruption show that out of 159 countries, only around one third are relatively free of corruption. In the remaining two-thirds, business decisions are presumed to be influenced by various degrees of corruption.

Quality

One of the central themes of today's management paradigm is the focus on customer value. Value chains, customer's customer approach and customer orientation are all well-known concepts where quality is regarded as a critical variable influencing the competitiveness and performance of enterprises. In most competitive firms, increased quality is just one more by-product of an approach that stresses continuous improvement in all aspects of the business process, from customer or client encounters by telephone switchboard personnel, to timely delivery service and satisfactory after-sales support. Better product quality coupled with a simultaneous stream of advances in productivity, flexibility and cost performance occur as a result of a dynamic, continuous improvement of the overall organization.

This focus on customer value, with its awareness of the need to satisfy customer requirements, places the individual at the centre. Meeting the needs and demands of the individual customer, not least regarding quality in products and service, is considered the guiding principle for good management. However, business managers need to be aware that there is also an upper limit to the provision of product and service quality. This upper limit is determined by the additional cost of providing high quality and is reached when the marginal cost of increasing customer value is less than the marginal benefit perceived by the customer or user. Discussion of the balance between what is too much and what is too little is of great importance to SME managers. They may otherwise feel tempted to adopt a business strategy that may turn out to be counterproductive: efforts to increase customer value beyond a reasonable limit may cost more than it generates in terms of increased revenue.

The idea of continuous improvement points at another weakness in many SMEs, not least in developing countries: the loyal involvement of the employees. Loyalty and commitment requires a win–win approach between the organization and its employees, in particular with skilled employees who are in short supply in most developing countries. The traditional role of managers as supervisors, i.e. to use employees as a resource to achieve company goals, needs to be complemented by an extended manager role: the manager as mentor. In this role, the manager uses the company as a resource to meet the individual goals of the employees, for example in further training as a step towards promotion and career. Here, too, greater awareness among managers is needed.

Supply of spare parts

Shortage of convertible currency restricts the ability of small firms in countries with non-convertible local currencies to import machinery and spare parts from abroad, since transactions are almost exclusively in hard currencies (USD, Yen, euro). Domestic supply of production equipment may be available as second-hand machinery, whose 'best-before date' has expired and the price is therefore lower. Development aid may contain assistance to acquire new production technology where budget frames are specified for new equipment. Spare parts that will be required after some time are mostly not part of the financial assistance. When the first need arises, the recommended spare parts cannot be obtained. Instead, improvised solutions are found locally which, in the long run, shorten the life for the original machines.

Aging machinery

The following example from an Egyptian industry illustrates how aging machinery or machinery with a high risk of break-down jeopardises productivity (Lind 1991). The production machinery in the example shows the following age distribution:

Age between 2 and 5 years	5%
Age between 5 and 10 years	15%
Age more than 10 years (some more than 25)	80%

In a typical production line where machines are arranged so that the output from one becomes the input to the next, it is important that each machine is kept working. This interdependency between machines makes the production system vulnerable: the risk of line breakdown can be significant even when individual machines have low failure rates.

Consider a production line made up of n machines, some working and some out of order. If q_i denotes the probability that machine number i has a breakdown, then the probability that all n machines are working is given by the statistical expression

$$(1 - q_1)(1 - q_2)(1 - q_3)...(1 - q_n)$$

The probability P that the job flow is interrupted due to machine breakdown somewhere in the line is given by

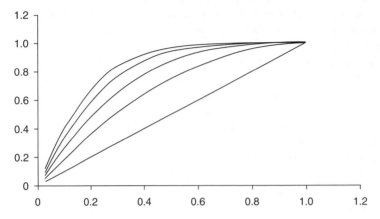

Figure 3.3 The probability of production line breakdown for different values of machine breakdown
probability q and number of machines n.

Source: Lind (1991).

$$P = 1 - (1 - q_1)(1 - q_2)(1 - q_3)\ldots(1 - q_n)$$

If, for simplicity, we assume all machines are equally reliable (i.e. $q_1 = q_2 = q_3 \ldots = q_n = q$),
the above formula reduces to

$$P = 1 - (1 - q)^n$$

Figure 3.3 illustrates the effect on P of different values of q and n.

Assuming the line breakdown probability P varies continuously with the machine breakdown probability q allows us to differentiate P with respect to q. The expression for this is

$$dP/dq = P' = n(1 - q)^{n-1}$$

Hence

$$P'(0) = n$$

Thus even when the machine breakdown probability is small ($q \sim 0$), the risk of a production line interruption is directly proportional to the number of machines in the line (n).
If work cannot be re-routed to alternative machines, the more machines there are in a production line the higher the risk of a total breakdown in production. A machine breakdown
probability q of 5 per cent (which is not alarmingly high) does, however, result in a 40 per
cent risk for the production line as a whole. This risk is significant enough to make any production planning hazardous, in particular as a breakdown may result in a longer stop.

There are two main reasons why this example and its negative effect on productivity is
particularly relevant in low-income countries. First, a general lack of capital makes it unaf-
fordable to implement a second production line to balance the risk of machine failures.
Second, the tendency to resort to *ad hoc* repair in the event of machine failures rather than
a strategy of planned maintenance makes the situation even more hazardous.

The concept of added value

Added value is one of the more fundamental concepts in business management (Meredith and Shaffer 2002; Jones and Tilley 2003). The significance of added value lies in the fact that value creation is what makes enterprises competitive, yet business strategies consciously focusing on adding value to products and services are still lacking in many small and medium enterprises, particularly in developing countries. Management awareness about the strong relationship between added value, customer value and profit is important, and needs to be strengthened, even if modern management principles of customer satisfaction and serviceability have been widely accepted among managers today. In practice, the management of small businesses is often still conducted in a traditional way, with decisions made incrementally from previous commitments, despite easy access to new approaches to business that could spur managers into new directions.

In spite of its significance as a measure of SME contribution to GDP, added value is not explicitly stated as a performance measure of firms in official statistics, not even as a measure of SME sector growth. The annual World Bank Development Report presents data on sector development according to their added value contribution to GDP. The annual UNIDO International Yearbook on Industrial Statistics shows added value data for countries and per industry sector according to ISIC code. Together with additional data on employment and number of enterprises, the UNIDIO data can provide indicators of added value per employee and per firm, but only at highly-aggregated levels (see Figure 3.5 below). This information on added value applies, however, only to the industry sector and thus represents less than half the contribution to total GDP in most countries.

The reason why added value data as a measure of enterprise performance is missing is due to the difficulty of retrieving the necessary data on sales revenue and production costs, data which are traditionally difficult to obtain, particularly from the informal sector. Registered companies are usually obliged by law to make this kind of data available, but there are various ways of evading the rules by omitting certain revenue or cost data from the accounts. In high-income countries with strict taxation rules, official and reliable company data is more easily retrievable and useful for analysing added value. Bannock makes the statement that

> what would be more significant from an economic point of view would be comparative data on SME contributions to value added as well as to employment. However, it is just not available. There are figures for sales turnover for some countries, but such data can be misleading. Turnover double counts aggregate economic activity, since the sales of one company may be inputs to others – for example, manufacturing and retailing. ... Value added which measures the contribution to GDP is a better measure but there are no official estimates.
>
> (Bannock 2005)

Box 3.1 Mini-encyclopaedia: added value

The concept of added value is used in many contexts.

Marxist theory uses the term *surplus value* (*Mehrwert* in German) as the difference between what the worker gets as labour salary and the production value he or she creates. As labour work is sold by the worker, he or she renounces that part of the value that he or she has produced. This *profit* in Marxist terminology goes to the owner of the capital needed for production. In the

Marxist view, capitalist production is not just the production of goods but primarily a production of surplus value. While added value includes all costs involved in the production of goods, the Marxist term of surplus value refers to the cost of labour.

Value Added Tax (VAT) is a type of consumption tax that is placed on a product whenever value is added at a stage of production and at final sale. The definition of added value as used in this book is the basis for VAT calculation. Value Added Tax is not applied in all countries.

Economic Value Added (EVA) is an economic measure used to value a firm by estimating the difference in value between profit and cost of creating shareholders' expected returns. Economic Value Added is thus the difference between a company's profit and the cost of its capital. The value of a firm is high when the capital employed to run the company returns a profit, the value of which is higher than the cost of using the capital (shareholders' return, interest etc.).

Definition of added value

The basic definition of added value is the difference between a product's market sales price and the cost of input materials. The definition points at one important aspect: a product's added value is not determined – or set – by the producer, but by the market. Economic theory states that the value of a product is not tied to the cost of production or inherent in the product but by judgment made by the user, and consists of the significance assigned to the satisfaction obtained through its usage or consumption (Menger 1950).

From a semantic point of view the definition of added value is incorrect since the production process of goods or services only involves costs, i.e. cost of labour, cost of energy and cost of using machinery and equipment. A better would therefore be *added costs*: the costs that contribute to the refinement process from input material to finished product. However, the product does not have a value until a price has been set and accepted by the market. It is meaningless to refer to the added value of an unfinished product still in production, since it cannot be assigned a price.

Added value in developing and developed countries

The following comparison between countries belonging to the low, middle and high-income levels is based on data from the UNIDO International Yearbook on Industrial Statistics. The measure used in the analysis is added value per employee, and ten different industry sectors have been selected, namely textiles (321), footwear (324), furniture (332), industrial chemicals (351), rubber products (355), plastic products (356), iron and steel (371), metal products (381), electrical machinery (383) and transport equipment (384). (The numbers in parentheses are the version 2 codes of the International Standard Industrial Classification for the sectors.)

In Figure 3.4, developing and developed countries have been grouped with respect to added value per employee in the selected industry sectors. The criterion is that total added value per employee and year is at least 40,000 USD. The diagram thus shows the percentage of developing and developed countries where the criterion is met.

The histogram shows there has been a slight increase in the average of added value per employee from 1999 to 2003 in developing countries and a small decrease for developed countries in the same period. With a definition of labour productivity as added value produced per employee, the chart shows a productivity factor of 6:1 in favour of the developed countries.

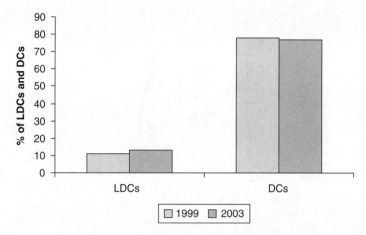

Figure 3.4 Percentage of developing countries (LDC) and developed countries (DC) with added value
per employee of 40,000 USD or more in 1999 and 2003.

Source: Compiled from (United Nations Industrial Development Organization 1999, 2003).

Box 3.2 Mini-encyclopaedia: international classification systems ISIC, SITC

The International Standard Industrial Classification (ISIC) is a United Nations system used to
classify data according to type of economic activity in the fields of production, employment,
gross domestic product and other statistical areas. ISIC is a basic tool for comparing industry
data. The ISIC code is a hierarchical; two digit broad product classification that can be broken
down into four digits for more specialized product classifications. The ISIC system has been
through several versions, the version current in 2010 being number 4.

The Standard International Trade Classification (SITC) is another United Nations system
used to facilitate international comparison of commodity trade data. SITC covers all goods
except monetary gold.

SITC is based on the Harmonized Commodity Description and Coding System (HS) of tariff
nomenclature, an internationally standardized system of names and numbers for classifying
traded products, developed and maintained by the World Customs Organization (WCO).

There are tables for converting between the various versions of ISIC and SITC.

In a more recent analysis from 2006, Figure 3.5 shows added value per employee for
selected developing countries in comparison with the EU-15 countries. The comparison
applies to the following sectors: textiles (171 and 172), footwear (192), furniture (361), rubber (251), metal products (289) and electrical machinery (311, 312 and 319). (Again, the
numbers in parentheses are ISIC codes, this time relating to version 3.)

The spread (standard deviation) around the average mean values from the selected countries is high. For example, average added value per employee in the textile sector in
Colombia is 22,800 USD but for Madagascar only 100 USD, and for India 3,700 USD.
Reasons for this variation differ and may be found in social and health conditions, in education and overall labour productivity. Comparing Madagascar and Colombia shows

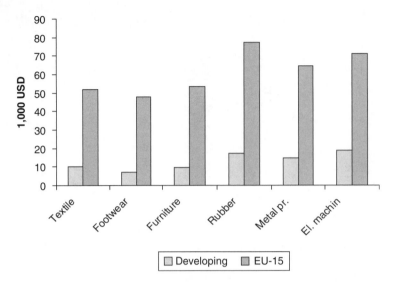

Figure 3.5 Average added value per employee and sector for selected developing countries and the EU-15 countries.

Source: United Nations Industrial Development Organization (2009).

significant differences in factors such as life expectancy (63 and 74 years respectively), literacy (69 and 90 per cent) and a factor of 1:10 in manufacturing labour productivity.

For the EU-15 countries, average added value per employee in the footwear sector in the Netherlands is 92,100 USD, but for Portugal only 14,100 USD. Still, the difference in added value per employee between developing and developed countries is significant and constitutes the background for this chapter.

Manufacturing and added value

The importance of the manufacturing sector as a driving force of economic development stems from its integration with other economic activities, generating up-stream as well as down-stream development in other sectors, each sector producing their share of added value.

Manufacture of high added value products is generally synonymous with an advanced technological level and high productivity, and therefore striving towards increased added value in the manufacturing sector has been an explicit strategy in many countries. However, the success of such a strategy is jeopardized by the deep-rooted and common pattern of many firms in the small and medium enterprise sectors to resort to price competition in their business practice. As a result, there is the tendency of the market to value low price at the expense of more intangible benefits that ought to be ascribed with values of their own such as quality in products and service. A strategy aiming at increased added value may therefore initially have counterproductive effects on the individual firm as increase in added value through higher quality may result in higher costs and thereby lower profit.

The significance of added value as an indicator of enterprise performance can be seen from two aspects. Added value in relation to the usage of material, capital and labour is a measure of productivity. But its significance also stems from the relationship between what is produced by the enterprise and how its products and services are valued by the market.

From economic theory we know that the value of a product does not depend on the costs of its production. Instead, added value is determined by the market rather than by the enterprise itself. Value is therefore not inherent in the product but is a judgment made by the user and consists of the significance assigned to the satisfaction obtained through its usage or consumption. High added value is thus an indicator of the ability of an enterprise to produce the value that the market is prepared to pay for. If a firm is faced with the situation that its product is considered too expensive by the market, it has two alternative options: to reduce the price (which also means reducing added value), or to retain and even increase the price while trying to increase the customer value.

Increase in productivity means that the same or more added value is produced with less or the same input (capital, labour), which at the level of the firm means production costs. Change in added value is the result of a change in output price or material costs, or of both, but not necessarily of production costs. However, with the same production costs, profit may rise with increased added value. Likewise, the refinement cost, i.e. the cost of producing the finished product from the input material, may increase with increasing added value if the added value stems from new product design, new features etc. In fact, a number of scenarios involving profit and refinement costs can be imagined as added value increases. One of the scenarios is higher added value but lower profit.

Increasing domestic added value is important to break away from a situation where countries export their natural resources and re-import the refined products. However, a precondition for this to happen is that enterprises can achieve a reasonable profit in their business and at the same time increase added value. The reverse situation where added value increases but profit goes down does not encourage a sustainable added value strategy. This gives rise to an important question: Why and when does profit go down as added value increases, and how can such a scenario be avoided?

Added value and customer value

In its simplest form, customer value can be defined as perceived benefits of a product or service in relation to perceived sacrifice in terms of price and other transaction costs (Naumann 1995). Customers are interested in quality at an acceptable price and they use product and service attributes to evaluate the benefits that will be received (Stock and Lambert 2001). In a sales situation involving a producer and a customer, it is possible to identify three business strategies depending on the success or lack of success of the producer's marketing strategy. If the seller (producer) fails to sell the product or service, the following strategies can be expected:

- Strategy 1: Reduce the price to produce a more attractive ratio between product performance and price, hoping that the customer will buy.
- Strategy 2: Improve performance (by adding new functions or providing better service) but without increasing the price, so becoming more attractive as a supplier.
- Strategy 3: Improve performance and also increase the price, under the assumption that the improved product performance will, in the eyes of the customer, justify the higher price.

Strategies 1 and 2 may be attractive to the customer, and ultimately even result in a sale. For the seller, however, both alternatives will result in lower profit and are therefore poor alternatives – in the first case because of lower revenue, in the second case because the enhanced performance is likely to result in higher production costs. Strategy 3 is therefore preferable, so long as the increased price can compensate for the added costs incurred by the higher product performance.

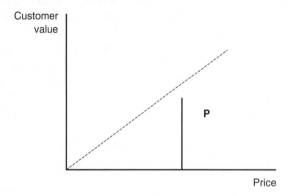

Figure 3.6 Illustration of the indifference curve.

To elaborate on the discussion above, we introduce the notion of the *indifference curve*. This is an imaginary optimal price–performance curve representing products and services that a consumer may acquire at price levels that in the consumer's subjective view are reasonable, but only just reasonable! An example is illustrated in Figure 3.6. Each point on the indifference curve renders the same level of satisfaction for the consumer. The vertical axis in the diagram shows the perceived customer value whereas the horizontal axis shows the monetary price of the product or service. Each point in the diagram corresponds to a particular combination of price and customer value. A consumer choosing among products located along the indifference curve would be indifferent among the offerings. Products offering price–value combinations located below the indifference curve yield a lower consumer preference than those along or above the indifference curve.

As customer value does not reach the price-performance curve for the actual price P in the diagram above, the perceived sacrifice (cost) is higher than the perceived benefits. The producer therefore has two options: either reduce the price of the product (or service) so that the price/performance ratio becomes attractive to the customer (arrow A in Figure 3.7), or enhance its performance or functionality so that the customer values the offering higher (arrow B).

Box 3.3 Mini-case: IE Electronics

IE Electronics is a manufacturer of electrical appliances such as TV antennas and other types of equipment for the consumer electronics market in Sri Lanka. Being customer-oriented is part of the company's strategy, and the company has therefore hired a new and dynamic sales staff to cope with market demand and customer requirements. However, this initiative has led to increased operating costs (salaries and overheads), and the owner-manager has advocated a price-cut on key products to meet competition, especially from overseas vendors now entering into the local Sri Lankan market. The resulting losses are expected to turn into profit as sales will grow, due to better customer service and lower prices.

There is an obvious risk that the losses will continue as higher volumes and improved customer service increase administration costs and require more employees. Reduction in both added value and profit margin may ultimately be the end effect of the price cuts.

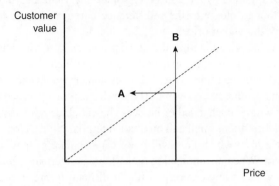

Figure 3.7 Two strategies.

This well-known scenario of competition based on price reduction has forced many small firms out of the market due to financial problems. Lower sales price is expected to result in higher volumes sold according to traditional price elasticity theory. Higher volumes will, however, lead to more production and higher material costs, more transportation for material input and product outputs and more administrative costs to manage the higher volumes. In addition, extra marketing and sales staff may be required to take care of the new customers.

Total sales revenue will increase due to higher sales volumes as sales price will be lower. By definition, the added value is reduced. The cost factor in this business scenario is critical since both the additional direct costs and indirect and hidden costs may increase due to the higher volumes, and the total costs may even turn out to be higher than the total revenue. Once the company becomes known on the market for its low price profile, it may be difficult for it to return to the previous price level in order to restore profit.

In alternative B in Figure 3.7, the producer adds functions and/or features to the product, thereby improving product performance while the sales price remains the same. The new product and service attributes do, however, result in increased costs for the supplier with the same end effect, namely reduced profit.

Box 3.4 Mini-case: price reduction

A Scandinavian travel agent has been highly successful for many years in the Nordic charter market offering all-inclusive tours to Southern Europe. Flights were booked and paid for long in advance. Growing competition in the charter market made the company stick to high passenger volumes and avoid jeopardizing good customer service by having insufficient seating capacity. The strategy was therefore to keep high volumes of seats; any sold two days before departure were offered in last-minute campaigns for a fraction of the full price. After the initial marketing success, the strategy became a deadly game for the company.

As it became known the company would offer seats at a very low price one or two days before departure, a growing number of prospective passengers began waiting until late and pay the low price. Gradually the low price strategy eroded the financial strength of the company and after some time it was out of the market.

In the next alternative (arrow C in Figure 3.8) the consumer value may yield a surplus, since the value–price combination, though closer to the indifference curve, is still in the region where the consumer will accept the higher price.

The ability of a producer to increase the price in return for added product and service attributes depends on his success in translating them into financial or other real benefits for the customer. If the producer fails in translating the improvements into customer benefits he may go unrewarded, result in extra costs that cannot be recovered. If the price can be increased to compensate for the extra costs, profit will be unchanged or higher. The variables price, costs and profit must therefore be balanced. Too often, small and medium enterprises in developing countries are caught in a vicious circle from which they will not escape as long as they are trapped in the price competition pattern. When encouraged to embark on an alternative business strategy aiming at higher added value, many enterprises find it difficult to break away from the traditional price competition pattern and instead compensate for higher production costs through increased sales price. Customer value as well as added value therefore remains at modest levels resulting in the following vicious circle:

> Lowest price to get the order → limited financial scope to develop new products, new materials, new types of service etc. → limited use of new skills to enhance present capacity → limited interest in bringing in new employees with new knowledge/ideas to act as change agents (albeit at a higher cost) → limited input of new ideas to develop new business concepts or add new product functions → little increase in customer value → price competition remains the primary business strategy → lowest price to get the order

The pattern may explain why so many manufacturing enterprises in the medium- to small-size industry sectors produce a great number of different products in small quantities. As added value is low, these enterprises have few, if any, competitive advantages and therefore have to accept orders that can be produced with existing production facilities at a price that the customers are willing to pay. Profits are mostly at low levels and the margin between profit and loss often so small that any extra costs incurred as a result of an added value strategy may seem too risky for many firms.

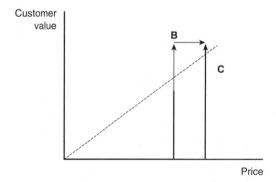

Figure 3.8 A third strategy.

The three alternatives mentioned above describe three business situations that are well known to any SME manager. Strategy 1 (price reduction) can be justified if the strategy is to break into a new market. The strategy may be to keep the low price for a period and later revert to the original price. Experience shows, however, that once the market has become accustomed to one price level there is resistance from the market to pay the original (higher) price unless there are obvious changes in the product offering. Often, however, price reduction is not a conscious strategy but more of desperation to come out of a competitive situation. Another motivation for using this strategy may be the desire to let the reduced price lead to higher volumes sold. Already depressed profit margins may, however, shrink even further if the extra volumes result in additional administrative and distribution costs.

In Strategy 2 (enhanced product/service) the decision to add customer value to the product/service at extra cost to the producer is a conscious strategy based on the assumption that the extra benefits will increase attractiveness of the product and lead to increased sales volumes. As with Strategy 1, the extra sales volumes may result in additional administrative and distribution costs.

Strategy 3 (enhanced product/service at higher price) is based on the assumption that the extra customer value justifies an increase in sales price leading to higher added value. Of the three strategies this strategy is therefore of greatest commercial interest. The crucial question is, however: Will the higher costs incurred by the additional functions and/or service yield enough customer service to justify a higher price? The question is important and relevant, for example when the additional function relates to better quality. It cannot be expected that customers will appreciate and pay higher price for ever increasing quality. Both services and products have mostly a lower and upper quality level outside which there is no profit for the producer. This is illustrated in Figure 3.9.

The diagram shows how low quality means increased cost due to customer complaints, rectification etc. Ensuring high quality means instituting frequent quality inspections, using special machinery etc. But low quality also means revenue will be low, since customers do not trust low quality products. Customer benefit tends to flatten out as quality increases

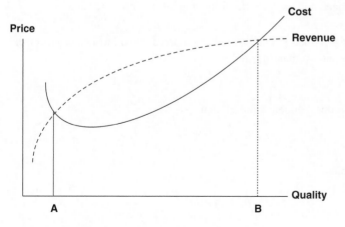

Figure 3.9 Preferred quality level (interval A to B).

beyond reasonable levels. A product that lasts for fifty years does not justify a much higher price if it can be guaranteed to last for sixty years.

> **Box 3.5 Mini-case: cigarette packaging**
>
> This German company produces machines that make cigarette packets.
>
> The market is characterized by small number of producers (no more than a handful in Europe), a small number of very big international customers and a somewhat larger number of medium-sized customers in national overseas markets (e.g. China). Quality requirements are higher for so-called crush-proof packets, but there is a continuing and growing demand for soft packets from international brands.
>
> The company produces packaging machines for crush-proof packets only, in which it has reached a high level of quality sophistication. In spite of this the company was not a market leader; indeed, it encountered severe competition from companies whose customers were not prepared to pay the price for the high quality. A contributing factor has been the general move to soft packets, which has reduced the emphasis on quality in cigarette packaging. Customer value seems to have changed focus!

The example shows that increasing the product quality beyond a certain limit may be difficult to justify. However, as the efficiency of production management is generally measured by factors such as product quality, production quality and production throughput, there are few incentives in the production department alone to set new, and lower quality targets. In the company considered, production and marketing were not within the same premises, and it can be assumed there was insufficient dialogue between the two departments to articulate the situation. As a consequence, the company's marketing department was faced with product prices that could perhaps be lower if production costs were lower as the product cost reflects the superior product quality.

Analysing the three alternatives

Three parameters are introduced and used for the following discussion. They are:

- cost of purchased material refined through a production process to a finished product (m);
- cost to produce the finished product (q); and
- sales price (Q).

It follows from the definition of added value aV that

$$aV = Q - m$$

which can also be expressed as

$$aV = (Q - q) + (q - m)$$

This transformation shows that added value has two components, namely sales surplus ($Q - q$) and in-house production costs ($q - m$).

Table 3.2 The three business strategies

	Sales surplus $(Q - q)$	Costs $(q - m)$	Added value $(Q - m)$
Alternative 1	Reduced	Unchanged	Reduced
Alternative 2	Unchanged	Increased?	Unchanged
Alternative 3	Increased	Increased?	Increased

Table 3.2 summarises the three strategic alternatives above with regard to changes in sales surplus, production costs and added value.

For alternatives 2 and 3 it is assumed that the costs $(q - m)$ are increased; for alternative 1 it is uncertain if the increased production costs are higher than the increase in added value. This is of importance as it will show if the increase in added value is also profitable for the firm.

Alternative 1

The alternative of reducing the price in order to increase sales can be justified if costs of production can also be cut, which may happen if new production techniques or new technologies are adopted. (Technology is here used in its broadest sense, i.e. not only techniques but also the way of organizing, managing techniques and related procedures, as well as its psychological and philosophical implications and aspects.) In Figure 3.10 the two technology trajectories illustrate how the use of a previous technology can produce a product at a certain unit cost and with a certain output variety (functions, features etc.) (A). Applying a newer technology means that the same product can be produced at a lower unit cost (A_1) with the same output variety or with additional output variety with the same cost as before (A_2), or a combination of the two.

In many developing countries, the issue of adopting a new technology is not as straightforward as may seem from the diagram. This was described by Francis Stewart in the following way:

> The technology available to a particular country is all those techniques it knows about (or may with not too much difficulty obtain knowledge about) and could acquire, while the technology in use is that subset of techniques it *has* acquired. It must be noted that the technology available to a country cannot be identified with all known techniques: on the one hand weak communication may mean that a particular country only knows about part of the total methods know to the world as a whole. This can be an important limitation on technological choice. On the other hand, methods may not be available because no one is producing the machinery or other inputs required. This too limits technological choice.
>
> (Stewart 1978)

Moving from one technology level to another that allows reduced production costs may be theoretically attractive and possible, but with practical limitations. For example, Internet is often mentioned as a tool that SME managers in Third World countries can use to gain access to information that was previously inaccessible, for example information about new technologies and techniques. However, a simple example illustrates the difficulties SME managers can face when using the Internet for this purpose.

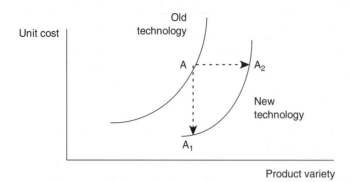

Figure 3.10 The effect on unit cost and product variety of a change in technology.

Suppose a manager wishes to research new types of lathe. In 2010, Google gave 5,160,000 responses. If we assume that 5 seconds is sufficient to retrieve and assess one response, it would take about 896 eight-hour working days or 2.5 years before all the responses had been viewed. In some countries with longer Internet response times, the total time needed to review all responses would double or triple. Even if the search terms are refined, the number of responses would still be very large, and few SME managers could spend the time needed to view all of them. Identifying, retrieving and assessing information about new techniques remains a bottleneck for small business managers.

Alternative 2

In this alternative, the sales price is unchanged as additional features and functions ('output variety') are added. The underlying strategy may be to increase customer value and thereby also increase sales volumes, since more potential clients are attracted by the greater variety. This will not result in increased added value either, since the price is unchanged. It may, however, result in higher costs, as higher volumes may ultimately result in more administration and additional sales staff.

If the new features and functions were based on newer technology, Figure 3.10 shows that this technology might allow an increase in output variety, but without changes in costs. However, local conditions, such as lack of skilled personnel and the need for technical adaptations, may result in additional costs. As a consequence, the extra output variety is often achieved only at a higher cost.

Alternative 3

International trade is dominated by the industrialized countries whose share is around the 80 per cent mark (by value), which should be compared to developing regions such as Latin America and Africa that account for 6 and 2 per cent respectively (O'Brien and Williams 2004). In contrast, the world's 48 poorest countries have seen their share of world trade decline by more than 40 per cent since 1980 to a mere 0.4 per cent in 2000 (Oxfam 2000). In many developing countries, trade means exporting primary commodities and importing high added-value products. Apart from being vulnerable to a price mechanism that the poorer countries have a limited chance of influencing, the high costs of imports give little margin for investments in technology and skills. In a few developing countries (e.g. China, India, Brazil) there was an early shift away from this traditional dependence on the export of primary commodities to more labour-intensive and low-technology manufactured products (O'Brien and Williams 2004). More recently, this process has partially developed into added-value production, and the Indian software industry is often cited in this context as an example of a highly-competitive and export-oriented industry sector based on human capital. Even so, this same industry is reported to represent the lower value-added end of the global software market (Forbes and Wield 2002).

Box 3.6 Mini-case: Sri Lanka

Sri Lanka has an annual income from spice exports amounting to 85 million USD. Ninety per cent of this export is sent in bulk form and not in added-value form, the highest being in the perfume industry. The amount of value that can be added in the perfumery industry ranges between 3 and 30 times.

An industry strategy that leads to improved added-value production must therefore be a high priority in developing countries, particularly as the gap between developing and developed countries (measured by added value per employee) is substantial (see below). It is therefore important to analyse what restricts added-value growth and what can and should be done to pave the way for increased added-value production.

This alternative results in increased added value (higher price), but may also lead to higher costs. The crucial question is therefore how to balance the higher costs with the increased price.

The critical point here is that in many commercial relationships in developing countries there is a lack of dialogue between supplier and customer. As we have seen, customer value is created when the perceived benefit is greater than the perceived sacrifice. It is therefore of utmost importance for the supplier to research the benefits expected or perceived by the customer. Such information can only be obtained though dialogue, and through the creation of sufficient trust between the two parties.

The aim of the supplier–customer dialogue should therefore be to understand how the supplier's products and services can contribute to improving the customer's business with its own customers. The Customer's Customer Concept is a simple way of highlighting the importance of a creative and explorative supplier–customer dialogue in which not only selling but also listening to customer requirements is of importance.

Traditionally, contact between supplier and customer is aimed at maximizing sales of the supplier's products and services. As such, the supplier has little knowledge about the customer's market situation and no real incentives to learn. By finding out more about the customer, and in particular about the customer's customer(s), the supplier can learn how its products and services contribute to the customer's business, leading ultimately to increased trust on the part of the customer and its dependence on the supplier. By taking advantage of every customer encounter, the customer-focused enterprise creates mutually-advantageous relations that transform customers into loyal advocates (Johnson 1992). Customer

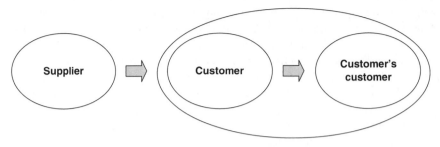

Figure 3.11 The Customer's Customer Concept.

encounters are seen as opportunities to learn and inform, not just as opportunities to present and sell. When trust has been created, such encounters will increase over time as customer and supplier learn more about each other's needs and opportunities and become more mutually dependent. This makes it much easier for the supplier to argue in favour of a reasonable price. As discussed above, increase in costs due to improved product performance may, however, be higher than the increase in price, which leads to a reduction in profit. The Customer's Customer Concept is illustrated in the following mini-case.

Box 3.7 Mini-case: Indian Casting Ltd.

Indian Casting Ltd. is a small casting company in Uttar Pradesh, India. One of its products is engine blocks. Durability and material strength are factors that determine the quality of engine blocks, and these are greatly influenced by the degree of impurities (e.g. carbon, magnesium) in the castings. An engine that malfunctions because of a low quality block may jeopardize the manufacturer's entire.

Indian Casting Ltd. has therefore invested in a computer-based control system for continuous monitoring the impurities of batches. The customer receives a statement with each delivery, showing the quality of the engine blocks in terms of impurity levels. The company is thereby in the position of guaranteeing product quality to its customers who are prepared to pay a higher price compared to other suppliers in the region who do not provide this service. Higher customer value has thus led to increased added value.

SMEs in international trade

In the discussion about SME contribution to economic development, we have focused on the creation of added value because the added value generated by the SME sector constitutes a significant part of GDP. Added value creation is also an important aspect for those small businesses aiming to export and participate in international trade, since overseas markets may be more profitable for a given product and have greater demand than the domestic market (which may be stagnant for certain products and profitability low). International trade is becoming complex and highly demanding, and continuous improvement and innovation in quality, price and services have driven the competition frontier of products and services to an unprecedented level. In addition, new opportunities have been created which address the challenges of: competitiveness; increased productivity; the formation of industrial clusters and value chains; and the need for greater technological innovation. As such, the success and survival of SMEs in international trade calls for preparations that are far more comprehensive than ever before.

SMEs tend to less capital to create jobs than larger enterprises. This is a salient feature, especially for developing economies abundant in labour but short of capital. SMEs are claimed to be the main potential source of economic growth and innovation as they are an important source of export revenue in some developing countries, given their lower exchange rate, cheaper cost of production, and government incentives. When referring to statistical data from different countries, one needs to bear in mind what has been previously stated: not only is the quality of statistical data uneven, but also the fact that virtually all businesses in many countries around the world are SMEs, the label 'SME' encompassing nearly the whole set of domestic enterprises.

The vast majority of SMEs remain local throughout their lives; this is particularly true of firms at the lower end. More recently, however, a small but gradually growing category of small firms – the so called 'born globals' – have entered the small business scene, focusing on international business from the outset. First appearing in the 1990s, these firms are mostly created by owners who have already acquired international business experienced from larger firms. To be counted as a 'born global', a business must derive a minimum of 10 per cent of its revenues from export.

A dilemma affecting international trade is still the imbalance between developed and developing countries with regard to which commodities are being traded. Most of the low-income and many middle-income countries rely on agriculture and minerals as the basis for their survival (Isaak 2005). Yet the price of these commodities typically stays flat or declines when compared with the prices of manufactured goods and services of developed countries. Developed countries are more capable of creating a diverse portfolio of products and services so their economies do not become unduly dependent on any one industry or product.

Note

1 This reasoning is based on the so called 'Cobb–Douglas Production function' as a neoclassic growth model. The model has been criticised for being more a mathematical model with limited reflection of economic realities.

References

Bannock, G. (2005) *The Economics and Management of Small Business.* London: Routledge.
Beck, T. and Demirgüç-Kunt, A. (2004) *SMEs, Growth, and Poverty: Do Pro-SME Policies Work?* Washington, DC: World Bank.
Cypher, J. and Dietz, J. (2009) *The Process of Economic Development.* London: Routledge.
Forbes, N. and Wield, D. (2002) *From Leaders to Followers – Managing Technology and Innovation.* London: Routledge.
Harvie, C. and Lee, B. (2005) *Sustaining Growth and Performance in East Asia: The Role of Small and Medium Sized Enterprises.* London: Edward Elgar.
Hoffman, K. (2005) *Enterprise Solutions to Poverty.* London: Shell Foundation.
International Labour Organization (2006) *Poverty Reduction Through Small Enterprises.* Geneva: ILO.
Isaak, R. (2005) *The Globalization Gap.* London: FT Prentice Hall.
Johnson, T. (1992) *Relevance Regained – From Top-Down Control to Bottom-Up Empowerment.* New York: The Free Press.

Jones, O. and Tilley, F. (eds) (2003) *Competitive Advantage in SMEs*. London: John Wiley.

Lewis, W. A. (1954) *Economic Development with Unlimited Supplies of Labour*. Manchester: School of Economic and Social Studies. Vol. 22.

Lind, P. (1991) *Computerisation in Developing Countries: Model and Reality*. London: Routledge.

McIntyre, R (2003) 'Small Enterprises in Transition Economies: Casual Puzzles and Policy-Related Research', in McIntyre, R. and Dallago, B. (eds) *Small and Medium Enterprises in Transitional Economies*. Basingstoke, Hampshire: Palgrave Macmillan.

Menger, C. (1950) *Principles of Economics*. New York: The Free Press.

Meredith, J. and Shaffer, S. (2002) *Operations Management for MBAs*. New York: John Wiley.

Mukras, M. (2003) 'Poverty Reduction Through Strengthening Small and Medium Enterprises'. *Botswana Journal of African Studies*, 17: 2.

Naumann, E. (1995) *Creating Customer Value: The Path to Sustainable Competitive Advantage*. Cincinnati, OH: Thomson Executive Press.

O'Brien, R. and Williams, M. (2004) *Global Political Economy – Evolution and Dynamics*. Basingstoke, Hampshire: Palgrave Macmillan.

Oxfam (2000) *Millennium Summit: Closing the Credibility Gap?* London: Oxfam. International Policy Paper 8/00.

Porter, M. (1985) *Competitive Advantage: Creating and Sustaining Superior Performance*. New York: The Free Press.

Porter, M. (1990) *The Competitive Advantage of Nations*. New York: The Free Press.

Schramm, C. J. (2004) *Building Entrepreneurial Economies*. Washington, DC: Foreign Affairs.

Schultz, P. (2008) *Handbook of Development Economics*. Amsterdam: Elsevier.

Sen, A. (1999) *Development as Freedom*. Oxford: Oxford University Press.

Stewart, F. (1978) *Technology and Underdevelopment*. London: Macmillan.

Stock, J. and Lambert, D. (2000) *Strategic Logistics Management*. New York: McGraw-Hill.

Storey, D. J. (1997) *Understanding the Small Business Sector*. London: Routledge.

Thirlwall, A. P. (2003) *Growth and Development*. Basingstoke, Hampshire: Palgrave Macmillan.

United Nations Industrial Development Organization (1999) *The UNIDO Yearbook on Industrial Statistics*. Cheltenham, UK: Edward Elgar Publishing.

United Nations Industrial Development Organization (2003) *The UNIDO Yearbook on Industrial Statistics*. Cheltenham, UK: Edward Elgar Publishing.

United Nations Industrial Development Organization (2009) *The UNIDO Yearbook on Industrial Statistics*. Cheltenham, UK: Edward Elgar Publishing.

World Bank (2004) *World Development Report 2004*. Oxford: Oxford University Press.

4 Entrepreneurship and small business

Introduction

In May 2005 the Swedish Foundation for Small Business Research organized a seminar in Brussels to consider perspectives on *Entrepreneurship and Economic Growth*. Despite an array of academic leaders in the field, no-one succeeded in answering the question as to whether entrepreneurship leads to economic growth. This conclusion contrasts with a recent OECD report that states it is abundantly clear that entrepreneurship is important for economic growth, productivity, innovation and employment, and many OECD countries have made entrepreneurship an explicit policy priority. As globalization reshapes the international economic landscape and technological change creates greater uncertainty in the world economy, entrepreneurship is believed to offer ways to help to meet new economic, social and environmental challenges (OECD 2010).

It is not the conclusion of the seminar as such that attracts our interest here, but rather the summary of the seminar published by Cobweb Information (2007). This shows there are more references to small and medium Enterprises (SMEs) than to entrepreneurship or entrepreneurs. In this international seminar there was no attention paid to the possibility that there is a difference between SMEs and entrepreneurship in their impact on economic growth. Also it is not clear from the OECD report whether its focus is on entrepreneurial activities alone, on small business activities, or both. Lack of definition of entrepreneurship is probably explains this ambiguity. Aidis (2005) points out that though entrepreneurship is an intensely-researched subject in the social sciences as well as an important issue for policy-related decision-making, it remains an ill-defined concept.

While several writers on entrepreneurship and small business do not see a reason to distinguish between the two, the view taken here is that a distinction between the meaning of entrepreneurship and small business *management* does make sense. This is not just a semantic issue, but has implications in a wider context. If a government launches a programme to promote entrepreneurship, does it mean that small firms are excluded from the programme? If not, what should be the qualifying factor for inclusion or exclusion? Should it be turnover or employment, or the operating history of a functioning SME? Bannock (2005) comments that the more one looks at the research on business success, and the more one reviews the life histories of outstandingly successful entrepreneurs, the more one realises that, with present knowledge, the whole process is somewhat mysterious.

Confusion has arisen because the word entrepreneur has gained many interpretations and connotations, for example:

* it is used as a *metaphor* for a dynamic, daring and risk-taking person;
* it refers to a business person in general as distinct from, for example a civil servant; and
* it refers to a person starting a business.

In this book, we use the terms *entrepreneur* and *risk-taking* distinct from a small business owner-manager operating in a business environment where established and successful customer relations reduce the need for entering into uncertain business activities. Small business owners/managers may be entrepreneurial in their approaches to find new business niches and search for opportunities in the market, but only very few are entrepreneurs in the Schumpeterian sense of *creative destruction* (see below), and a majority of small businesses are not engaged in spectacular innovations or aspire to do so. There is an implicit question in the title of this chapter: Are entrepreneurship and small business the same?

Some entrepreneurship definitions

The meaning of entrepreneurship is vague, and looking for a common definition does not bring much clarity. The following list is just a sample of the many definitions that have been proposed.

- Webster's Dictionary defines the entrepreneur as the one who organizes, manages and assumes the risks of a business or enterprise.
- Entrepreneurship is the act of being an entrepreneur, which is a French word meaning 'one who undertakes an endeavour'. Entrepreneurs assemble resources, including innovations, finance and business acumen, in an effort to transform innovations into economic goods.
- Entrepreneurship is the art or science of innovation and risk-taking for profit in business; the quality of being an entrepreneur.
- An entrepreneur is a person who has possession of a new enterprise, venture or idea and assumes significant accountability for the inherent risks and the outcome. The term was originally borrowed from the French and first used in this way by the Irish economist Richard Cantillon.
- An entrepreneur is someone who organizes a business venture and assumes the risk for it.
- Entrepreneurship is one special form of human capital that is important in an economic setting (often thought of as the fourth factor of production). Entrepreneurial abilities are needed to improve what we have and to create new goods and services.
- An entrepreneur is a risk-taker in the business world. Usually applied to a person who sets themselves up as a business owner using their own money or borrowed money.
- An entrepreneur is an individual or group of individuals who take on the risk of starting a venture.
- An entrepreneur is a person who engages in the process of entrepreneurship.
- An entrepreneur is someone who is willing to assume the responsibility, risk and rewards of starting and operating a business.
- An entrepreneur is a person who is innovative and takes the risk of bringing the other factors of production together in a business concern to try and satisfy the needs and wants of a particular segment of a market at a profit.
- An entrepreneur is an individual who starts his/her own business.
- An entrepreneur is a dare-devil who also carries primary responsibility for operating a venture.
- Entrepreneur is a French word that translates roughly as 'enterpriser'. In capitalism, he or she is a speculator who invests capital in stocks, land and machinery, as well as the exploitation of wage labour, in the pursuit of profits.

Of these fourteen definitions, six can be interpreted as general management, six can be interpreted as specifically starting a new business, and two definitions are somewhat unclear. Does this lack of consistency between definitions create a problem, or is it purely of semantic interest?

An individual who starts his or her own business (as in one of the definitions) and maintains it as a sole trader type organization is facing an entirely different situation compared to a small business manager with responsibility for employees, for loans to be repaid and with the need to meet budget. To refer to the entrepreneur and the small business manager as one and the same person is not only misleading but basically wrong.

Risk-taking is inherent in all business ventures, but it means different things to the entrepreneur only responsible for him- or herself, with either no or limited commitments to customers and market. The small business manager is responsible for employees but also to customers, suppliers and other stakeholders. The same applies to the entrepreneur albeit on a different scale, since the number of stakeholders can be assumed to be lower compared to a small firm with far-reaching commitments. While many small businesses are constantly struggling to survive financially in harsh competitive climates, the entrepreneur who recently started a new business will lose the start-up capital if it fails, but this will have limited effect on other stakeholders

Entrepreneurship research

The concept of entrepreneurship was introduced in the eighteenth century by Richard Cantillon[1] who was one of the first economists to develop insights into the entrepreneur and the role entrepreneurship plays in the economy. Since market prices tend to fluctuate due of the cost of production, this fluctuation, according to Cantillon, is a risk the entrepreneur has to face:

> Entrepreneurs can never know how great will be the demand in their City, nor how long the customers will buy of them since their rivals will try all sorts of means to attract customers from them. All this causes so much uncertainty among these Entrepreneurs that every day one sees some of them become bankrupt.
>
> (Cantillon 1775)

Uncertainty was thus what characterized entrepreneurship in Cantillon's view, as the entrepreneur will never know how much demand there will be, how long it will last, and what price can be charged.

In the late nineteenth and early twentieth centuries a number of alternative economic theories were developed in Western academic circles, among which was the Austrian School. It argued that life in general and economic life in particular are characterized by genuine uncertainty. The entrepreneur (described as a person willing to take risks) was therefore a suitable actor in this uncertain context, and was seen specifically as someone alert to opportunities for making money. The entrepreneur's profit does not arise from sophisticated market analysis or from deep understanding of consumer behaviour; rather it comes from the entrepreneur's observation of unexploited business opportunities. The entrepreneur was thought of as someone having specific talents for serendipity and the ability of interpreting market opportunities! A researcher adopting these ideas and who further developed theories about entrepreneurs and entrepreneurship was Joseph Schumpeter.

Box 4.1 Schumpeter (1883–1950)

Schumpeter's work on entrepreneurship extends over almost the entire first half of the twentieth century, and arose from his attempts to construct a comprehensive theory of economic development into which the entrepreneur was introduced as the *agent of change*. Schumpeter made a distinction between two types of processes in economic development, namely *adaptive response* and *creative response*. This distinction is based on the idea that actors respond to changes in their environments and that the character of the response may be either creative or adaptive. To make an adaptive response means that no drastic changes are made to the activities of an enterprise. It means staying with existing practices, while adjusting the quantities and perhaps qualities of outputs and/or inputs. In short, the consequence of an adaptive response is a development along lines that could be anticipated from existing practice. On the other hand, making a creative response entails doing something that is outside the range of existing practices, such as innovating to replace obsolete products and designs, so destroying the old and creating the new.

Schumpeter coined the expression *creative destruction* which has become widely interpreted to characterize the successful entrepreneur (Schumpeter 1942). The meaning is that the dynamic economic change inherent in capitalism requires capitalist society to demand ever newer goods and services, so creating business opportunities for the entrepreneur to tap. Later in life, Schumpeter found the word *destruction* less appropriate, preferring *creative transformation* instead (Adler 2005).

More recent research

In recent years there has been a growing interest in research on entrepreneurship and entrepreneurial activities. There are several reasons behind this. The 1971 publication of the Bolton Report (discussed in Chapter 5) created a renewed interest in entrepreneurship and small business, and governments began launching programmes in their industry strategies to promote entrepreneurships as a means of creating more jobs. This led to a considerable number of grant aid programmes and projects to support the strategy, which in turn encouraged growth in entrepreneurial research involving a significant number of academics. However, it is uncertain whether research into the growth of the entrepreneur sector has grown as much as the number of professors of entrepreneurship!

In a recent report (Frontiers of Entrepreneurship Research 2009) summarising international research on entrepreneurship in the period 1981–1990 the main research areas (judged by number of accepted papers) were found to be:

The entrepreneur and entrepreneur characteristics	(42)
Entrepreneurial cognition	(25)
Strategy	(24)
The entrepreneur and networks	(16)
Venture capital	(16)
Environment	(13)
Corporate entrepreneurship	(12)
Business angel financing	(10)
Family enterprise	(10)
Teams	(10)

Entrepreneurship financing   (8)
International entrepreneurship   (8)
Opportunity recognition   (7)
The organization   (7)
The organization and networks   (7)
Women and entrepreneurship   (7)
Ethnic entrepreneurship   (6)
Governance   (6)
Public policy   (2)
Social entrepreneurship   (8)

A significant majority of all academic papers represented in the selection above is devoted to starting and operating the entrepreneurship (financing, organization etc, 40 per cent), how to characterize the entrepreneur (30 per cent) and different types of entrepreneurships (17 per cent). None of the papers deals explicitly with entrepreneurship and economic growth. This is quite remarkable considering the number of policy statements dealing with this particular issue. A serious approach to economic growth and entrepreneurship would need to be addressed both from a macro and micro perspective, where contextual, cultural and other socioeconomic aspects *are* compared with entrepreneurial and small business initiatives and traditions.

The Global Entrepreneurship Monitor

A source often referred to for data about entrepreneurship is the Global Entrepreneurship Monitor (GEM), a non-profit academic research consortium whose aim is to provide information on global entrepreneurial activities. For its 2009 report, GEM interviewed about 2,000 entrepreneurs in 54 countries, asking them if they were running an entrepreneurial activity or about to start a business. Table 4.1 shows the countries currently included in the GEM report.

The reference to countries as being either factor-driven, efficiency-driven or innovation-driven, relates to growing complexity in the operation of the economy. The definitions are as follows:

•   Factor-driven: Competition is based on inherited factors, primarily unskilled labour and natural resources.

Table 4.1 Countries represented in the Global Entrepreneurship Monitor, 2009

Type of country	*Countries*
Factor-driven economies	Algeria, Guatemala, Jamaica, Lebanon, Morocco, Saudi Arabia, Syria, Kingdom of Tonga, Uganda, Venezuela, West Bank and Gaza Strip, Yemen
Efficiency-driven economies	Argentina, Bosnia–Herzegovina, Brazil, Chile, China, Colombia, Croatia, Dominican Republic, Ecuador, Hungary, Iran, Jordan, Latvia, Malaysia, Panama, Peru, Romania, Russia, Serbia, South Africa, Tunisia, Uruguay
Innovation-driven economies	Belgium, Denmark, Finland, France, Germany, Greece, Hong Kong, Iceland, Israel, Italy, Japan, Republic of Korea, Netherlands, Norway, Slovenia, Spain, Switzerland, United Kingdom, United Arab Emirates, United States

- Efficiency-driven: Competition is based on prices and the sale of basic products or commodities, with their low productivity reflected in low wages.
- Innovation-driven: Competition is based mainly on well-functioning public and private institutions, appropriate infrastructure, a stable macroeconomic framework, good health and primary education.

The responses are used to calculate indicators that compare entrepreneurial activities between countries. The basic indicator, the Early Entrepreneurial Activity (EEA) measures the share of population in a country that is either participating in an activity that will ultimately lead to a new enterprise or is running an enterprise younger than 42 months. The EEA indicator is thus different from merely measuring newly-established enterprises.

Entrepreneurial activity[2]

One of the principal measures in GEM is Total Early Stage Entrepreneurial Activity (TEA), that is, the proportion of people who are involved in setting up a business or owners-managers of new businesses. The general picture shows a decline in overall levels of TEA with increasing economic development. However, there are large variations in early-stage entrepreneurial activity within the three chosen phases of economic development. The GEM results confirm that countries have unique sets of economic and social conditions that affect entrepreneurial activity.

Entrepreneurial aspirations

Analysis of GEM data over a five-year period confirms that a small number of new firms plan to contribute a disproportionate share of new jobs. About 70 per cent of new start-ups expected some job creation, but only 14 per cent expected to create 20 or more new jobs. GEM also found a clear negative relationship between the strictness of employment protection and the prevailing rate of adults involved in 'high-aspiration' entrepreneurship in terms of job growth expectations. In other words, countries with high levels of employment protection also exhibited lower rates of business start-ups that expect to generate large numbers of new jobs. One reason for this may be that entrepreneurs faced with fierce employment protection will perceive this as a barrier to growing their businesses. A second reason may be that individuals with potential for high aspiration entrepreneurship may see employment as a more attractive option than starting their own business.

A shortcoming of the GEM report is the limited number of interviews conducted in each country. The consequence is considerable statistical uncertainty and variation in country data, making comparison between countries hazardous. The quality of the GEM analysis is also influenced by the general lack of consensus of the meaning of 'entrepreneurial activity' on the one hand and traditional small business activities on the other.

Entrepreneurship versus SMEs

Writers in general do not distinguish between entrepreneurs and SMEs. For example Steward and Gorrino (1997) claim that it is evident a critical role is played by entrepreneurial individuals in establishing both the technical and managerial capabilities of the innovative fast-growing SMEs. It is the entrepreneurial personality type that is referred to. Many writers on entrepreneurship, not least authors of texts used in business schools, reserve the term 'entrepreneur' to broadly cover the entrepreneurial functions in a growth business.

The entrepreneur as a type – the Mars typology

It has been widely assumed that the typical entrepreneur has specific characteristics that make him or her particularly suited to starting a business, and that *entrepreneurism* is a state of mind. Among writers supporting this view are Perren (1999), Smallbone (1995) and Chell (1999). Gatley *et al.* (1996) present several models of work roles that place the entrepreneur in a typological context. Mars[3] introduced a typology model classifying different occupations along the dimensions of 'grid' and 'group'. In his model, Mars makes allusion to the animal world as a means of communicating imagery and its associated meaning.

The Group (the horizontal dimension) represents the extent to which people are driven by or restricted in thought and action by their commitment to a social unit larger than the person. High group strength results when people devote considerable time and attach great importance to interacting with other members of their unit. The Grid (the vertical dimension) is the complementary bundle of constraints on social interaction – a composite index of the extent to which people's behaviour is constrained by normative role differentiation. A strong grid applies to common social roles whereas a weak grid social environment is one in which access to roles depends on personal abilities and skills to compete.

This is how Mars describes the four work roles by using the typologies in Figure 4.1.

1   Hawks (weak group/weak grid in Figure 4.1): Mars claims that the typical individual entrepreneur is found among the hawks. Hawks are entrepreneurial managers, owner businessmen, successful academics and pundits, the prima donnas among salesmen, the more independent professionals and journalists. Hawkish entrepreneurialism is also inherent in occupations such as waiters, fairground buskers and owner taxi drivers. Since competition is a dominant characteristic of this type, and because the group dimension is weak, Mars assumes that alliances among hawks tend to shift with expediency and that a climate of suspicion is more common than one of trust.

2   Vultures (strong group/weak grid, i.e. loose work groups): Vultures include sales representatives, travellers and roundsmen (persons making inspections or deliveries of various kinds). The classic examples are driver deliverers, linked collectively by their common employer, common work base and common task, but who have considerable

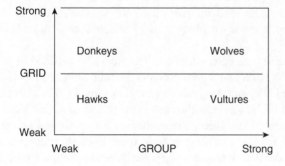

Figure 4.1 The Mars typology of work roles.

freedom and discretion during their working day. Workers in these occupations are, therefore, members of a group of co-workers for some purposes only and they act individualistically and competitively for others.

3   Wolves (tight work groups): Wolves are found in occupations based on groups with interdependent and stratified roles. As well as longshoremen and teams of miners, it includes garbage collection crews, aeroplane crews and stratified groups who both live and work in 'total institutions' such as prisons, hospitals, oil rigs and some hotels.

4   Donkeys (weak group/strong grid): The classic example of a donkey is probably the skivvy (maid) in a nineteenth-century one-servant household. Isolated from social contact with others, unable to relate to fellow servants or the family she served, she was even excluded from contact with 'followers', that is, from male admirers. She was tightly controlled, not only in terms of time and space, but also in work and leisure with a programme of activities that minutely regulated all aspects of her life.

Doubt about the entrepreneurial type

Other views claim there are no ideal types of personality or a set of entrepreneurial attributes that guarantees success for new ventures (Ray 1993). Osborne (1993) argues that the success of the newly established firm is not related to entrepreneurial competence but to the firm's underlying business concept and capacity to accumulate capital. This leads to a shift in focus from the personality and characteristics of the business founder to other less personal factors. Wickham (2001) finally concludes that there is very little evidence to suggest that any particular trait leads to successful entrepreneurship!

Like Schumpeter, Marris and Somerset (1971) did not want to focus on the individual in defining an entrepreneur. They argued that businessmen are merely entrepreneurs during one or more very short periods of their business life. Identifying entrepreneurs on the grounds that they have succeeded before excludes individuals with innovative capacities.

Many writers on entrepreneurship in smaller firms focus on personality types (extrovert, introvert) and traits (need for control, achievement, etc.) as the explanation for organizational success (Chell *et al.* 1991; Chell, 1999). Generally such types and traits are regarded as biologically or genetically determined, although occasionally some degree of environmental influence is acknowledged. It is now accepted that there is very little evidence to suggest that any particular trait leads to successful entrepreneurship (Wickham 2001: 16).

In the same fashion, Sokol and Shapero (1982) have made the case for an approach where the actor is emphasized less and the event itself is given prominence. Focusing on the entrepreneurial event, they argue for the importance of avoiding such questions as to whether an individual who has carried out one entrepreneurial act is or is not an entrepreneur. It permits one to consider the one-time entrepreneur, and the part-time entrepreneur as well as the repetitive full-time entrepreneur, and to consider a large variety of activities without being tied to a particular individual.

The lack of consensus about whether entrepreneurial success should be ascribed to personal traits or to generally favourable market situations prompts the following comments by Minniti and colleagues suggests a middle way. In general, individuals involved in entrepreneurial activities are more confident of their own skills when compared to those individuals that are not involved in entrepreneurial activities, given the same age, education, etc. Furthermore, they are less likely to let fear of failure prevent them from starting up their own business activity, even though the decision to start up a business is a complex process with many contingent factors affecting the process. The presence of role models is important when considering the transfer from paid employment to self-employment and confidence in one's own skills and abilities is crucial. A positive attitude to risk and a willingness to take risks is needed; alertness to unexploited opportunities is important in the recognition of business start-up possibilities (Minniti *el al.* 2005).

Entrepreneurship as part of the organization

By relating the entrepreneurial activity to the life-cycle perspective of an organization, Robbins (1990) noted how an organization is born, grows and eventually dies. In this cycle the entrepreneurial stage is well defined as the initial life cycle stage and synonymous with the formation stage in the product life cycle. The organization is at its infancy. Goals tend to be ambiguous and creativity is high. Progress to the next stage demands acquiring and maintaining a steady supply of resources.

In the subsequent collectivistic step, the innovation of the previous stage continues, but now the organization's mission is clarified. Communication and structure within the organization remains essentially informal. The formalization-and-control phase follows as the third stage. Formal rules and procedures are introduced and innovation is de-emphasized, while efficiency and stability are emphasized. This phase is followed by the elaboration of structure, where the organization diversifies its product and service markets. The last phase is the decline stage, which can take various forms. This life-cycle view places the entrepreneurial activity as the first step in a chain from start-up through micro firm to a small and later a medium-sized firm (Figure 4.2).

In an attempt at summarising the many and varying pictures, it seems that an entrepreneur belongs to the same category as a manager or a business owner and performs similar duties albeit on different scales. An entrepreneur is, however, not a SME manager. Scale and scope of the business activities create a significant difference when it comes to responsibility, endurance, competence etc. If, on the other hand, an entrepreneur were the same as a manager, there would be no reason to explicitly define entrepreneur. Penrose (2009) claims that entrepreneurial services are distinct from managerial services, which relate to the execution to the entrepreneurial ideas and proposals, and to the supervision of existing operations respectively. References to other traits like openness to opportunities, inclination to challenges, risk-taking and the like are not exclusive to entrepreneurs but apply to management in general.

Entrepreneurship is an activity of creating a business and therefore a process rather than a condition. The process of creating a business is thus limited in time, and once the business is in operation it qualifies to be referred to as a firm. As long as the firm is operated by the founder – the entrepreneur – it is an entrepreneurial or a one-person firm. When the firm grows by employment, it becomes first a micro firm and later it may grow into a small or medium-sized firm.

In starting up a business, the search for – and openness to – opportunities is essential. A restricted or short-sighted business focus may hamper creativity and reduce the number of

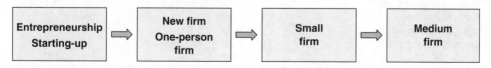

Figure 4.2 A schematic view of entrepreneurship and small business.

potential strategies, which should be numerous in the initial stage. The opposite can be said about the small business that has passed the start-up stage and requires consolidation. This generally means a more focused strategy with a well-defined and comprehensible business profile.

Many researchers have tried to identify the prior characteristics of successful entrepreneurs and fast-growth firms. Bannock (2005) refers to Storey (1994) who reviewed 18 studies of characteristics of entrepreneurs that could in principle be identified prior to start-up, and their relationship to growth performance. Although higher levels of education, prior managerial experience and middle age are more likely among founders of fast-growing firms (and such firms are more likely to be founded by groups rather than single individuals), Storey found that the patterns were not strong. He concluded that, prior to start-up, the identikit picture of the entrepreneur whose business is likely to grow is extremely fuzzy. Storey carried a similar review of research on the strategies adopted by firms. This revealed only a *tendency* for rapidly-growing firms to be more likely to have introduced new products, to have made a conscious decision on market positioning, and to be willing to share equity with external organizations or individuals. This last point, sharing equity, might merely reflect necessity rather than a positive attitude to collaborative equity, or it might suggest that multiple investors bring a wider range of skills and contacts to the firm.

Entrepreneurial success factors

Attempts have been made to identify factors that create a successful entrepreneur. However, there does not seem to be a typical mould from which the typical entrepreneur can be shaped. By studying a successful entrepreneur, his or her characteristics may seem to fit with the perception of what makes the successful entrepreneur. The reverse approach of using those characteristics to create a generic model of the successful entrepreneur does not seem to work. Table 4.2 summarises some of the factors thought important by the public and researchers to make a successful entrepreneur. The result shows a distinct lack of consensus between these two groups.

A factor that has gained support, not least in academia, is the reference to a *complex set of interrelated factors*. This would indicate that the typical entrepreneur is a construct which is both individual and context dependent.

Table 4.2 Entrepreneurial success factors according to the public and researchers

Factors perceived as being important	Public Opinion	Research Opinion
Entrepreneurial drive	Widely supported	Uncertain
Level of education	Seldom heard	Highly supported
General criteria identifiable	Widely supported	Uncertain
Complex set of interrelated factors	Seldom heard	Widely supported
Age/family/gender, background	Uncertain	No support
Access to venture capital	Widely supported	No direct support
Access to markets	Uncertain	Support
Employment legislation	Supported	No support
Generation of jobs	Widely supported	No support
Growth orientation	Uncertain	No support

Source: Compiled by author.

Social entrepreneurship

The term 'social entrepreneurship' was coined in 1981 and led to the formation of Ashoka, a global association of the world's leading social entrepreneurs whose aim is to address the world's most urgent social problems by using market-driven business models. As a result, a variety of social entrepreneurship schemes were established in different countries during the 1980s.

Social entrepreneurship uses a different measure for performance assessment compared to traditional business activity. Success for a social entrepreneurship is measured by its social or environmental impact. The financial bottom line should show profit or financial stability just in order to sustain the social mission. Social entrepreneurship is therefore not about balancing profit and social impact as though they are equally important. There can be no social mission without money, but the first goal is *social* mission.

The concept of social entrepreneurship gained international recognition when the Nobel Peace Prize was awarded to the Grameen Bank and its founder, Muhammad Yunus, in 2006. The bank makes small loans as start-up capital to poor individuals and communities in Bangladesh for entrepreneurial activities in rural areas. The Grameen Bank started in 1976 as a social entrepreneur with the objective of enabling poor villagers to invest in a cow or a hand loom and thereby generate an income. Preference was given to women as loan takers and, of the total number of 8 million loan takers about 97 per cent are women.

Corporate social responsibility has recently developed into a widespread and important concept that calls attention to the fact that large as well as small enterprises share responsibility with the rest of society for social fairness and human rights, similar to the environmental aspects which have nowadays turned into business assets. Social entrepreneurship is developing in a similar way.

Measuring the start-up activity

The most common method to measure the number of start-up companies is based on 'business demography' that counts the number of newly-created firms. A problem here is the great variation between enterprise registers in different countries. The most common indicator in business demography statistics is based on the ratio between the number of new firms and the existing enterprise base. However, since the existing enterprise base is related to the population of the country, it needs to be compensated for population size. There are therefore two measures, one is the total number of start-ups compared to the total number of existing firms, the other is the proportion of new firms to total enterprise stock and divided by the population. A third measure is the number of new firms divided by the total enterprise stock, as if all countries had the same number of firms per 1,000 population (normalization).

Figure 4.3 shows how the number of new firms in a selection of European countries varies depending on measures used.

An alternative measure is used in the Global Entrepreneurial Monitor (GEM) reports. A Total Entrepreneurial Activity (TEA) indicator is determined for individual countries based on local interviews in which subjects respond to a set of statements using a Likert scale (fully agree, partly agree, partly disagree, fully disagree):

- they see good opportunities for starting a business in the next six months;
- fear of failure prevents them starting a business;
- they personally know someone who started a business in the past two years;

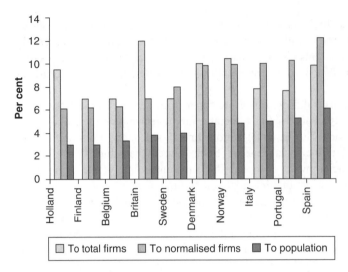

Figure 4.3 Number of new firms in selected countries in relation to total enterprise stock, to normalised enterprise stock and to population.

Source: Eurostat, 2000.

- they have the required knowledge and skills to start a business; and
- they expect to start a business in the next three years.

They are also asked about their perception of national attitudes to entrepreneurship:

- entrepreneurship is considered desirable career choice; and
- entrepreneurship attracts media attention.

This TEA measure shows that entrepreneurial activity tends to decline in more wealthy nations, which is explained as follows (GEM 2008): in countries with low levels of per capita income, the national economy is characterized by a prevalence of many very small businesses. As per capita income increases, industrialization and economies of scale allow larger and established firms to satisfy the increasing demand of growing markets, increasing their relative role in the economy. An important factor for achieving growth is the presence of macroeconomic and political stability, which is reflected by the development of strong supporting government institutions and non-governmental organizations. The increase in the role of large firms may be accompanied by a reduction in the number of new businesses, since a growing number of people find stable employment in large industrial plants.

A similar trend indicating that entrepreneurship and self-employment decline with increasing GDP per capita was observed in an OECD study from 2005 and illustrated in Figure 4.4.

The nature of entrepreneurship in cross-cultural environments

Understanding entrepreneurial activities as social processes implies a contextual perspective on entrepreneurship which downplays the importance of psychological attributes of the

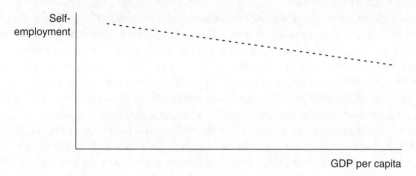

Figure 4.4 Self-employment versus GDP per capita.
Source: OECD (2005).

individual. Psychological characteristics of entrepreneurs are still considered important, but they are not understood to be sufficient to explain the rise of entrepreneurial activity by themselves. Buame (1996) contends that, in spite of its Western origin, from the point of view of individual characteristics, the concept of entrepreneurship may be universal, but its manifestation in praxis differs. In making this statement he also argues that what is *entrepreneurial* must be judged in relation to the context where the label is attached, which means that the concept must be re-embedded.

From this contextual perspective, Buame (ibid.) designates four levels of investigation that together make up a 'holistic' approach: the historical, political and economic and sociocultural contexts. Entrepreneurial activities therefore vary from one socioeconomic context to another for a variety of reasons including differences in: the distribution of resources; economic, political and historical circumstances; regulations, laws and levels of state involvement; sociocultural institutions; and overall social structures.

The following is a brief survey of entrepreneurship and new business start-up in some regions, which assumes that the entrepreneurial action is embedded in the social context where it is performed.

Transition countries

By transition we mean the radical change process that certain countries undergo as societies change from one type of political and economic system to another. In this context we focus on the significant change that took place towards the end of the twentieth century in the former Soviet Union and also to some extent in China. In both regions there has been a transition from closed state-controlled economic systems to more open economies with tangible elements of market capitalism. Politically, the states still have decisive impact on their societies.

Entrepreneurship during the transition process in countries of Eastern Europe has been characterized by consumption of generated surplus, trading of consumer goods and survival under harsh conditions.

The government in many transition countries has proclaimed self-employment to be an efficient means to achieve success in life. This view ignores world experience and overestimates the role of self-employment in the advanced capitalistic economies.

A considerable share of entrepreneurial activities takes place in the grey zone between the official and unofficial economy. This has both positive and negative effects. The positive effects are that for many it is a means of survival in an economic system being restructured from large state owned enterprises with employment guarantees to an open market economy without any guarantee of a job. The transition from the old economic system has also resulted in the dismantling of previous social institutions, while new social organizations have not yet been fully installed. The more successful entrepreneurs may be able to create personal small welfare and pension plan benefits to replace the national system.

With a majority of entrepreneurships engaged in the trading and re-selling of consumer goods, not least in areas bordering on more affluent countries, they contribute to the saturation of the consumer market which, in turn, results in downward pressure on price levels. Under constrained economic conditions, the provision of consumer products at affordable price levels is also important for political stability. As the positive transition process continues the formal economy will grow both in importance and extent.

However, the grey zone economy also has negative effects. The role of the state in controlling the economy for taxation and legislative purposes is eroded, as well as its role as facilitator of stable markets and financial systems. The grey zone economy also leads to high volumes of hidden transactions, which can easily lead to bribery and corruption, which in turn creates opportunities for criminality. In the long run, grey zone activities lead to a shrinking economy, as the large number of small unofficial businesses leads to high competition, with price dumping and decreasing profit margins. Unregistered wages and lack of labour unions who could strive for higher salary levels reduce family income and the standard of living.

Survey of selected regions

Africa

Africa is not a homogenous concept but is divided into regions and countries each having their own history and culturally-distinctive features. The African continent is today divided into four main regions: North Africa (with predominantly Muslim states), West Africa, East Africa and Southern Africa south of the Sahara desert. Southern Africa is also referred to as the SADC (Southern African Development Community) region. There is a big variation in economic development levels between African states, ranging from middle-income countries (e.g. South Africa, Egypt) to low-income countries (e.g. Malawi, Senegal). At present, no country in Africa fulfils the World Bank criteria of being a high-income country.

The motives for starting up a business in an African country have been described either as *necessity-based*, i.e. no better options for work, or *opportunity based*, where the market offers business opportunities that are more attractive than being employed. In a study, the GEM reports that necessity-based reasons for starting up a business tend to decline with growing GDP per capita. In many African countries the start-up of a business is a necessity in order to get an income, but it also creates an opportunity for family members and relatives to get jobs and receive an income. Iguisi (2005) reports from a study of selected European countries and Nigeria that the Nigerian respondents had many family members who depended on the business man for financial support. As the family may be an important source of capital to start a small enterprise, family responsibilities may also tap the enterprise for resources at a later stage and make it difficult to maintain the accumulated financial resources needed to develop the enterprise. Writing on Uganda, Whyte and Whyte

(1996) mention that while success in business is highly respected, this success is a public good which the business-owner must be prepared to share. Therefore a business needs to grow beyond a certain threshold before it is able both to accumulate finance and honour its social responsibilities.

In most African countries large parts of the population have little or no access to the state's social security and legal systems. Income transfers through informal social institutions and ethnically-based patron–client relations therefore play a major role for small entrepreneurs as safety net in case of illness, fire, theft, robbery, traffic accidents, bad luck in business, job loss and other unforeseen events. The social requirement to transfer of resources especially rests on liquid income. Based on an investigation in Senegal, Dia (1996) found that people invest in fixed assets and consumer durables to reduce their income transfers. This may be one of the reasons for the recurring cash flow problems which seem to be typical for small African businessmen, and for the tendency to overinvest in fixed assets, like shop buildings and machinery, which end up unused for lack of cash (Pedersen 1997).

South-East Asia

Entrepreneurship in the more dynamic South-East Asian countries such as China, Thailand, Vietnam and others is characterized by a strong work ethic, the booming economies of recent years and a focus on trading in consumer goods. Dyadic authority relations between supervisors, managers and the owning patriarch imply high levels of centralization in South-East Asian family businesses. According to Redding (1990), this was especially so for financial, marketing and personnel decisions, which were usually made by the owner, who also maintained considerable secrecy over financial transactions. While there was some delegation of operational control over production activities and greater reliance on formal control systems, planning decisions remained centralized. This central control of decisions in the family business is forced by the common view that leadership is a moral quality of individuals rather than a technical skill which can be modified and taught. This emphasis on the moral superiority of the leader in Chinese society, for example, means that authority cannot be easily delegated or shared, since this would suggest a reduction in moral worth. It also encourages considerable distance between the owner and all employees, including managers.

In his overview of South-East Asian management, Whitley (1996) concludes that the moral superiority of leaders of firms influenced by Chinese business ethics is manifested by their economic success, which follows from their superior insight into business affairs and ability to control egocentric impulses. Loyalty to these leaders is therefore conditional on the firm's continuing success and thus the owner's demonstrated superior rationality. When it fails, employees can legitimately withdraw their commitment to the leader and move elsewhere. As a result, employers display relatively little trust and commitment to employees with whom they do not have strong personal 'family-like' connections (Wong 1988), and employees display formal subordination to business owners without strong emotional commitments. Essentially, they follow the role performance model of filial piety which specifies appropriate patterns behaviour rather than personal commitment to the individual leader of the firm.

This emphasis on the moral superiority and greater rationality of successful business owners is linked to a didactic or pedagogic leadership role in which the leader conveys to subordinates the methods by which he has achieved success. However, because of his superiority, social distance and concern for secrecy, these methods are rarely spelled out as formal rules. Rather, the successful subordinates are those who correctly understand the leader's beliefs and thoughts and can be relied upon to follow them. As moral inferiors they cannot question these beliefs, or even discuss them formally; they are expected to accept the owner's decisions as the product of superior wisdom.

Family ownership combined with lack of institutionalized trust relations between non-kin and non-close-friends in the family business leads to strong reliance on family members and people with strong personal ties to the owner for filling senior positions. Thus the dominant coalitions of firms influenced by Chinese ethics are usually made up of close kin, and economic issues become fused with family ones. Since the firm is typically seen as an instrument for the service of the family, its decisions and activities are essentially family ones, so that salaried managers without close family-type links to the owning group cannot be involved in major choices. This does not mean that nepotism leads to incompetence, since most owners of family businesses invest heavily in the education and training of their successors and take pains to teach them the craft of deal making (Limlingan 1986). Often the patriarch selects the son or son-in-law who displays the most talent as an entrepreneur rather than the best qualified in formal terms, since it is this skill which is regarded as crucial, and he does not hesitate to sideline incompetent sons. Occasionally adopted children are given major responsibilities if they demonstrate the required talents, but Chinese families place greater emphasis on blood ties than Japanese families (Pelzel 1970).

The highly personal nature of authority relations in the family business, the limited separation of the firm from the family and the conditional nature of employee loyalty together restrict the longevity and size of firms. Succession to the patriarchal role is decided by the founder, but the principle of equal division of his assets among his descendants encourages division, conflict and fragmentation. As Wong (1985) points out, the typical successful family business goes through four distinct phases in three generations: emergent, centralized, segmented and disintegrative. Because each son expects to run his own business, the brothers who do not succeed to the top position are often given a subsidiary to run. If successful this leads to demands for more control and more resources which can result in fission. By the third generation, many prefer to sell the family business to realize their assets, perhaps to start their own firm independently, and so fragmentation and collapse of family businesses are frequent. Together with the continuing movement of employees away to start their own firms, this is assumed to lead to the perpetual destruction and creation of Chinese businesses as a centrifugal process (Tam 1990).

Latin America

Latin America is the generic term for those American countries having Spanish or Portuguese as their mother tongue, which identifies a group of countries stretching from Mexico in the north to Chile and Argentina in the south. As a geographic term, the same region is divided into South America and Central America, the latter ranging from Mexico in the north as far as Panama in the south. The Caribbean countries are also part of Latin America.

Entrepreneurship is vital for social and economic development in Latin America according to a study with contributions from 13 authors that shows rapidly increasing interest and involvement in nearly all countries of the region. Even though there have been several ambitious research efforts to determine the level of entrepreneurship in the region, views differ. While the GEM studies consistently place Latin American countries among the most entrepreneurial in the world, other sources operating outside the GEM methodology show considerably lower entrepreneurial achievements compared with other emerging economies like South-East Asian countries (Casas *et al.* 2005).

Amorós and Cristi (2008) analyse the relationship between entrepreneurial dynamics in Latin-American countries and the level of competitiveness these countries show by referring to various studies. Many Latin-American countries have experienced high economic growth rates during the last 20 years. Exports of natural resources and some low value-added products led the economic expansion in these countries until the mid-1990s, but in the last few years economic growth rates have slowed down considerably. Latin-American countries have a big potential to generate competitiveness and well-being through the creation of new firms, but they have not managed to consolidate the entrepreneurial dynamics. Some countries of emergent regions other than Latin America have made an important bet on entrepreneurship. The economies of Latin America need to transform self-employment or isolated new ventures with little value-added into innovation-based firms and create business networks that allow them to compete globally. This translates into an emerging interest on how to develop more industries to produce value-added products or services. Entrepreneurship and innovation processes are key factors to increase economic dynamism.

Summary and conclusion

Summary

This chapter has discussed and summarized various aspects of entrepreneurship and small business in various regional contexts. Since some of the general opinions about entrepreneurs and entrepreneurship have little or no support in related studies, they tend to be based more on assumptions and myths rather than serious comment. Others, on the other hand, are based on studies and analyses of research papers and books.

Conclusion

What is an 'entrepreneur'? When talking about an entrepreneur, everyone seems to have a clear idea of who they mean. However, when questions are posed about the defining features of the entrepreneur, opinions start to diverge.

And the distinct agent that Schumpeter envisaged is to be sought in relation to his idea of the entrepreneurial function. By focusing on the entrepreneurial function one may discuss entrepreneurship without being concerned about the individual, or even the actor. Schumpeter himself pointed out that 'the entrepreneurial function need not be embodied in a physical person and in particular single physical person'. Consequently, the entrepreneurial function might just as well be performed by collectives of people or even state institutions.

Schumpeter defined the entrepreneurial function simply in terms 'innovation': to do new things or to do things in novel ways. In other words breaking old habits and embarking on new ones.

Notes

1 Richard Cantillon (1680–1734) was an Irish-born economist living in Paris.
2 The following paragraphs are extracts from the GEM report.
3 Gerald Mars, Professor of Anthropology at London University.

References

Adler, P. (2005) 'Market, Hierarchy and Trust: The Knowledge Economy and the Future of Capitalism', in Grey, C. and Willmott, H. (eds) *Critical Management Studies*. London: Oxford University Press.

Aidis, R. (2005) *Entrepreneurship in Transition Countries: A Review*. London: SSEES, University College.

Amorós, J. and Cristi, O. (2008) *Longitudinal Analysis of Entrepreneurship and Competitiveness Dynamics in Latin America*. Berlin: Springer Verlag.

Bannock, G. (2005) *The Economics and Management of Small Business*. London: Routledge.

Buame, S. (1996) *Entrepreneurship: A Contextual Perspective, Discourse and Praxis of Entrepreneurial Activities within the Institutional Context of Ghana*. Lund: Lund University Press.

Cantillon, R. (1755) *Essai sur la Nature du Commerce en Général*. Paris. English translation in Thornton, M. (2010) *Economic Theory*. Auburn, AL.: Ludwig von Mises Institute.

Casas, R., Etzkowitiz, H. and Carvalho de Mello, J. (2005) *Knowledge for Innovation: New Directions for Latin American University–Industry–Government Interactions*. New York: SUNY Press.

Chell, E. (1999) 'The Entrepreneurial Personality; Past, Present and Future'. *Occupational Psychologist*, 38.

Chell, E., Haworth, J. and Brealey, S. (1991) *The Entrepreneurial Personality: Concepts, Cases and Categories*. London: Routledge.

Cobweb Information (2007). Gateshead, UK: Cobweb Information Ltd.

Dia, M. (1996) *Africa's Management in the 1990s and Beyond: Reconciling Indigenous and Transplanted Institutions*. Washington, DC: World Bank.

Frontiers of Entrepreneurship Research (2009) *Proceedings of the Twenty-Ninth Annual Entrepreneurship Research Conference* at the Arthur M. Blank Center for Entrepreneurship. Babson Park, MA: Babson College.

Gatley, S., Lessem, R. and Altman, Y. (1996) *Comparative Management: A Transcultural Odyssey*. Maidenhead, Berkshire: McGraw-Hill.

Global Enterprise Monitor (GEM) (2008) *Report (The Global Entrepreneurship Monitor)*. London: Global Entrepreneurship Research Association.

Iguisi, O. (2005) *Management and Indigenous Knowledge Systems: An Analysis of Motivational Values Across Cultures*. Maastricht: Euro-African Research Centre.

Limlingan, V. S. (1986) *The Overseas Chinese in ASEAN: Business Strategies and Management Practices*. Pasig, Metro Manila: Vita Development Corporation.

Marris, P. and Somerset, A. (1971) *African Businessmen – A Study of Entrepreneurship and Development in Kenya*. London: Routledge.

Minniti, M., Bygrave, W. and Autio, E. (2005) *The GEM Report 2005*. London: Babson College and London Business School.

OECD (2005) *Labour Force Statistics*. Paris: OECD.

OECD (2010) *Measuring Entrepreneurship: A Digest of Indicators* [2009 edition]. Paris: OECD.

Osborne R. L. (1993) *Why Entrepreneurs Fail: How to Avoid the Traps. Management Decisions*, 31:1.

Pedersen, P. (1997) *Small African Towns Between Rural Networks and Urban Hierarchies*. London: Averbury.

Pelzel, J. C. (1970) 'Japanese Kinship: A Comparison', in Freedman, M. (ed.) *Family and Kinship in Chinese Society*. Stanford, CA: Stanford University Press.

Penrose, E. (2009) *The Growth of the Firm*. Oxford: Oxford University Press.

Perren, L. (1999) 'Factors in the Growth of Micro-Enterprises: Part 1, Developing a Framework'. *Journal of Small Business and Enterprise Development*, 6: 4.

Ray, D. M. (1993) 'Understanding the Entrepreneur: Entrepreneurial Attributes, Experiences and Skills'. *Entrepreneurship and Regional Development*, 5.

Redding, S. G. (1990) *The Spirit of Chinese Capitalism*. Berlin: de Gruyter.

Robbins, S. (1990) *Organisation Theory: Structure, Design and Applications*. New York: Prentice Hall.

Schumpeter, J. (1942) *Capitalism, Socialism and Democracy*. New York: Harper.

Smallbone, D. (1995) 'The Characteristics and Strategies of High Growth SMEs'. *International Journal of Entrepreneurial Behaviour & Research*, 1.

Sokol, L. and Shapero, A. (1982) *The Social Dimensions of Entrepreneurship in Kent, Sexton and Vesper: Encyclopaedia of Entrepreneurship*. New York: Prentice Hall.

Steward, F. and Gorrino, I. (1997) *Innovative Fast-Growing SMEs*. Luxembourg: European Innovation Monitoring System. Publication 42.

Storey, D. J. (1994) *Understanding the Small Business Sector*. London: Routledge.

Tam, S. (1990) 'Centrifugal versus Centripetal Growth Processes: Contrasting Ideal Types for Conceptualising the Development Patterns of Chinese and Japanese Firms', in Clegg, S. and Redding, G. (eds) *Capitalism in Contrasting Cultures*. Berlin: de Gruyter.

Whitley, R. (1996) *Business Systems in East Asia: Firms, Markets and Societies*. London: Sage Publications.

Whyte, S. and Whyte, M. (1996) 'The Value of Development: Concerning Growth and Progress', in Whitley, R. (ed.) *Business Systems in East Asia: Firms, Markets and Societies*. London: Sage.

Wickham, P. A. (2001) *Strategic Entrepreneurship: A Decision-Making Approach to New Venture Creation and Management*. Harlow: Pearson Education.

Wong, S.-L. (1985) 'The Chinese Family Firm: A Model'. *British Journal of Sociology*, 36.

Wong, S.-L. (1988) *Emigrant Entrepreneurs*. Hong Kong: Oxford University Press.

5   Government: facilitator or trouble-maker for SME growth?

Introduction

Small and medium Enterprises (SMEs) constitute the numeric majority of all enterprises in most economies in the world. In most industrialized countries, the SME sector as a whole accounts for around 99 per cent of all firms, micro and small firms for a little less. The situation in less developed countries is not very different. For example, in the Lao People's Democratic Republic SMEs account for 99.5 per cent. When it comes to employment and a country's ability to generate wealth as measured by gross domestic product (GDP), however, the large enterprise sector has a significantly higher share of the total in industrialized countries, where large firms account for around half of employment and half of the contribution to GDP. For the less-developed countries employment, the share is higher in the SME sector and its contribution to GDP less than half of what is achieved in the industrialized countries (see Chapter 2).

In low- and middle-income countries, the contribution by small firms to wealth creation is less than 50 per cent of the total. However, the sector's contribution to employment is higher and appears to be increasing over time. Officially, the aim of government assistance to the SME sector is to provide potential benefits by creating employment opportunities and establishing a seedbed of growing firms as well as improving innovation and competitiveness. The widespread view that SMEs create new jobs is partly based on earlier studies which concluded that small firms (less than 20 employees) in the United States generated 66 per cent of all new jobs between 1969 and 1976. The belief that new jobs would automatically be created through rapid small sector growth was predominant in that period. Like many other claims made of SMEs, this one has also been contested by other researchers. However, there is a general consensus among politicians and researchers that small firms shall be included in public policy interventions.

During the last 30 years, governments have taken many different support initiatives resulting in development programmes for the SME sector, ranging from deregulation measures aimed at reducing bureaucratic and administrative demands burdensome to owner-managers, to programmes of advice, consultancy, information and training. There is also a growing interest among governments to foster stronger links between the SME sector and universities, as there is a strong belief that small and medium firms will benefit by interactions and partnerships between the two.

Government support programmes towards a thriving and prosperous small business sector can sometimes have counter-productive effects and hamper rather than encourage small business initiatives. Formulation of rules and regulations for the protection of patents as well as legislation to protect business agreements are essential for setting up and running any business

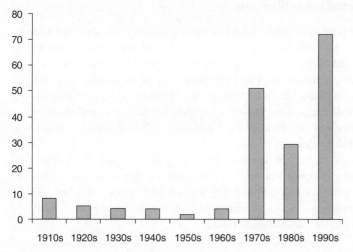

Figure 5.1 Number of new laws regulating SME activities in Sweden.
Source: Fölster (2004).

venture. An overly-complex set of regulations not easily comprehended by the small business manager creates uncertainty. Fewer potential entrepreneurs will take the initiative to start a business and fewer small business managers will feel encouraged to grow if they feel entangled by over-ambitious rules and regulations. A Swedish survey estimates that, for a business with fewer than ten employees, the costs of compliance per employee is the equivalent of 4,500 USD per year. For firms with more than ten employees the corresponding sum is around 1,400 US dollars (Fölster 2004). The set of rules and regulations surrounding business and business management is complex, and in Sweden it is contained in 20,000 pages with a total of 10,000 laws and regulations. The number of new laws regulating the greater part of small business activities has been increasing significantly in recent years, as shown by Figure 5.1.

From an enterprise manager's view, government rules and regulations should be easy to understand, fair and predictable. This will engender a positive business climate and encourage firms to grow.

Government interventions

In the 1980s, great changes swept through the developing world as governments turned against economic interventionism and put their trust in market forces, under the assumption that imperfect markets work better than imperfect governments. The debate at the time was between the neo-liberals and the more traditional economists who did not share the neo-liberal ideas. The neo-liberals had on their side several facts, including the comprehensive failure of massive intervention to spur growth in the 1960s and 1970s (in Latin America, Africa and India), and what seemed to be the comparative success of liberal – or liberalising – regimes (the East Asian 'dragons', Chile, China and Turkey). The ideas included the assertion – long denied by traditional development economics – that governments in the real world are usually incompetent or dishonest, and frequently both, against which it was suggested that the world is complicated. The more balanced opinion was that it is reckless to generalize and that, in many areas, the right sort of government intervention is essential.

Box 5.1 Mini-encyclopaedia: neo-liberalism

The neo-liberal economy developed during the 1980s and 90s as a reaction to the traditional economy that had dominated the post-war period of the 1960s and 70s by which governments had sought to balance inflation and unemployment using techniques promoted by Keynes. These balancing efforts failed in the 1970s in the wake of financial crises partly due to escalating oil prices.

The emerging neo-liberals claimed that any attempts by government to regulate the economy will simply result in individuals acting rationally to counteract the government initiatives by redefining their own ambitions. A better alternative, according to the neo-liberals, was to let market mechanisms work independently!

Neo-liberalism has been criticized for its unrealistic assumptions and lack of accordance with economic realities. The assumption that individuals act rationally may be viewed as ignoring important aspects of human behaviour. Neo-liberalism is highly theory-based, and their approach to modelling a system as complex as a modern economy using mathematical models is considered by many as unrealistic and doomed to failure.

The tragedy of energetic intervention in the Third World is that it was so misdirected. Governments ran industries, monopolized trade in farm produce and turned away imports. In these and other ways they supplanted functioning markets. Where markets were certain to fail, and where intervention was therefore necessary (in providing law and order, infrastructure, primary health care and education), governments did far too little. For example, a weak understanding of rural irrigation led policy-makers to design infrastructure that was of little or no use to the rural poor.

For government to intervene in the small business sector with relevant and creative support measures and programmes, they need to have adequate knowledge about problems and conditions related to the sector in general and, in particular, about the improvements needed for growth and development. However, in locations where many state interventions exist merely for control and taxation purposes, entrepreneurs and small business managers consciously keep a low profile to escape control measures (Tripp 1997). The Sri Lankan government's ambitious 1990s project to implement an Industry Monitoring and Performance Analysis System for the benefit of the small and medium enterprise sector was cancelled due to lack of adequate and necessary information about the firms. Out of the total number of firms selected for interviews, only a fraction responded to the questions asked. The majority shunned participation in the project for fear of state control and close intervention by government officials.

Box 5.2 Mini-case: 'Two Sisters and a Cook' – a lunch café in Stockholm, Sweden

Susanna runs the café with her sister and one full-time and three part time employees. The number of customers is gradually increasing which, unfortunately, cannot be said about the economy of the firm. Increasing business revenues are spent on costs that are partly incurred by an increasing burden of government rules and regulations with which the company has to comply. Susanna gives some examples:

> One regulation requires an annual visit by a chimney sweep, who spends five minutes looking through a pipe. The cost of this inspection is about 250 USD. Regular visits by the Community's Environment and Health Inspector can lead to

random demands. Recently we had to install stronger strip lightning in one location, which cost us 550 USD. It seems these official people have no idea of the
circumstances under which small firms operate!

Sandra's conclusion:

From time to time, the politicians should spend a few hours with a small business
manager to see the effects of government rules being implemented. We work 60
hours a week and take minimal salaries. The politicians should consider this when
they argue for more small businesses!

Structured and politically-driven interventions in the small business sector was unusual
in most countries before the 1960s, the main reason being that the SME sector was not considered central to economic development, in a period when economies of scale and large
business was the focus of governments and academics. SMEs were regarded as being
poorly-managed, badly-organized and reliant on outmoded technologies to produce inferior
products and services (Mason and Harrison 1990). As late as 1991 the common perception
was that in industrialized nations small and medium firms were of little relevance to economic progress or competitiveness (Stanworth and Gray 1991) and therefore received little
attention in government economic and industrial policies of the period.

In the 1980s, however, circumstances led to a new and different view on small firms and
their relevance to economic development. Many development regions saw the advent of privatization through which large state-owned companies were broken up into smaller units as
small and medium-sized firms. In industrialized countries, defensive industrial policies
became necessary to cope with the decline in key industry sectors, such as textile, steel and
shipbuilding. The result was aggressive technology policies with generic stimulation of new
advanced technologies and application areas. With more capital-intensive production, firms
could not just maintain productivity with fewer people but increase it too. Government interest in promoting growth of the SME sector was thus stimulated by rising unemployment.

Government SME promotion programmes

Practically all countries have programmes to promote small business growth. It is not within
the scope of this chapter to review the different programmes. A detailed survey is provided
in Bannock (2005); Whitley (1996) gives a detailed and more general account of the institutional influence on industrialization and economic development in some Asia countries,
without specific focus on the small and medium businesses. The concentrated and structured
approach by governments towards the small business sector was rare 50 years ago when
small firms were still seen as peripheral actors in business circles. It is fair to say that the
present focus on SMEs began with the publication in 1971 of the Bolton Report in Britain.

Box 5.3 Mini-encyclopaedia: the Bolton Report

In 1971, the British government established a *Committee of Inquiry on Small Firms* chaired by
the late John Bolton, and its report has become known as the Bolton Report.

The report formulated and discussed issues relating to the small firm sector in the economy,
and became the agenda of small firm policy intervention for several governments besides

---

Britain. Since the report was issued, relatively little has changed ideologically, and small businesses are still portrayed as components within a market-driven economy, resulting in a bewildering array of government support agendas for small businesses. Academics have also probed, promoted, suggested, evaluated and discussed these policy agendas.

The report raised a number of issues which have been debated ever since. Some issues have been confirmed today, others refuted. As an example, the report argued that business success is primarily related to the desire of the owner-manager to achieve personal involvement and an independent lifestyle. The development of competitive advantage is therefore seldom a readily-visible process but often arises accidentally out of particular circumstances and is linked to the aspirations, perceptions and capabilities of the owner-manager.

The report refers to a paradox: conditions of employment in SMEs were generally worse than in large firms but employees were more satisfied. This was partly explained by the friendlier atmosphere which prevails in small firms. More recent research cast doubt on the validity of this paradox, claiming that employee legislation has resulted in better conditions for SME employment.

Nature of government promotion schemes

The overriding aim of government programmes to promote growth of the small business sector is to create jobs. Even if unemployment is not evenly distributed among countries, it is serious enough for the more affluent nations to come to grips with high unemployment figures. Policy-makers and academics alike try desperately to identify the mechanisms that will make small business grow. As long as economic growth was the primary objective of government programmes, the creation of jobs was assumed to follow suit. In periods of financial depression, governments have tried various means to stimulate the economy, for example by direct job interventions in line with the Keynesian model.

The many efforts aimed at job creation among SMEs have generally not been successful as unemployment remains high. Governments have been criticized on the ground of their persistent policy of promoting new-firm start-ups at the expense of stimulating and promoting established firms by reducing bureaucracy, reducing administrative burdens and initiating long-term and favourable financial programmes for investment in technology and skills. The high termination rate of between 30 and 50 per cent of new firms within three years is well known to governments; even if the entrepreneurs behind the failures start new businesses, there is no guarantee of the sustainability of the new ventures. The high termination rate applies to most regions of the world; in some countries the rate is even higher.

Facilitating small business growth as a means of creating jobs should have a higher priority for government support to the SME sector than starting new firms. The importance of creating an effective business environment for growth has support in research undertaken by the World Bank (Beck *et al.* 2004). Cross-country regressions on GDP per capita growth and business environment indicators and an array of other potential growth factors show a strong relationship between an effective business environment and economic growth. Moreover, they show that this relationship still holds when the analysis takes into account the possibility that faster-growing countries might adopt more effective business regulations or that a third factor might drive both an effective business environment and economic growth. So, unlike for SMEs, there is evidence that an effective business environment is not just a characteristic of successful economics but also plays an important part in their success. Cross-country

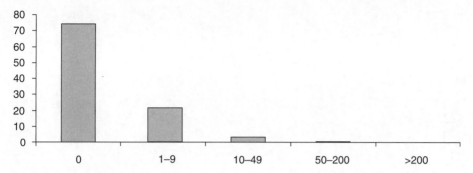

Figure 5.2 Average number of firms by group size in the period 2000–2008 (per cent).
Source: Swedish Statistical Office (SCB).

comparisons show the positive relationship between an effective business environment and income growth holds as much for the lowest income quintile as for the rest of society. But there are limits: the results do not show that a good business environment has an effect on poverty reduction beyond its positive effect on GDP per capita growth.

A result of active government support – the case of Sweden

Small Swedish firms are generally not growth-oriented – that is obvious from statistical data from national statistical offices. In the period 2000–2008, the share of one-person firms (zero employees) to total enterprise stock has been stable at 74 per cent. The number of micro firms employing from 1 to 9 persons was stable at 21 per cent and small business (10 to 49 employees) at 3 per cent. If growth had taken place it should have been noticed for these last two enterprise groups. The small business sector, 98 per cent of the total stock, is very stable and there is no significant movement between the size groups. The chart in Figure 5.2 has looked the same for several years.

Small business creates relatively few new jobs. The average number of employees per micro firm (1 to 9) has been 2.7 during the last eight years. For small firms (10 to 49 persons) average around 19 employees per firm during the same period. Total employment growth in the country during the actual period is approximately the same as growth in the number of small firms. In other words, the average number of employees per firm is more or less constant.

Figure 5.3 illustrates how growth in the number of firms and employment decreases with increasing size of group. Growth in the number of one-person and micro firms (0 to 9 persons) is the highest, with an average of 16 per cent per year in the same period. Large enterprise growth is just below 2 per cent. With regard to the average number of employees per firm, the large enterprises show the highest growth rate. Figure 5.3 shows that employment growth in small firms is lower than growth in the number of small firms, while the opposite is true for large firms with more than 200 employees. The expectations are – and have been – that employment growth should also be faster and higher for the smaller firms!

New start-ups have a generally slow growth rate and are therefore a doubtful measure of an expansive economy. From a societal perspective, new firms have limited importance, as many (around 30 per cent) disappear within three years and the remaining ones remain very small for a long time, with a statistical average of 1.7 persons per firm. From the individual's perspective, there are many arguments for government support to self-employment, and it is

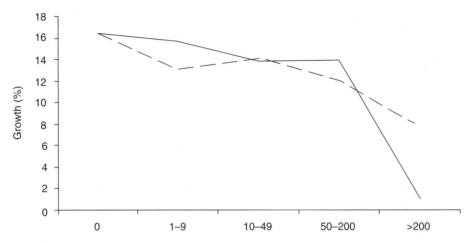

Figure 5.3 Average growth rates of firms (solid line) and employment (dotted line) for different group
sizes.

tempting among politicians to refer to the creation of new firms. From a macroeconomic perspective, however, where aspects such as national competitiveness and productivity come into the foreground, the political rhetoric has limited value.

It remains important for existing small firms to grow and develop the ability to produce added value that can compete internationally. Jobs will come as volumes and revenues increase as a result of products and services with high added value. If every micro firm (1 to 9 employees) could increase employment by just one person, Sweden would see the creation of 200,000 new jobs.

One of the recent government proposals to create jobs was to reduce employment taxes 1 per cent which it is hoped will create thousands of new jobs. However, some calculation reveal that, while the small firm may save around 1,000 US dollars, large firms with more than 200 employees will save considerably more. Government action will not result in many small firms buying new machines or employing more people: 1,000 USD is not enough.

A result of active government support – the case of Singapore

According to Chatterjee and Nankervis (2007), the particular characteristics of the entrepreneurial culture of Singapore lie at the heart of managing the island's post-independence economic and community development success. A debate is currently going on how to further develop that entrepreneurial culture. The ramifications of this issue were previously examined by the government almost two decades ago. Following an economic recession in the years 1985 1986, the Singaporean government realized the increasingly important role that small and medium enterprises were playing in the country's long-term future (Tan and Tay 1994). Consequently, the government set up a subcommittee on entrepreneurship development (Ang 1985), which assessed how the government's development policies had affected the entrepreneurial environment in Singapore. The report found that:

- the government's continuing efforts to attract multi-national companies and establish large Government Lead Companies (GLC) had stifled local entrepreneurship; and

- high employment levels, high salaries and high job security have led to Singaporeans becoming accustomed to the associated high levels of security.

These circumstances contributed to the reluctance of Singaporeans to start their own businesses. Essentially, under the existing system and structure, there were no incentives or motivations to venture take on the risks associated with developing their own businesses.

It is noteworthy that the government has, over the years, actively expressed and supported the development of SMEs as a key strategy to enhance local entrepreneurial culture. This strategic approach is consistent with the government's philosophy of playing the dominant role in the economy, as was the case in its previous strategic efforts designed to attract multi-national firms and to develop government companies in order to spur employment levels and to develop the economy. Despite the far-reaching government role in assisting local businesses and promoting the spirit of entrepreneurship in Singapore, the island-state remains less entrepreneurial than many other countries in the world (Chatterjee and Nankervis 2007).

Government: facilitator or trouble-maker?

Rules to regulate a country's economy are despised or welcomed depending on one's own interests and perspectives. The SME sector makes demands on government policy that must be balanced with other demands and requirements. However, most small businesses consider administrative burdens and hampering bureaucracy to be serious obstacles to growth. While governments have limited influence on factors such as market behaviour and organizational efficiency, they have a more decisive influence on security of property rights, on taxation, on infrastructure and on financial and labour markets. In particular, governments are expected to take responsibility for creating and maintaining stable and secure business environments free from criminality, bribery and corruption. No-one is prepared to set up a business venture if there is risk of political and financial instability and uncertainty.

Dynamic governments open to necessary adjustments of rules and regulations are often aware of the need for change, although political commitments to various stakeholder groups may render certain changes politically unacceptable. However, the creation of job opportunities is a high-priority political goal in most countries with general political consensus. Since relatively little has been achieved in the recent past in this context, governments need to make laws and policies to facilitate real growth in the small business sector. A World Bank report maintains that progress requires more than changes in formal policies:

> Many investment climate improvements require changes to laws and policies. But more is required. Over 90 per cent of firms in developing countries report gaps between formal policies and what happens in practice. And the content, as well as the implementation of policies, is vulnerable to a deeper set of policy failures. At the heart of the problem lies a basic tension: Societies benefit greatly from the activities of firms, but the preferences of firms don't fully match those of society. This tension is most evident in taxation and regulation. Most firms complain about taxes, but taxes finance public services that benefit the investment climate and other social goals. Many firms would also prefer to comply with fewer regulations, but sound regulation addresses market failures and can therefore improve the investment climate and protect other social interests. Similar tensions can occur across most areas of investment climate policymaking.

Creating a good investment climate requires governments to balance these interests. Complicating this task are the differences in preferences and priorities between firms. Firms have common perspectives on many issues, but their views can diverge on others – whether on market restrictions, the structure of taxation, or the priority given to infrastructure improvements in different locations. There can also be differences in policy preferences within firms, between owners and managers on matters of corporate governance, or between owners and workers on labour market policies. All governments must arbitrate those differences in an environment where firms, officials and other stakeholders seek to tilt the outcome to their advantage.

(World Bank 2008)

Responding to this tension requires governments to navigate four interrelated challenges that cut across all areas of investment climate policy. The way governments respond to those challenges has a big impact on investment climates and thus on growth and poverty. And each involves going beyond changes in formal policies to confront deeper sources of policy failure.

First challenge: Investment climate policies are an enticing target for rent-seeking by firms, officials and other groups. Corruption can increase the cost of doing business – and when it extends to higher echelons of government, it can lead to deep distortion in policies. Surveys show that the majority of firms in developing countries expect to pay bribes when dealing with officials, but with big variations across countries (see table below). Capture and patron-clientelism (reflecting unequal information and influence in policymaking) can also create large distortions, tilting policies in favour of some groups at the expense of others. Eliminating unjustified interventions in the economy, curbing discretion and improving the accountability of governments, particularly through greater transparency, help to restrain rent-seeking.

Second challenge: Establishing credibility is of vital importance since the confidence firms have in the future – including the credibility of government policies – determines whether and how they invest. Policies that lack credibility will fail to elicit the intended investment response. Policy credibility can be undermined by many things, including the temptations governments face to compromise sound long-term policies to meet shorter-term or narrower goals (such as extracting rents for policy-makers or currying favour with some voters). Mechanisms that allow governments to commit to sound policies, discipline and persistence all play a role.

Third challenge: Fostering public trust and legitimacy. Good investment climates are nurtured by broad public support: a consensus in favour of building a more productive society can facilitate policy improvements regardless of the political party or group in office. Absence of such support can make policy reform more difficult and undermine the sustainability (and hence the credibility) of reforms. Open and participatory policymaking and efforts to ensure that the benefits of a better investment climate extend widely in society can help to build that support.

Fourth challenge: Ensuring policy responses fit local conditions. To be effective, policy interventions need to take into account sources of potential government failure and differences in local conditions. Failure to do so can lead to poor or even perverse results. Approaches that demand enforcement capacity beyond that available will not only fail to meet their intended objective but also contribute to informality and corruption and undermine credibility. Approaches that involve high levels of discretion can expose firms to considerable uncertainty and risk when effective safeguards against the misuse of that discretion are not yet developed. While approaches in today's developed countries can provide a

Table 5.1 Distribution of respondents reporting they paid a bribe to obtain a service

Quintile	Range	Countries
1 (top)	> 32%	Albania, Cambodia, Cameroon, Macedonia, Kosovo, Nigeria, Pakistan, Philippines, Romania, Senegal
2	18–32%	Bolivia, Dominican Republic, Greece, India, Indonesia, Lithuania, Moldova, Peru, Serbia, Ukraine
3	6–18%	Bulgaria, Croatia, Czech Republic, Luxembourg, Malaysia, Panama, Russia, Turkey, Venezuela, Vietnam
4	2–6%	Argentina, Bosnia-Herzegovina, Finland, Hong Kong, Ireland, Portugal, South Africa, Spain, United Kingdom, United States
5 (bottom)	< 2%	Austria, Canada, Denmark, France, Iceland, Japan, South Korea, Netherlands, Sweden, Switzerland

Source: Transparency International Global Corruption Barometer, 2007.

valuable source of inspiration, care needs to be taken to adapt approaches to local conditions. In some cases this may involve the choice of simpler rules with less discretion and additional measures to restrain arbitrary behaviour.

Both corruption and poor institutions have been characteristic of many Latin American countries, which explains why Latin America has had a long series of crises in their economic growth. A growth crisis is defined as a year of negative GDP growth. Some of these crises were triggered by common external shocks, such as the debt crisis of the early 1980s. However, domestic policies and country-specific volatility (inflation, fiscal deficits, exchange-rate volatility) also came into play at various times in various Latin American countries. Table 5.2 shows the number of crises in selected Latin American countries in the period 1960–2002.

Government institutions

The Global Competitiveness Report, published annually by the World Economic Forum is an assessment of competitive strength among countries, measured by 90 variables that are structured into nine sections, or *pillars*. The nine pillars are: institutions; infrastructure; macro economy; health and primary education; higher education and training; market efficiency; technological readiness; business sophistication; and innovation. In 2009–2010, countries were ranked as shown in Table 5.3.

Countries are divided into three specific stages or categories; referred to as: factor-driven; efficiency-driven; and innovation-driven. Each of these implies a growing degree of complexity in the operation of the economy (see Chapter 4). Innovation-driven countries belong to the most competitive group where competition is based mainly on well-functioning public and private institutions, appropriate infrastructure, a stable macroeconomic framework and good health and primary education. All these functions belong under the umbrella of government responsibility.

Strong, efficient and reliable institutions to support entrepreneurs and small business managers without the need for bribes or corruption are necessary (although not sufficient) to encourage initiatives leading to business growth. Institutional efficiency has many parameters and is difficult to generalize across cultural and socioeconomic contexts. In order to grade the efficiency of government institutions in relation to small business support, the following two procedures are sometimes taken as measures of institutional efficiency, namely

Table 5.2 Growth crises in Latin America in the period 1960–2002

Country	Crisis years (per cent)
Argentina	41.5
Bolivia	34.1
Brazil	29.3
Chile	22.0
Colombia	17.1
Costa Rica	24.4
Ecuador	24.4
Mexico	19.5
Peru	36.6
Uruguay	36.6
Venezuela	43.9

Source: Economic Survey of Latin America; ECLAC, Santiago, 2003.

Table 5.3 Global competitiveness rankings, 2009–2010

Most competitive	Ranking	Least competitive	Ranking
Switzerland	1	Nepal	130
Sweden	2	Mozambique	131
Singapore	3	Mali	132
United States	4	Timor-Leste	133
Germany	5	Burkina Faso	134
Japan	6	Mauritania	135
Finland	7	Zimbabwe	136
Netherlands	8	Burundi	137
Denmark	9	Angola	138
Canada	10	Chad	139

Source: Global Competiveness Report 2010–2011.

the time required to start a new business and the time required to enforce a contract. One reason why these measures are so widely used in international statistics is because both parameters are easy to determine.

Table 5.4 shows number of days required to start a business, i.e. days needed to complete the procedures to legally operate a business. Table 5.5 shows the inconvenience in the form of procedures, time, cost and minimum paid-up capital for starting a business. Table 5.6 shows the time required to enforce a contract in number of calendar days from the filing of the lawsuit in court until the final determination and, in appropriate cases, payment.

Government support for SME–university collaboration

Many small firms lack the time, resources, technology and expertise to research and develop new business ideas and innovations. Universities can potentially provide access to expertise, technology and resources that could be of assistance to SMEs. Working in partnership with research departments can lead to new commercial developments that an SME may have been unable to achieve on its own. Student projects and placements offer SMEs access to a

Table 5.4 Days required to set up a business

Fastest countries	Days	Slowest countries	Days
New Zealand	1	Laos	100
Australia	2	Brunei	116
Georgia	3	Brazil	120
Rwanda	3	Equatorial Guinea	136
Singapore	3	Venezuela	141
Belgium	4	Sao Tome and Principe	144
Hungary	4	Democratic Republic of Congo	149
Macedonia	4	Haiti	195
Albania	5	Guinea–Bissau	213
Canada	5	Suriname	694

Source: World Bank 2010; Doing Business 2010.

Table 5.5 Rankings of procedures, time, cost and minimum paid-up capital for starting a business

Least onerous	Ranking	Most onerous	Ranking
New Zealand	1	Cameroon	174
Canada	2	Iraq	175
Australia	3	West Bank and Gaza	176
Singapore	4	Djibouti	177
Georgia	5	Equatorial Guinea	178
Macedonia	6	Guinea	179
Belarus	7	Haiti	180
United States	8	Eritrea	181
Ireland	9	Chad	182
Mauritius	10	Guinea–Bissau	183

Source: Word Bank Report, 2008.

Table 5.6 Days required to enforce a contract in 2006

Fastest countries	Days	Slowest countries	Days
Denmark	190	Afghanistan	1,642
Armenia	185	Guatemala	1,459
Kazakhstan	183	Bangladesh	1,442
Ukraine	183	India	1,420
Australia	181	Slovenia	1,350
Russia	178	Colombia	1,346
Lithuania	166	Trinidad and Tobago	1,340
Kyrgyzstan	140	Suriname	1,290
Singapore	120	Djibouti	1,225
New Zealand	109	Italy	1,210

Source: World Development Indicators database, World Bank Report.

wide range of knowledge, expertise and resources. Furthermore, recruiting more graduates will result in a greater flow of talent, energy and innovation into the SME sector.

SMEs may not always operate at the optimal technological level. A study undertaken on technology transfer between SMEs in the UK and the local research base stated that:

Table 5.7 Summary of characteristics hampering and fostering competitiveness

Hampering competitiveness[a]	Fostering competitiveness[a]
Lack of property rights	**Good macroeconomic management**
Corruption	Modern institutions
Favouritism of government officials	**Efficient public institutions**
Low quality of public institutions	High rank in technology
Poor management of public finances	Sound public finances
Institutional weaknesses	**Low levels of corruption**

Source: World Economic Forum report (2005).

Note
a   Characteristics in **bold** were thought especially important.

'although technology transfer is increasingly recognised as being of great importance, getting it to work in practice can be difficult'. The study concluded that technology transfer was making an important contribution to local manufacturing and technology-based firms, but SMEs were still concerned with their own lack of know-how in accessing assistance from universities. Nevertheless, universities are repositories of specialist technology and expertise which can be of enormous benefit to SMEs willing to engage with academia.

Owner-managers often possess the entrepreneurial drive but lack formal management training. This weakness can eventually become a critical factor limiting growth and expansion. Developing high-level workforce skills has been identified as central to improving competitiveness. It can also be argued that SMEs would benefit from improvements in their commitment to management training.

SMEs could make better use of skills available in the graduate labour market. Graduates are under-represented in the SME sector, but this is seen as the most likely growth area for future graduate employment. Owner-managers are often wary of employing highly-qualified staff because graduates are perceived as unlikely to remain committed over the longer term due to ambitious career plans.

Conclusion

Governments can facilitate small business growth by implementing and actively supporting anti-corruption programmes, by building efficient institutions and by guaranteeing a sustained macroeconomic environment. Governments can also hamper small businesses by neglecting – or failing to support – essential functions for business development. These essential functions are legislation to support property rights, institutions that act as intermediaries between the small business sector and institutions like banks, non-governmental organizations and local governments.

Table 5.7 shows factors perceived as hampering and fostering competitiveness in a country.

References

Ang, K. H. (1985) *Subcommittee Report on Economic Development*. Singapore: Economic Committee.
Bannock, G. (2005) *The Economics and Management of Small Business*. London: Routledge.
Beck, T. and Demirgüç-Kunt, A. (2004) *SMEs, Growth, and Poverty: Do Pro-SME Policies Work?* Washington, DC: World Bank. Private Sector Note 268.

Chatterjee, S. and Nankervis, A. (2007) *Asian Management in Transition: Emerging Themes*. London: Palgrave.

Fölster, S. (2004) *Missing: 70,000 New Enterprises*. Stockholm: Confederation of Swedish Enterprise.

Mason, C. and Harrison, R. (1990) 'Small Firms: Phoenix from the Ashes', in Pinder, D. (ed) *Western Europe: Challenge and Change*. London: Belhaven Press.

Stanworth, J. and Gray, C. (1991) *Bolton 20 Years on: The Small Firm in the 1990s*. London: Chapman Publishing.

Tan, W. and Tay, R. (1994) 'Factors Contributing to the Growth of SMEs: The Singapore Case', in *Proceedings of the 5th ENDEC World Conference on Entrepreneurship*. Singapore: Nanyang Technological University.

Tripp, A. M. (1997) *Changing the Rules: The Politics of Liberalization and the Urban Informal Economy in Tanzania*. Berkeley, CA: University of California Press.

Whitley, R. (1996) *Business Systems in East Asia: Firms, Markets and Societies*. London: Sage Publications.

World Bank (2008) *World Development Report 2008*. Oxford: Oxford University Press.

Part 2

SME management in a cross-cultural perspective

Judging by a Google search for 'small business management' that gave over 20 million hits, there is no shortage of views, ideas and recipes about how to manage a small business! Many of these may be the same, some are probably trivial or uninteresting and many can be excluded for various reasons. Nevertheless, the topic is attractive and keeps policy-makers, researchers and professionals involved in small business busy with questions about small and medium enterprise growth and development.

An important question relates to the growth of small firms, since growth is a precondition for the creation of jobs, for contributing to economic development and for income generation. A combination of factors has been assumed to be crucial for growth, such as government support programmes, improved management capability and improved productivity through technology. In spite of substantial government investments in the small and medium (SME) sectors, and in spite of an endless number of management training programmes, growth has been very modest. Many theories and models presented in training programmes originate from academic circles and are far from being based on a thorough familiarity with the realities of small business. The debate that has been going on for some years as whether small firms are merely small versions of large firms seems to have concluded that this is not the case, even if the conclusion may not yet have been accepted everywhere within the academic sphere.

Enterprise growth is not an intrinsic phenomenon that happens as a result of a strategy or an ambition. Growth is the result of a demand for products and services that have value for a user. The concepts of 'added value' and 'customer value', and the linkage between the two, are therefore the focus of the following chapters. Adding value to products and services is the alternative to the more common approach among small firms in many countries of price competition. Continuously reducing price to obtain customer orders is generally sure route to bankruptcy. Creating management awareness about this requires neither sophisticated theories nor models.

Current organization and management theories and models are predominantly of Western origin and formulated in response to conditions prevailing in the West. Their applicability in non-Western contexts has been a topic for discussion over the years and is still a matter of concern as noted from a quotation by the Director of the Business School at the University of Cape Town in March 2011:

> The current influx of incoming business schools to Africa talk about bringing pre-existing European and US models to Africa as if this will be the answer to all of the continent's problems. None, it seems, have paused to consider whether Africa really will benefit from what they are offering or if they are missing an opportunity to create something better.

Theoretical reasoning that aims at the creation of models for cause-effect understanding and which are based on assumptions about economic and political stability for long periods are of course less suited in contexts where such assumptions do not hold. Strategic planning and long-term investment analyses are examples that cannot be justified for small firms where adaption to unpredictable changes is a way of life. On the other hand, models promoting customer dialogues and assisting managers in building close customer relations are less context-dependent and therefore widely applicable in current business principles aiming at a more personal approach to stakeholders and customers.

In the following chapters, the two main emphases are on management and small business growth. The two are of course connected but not identical. Management development and training are essential aspects for understanding the principles that guide managers in different cross-cultural environments. Training programmes based on theories that are alien to the cultural context will not be suitable to promote business growth.

Chapter 6 is devoted to growth and the means of achieving growth. The concept of added value is discussed in detail together with customer value and its definition. The strategy of innovations is introduced as a path to further growth.

In Chapter 7 the theory and practice of small firm management is the main topic, which also includes a brief survey of how management ideologies have developed in the past. In this chapter, various aspects of management and culture are discussed.

Chapter 8 focuses on the different management roles from strategist through operator to mentor, which relates to the different hierarchical levels in the organization where the small business manager must be active.

Chapter 9 introduces a number of strategic and operational tools which assist the small business manager. Some of the tools are introduced together with how-to-use guidelines.

In Chapter 10, networking between firms is the main theme, and it introduces a typology for different forms of networks. A special form of networking, namely partnerships, is discussed.

Chapter 11 contains a general discussion of the opportunities and threats related to the small business sector in the global context, and ends with a consideration of communication in international business contexts.

6 Small business growth

Measures and means

Introduction

In 1962, the American economic historian Alfred Chandler published a book entitled *Strategy and Structure* that contained in-depth studies and comparisons of large American companies. Chandler concluded that the strategic orientation of a large company is a determining factor in the way the company structures its organization. The comparison emphasized that, in time, a company's strategy determined its structure, and that the common denominator between structure and strategy was the application of the enterprise's resources to market demand. Structure had been used to adapt the enterprise's existing resources to current demand; strategy had been used to plan for the allocation of resources to anticipated demand (Chandler 1984). In his research, Chandler explored how large businesses adapted their administrative structures to accommodate strategies of growth (Heracleous 2003). The importance of formulating and implementing a business strategy to strengthen competitiveness and growth has often been stressed in the literature on organization and management (Ansoff 1965; Stern and Stalk 1995; Porter 1996).

To what extent can we assume that similar views on strategy and structure apply in the context of small business? Do small firms in general set up a business strategy from which they structure their organization and administrative routines? In the so-called 'top-down' approach to SME research, it is assumed that small firms are much like larger firms: though smaller, they have applied general models developed for large business (Marsden and Forbes 2003). However, Porter's (1985) support of the idea that generic strategies are applicable to all kinds of firms was controversial, and various writers maintained that firm size should be the determinant for choosing strategic approach (Marsden and Forbes ibid.). The 'bottom-up' approach to research rejected the application of large scale strategic management concepts to small firms (Jennings and Beaver 1997).

Small and medium enterprises (SMEs) operate under conditions that are largely different from those of large firms, and it cannot be taken for granted that a conscious long-term business strategy is decisive for their growth. The business strategy of the large firm may involve high-cost product innovation plans, long-term penetration of export markets to open-up new business potentials or the acquisition of competitors to ensure market leadership. These strategic considerations require structural changes and modifications for their implementation. SMEs – and particularly the small firms – seldom have the financial resources for costly long-range strategies, where the pay-off from investments made today will happen sometime in the future. The competitive advantage of the small firm is rather to react to and take advantage of sudden changes in the market.

Likening the large firm to ponderous oil tanker, the small firm is more like a canoe, quick to change direction and capable of navigating in most waters. The strengths of a small firm should be its adaptability to new and changing business conditions, where a predetermined business strategy could be restrictive. However, various studies have shown that small firms are generally not very good at making use of their small size and flexibility. It is obvious that growth factors for SMEs cannot be found in a simple, one-dimensional recipe, but are rather the result of various factors (Gibb and Davies 1992; Storey 1994).

It is not meaningful to search for a generic strategy pattern for small business, rather the strategy must emanate from the model selected to describe a firm. In the case of the 'resource-based' approach, the strategy is geared to the optimal mobilization of internal resources.

SME growth

Small business growth has interested and motivated many writers and scholars to develop models and theories for small business managers to follow (for example, Storey 1994; Smallbone and Wyer 2000; Gibb and Davies 1992). As already discussed, certain theories have endured and continue to be sources of inspiration for research, Penrose's *The Theory of the Growth of the Firm* (1959) among them. Some of the theories that have been developed contradict each other, notably the 'top-down' approach ('small firms are smaller versions of large firms') and the 'bottom-up' approach ('theories developed for large firms cannot be applied in small firm research').

To measure the growth of small business, we need to be clear about what we mean by growth. Revenue from sales (also referred to as sales turnover) can be a relevant growth measure, like profit. However, results from one year may be misleading due to an extraordinary situation, thus the trend during a sequence of years gives a more reliable picture. If growth measured as the percentage increase in total revenue over a period (a year) is the same as inflation there is no growth in real terms.

In fact there is no general consensus among researchers on how to measure the growth of SMEs; instead, a variety of different indicators are in use. Increase in sales revenue is one, growth in total assets is another, added-value growth yet another. Table 6.1 summarises some of the more common measures and definitions of SME growth.

Sales revenue, added value and profit are suitable measures of growth, since data can be monitored over a period of time and variations observed. However, the difficulty of

Table 6.1 Some common measures of SME growth

Growth measure	Direct/indirect	References (examples)
Sales revenue	Direct	Wiklund *et al.* (2003); Barkham (1996)
Total assets	Direct	Wiklund *et al.*(2003)
Change orientation	Indirect	
Added value	Direct	Jones (2003); Barkham (1996)
Innovations	Indirect	Forbes and Wield (2002)
Profit	Direct	Jones and Tilley (2003)
Employment	Direct	Wiklund *et al.*(2003); Barkham (1996)
Return on Investment	Indirect	Gadenne (1998)

Source: Author.

collecting financial data from small firms is a problem in many low- and middle-income countries. In high-income countries, where firms are formally registered and hence obliged to publish results, the collection of financial data may be easier. The direct/indirect criterion in Table 6.1 distinguished between measures such as added value that directly measure growth and others such as innovations that may indirectly reveal growth potential of the firm.

Although a majority of theories and models related to SMEs focus on growth, there are no blueprints offering managers recipes for success! There is no shortage of success stories with examples from individual small businesses, but specific conditions in each case make generalization too hazardous. Tables 6.2 and 6.3 contain examples of success factors given by small businesses in Europe. Table 6.2 is based on interviews with 100 Swedish SME managers selected from a database of the Swedish Federation of Small Enterprises. In these interviews, the managers were asked the following:

> By success factors we refer to those positive characteristics of your company that you consider have or have had significant importance for the successful development and growth of the company. Please identify the five most relevant success factors in priority order.

Table 6.3 presents the findings are of a study conducted by the economic secretariat of the Swedish Saving Banks among 50 industrial and banking economists in 12 European countries. The five factors were identified as common for successful firms operating in weak markets in periods of economic recession.

A number of factors, such as knowledge of company products and customer orientation, are among those common to the two studies. Listening to and understanding customers' requirements, striving towards increased customer value content in products and services and making customer demands become govern product and service updates and

Table 6.2 Examples of suggested SME growth factors

Category	Growth factors[a]
Business Concept	Good knowledge of our products
	Good knowledge and understanding of the market
	Competent and efficient management
	Close monitoring of the market development
Serviceability	Satisfactory customer service
	Positive approach to problem solving
	Qualified and efficient sales and service networks
Quality	ISO certification
	Attractive and logical price/quality ratio
	Efficient maintenance system
	Efficient and adequate organization
Economy	Good banking contacts
	Good liquidity
Employment	Qualified and loyal employees
	Efficient recruitment routines

Source: Author's survey.

Note
a Most popular response in category first.

Table 6.3 Common factors for successful companies in 12 European countries

Success factor	Example techniques
Focus on customer	Be main supplier to fewer customers
	Focus marketing on geographical growth areas
	Be receptive to customer complaints
	Improve understanding of customer's business
	Develop knowledge and understanding of our products
Concentration on profitable products	Find product niches
	Strive towards higher product added value
	Adopt a flexible price strategy/target pricing
Reduction of lead-times	Make changes for faster throughput
	Catch 'time thieves'
	Identify cost drivers
Improvements to purchasing	Reduce number of suppliers
	Co-ordinate between production and sales
Personnel management	Introduce individual training and planning

Source: Swedish Saving Banks, 2002.

improvements are all findings associated with growth. Small business strategies must therefore concentrate on making use of opportunities coming from change in technology, markets and ways of organizing work, by adding value to products and services through creative and innovative thinking and behaviour. But strategies must also mindful of factors that hamper business growth.

Barriers to SME growth

Business success and competitiveness depend on a range of situational and contextual factors, internal as well as external. Improving the competitiveness of SMEs thus involves understanding the barriers that hamper the ability of small and medium firms to reduce internal obstacles and to navigate or to reduce the impact of external factors. Small firms encounter a number of barriers to success not only during the start-up period but also more generally. Internal barriers may range from the lack of an adequate business idea to low management capability; external barriers may include bureaucracy in the form of over-ambitious government controls, or shortness of skilled labour. The following discussion identifies some of these internal and external barriers.

External factors hampering SME growth

Morrison (2006) claims that businesses are affected by external factors which they cannot control. Such factors can rarely be influenced by management decisions, and include political, economic, social, technological, environmental and legal factors.

Competition

The Office of Small and Medium Enterprises Promotion in Thailand (OSMEP 2007a) claims that SMEs are generally facing low competitiveness in terms of knowledge, innovation, prudent investment, business operation and good management, all important for raising quality.

In spite of increasing global trade, small firms in low-and middle-income countries are facing increased competition from transnational firms with higher levels of management skills and financial strength. Small firms in developing countries also have difficulties in complying with regulations set up by the World Trade Organization (WTO) on technical barriers to trade, which makes it difficult for them to compete initially on the global market due to low quality and unsuitable materials (Lind 2009).

Economic crisis

The world economy has been hit by downturns in the past, and since these global economic fluctuations are a reoccurring phenomenon, enterprises must learn to accept them. It has been argued that small firms are more vulnerable to economic crisis than large firms, since their size makes them less financially sustainable and limits their choice of survival strategies due to more limited skills, technology and management capacity.

Governmental policies

Government rules and regulations that may hinder SME growth have been discussed in detail in Chapter 5.

Access to finance

It is difficult to find a clear picture as to whether finance is a constraint or not for small business growth. Some writers argue that insufficient capital or lack of financial sources is the major obstacle for SMEs (Schleuwagen and Goedhuys 2002) whereas others (for example Gadenne 1998) claim that firms which rely on large amounts of external finance perform worse in the short term than those that generate funds internally. Small business managers who approach financial institutions like banks for loans for investments or to improve liquidity can go away empty-handed if their business plans are vague or not properly elaborated. Banks take risks when lending money and therefore need to have sufficient security for it. Many small business managers fail to realize that a visit to the bank requires proper preparation of their case.

Corruption

Corruption is a significant hindering factor for SME growth in many parts of the world, and it has been shown that government accountability reduces the possibility of corruption. The World Wide Governance Indicators (WGI) produced by The World Bank show that most countries in Africa perform badly on all aspects good governance (Padayachee 2010). The WGI indicators place the vast majority of African countries in the bottom fifth percentile of their six dimensions of governance, meaning that Africa performs worse than any other region except the former Soviet Union. In the Corruption Perceptions Index (CPI), produced by Transparency International, 30 out of the 47 countries where corruption was measured in Africa were found to have rampant corruption while only three (Botswana, Cape Verde and Mauritius) scored above the global average for corruption (Transparency International 2008).

   In China, despite repeated party-led anticorruption drives, the corruption record has probably deteriorated since the mid-1990s. China may not be the most corrupt country in the world, but it has certainly fallen from grace. It is sometimes claimed that greater transparency and a more market-orientated system reduces corruption, but this is offset by the fact that the growth of capitalism has increased exponentially the gains to be made from corruption; many prominently-placed Chinese have been unable to resist its lure (Bramall 2009).

In many transitional societies, criminality in everyday life has been the subject of much sensationalized discussion, but remains a serious and complex problem. Embedded criminality caused by transition is among the most vivid examples of the misguided character of policy driven by unprepared liberalisation and 'faster-is-better' ideology (McIntyre 2003).

Bribery and corruption are related, but Transparency International (2008) highlights that in the case of SMEs, bribery is even more problematic since they can feel powerless in the face of demands for bribes, and are often unaware that bribery can be resisted.

Internal factors hampering SME growth

According to Morrison (2006), internal factors within an organization reveal how management decisions and the attitudes of a company can affect decisions taken regarding the growth of a firm. Factors that are frequently considered part of the internal environment include marketing objectives, human resource (HR) strategies (such as employee motivation), staff turnover and the provision of training, leadership styles, investment in research and development (R&D) and the organizational culture.

Management competence

Macpherson and Holt (2007) and Barratt-Pugh (2005) claim that the growth of firms is dependent on managerial knowledge. Small business managers are less well trained than their large firm counterparts (Tannock *et al.* 2002) and hence tend to choose poor production technology, do not use proper accounting systems and underestimate funding required (APO 2001). Like in so many other general views on small business management, this perspective is predominantly a Western one. For example, managing a small firm in the United States is different from Mozambique, and even if factors hamper growth in both countries the factors are different. Abundance of resources in the United States may be the reverse in Mozambique, and while use of technology in Mozambique is hampered by access to spare parts their availability is no problem in the United States.

Generally, SMEs spend less on formal training than large enterprises due to financial limitations and the fact that it can be difficult to take employees out of production (Tannock *et al.* 2002). Training is crucial for productivity and quality as it influences the effectiveness, efficiency and motivation of the employees. Managers of SMEs often fail to listen to employees who really understand the process and product (Tannock *et al.* 2002).

Lack of skilled labour

Lack of skilled labour hinders SMEs in developing countries (Sleuwaegen and Goedhuys 2002). According to Holden *et al.* (2007) firms in all sectors and of all sizes can progress through greater use of graduate labour, but there is generally a mutual distrust between graduates and SMEs. APO (2001) highlights lack of skilled labour as one of the most crucial obstacles for SMEs, making it difficult for them to attract highly-educated workers and retain skilled employees (high labour turnover), since they prefer to work for large enterprises that can offer higher salaries, job security and better career opportunities, resulting in a slowdown in workforce development which has a negative impact on the quality of goods and services (OSMEP 2007b).

Marketing

According to Brush *et al.* (2009), marketing is another obstacle to companies' growth. To maintain sales, businesses face challenges in: establishing effective distribution channels; communicating product features; pricing products and services in an attractive way; implementing sales and marketing efforts to win and retain customers; and undertaking constant product development. Moreover, OSMEP (2009) identifies other aspects, such as: the need to understand domestic and international marketing; lack of capabilities to create innovation, image and exclusive branding; and the lack of appropriate support from a marketing infrastructure.

SMEs generally do not have the knowledge or information about other markets, thus limiting their ability to market their products to larger groups of customers and expand their business (APO 2001). On the other hand, Brush *et al.* (2009) argue that massive marketing campaigns are not the best way to achieve success, rather close personal relationships, word-of-mouth referrals, repeat business and niche marketing efforts have proven to be more cost-effective and successful.

Technology

SMEs tend to have low productivity and lack competitiveness, the result of using old technology, inefficient use of the machinery they have, their inability to improve technology due to funding limitations, and the fact that most SMEs are users of technology, not adaptors of technology (OSMEP 2007b). Many managers are not aware of the appropriate technology for their business and they do not have the ability to choose.

Managing change

As present-day companies find business partners, customers and suppliers in ever more remote geographical areas, so competition between firms is increasing. There is growing awareness that existing ways of competing and thinking are not enough for future competitive success, and that organizations must learn to compete and think in new ways (Heracleous 2003). Emerging strategic imperatives include the goals of optimization within the organization's current industry and the generation of ground-breaking strategies that will create new niches and markets and re-define whole industries (Porter 1997). In other words, in a world of continuous re-definition of industry boundaries and commingling technologies, competition not just about share of existing markets but about 'opportunity share' in future markets, (Prahalad 1997). This means that companies should not merely or exclusively be trying to catch up with the best performers in current competitive games, but be aiming to invent new games, re-write the rules and create new competitive space (Hammel 1997).

Change and *learning* have become key concepts whereby organizations are advised to listen and respond to the needs and requirements of users. Specifically, a successful organization is the one that can change to apply the new paradigm for prosperity in today's global environment. Table 6.4 summarises some of the changes that are considered essential for firms to follow to comply with the new paradigm that is emerging.

Table 6.4 Changes in organizations

Old approach	New approach
If it's not broken, don't fix it	Continuous improvement
Inspection of poor quality	Prevention of poor quality
Quality not important	Quality critical
Accept current processes	Question current processes
Development	Innovation
Rigid organizational structure	Flexible organizational structure
Many organizational layers	Few organizational layers
Compete	Co-operate
Individual performance	Team performance
People are specialized, controlled or eliminated	People add value, are flexible, empowered
Strong management	Strong management and leadership
Leadership only at the top	Leadership throughout the organization
Short-term outlook	Long-term vision
Individual merit reward system	Team performance reward system
Education for management	Education and training for everyone
Focus on cost and profit	Driven by total client satisfaction

Source: Lind (2007).

The following comments germane to Table 6.4 have been collected from various sources such as Barcly and Saylor (2001). Continuous improvement of processes, people, products and services aimed at client satisfaction is essential. The 'if it's not broke, don't fix it' attitude does not promote the critical thinking necessary for growth and sustainability. Continuous improvement is important for a firm to stay competitive in the marketplace, the proactive approach to change. The view that 'everything can be made better through process improvement' stimulates the creativity and innovation needed for constant development. In addition to continuous improvement of processes, individuals must take responsibility for upgrading their knowledge and skills through a lifelong learning system. Further, products and/or services require progressive enhancement to meet or exceed the changing needs and expectations of clients.

It is important to realize that all organizations – private as well as government and non-government – have clients, individuals or other organizations that will benefit from the services provided. This comment may seem trivial, but the opposite would have serious implications: if there were no clients there would be no reason for the organization to exist.

Inspection-based quality assurance needs to be superseded by prevention techniques. The industrial mind-set that has dominated organizational thinking for a long time is one which expects defects. Therefore as non-industrial organizations – public as well as private – have borrowed their organizational paradigm and behaviour from industry, so a certain level of defects in services provided to clients and society has become accepted as unavoidable. To reduce the effects of these defects, different inspection regimes have been adopted. But this inspection-based viewpoint adds cost to the product or service – a cost that most organizations should no longer afford and that clients should not tolerate. By shifting the emphasis to prevention, thing are 'right the first time': cost is reduced, while product and service quality is increased. Prevention techniques focus on improvement of all the processes in an organization to maximize the capabilities of its processes.

Quality needs to be focused on satisfying users and clients. Disregard for quality or concern for just conformance to requirements is not good enough to keep and maintain clients. Today's knowledgeable clients demand satisfaction. This is how they define quality. Hence, organizations must determine what will satisfy their clients and then focus on striving to meet their needs and expectations. To accomplish this goal the organization must identify the elements of quality that are of vital importance to their particular users. The key elements of quality for a user might include, among other things, the following items: perceived product and/or service quality, performance, reliability, supportability, durability, features, availability, aesthetics, serviceability, maintainability, usability, environmental impact, conformance to requirements, client service, logistics, training, warranty and life-cycle cost, all depending on the kind of service provided. For instance, some clients demand reliability as a key element of client satisfaction. In other cases, clients might value performance as the critical element. For still other clients, the key element of quality may be availability. For such a client, it is of primary importance that the product or service be available in the right quantity, at the right time and at the right place.

Innovation through constant incremental improvement must be pursued by all organizations and industries. Building on the old and creating new uses are critical for future survival. Economic considerations dictate making do with what is already available. Such an approach targets innovative enhancements of existing systems and deliverables as a major method of satisfying requirements.

Flexible organizational structures with as few layers as possible are best able to respond rapidly to clients' changing demands. Rigid structures cannot react fast enough to keep pace with a formidable competitor, whereas an organization with only a few layers has the 'lean and mean' structure needed for today's world. Clients will no longer subsidize the cost of the huge waste created by large bureaucratic organizations. Organizations must be trimmed to the absolute core, with decision-making devolved to the people closest to the clients and the processes. Such organizations have fewer managers.

Cooperation among governments, industries, companies, organizations, teams and individuals is essential for survival. Cooperation among government, industry, labour and education is critical to a high-growth, high-wage economy. In addition, management and labour must learn to cooperate for a prosperous economy. Further, departments and functional organizations must break down barriers to optimize organizational productivity. Also, individuals need to work together in teams to respond rapidly to clients. All cooperative efforts aim at win/win solutions instead of the win/lose situation fostered by competition. Only through cooperative relationships can global success be realised.

Groups, especially teams, are the organizational structures of choice. Although individuality is important, teams multiply the capabilities of each team member. In today's complex workplace, teams are the only structure capable of providing the high level of performance, flexibility and adaptability necessary to respond rapidly to clients and to provide deliverables that delight them.

People are the most important, flexible and versatile resource capable of adding client value to a product or service. Empowered people are the only resource with the ability to respond quickly to clients by optimizing the output of a process based on a thorough analysis of the client requirements and the process. Therefore, specializing or eliminating people greatly reduces an organization's ability to keep or gain clients, and that significantly decreases its chances of survival. People are the most important resource for gaining an advantage over the competition. To optimize this essential resource, forward-thinking organizations must strive to provide a high quality work environment, where both individual and organizational needs are satisfied while striving to delight clients.

Strong leadership at the top and at all levels is needed, instead of strong management. Guiding people to achieve a common goal is the focus of improved performance in any organization. Strong management is still required to ensure that a project is completed as required, but leadership is essential to maximize the human potential to care about and satisfy clients. Managers simply ordering achievement will not make an excellent organization. Leadership involves the sustained, active, hands-on participation of all leaders, continuously setting the example, coaching, training, mentoring and facilitating empowered people.

The reward and recognition system must shift from individual merit to team-performance systems. A team-performance reward and recognition system provides the incentive for optimizing the results of teamwork to accomplish a mission. The team-performance system should credit the individual's contributions to the success of the team, while at the same time providing a reward for effective teamwork. All reward and recognition systems should be geared to each individual team member wanting to contribute to the best of his or her abilities for the ultimate successful outcome of the team.

Investment in education and training for everyone in the organization must be the cornerstone of any organization using a continuous improvement system to persevere in today's environment. Improvement through education and training must continuous, and have an eye to the future. High-growth labour markets demand people with specific higher-level education and skills. These conditions require organizations to adopt a viewpoint that people truly make the difference in the competitive world economic environment, and such organizations must make an investment to create a lifelong learning system. The satisfaction of clients through its processes and deliverables must be the driving force in the organization.

An Asian example of SME change

During a period of four years small and medium enterprise managers from 14 Asian countries were interviewed regarding their approach to various factors of relevance for managing the small business. The countries were India, Nepal, Bhutan, Malaysia, Bangladesh, Vietnam, Lao, Cambodia, Indonesia, Thailand, Philippines, Sri Lanka, China and Mongolia. Managers were asked to rate the 12 statements in Table 6.5 for the SMEs in their country

Table 6.5 Statements used in interviews of SME managers in selected Asian countries

1	In my country, SMEs in general have close customer contacts and are keen to meet customer needs
2	In my country, uncertainty about the future is a hampering factor for SME business
3	In my country, SME development is primarily constrained by lack of capital
4	In my country, there is a general awareness among SME managers that concern about environmental issues is becoming a true business asset
5	In my country, women are encouraged to actively participate in the business process as entrepreneurs and managers
6	In my country, SME development is hampered by a general lack of technology
7	In my country it happens quite often that SMEs co-operate in networks to win customer orders
8	In my country, SMEs are in general very quality minded in the products and services they provide
9	In my country, SMEs compete primarily with the help of price
10	In my country, SMEs in general consider employees as their most important resources
11	In my country, SMEs are innovative in exploiting new product and service niches
12	In my country, it is acceptable for an employee to argue with the manager

Table 6.6 Attempt at characterizing managers' responses

Statement	Category	In agreement (%)
1	Open	96
2	Constrained	90
3	Constrained	83
4	Dynamic	61
5	Open	77
6	Constrained	99
7	Closed	15
8	Dynamic	54
9	Constrained	86
10	Open	60
11	Closed	35
12	Closed	41

Source: Author.

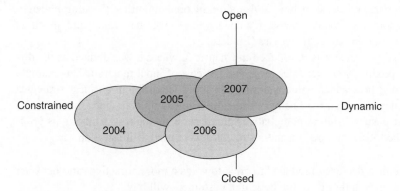

Figure 6.1 Change in SME managers' attitudes.

on a Likert scale (fully agree, partly agree, ...). Although there was no continuity of managers over the four years, statistical analysis showed strong correlations between responses from each country.

Agreement with the statements was classified as indicative of openness, closedness, dynamism or constraint. A table was compiled for each year. Table 6.6 summarizes the results over the four years.

Figure 6.1 shows how the attitudes of the managers interviewed changed over the four years.

The trend over the four years shows changes in management attitudes from more constrained towards more dynamic. On the open–closed axis it was not possible to observe any significant changes.

Added value

The significance of *added value* comes from the fact that value creation is the *raison d'être* for a business and what makes enterprises competitive. However, a conscious business

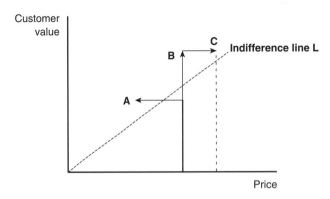

Figure 6.2 Three strategic alternatives.

strategy focusing on adding value to products and services is still lacking in many small and medium enterprises, not least in low- and middle-income countries. Creating management awareness about the linkage between added value, customer value and profit is therefore an urgent issue for small businesses (Lind 2005).

The concept of added value was introduced in Chapter 3, where it was defined as the difference between a product's market sales price and the cost of input material. The example from Chapter 3 shows how added value is used to illustrate the different business strategies a firm can follow depending on the business situation. The example assumes that the sales efforts of a firm are unsuccessful, as potential customers show no interest in buying its products or services. The following three business strategies were used as illustration:

1   Strategy A: the firm decides to reduce the price towards a more attractive ratio between product performance and price in the hope that customers will buy.
2   Strategy B: the firm decides to improve performance (new functions, better service etc.) but without increasing the price in the hope that customers will buy.
3   Strategy C: the firm decides to improve performance and also to increase the price in the hope that the improved product performance will justify the higher price and the customers will buy.

The three strategies are illustrated in Figure 6.2 in relation to the *indifference line* (explained in Chapter 3).

In the example it is only in strategy C that added value is increased according to definition of sales price less cost of input material (which is here assumed to be constant). As in strategy B, the improved product or service performance is likely to result in increased production costs. Strategy C is profitable only as long as the increase in costs is no higher than the price increase, otherwise the increased added value might result in less.

Added value in individual firms is important because it is the sum value added by all firms that constitutes a country's gross domestic product (GDP). However, promoting added value creation and making small business managers aware of the strategic importance of added value requires knowledge of the conditions under which increased added value could result in reduced profit. For the following discussion, we need to introduce several parameters.

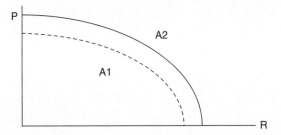

Figure 6.3 Relationship between parameters *A*, *P* and *R*.

Analysing added value parameters

In Chapter 3, the following economic factors were used:

- cost of purchased material (*m*);
- cost to produce the finished product (*q*); and
- sales price (*Q*).

Added value (aV) was defined as:

$$aV = Q - m$$

For the analysis three further parameters are introduced.
Added value grade (*A*), defined as the ratio of added value to total sales revenue:

$$A = (Q - m)/Q$$

Profit margin (*P*), defined as the ratio of profit to total sales revenue:

$$P = (Q - q)/Q$$

Refinement cost grade (*R*), defined as the ratio of in-house production cost to total cost:

$$R = (q - m)/q$$

By eliminating *m*, *q* and *Q*, we arrive at the following relation between *A*, *P* and *R*:

$$P = (A - R)/(1 - R) \tag{1}$$

The relationship between *P* and *R* for specific values of *A* is illustrated in Figure 6.3.

From the relationship (1) above and Figure 6.3, it will be noticed that the values of *P* (profit margin) and *R* (refinement grade) can never be higher than *A* (added value grade). A_1 and A_2 in the diagram denote two levels of added value grade, where A_2 has higher value than A_1.

As noted in Chapter 3, the expression for added value can be reformulated by introducing the parameter *q* as

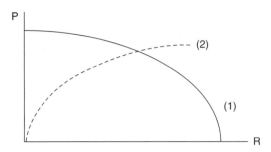

Figure 6.4 Expressions (1) and (2) in the same *P–R* diagram.

$$aV = Q - m = (Q - q) + (q - m)$$

which shows that added value has two components: profit (or surplus) and value of in-house production. By comparing these two components, it is possible to assess how much of the added value is profit and how much comes from value of in-house production. The parameter L (surplus grade) is therefore introduced as the ratio between surplus $(Q - q)$ and costs $(q - m)$. P can be expressed in terms of L and R as follows:

$$P = L \times R / (1 + L \times R) \qquad (2)$$

Figure 6.4 is a graphic representation of the two expressions given by (1) and (2) above.

The diagram in Figure 6.3 can be used to illustrate the strategy C above where additional product or service functions justifies a product price increase with the risk that the additional production cost may jeopardize profit. Two possible situations are illustrated in Figure 6.5 below:

1   Price is increased, cost of material unchanged and parameter L is unchanged, which means the ratio between surplus and in-house costs is unchanged.
2   As situation 1, except that in-house production costs increase with the result that parameter L is lower.

In situation 1, price is increased, which means added value grade increases from A_1 to A_2. With L unchanged (L_1) profit margin is higher – the intersection between the A and L curves. If, however, the in-house production costs increase due to new production functions that justified the price increase, the value of L is lower (L_2) and profit margin is lower (intersection between A_2 and L_2). As long as the ratio (L) between surplus and production cost remains the same, an increase in added value grade always results in a higher profit margin. It is not until the value of L is below a certain level that increase in added value will not result in higher profit margin. It is easily proved that this happens when L is less than a value of P given by the expression

$$A_1 \times L_1 / (A_2 + L_1 (A_2 - A_1))$$

Production costs and profit margin

The diagram in Figure 6.3 is used for the following brief discussion about variation in profit margin depending on the refinement grade R.

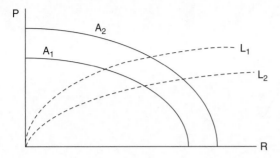

Figure 6.5 Expressions (1) and (2) in the same *P–R* diagram for different values of *L*.

The point R_0 in Figure 6.6 occurs where the slope of the curve is equal to -1 (i.e. the derivative of expression (1) above has the value -1). It can be proved that this happens when R takes the value:

$$R_0 = 1 - \sqrt{(1 - A)}$$

The significance of R_0 can be described as follows. For a refinement grade R less than R_0, changes in R result in less change in profit margin P, whereas to the right of R_0 in the diagram even a small increase in refinement grade will result in a big change (decline) in profit margin. The conclusion is therefore that it is important for a firm to strive for a position lower than the value R_0, since variation in production costs will have less impact on profit margin than in case of higher *R*-values.

Added value, surplus grade and GDP

The accumulated production added value of a country makes up the country's total GDP, defined as the sum of private consumption, gross investments, government spending and exports less imports. Since added value consists of both surplus and in-house production value, the surplus is also part of the GDP value. If surplus is not used for consumption or investments, GDP becomes over-valued, and high values of surplus grade *L* mean that significant amounts of the accumulated added value is profit that may distort the GDP figures. This can be the case in trading businesses where the difference between productions cost *q* and input material cost is low, and hence the surplus value *L* very high.

Analysing cost structure in the firm

The UNIDO International Yearbooks of Industrial Statistics present data *inter alia* on gross manufacturing output, added value, material costs and salary costs for the principle manufacturing sectors of selected countries. In line with earlier comments, it must be underlined that the reliability of this kind of accumulated data is not guaranteed, and the discussion below should be seen merely as an example of a method to determine the total production costs in a firm where overhead costs are not usually available in official statistics. Using the terminology introduced above we denote gross output by *Q* and added value by $(Q - m)$. Salaries and overhead costs are part of the production costs (*q*). Overhead costs are seldom provided by firms and therefore difficult to assess. This in turn makes cost calculation difficult and the following discussion suggests a method to address this situation.

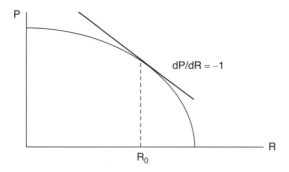

Figure 6.6 Identification of the significant *R*-value R$_0$.

By denoting over-head costs by the Greek letter ε, production costs q can be described as

$$q = m + w + \varepsilon$$

It should be noted that overhead costs ε are mostly not available in international industry statistics, in spite of their importance for estimating production costs. The following method is used to estimate overhead costs and their impact on profit.

With the new expression for q, the surplus grade L can now be written as

$$L = (Q - m - w - \varepsilon)/(w + \varepsilon)$$

In case of no overhead costs ($\varepsilon = 0$), $L = (Q - m - w) / w$; for $\varepsilon = Q - m - w$, $L = 0$. As these two extremes are unlikely to happen, and since ε is a factor that is not present in international statistics, we assume that the overhead costs can be calculated as a percentage of the total production costs, $\varepsilon = x$ per cent of q. This will result in the following expression for q:

$$q = 100(m + w)/(100 - x)$$

In the following example the three countries Indonesia, Ethiopia and Peru are used to demonstrate how industry sector performance can be analysed with the use of data from the UNIDO International Yearbook on Industrial Statistics and further elaborated using some of the relationships discussed above. To illustrate the analysis, data was selected for the Footwear sector in the three countries. In addition to general uncertainty about accuracy in statistical data, there are also difficulties to access certain types of data, for example overhead cost data in firms. In the following example it has been assumed that overhead costs are 20 per cent of total production cost, i.e.

$$q = 100(m + w)/(100 - 20) = (m + w)/0.8$$

Footwear sector in Indonesia, Ethiopia and Peru

In Table 6.7, gross output (Q), added value ($Q - m$) and wages (w) are taken from the UNIDO International Yearbook of Industrial Statistics (United Nations Industrial Development Organization 1999, 2009). Data that is marked have been calculated.

Table 6.7 Economic data for the footwear sector (ISIC 324, ISIC 1920) of three countries

Parameter	Indonesia (billion Rupiahs)		Ethiopia (million Birr)		Peru (million New Sole)	
	1995	2005	1995	2005	1994	2005
Q	5,503	16,020	119	243	219	248
Q – m	2,117	6,283	47	87	50	90
m^a	3,386	9,737	72	156	169	158
w	747	2,385	6	28	12	51
A^a	0.38	0.39	0.39	0.36	0.23	0.36
q^a	5,166	15,152	98	230	226	261
P^a	0.06	0.05	0.18	0.05	< 0	< 0
Break-even	24.9%	24.2%	34.5%	24.3%	17.3%	16%

Source: UNIDO Yearbook of Industrial Statistics 1999, 2009.

Note
a Calculated.

The values for production costs q and profit margin P in the table are based on the assumption ratio of overhead costs to production costs is 20 per cent – value that is sometimes used in examples. Break-even in the table refers to the overhead cost percentage of production cost that makes cost of production equal to sales revenue, in other words, when profit is equal to zero. In the case of Peru, for example, the break-even in 2005 was 16 per cent, the assumption of 20 per cent obviously being too high a fact which can also be noted from the negative value of P.

Innovation in SMEs

Price reduction is the easy way out for many SMEs competing for customer orders. Reducing the price will result in lower or no profit, lower wages, lower quality due to inferior input materials or a combination of all these factors. The negative effect of price competition is that business does not generate the surplus needed for investment in the kind of resources that would lead to products and services with higher customer value that would justify a higher price. An alternative to either holding down wages in traditional industries or abandoning them in favour of higher technology industries is to add value in existing and new industries. Adding value by strengthening its capacity to innovate is a means for a firm to avoid ending up in the vicious circle.

The innovation process

It is now generally accepted that innovation is a process rather than a single event (Jones 2003). Figure 6.7 is a schematic view of the major activities involved in innovation. Innovation is closely connected with the firm's strategy and must be geared both to opportunities in the market and internal capabilities (competencies and capacities).

Innovations can be divided into product innovations related to goods and services, and process innovations can be both technological and organizational (Edquist 2001). Forbes and Wield (2002) argue, though process and product innovations are both important, their importance is different at different stages of industrial development. Process innovation – making things better – is often the first step towards product innovation – making better things. The process innovation step often takes place on the shop floor, where bottlenecks

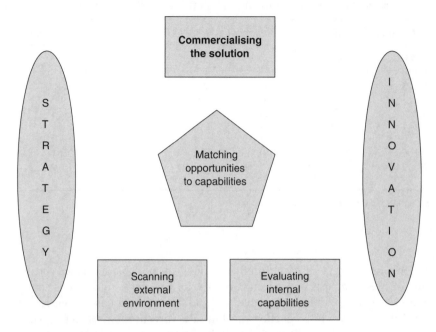

Figure 6.7 Atherton and Hannon's innovation process.
Source: Atherton and Hannon (2001).

hinder material flows and the production process. Process innovations are often about small improvements rather than radical leaps and have the goal of cutting costs.

Product innovation is oriented towards the market and to increasing added value in products and services. Edquist (ibid.) points out that some product innovations are transformed into process innovations in a 'second incarnation', but this concerns only 'investment products', not products intended for immediate consumption. For example, an industry robot is a product when it is produced and a process when it is used in production. Product and process innovations are also closely related to each other in many other ways. In spite of this, it is important to make distinctions between different kinds of innovation. Edquist's taxonomy, only goods and technological process innovations can be considered 'technological innovations' of a material kind. Organizational process innovations and services are 'intangibles'. It is crucial to take these intangible innovations into account as well, since they are increasingly important for economic growth and employment. Figure 6.8 presents Edquist's taxonomy.

Edquist and others use the distinction between process and product innovation to discuss the significance of innovations to employment creation. It is thus assumed that process innovations are labour saving whereas product innovations contribute to creating labour. However, this one-dimensional view can be challenged within the context of added value and innovations: technological process innovations in production can result in superior products with higher added value, more sales and ultimately even more employment. This notion is contained in what Schumpeter referred to as the *creative destruction* of the dynamic businessman, who starts new production, invests in new technology, in new products, in new markets and who creates and impels development, changes the world and

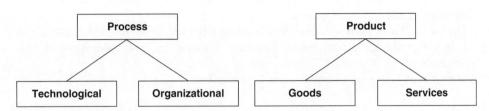

Figure 6.8 Edquist's taxonomy of innovations.
Source: Edquist (2001).

thereby eliminates old technology and production. Schumpeter used the term to indicate how old and obsolete technology and outmoded economic institutions are replaced by modern product and process innovations (Lundberg 1994).

Costs of innovations

The costs incurred by innovations are of different kinds. Technological innovations in the production process require skills and equipment, but also implementation efforts that may lead to indirect costs in the form of temporarily reduced productivity. Organizational innovations and changes may result in immediate but temporary implementation costs. Product innovations may require new types of material and equipment, and skills to be acquired from outside the firm. All these costs must be compensated for through a higher sales price. However, for various reasons (e.g. competition) the market may dictate an upper price level. As already discussed in relation to added value strategy, the increase in costs may therefore be higher than the increase in price, which leads to a reduction in profit.

Process and product innovations – some examples

Process innovations aim at reducing costs in the production of services and products. Some examples are:

- Barcode and scanner technology, used in shops and supermarkets for price scanning and in industrial conveyor systems for monitoring material flows.
- Robots, to eliminate manual work on production lines, to increase accuracy, productivity and efficiency.
- Direct transmission of customer orders to the computer-based production plan of the supplier, to eliminate administrative work, to speed up order handling and to increase accuracy.
- Tracking shipments, where clients can query the shippers database directly to determine expected delivery dates and related information.
- The use of standard components for different but related products, such as standard caps for various types of bottle.

Product innovations aim at the market and increased customer value. Examples include:

- Low consumption engines resulting in less pollution and lower fuel costs where governments have introduced tax reduction policies.
- Cameras based on new digital technology, improving picture quality and facilitating the copying and editing of images.
- The way cell phones have fundamentally changed the telecommunication market, from a state-directed service to private business, resulting in cost reduction and new functions.
- Microwave ovens with their impact on food handling.

Service innovations are aiming at the market and increased customer value. Some examples are:

- Twenty-four-hour banking, which has facilitated personal financial management, for example, regarding payment of bills.
- Medical diagnosis, where individuals with access to computers can enquire about health problems and obtain medical diagnoses.
- Travel planning, making it possible to enquire about prices and make reservations.
- Weather forecasts updated more frequently and for ever smaller regions, of importance to industries such as shipping, construction and agriculture.

Innovation strategies

Figure 6.9 refers to the need to evaluate internal capabilities before framing an innovation strategy. The capabilities include the firm's proprietary capability which refers to its unique knowledge and skills, for example intellectual property, such as patents, copyrights and various forms of design. Also included are various specifics skill and knowledge, such as deep experience and familiarity with certain kinds of material and production techniques, highly-competent management and so-called *tacit* knowledge that is not easily copied or possible to communicate to others. Tacit knowledge may be found in sophisticated craft production. A firm has developed tacit knowledge if it can to add value ahead of its competitors.

The innovation strategy a firm chooses depends on the market situation, the development level of the country and its internal capacity. If cost reduction is of primary importance, process innovation is what matters most. Overall, incremental innovation is associated with the Japanese management style, with concepts such as quality circles, suggestion schemes and the *kaizen* continuous improvement programmes. Forbes and Wield represent the different paths a firm may follow to increase competitiveness through innovation using the process–product–proprietary grid shown in Figure 6.9.

The diagram shows the different trajectories a firm may follow in its innovation strategy aiming at increased added value. Point A in the diagram marks the point of departure and characterizes the current situation in terms of process, product and proprietary capability. An innovation strategy leading to increased added value may follow the path from improved process capability making it possible to produce products with higher customer value. Innovation to point L in the diagram involves all three capabilities.

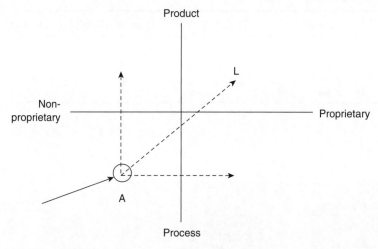

Figure 6.9 Forbes and Wield's process–product–proprietary grid.
Source: Forbes and Wield (2002).

Box 6.1 Mini-case: Tanzania Breweries Ltd.

Tanzania Breweries Ltd. (TBL) was established in the 1920s, nationalized in 1976 and subsequently merged with another nationalized brewery. TBL was privatized in 1993 and taken over by South African Breweries Ltd. as a means of increasing its presence in neighbouring countries. Following the takeover, profit and product quality improved as old and obsolete technology was replaced and sophisticated quality control systems introduced. Key improvement issues relate to management capability, export orientation and coping with poor infrastructure.

How can TBL improve its added value? New products must be developed and exports must be strengthened. But state tax is high for exports in Tanzania, and there is uncertainty regarding the extent South African Breweries wants to see TBL expand its products beyond a certain level in the region. If it is decided that TBL needs new brands and develop skilled strategic management, in terms of Forbes and Wield's process-product-proprietary grid, TBL's innovation trajectory might look as follows:

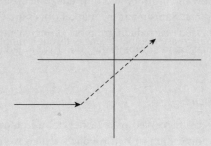

Table 6.8 Cost structure for microwave oven production

Cost type	General Electric, USA (USD)	Samsung, South Korea (USD)
Assembly labour	8	0.63
Set-up, maintenance	30	0.73
Materials handling	4	0.12
Total Product	218	155

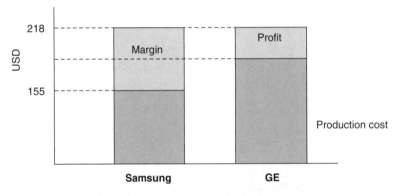

Figure 6.10 Competitiveness through process innovation.

An example of process innovation

The following example from the 1990s illustrates the importance of process innovations. It may also shed some light on the economic development in East Asia that led to growing regional competitiveness. The example compares the production costs per unit for identical microwave ovens in United States and South Korea respectively. Table 6.8 shows the major cost types in USD.

The cost difference might not be the same today due to changes in currency and price levels. However, the example illustrates the effect of an innovation strategy focused on cost reduction on the shop floor. The difference in production costs had significant impact on competitiveness between the two firms as shown in the Figure 6.10.

Figure 6.10 illustrates how the profit on top of production costs at General Electric gives room for a substantial margin at Samsung if the market prices are the same. This margin can be utilized in various ways, such as reducing the price, increasing profit or investments in further process improvements or in climbing the added value ladder by product design and development.

How does innovation happen?

Innovations come from needs, perceived or real, but not all innovations lead to needs. An illustrative example is the innovation of two products which were both based on sophisticated scientific research, one within the optical field, the other in electronics. Both products were available to the market in the same year (1947). One became a tremendous success;

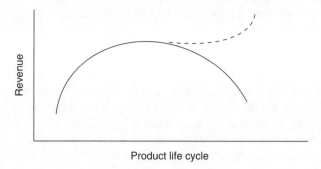

Figure 6.11 Incremental product innovation.

the other has not yet found a comparable use. The two innovations were the transistor and the hologram. The transistor is an electronic component based on a semiconducting material and able to amplify and switch electronic signals. The transistor fundamentally changed electronics and paved the way for today's information technology. The hologram works on the principle of light beams and their reflections from a surface. The potential usefulness of hologram grew in the 1960s with the introduction of the laser technique. An application today is in improving the security of credit cards. But the market success of the two innovations is not comparable.

While large firms can set aside considerable sums for research and development, smaller firms are mostly reluctant to risk scarce capital on uncertain innovation projects, which is a reason why high-growth, innovative SMEs are in short supply. SMEs tend to prefer commercial caution and financial safety, since innovative activities can sometimes be intangible and the assessment of returns from the innovation project difficult to make. For the same reason, entering into joint innovation projects with government bodies may seem less attractive for the SME manager due to uncertainty in risk assessment.

A large part of innovations in SMEs therefore comes from ideas originating at the customer site and in dialogue with customers. Often there are incremental innovations to current products and services as illustrated in Figure 6.11.

The diagram shows the typical life-cycle of a product supplied to a customer by a supplier. Through a supplier–customer dialogue, the supplier realizes the potential business opportunity of making incremental improvement to the current product, as represented by the dotted line.

The innovation step required has limited risk since both supplier and customer share the interest of the successful innovation. The importance of a good supplier–customer dialogue was further discussed in Chapter 3 in connection with Figure 3.11.

SME business strategy

Business strategy and strategic planning do not necessarily overlap, and need to be considered separately. Strategic planning once received an enthusiastic reception from the business community, but subsequent experience led to mixed results. In some SMEs, strategic planning restored their profitability and became an established part of the management process. In a majority of firms, however, a phenomenon was encountered that was referred to as 'analysis paralysis': strategic plans were made but remained unimplemented, and did therefore not have an impact on business growth. A strategic plan refers to the future and can be restrictive for a small firm, which should rather capitalize on its small size by being flexible and adapting to new situations.

What is a business strategy?

There is certain confusion as to what strategy actually is. This can be attributed to a number of factors. There is confusion between what firms are actually doing, what they claim to be doing and what they should be doing. In practice, strategy tends to embrace all three. In addition, 'strategy' is sometimes mistakenly considered the same as 'goals'. Goals refer to ends, to a planned and expected achievement, whereas strategy refers not only to the ends but also to the means of reaching the ends. As such, goals are part of strategy.

A good strategy is the commercial logic of a business and it suggests a path for a firm to follow that may ultimately result in a competitive advantage. To be complete, a strategy must include a definition of the domain – the lines of business, types of customer and geographical reach – in which the firm competes. It must also include a definition of the firm's *unique selling proposition* and the special hold this gives the firm on its chosen business domain. Strategy also means what a company does, not what it says, or what its strategy documents propound. In this sense, a strategy is how a firm actually positions itself commercially and conducts the competitive battle.

It would seem that the days of highly analytical, rational strategy creation are past. But, strategy can neither be purely rational nor purely intuitive. Indeed, one of the core skills of managers is to know when and how to use their intuitive judgement.

Management and leadership – strategic management

Management and leadership are two distinct and complementary systems of action, even if they coincide in the same person in small firms. A simplified distinction between management and leadership activities is that management is about operational complexity while leadership is about coping with change. Good management brings a degree of order and consistency to key dimensions, like the quality and profitability of products. Good leadership motivates, inspires and aligns people to move in a desired direction, despite major obstacles to change, by appealing to basic human needs, values and emotions. In small firms it is not possible – or meaningful – to separate the two, and balancing between being a leader with a long-term view and being a manager with responsibility for day-to-day operations is difficult. Small businesses are often accused of being short-sighted and not focusing enough on long-term development such as training.

The need to understand and to adapt to continuous change in the environment requires continuous learning by members of the organization. Learning implies that each employee has the freedom to observe, reflect and to identify changes relating to work activities, but also to be empowered to recommend opportunities for improvement. Freedom and power requires that employees have command of all information from their own processes, the key to organizational learning. Having command of information means that the work process must be observed in such a way that actual performance can be measured and that trends in performance can be assessed. To make the information meaningful, the individual employee must be able to associate himself or his group with the observations.

In non-learning organizations, companies learn and change in big steps that are often initiated by external consultants or from external knowledge. Information generated in this way stays with top management that plans, makes decisions and passes down instructions to subordinates and workers. There is no genuine learning in this way. The consequence is that next time the company needs to adapt to changes in the environment, knowledge must again be brought in from outside, since there is no tradition of making use of knowledge accumulated within the company.

A most important aspect of continuous learning is an understanding of improvement as a continuous *process of discovery*, not as a series of solutions to overwhelming problems. The latter view implies that things must be fixed once they are broken. The former approach implies never stopping looking for better ways to do the job! In the new business principles, improvements are viewed as opportunities created by a process, designed to increase customer loyalty and to improve the abilities of the employees. One of the methods used to encourage employees to become involved in this process is the reward programme.

From strategy to action

In order to implement a strategy, the starting point must always be a solid understanding of where one is starting from and the dilemmas one is facing. If a firm is not in touch with the reality of its situation, there is limited hope of moving forward. The starting point is thus to determine the firm's overall goals or objectives. If one does not know where one wants to go, then one is unlikely to get there.

In pursuit of this, many firms develop ambitious so-called mission statements, also referred to as strategic intent, core objectives, visions etc. As strategic business guidelines, such mission statements are useless as they take on many different forms, from bizarre aspirations to jargon-infested nonsense. Mission statements are – or should be – a pithy explanation of why a company is in business, what it intends to achieve and by what methods. Instead, most mission statements have become meaningless exercises, pinned on notice boards, printed on corporate keepsakes and generally ignored by the people they aim to influence.

Strategy to action requires seeing how the activities of a business can be divided into the following four categories:

1 Peripheral activities: Providing no source of competitive advantage; not essential to the core purpose of the business.
2 Supportive activities: Essential, but not core activities – failure in this area would cause serious damage to the business.
3 Strategic activities: An actual or potential source of competitive advantage.
4 Core activities: The primary activities of the business.

The structure of management control

The different functions of leadership and management also shape the characteristic activities of management control. While leadership involves the development of visions and the setting of directions, management is oriented towards the short term and complex operational issues. Management control starts with setting targets, based on the more long-term vision and direction. A typical target is the sales goal for the next month or for the current year. The targets are transformed into plans (for activities) and budgets (for revenues and costs).

Management control also involves ensuring that resources are available and that the organization structure is shaped to accomplish the plan's requirements. Management control furthermore involves staffing the jobs with qualified individuals, communicating the plan to those people, delegating responsibility for carrying out the plan and devising systems to monitor implementation. Once implemented, results need to be monitored against the plan in order to detect deviations. Deviation from the plan gives an account of performance, and management control should therefore involve efforts to analyse the background to and reasons for deviations. The final step is to take appropriate action as a result of the performance analysis. If the performance analysis indicates major changes are required to improve business performance, a change in the direction of the enterprise's long-term goals may be called for.

Concluding remarks

It is often emphasized (e.g. by Michael Porter) that the only meaningful concept of competitiveness at the national level is national productivity. A rising standard of living depends on the capacity of a nation's firms to achieve high levels of productivity, and to increase productivity over time (Porter 1990). As productivity is mostly measured by the amount of added value being produced with the input of resources (capital, labour), added value has become a frequently-used measure at macroeconomic levels. It has also been claimed that the best measure of competitive advantage for SMEs is added value, rather than profit, return on investment or market share. Improvements in added value provide an indication of more effective internal processes and stronger market performance (Johns and Tilley 2003).

An increase in productivity means that the same or more added value is produced with less or the same input (capital, labour), which at the level of the firm means production costs. Change in added value is the result of a change in output price or material costs or both. With the same production costs, however, profit may rise with increased added value. Likewise, the refinement cost may also increase with increasing added value as a result of extra costs that stem from new product design, new features, etc. In fact, a number of scenarios with changes in profit and refinement costs can be envisaged as added value increases. One of the scenarios, as mentioned above, is higher added value but lower profit.

Encouraging the growth of SMEs is widely seen as an important strategy in the economic development process in most developing countries. A stronger SME sector is expected to contribute to creating new jobs and alleviating poverty, as well as enhancing managerial capacity and increasing vertical integration in industry. In addition, SMEs need to contribute to expanding the added value part of the industry. In countries having their own natural resources, it is important to refine these resources into added value products. In countries lacking natural resources, finding niches for high added-value export production is an important way of generating export incomes.

It is therefore important to encourage the SME sector to strive for higher production added value while at the same time keeping costs under control. Studies have shown that administrative overhead costs tend to increase as the service content represents a bigger portion of the final product offering. Overhead costs therefore represent a potential cost saver in many SMEs.

SMEs in developing countries should therefore include added value grade in their strategic parameters, and embark on a business strategy of continuous added value grade increase. The model presented in this chapter can be implemented as a management tool to track added value grade and surplus, which together assist managers in this monitoring process.

To embark on an added value strategy, a firm should consider following a number of steps, such as identifying the needs of its most important customers through an intensive customer dialogue. From the customer dialogue the firm should furthermore improve own products and service offerings in accordance with what the most important customers need, and make the necessary investments in equipment, skills and materials needed to realise product improvements. The firm should also learn to argue why the improved products and services justify higher market price, and gain acceptance from the customer of the mutual benefits for a business relationship based on a win–win approach. The value that has thus been added should create opportunities for further product innovations and business development.

References

Ansoff, H. I. (1965) *Corporate Strategy: An Analytic Approach to Business Policy for Growth and Expansion*. New York: McGraw-Hill.

APO (2001) *Export Orientation for Small and Medium Enterprises: Policies, Strategies and Programs*. Surabaya, Indonesia: Asian Productivity Organisation.

Atherton, A. and Hannon, P. (2001) 'Innovation Processes in the Small Business: A Conceptual Analysis'. *International Journal of Business Performance Management*, 2: 4.

Barcly, B. and Saylor, J. (2001) *Building Quality into Project Process*. New York: McGraw-Hill.

Barkham, R. (1996) *The Determinants of Small Firm Growth: An Inter-Regional Study in the United Kingdom, 1986–90*. London: Jessica Kingsley Publishers.

Barratt-Pugh, L. (2005) 'Managing Knowledge Development in SMEs: No Longer the Poor Cousin, as Training Changes to Learning?', in Harvie, C. and Lee, B. (eds) *Sustaining Growth and Performance in East Asia: The Role of Small and Medium Sized Enterprises*, Vol III. London: Edward Elgar.

Bramall, C. (2009) *Chinese Economic Development*. London: Routledge.

Brush, C., Dennis, C. and Blackburn, R. (2009) 'Pathways to Entrepreneurial Growth: The Influence of Management, Marketing and Money'. *Business Horizons*, Vol. 52.

Chandler, A. (1984) *Strategy and Structure*. Cambridge, MA: MIT Press.

Edquist, C. (2001) *Innovation and Employment: Process Versus Product Innovation*. London: Edward Elgar Publishing.

Forbes, N. and Wield, D. (2002) *From Leaders to Followers – Managing Technology and Innovation*. London: Routledge.

Gadenne, D. (1998) 'Critical Factors for Small Business: An Inter-Industry Comparison'. *International Small Business Journal*, 17: 1.

Gibb, A. and Davies, L. (1992) *Methodological Problems in the Development and Testing of a Growth Model of Business Enterprise Development: Resent Research in Entrepreneurship*. Aldershot: Avebury.

Hammel, G. (1997) 'Killer Strategies that Make Shareholders Rich'. *Fortune*, June 23.

Heracleous, L. (2001) 'An Ethnographic Study of Culture in the Context of Organisational Change'. *Journal of Applied Behavioural Science*, 37: 4.

Heracleous, L. (2003) *Strategy and Organization*. Cambridge: Cambridge University Press.

Holden, R., Jameson, S. and Walmsley, A. (2007) 'New Graduate Employment within SMEs: Still in the Dark?'. *Journal of Small Business and Enterprise Development*, 14: 2.

Jennings, P. and Beaver, G. (1997) 'The Performance and Competitive Advantage of Small Firms: A Management Perspective'. *International Small Business Journal*, 15: 1.

Jones, O. (2003) 'Innovations in SMEs', in Jones, O. and Tilley, F. (eds) *Competitive Advantage in SMEs*. London: Wiley.

Jones, O. and Tilley, F. (eds) (2003) *Competitive Advantage in SMEs*. London: Wiley.

Lind, P. (2005) 'Competitiveness Through Increased Added Value: A Challenge for Developing Countries'. *Journal of Comparative International Management*, 8: 1.

Lind, P. (2007) *Management of Change Processes*. Linkoping: Linkoping University.

Lind, P. (2009) *The SME in a Changing World – Opportunities and Threats*. Unpublished paper. Visby: Gotland University.

Lundberg, E. (1994) *Studies in Economic Instability and Change*. Stockholm: Centre for Business and Policy Studies.

McIntyre, R. (2003) 'Small Enterprises in Transition Economies: Casual Puzzles and Policy-Relevant Research', in McIntyre, R. and Dallago, B. (eds.) *Small and Medium Enterprises in Transitional Economies*. Basingstoke, Hampshire: Palgrave Macmillan.

Macpherson, A. and Holt, R. (2007) 'Knowledge, Learning and Small Firm Growth: A Systematic Review of the Evidence'. *Research Policy*, 36.

Marsden, A. and Forbes, C. (2003) 'Strategic Management for Small and Medium-Sized Enterprises' in Oswald, J. and Tilley, F. (eds) *Competitive Advantage in SMEs*. London: Wiley.

Morrison, J. (2006) *The International Business Environment*. London: Palgrave.

OSMEP (2007a) *Situation and Structural Indicators of SMEs in 2008 and the Five-Year Change*. Bangkok: Office for Small and Medium Enterprise Promotion.

OSMEP (2007b) *The 2nd SMEs Promotion Plan (2007–2011)*. Bangkok: Office for Small and Medium Enterprise Promotion.

OSMEP (2009) *Situation and Structural Indicators of SMEs in 2010*. Bangkok: Office for Small and Medium Enterprise Promotion.

Padayachee, V. (ed.) (2010) *The Political Economy of Africa*. London: Routledge.

Penrose, E. (1959) *The Theory of the Growth of the Firm*. Oxford: Oxford University Press.

Porter, M. (1985) *Competitive Advantage: Creating and Sustaining Superior Performance*. New York: The Free Press.

Porter, M. (1990) *The Competitive Advantage of Nations*. New York: The Free Press.

Porter, M. (1996) 'What is Strategy?'. *Harvard Business Review*, November–December.

Porter, M. (1997) 'How Much Does Industry Matter Really?' *Strategic Management Journal*, 18 (Summer Special Issue).

Prahalad, C. K. (1997) 'Companies Will Have to Unlearn their Past and Forget It! The Future Will Not be an Extrapolation of the Past', in Rowan, G. (ed.) *Rethinking the Future: Business, Principles, Competition, Control, Leadership, Markets and the World*. London: Nicholas Brealey Publishing.

Schleuwagen, L. and Goedhuys, M. (2002) 'Growth of Firms in Developing Countries: Evidence from Côte d'Ivoir'. *Journal of Development Economies*, 68.

Smallbone, D. and Wyer, P. (2000) 'Growth and Development in the Small Firm', in Carter, S. and Jones-Evans, D. (eds.) *Enterprise and Small Business: Principles Practices and Policies*. Harlow, Essex: Financial Times/Prentice Hall.

Stern, C. W. and Stalk, G. (eds) (1995) *Perspectives on Strategy*. New York: John Wiley.

Storey, D. J. (1994) *Understanding the Small Business Sector*. London: Routledge.

Tannock, J., Krasachol, L. and Ruangpermpool, S. (2002) 'The Development of Total Quality Management in Thai Manufacturing SMEs: A Case Study Approach'. *International Journal of Quality and Reliability Management*, 19: 4.

Transparency International (2008) *Business Principles for Countering Bribery in SMEs*. Berlin: Transparency International Secretariat.

United Nations Industrial Development Organization (1999) *The UNIDO Yearbook on Industrial Statistics*. Cheltenham, UK: Edward Elgar Publishing.

United Nations Industrial Development Organization (2009) *The UNIDO Yearbook on Industrial Statistics*. Cheltenham, UK: Edward Elgar Publishing.

Wiklund, J., Davidsson, P. and Delmar, F. (2003) 'What do they Think and Feel About Growth? An Expectancy-Value Approach to Small Business Managers' Attitudes Toward Growth'. *Entrepreneurship, Theory and Practice*, 27: 3.

7 Managing the small firm
Theory and practice

Introduction

Encouraging the growth of the small and medium enterprise (SME) sector has become an important government strategy in most countries. Motivations behind the government support programmes range from the necessary and laudable aims of creating jobs to alleviating poverty, from the creation of entrepreneurial capabilities to raising skills among managers and workers. The emphasis that has thus come to be placed on small firms and entrepreneurship is associated with the failure of the large-scale public firms in meeting many of these objectives. Moving away from tight state control, new policies have set in motion various forms of restructuring of the enterprise sector.

Having been pulled into the global business system, success or failure of developing countries will depend on their competitive abilities. However, since competitive pressures reduce the direct subsidies and protection states can offer following trade liberalisation and deregulation, greater importance will be attached to strengthening management competence and skills. Enterprises in developing countries should find business advantages if managers can adapt modern business theories to local business practices and norms. If low- and middle-income countries fail to strengthen their relative business competitiveness, their role in the global business system will remain as marketing platforms for the industrialized countries only! Strengthening management capabilities in modern business practices is part of the recipe often recommended for small business managers. However, there are many different views about what constitutes good management, and there is a growing awareness that business is context dependent and that a recipe for all contexts is not sufficient.

With its root in Western culture (with some influence from Japan), the prevailing global management ideology is in the first place aimed at solving organizational problems in Western organizations and enterprises. To improve competitiveness and organizational efficiency in other cultures, a more pluralistic perspective on management education and training is required. The change in economic power as a result of the increasing importance of countries like Brazil, Russia, India, China and South Africa (the so-called BRICS countries) is likely to alter the hegemony in industry and world trade politics dominated by the traditional industrialized countries. In the wake of this change, new approaches to organization and management may emerge which result in new theories and models.

But the training of leaders and managers of tomorrow's enterprises and organizations – both in more traditional developing countries as in the more dynamic middle-income countries – is still carried out within the framework of theories and models developed in the most advanced industrialized countries, primarily in the United States and Britain. For a long time, management and organization models and theories were considered general and context free and therefore ought to be applicable in any country. In recent years, however, there has been a growing awareness that management and organizational behaviour is deeply culturally and context dependent, from which it follows that models originating in the West are characterized by views, norms and values that are deeply rooted in the Western cultures. They have developed gradually in response to needs that emerged from structural changes in Western societies. Such changes took place as political, economic, legal and technical structures have changed and developed.

There are many example of the lack of correspondence between models and reality. While Western models tend to focus on time optimization and assume flat democratic organization structures, many non-Western cultures in Asia and Africa have different conceptions of time and tend to organize work in more hierarchical structures. The education and training of tomorrow's managers must therefore not be restricted to uncritically delivering general theories and models thereby sacrificing deeper cultural and social understanding. Today's dominant theories of management and organization lack a historical and critical perspective, and tend to be both ethnocentric and unilateral. In these theories, cultural traits tend to be perceived as contingencies when viewed through the established Western models. Iguisi, a former director of the Euro-Africa Management Research Centre in the Netherlands, claims that while the African elite is very knowledgeable about the accepted models and theories of the West, knowledge about the cultures and values of their society is limited.

> The African elite is not equipped enough to understand the obligations imposed on him by Western cultures in which they have been socialised and the traditional environment in which they are born and raised, thus making their ability to contribute something original to development of their society limited.
>
> (Iguisi 1997)

Managing the small firm – theory

The globalization process

Developing countries are becoming increasingly challenged by the global economy and by the globalization process, as many of them have yet to find any meaningful market access opportunities for their products. Globalization has so far been confined to developed countries and a few developing countries only. Empirical evidence shows that globalization has contributed to further marginalisation of a large number of countries, in particular small and vulnerable economies and the lowest income countries.[1]

From the short term perspective, business opportunities in a majority of developing countries will emerge from partnerships between local and foreign enterprises, facilitated by the levelling of the playing field in world economic relations. However, a necessary precondition for such partnerships is that the business communities in the developing countries learn to integrate modern management practices and adapt them to local practices and norms. The predominant management, organization, and economic principles and models are still characterized by views, norms and values that have deep roots in Western culture. Importing them into other cultural settings without integrating them with the local culture and values, the models remain alien and do not contribute to the development of indigenous and more appropriate management concepts and theories.

In the training context, indigenous managers need technical and social knowledge: opportunities for training in technical and social skills enable them to improve and develop their professional competence at a conscious level. To achieve these goals, management training might take the participant's job situation as its starting point, thus achieving the transmission of relevant knowledge, the exchange of experience and hence the refinement of professional skills (Björkegren 1989).

SME management training

Management practice has its roots in business reality as well as in the concepts and ideas conveyed through management training institutions. However, the influence is bi-directional, as management training is also based on theories and models codified from management practice. The calculation of product costs is an example of a practice that gradually developed in response to the need to improve the pricing of products. This practice, codified in accounting principles and models at the beginning of the previous century, still constitutes the basis for cost accounting in management training.

The second source of management training is based on more recent concepts and modes developed in response to technological innovations and changes in views and values. Such concepts and models emerge from changes in society, but also from academic interdisciplinary discourses and debates, with ideas borrowed from disciplines such as sociology, psychology and anthropology. Once adopted, such models tend to remain influential on management behaviour for relatively long periods as paradigms thoroughly permeating management training.

Both the codification of management practice and current management ideology thus has impact on management training, which in turn influences management practice. The simplified diagram in Figure 7.1 suggests that organizations are units that can be observed in a context characterized by traditions and history, by values and norms and by their people. Values, norms and traditions may constrain their behaviour but, at the same time, offer competitive opportunities. History constrains the degrees of freedom of the organization, as do various forms of contingencies that constitute the business reality of organizations and enterprises.

Management practice develops in response to challenges and business realities. Management practice may, for example, develop from the need to cope with legislation and accounting principles. Such management practice is interpreted, analysed and codified into management theories and models and, in turn, into models and theories used in management education and development programmes. However, it must be stressed that management theories developed in this way generally do not focus on small and medium firms in the first instance, but what is appropriate and interesting for large business.

Organizational behaviour and business practices are observed and analysed by researchers and others having a professional interest in organization and management development. Their aim is not only to codify practice but also to describe, understand and analyse and so contribute to new theories and models. The tentative theories and models suggested and developed lead to discussions and debates. As a result, these discussions may gradually converge towards a consensus, becoming unified into a coherent theory or paradigm. This may challenge the prevailing theory, which is likely to have emerged from a similar process. Paradigms developed in such processes tend to last for several years.

This method of developing paradigms has similarities with the evolution of organization theory as suggested by Robbins (1990). He refers to two underlying dimensions in the evolution of organization theory: in the first, organizations are perceived as systems, in the

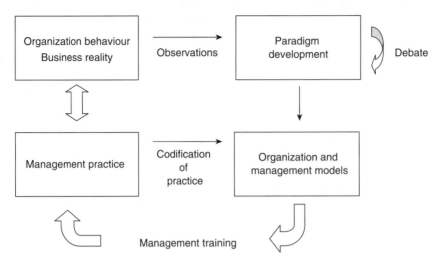

Figure 7.1 Observations and codification as the background to management models.

Table 7.1 Evolution of contemporary organization theory

Period	Systems perspective	Type	Central theme
1900–1930	Closed	Rational	Mechanical efficiency
1930–1960	Closed	Social	Human relations
1960–1975	Open	Rational	Contingency designs
1975 to date	Open	Social	Power and politics

Source: Robbins (1990).

second, the organization is characterized in terms of the way it achieves its objectives. Prior to 1960, organizations were seen as essentially autonomous and sealed off from their environment, i.e. the closed system perspective (Robbins ibid.). The closed approach was followed by the view that organizations are exposed to and influenced by external events and processes. The second dimension took two opposed positions: the rational perspective arguing that organizational structure is essential to achieve objectives, and the social perspective arguing that structure is essentially the result of conflicting forces seeking power and control. Robbins suggested (ibid.) that the evolution of contemporary organization theory can be divided into the periods shown in Table 7.1. In each period, organization theorists sought to identify central themes that characterized the period.

Management paradigms

As major technological innovations take place, and as values change and gradually influence working methods and organization structures, management behaviour is affected. A similar view on the development of management paradigms to that shown in Table 7.1 was suggested by Barley and Kunda (1992), who referred to the five different phases or paradigms through which American management discourse passed during the last hundred years.

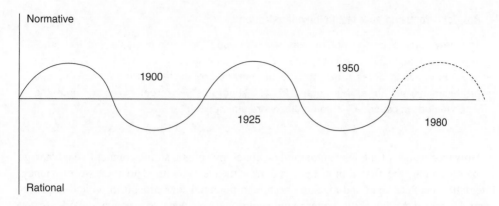

Figure 7.2 Barley and Kunda's normative–rational shifts in management paradigms.
Source: Barley and Kunda (1992).

With minor local deviations, the same development process took place in most countries in the industrialized world, particularly as American management principles were adopted by the vast majority of countries, both directly and indirectly through management guidelines and textbooks.

Barley and Kunda (ibid.) identified five management paradigms, or ideologies from the late nineteenth century until today. The authors characterise each paradigm as normative or rational if focus were on the human aspects or technological, as when a technological break-through happened that required and led to structural changes in organizations. The five paradigms were:

1 industrial betterment (1870–1900) – normative;
2 scientific management (1900–1923) – rational;
3 human relations (1923–1955) – normative;
4 systems rationalism (1955–1980) – rational; and
5 organizational culture (1980 to date) – normative.

What is the background to this alternation between normative rhetoric (focusing on humans) and rational rhetoric (focusing on technology), where each phase seems to last for between 20 and 30 years? It cannot be concluded that when one phase ends the next starts, since there is considerable overlap between the phases. This discussion should probably belong to the family of issues referred to as 'long wave' issues. Figure 7.2 illustrates the paradigm shifts.

According to the authors, each shift from a normative to a rational management paradigm coincides with major technological shifts in the world economy. The introduction of the automobile around the year 1900 marked a significant technological innovation that spread very fast with spin-off effects in the form of new demands for spare parts, petrol stations, repair shops, driving schools, improved road systems etc. The new technology thus gave raise to further technological innovations with substantial financial investments. For the time being the promising new technology had so much potential that focus on human requirements such as working conditions became overshadowed by the technological race.

> **Box 7.1 Promising new technology: illustration**
>
> The new automobile technology was much praised for its efficiency – and its clean-ness. An article in the *New York Times* from 1906 blessed the automobiles as an attrac-tive alternative to horse transport. On an average day in New York that year, horses produced 120,000 litres of urine and 220,000 kilograms of excrement. At that time, the inconveniences caused by automobiles were still negligible.

However, as use of the new automobile technology spread, so the competitive advantage of being among the first diminished, and new means were tried to increase efficiency. Interaction between man and machine became a potential for rationalization and improve-ment. Improved driving skills, better maintenance and new ways of organizing work created challenging new possibilities with the help of the new technology. This required closer and more carefully-prepared interaction between man and machine, and new knowledge from various studies, for example, the Hawthorne studies which had a 'dramatic impact on the direction of management and organization theory' (Robbins, 1990), paved the way for the next management paradigm of normative nature.

The next paradigm shift with a similar pattern came around 1950 with the next major technological break through – the computer. The following two periods show more or less the same development as the one just described.

Management rhetoric thus evolves around what is taking place in the industrialized coun-tries, and the paradigm that emerges is a response to new demands on management. This demand is therefore closely linked to Western conditions, and its relevance for management in developing countries is by no means evident. In spite of this, the concepts and principles of the current ideology occupy management training programmes to the same extent in developing as in developed countries.

Codification of practice

Codification of practice has been the primary input to the formal development of manage-ment theory. Names like Chandler, James Thompson, Trist and Woodward, just to mention a few, are associated with the study and codification of organizational behaviour. But practi-tioners and management consultants have also contributed to better understanding of manage-ment practice and to the formulation of new theories. Inadequate codification of management practice in developing countries has been attributed mainly to weak links between industry and academic institutions, hampered by the lack of academic tradition in cooperation with local industry. This absence of a dialogue had its roots in a mutual distrust on both sides about the other party's ability to contribute to improved understanding and knowledge.

As long as industry paid little attention to academic theorizing about industry problems, the gap between theory and practice did not cause any major problems. Today, however, as industry in developing countries is gradually opening up for academic research, and as soci-ety expects universities to take a more active part in and responsibility for economic devel-opment, inadequate theories and models of management and organizational behaviour will have negative consequences. Industry-related research at universities therefore needs to enquire into the nature of local management and organization behaviour, which should have priority over the implementation of ready-made solutions of Western origin.

Inadequate codification of management practice in developing countries leads to weak understanding and perception of local management and organization problems. Management training programmes in these countries are therefore often more in tune with global management trends and ideologies than with the working environment of local enterprises and the working conditions of local managers.

Codification of practice may seem trivial and of little importance to local researchers who instead set as their objectives the promotion of local business development by acting as intermediaries (or change agents) in bringing the general management paradigm down to local business levels. At first sight this does not seem particularly controversial, since the 'field of action' on local levels has adopted the same business and organizational 'heroes, rituals and symbols' as the global level, and which can be readily copied and imitated from one culture to another. But when it comes to value systems, being more deeply culturally rooted and hence less readily transferred between cultures, the codification and understanding of local management practice requires knowledge and insight into cultural traits and local value systems. Without this, training will be incapable of reinforcing the latent strengths embedded in local value structures.

In this simplified description, the underlying models and theories of management training have two main inputs: codification of management practice and the prevailing management ideology. In some countries the balance between the two inputs is better maintained than in others. In many developing countries the codification of local management practice has a low status among researchers. In such countries, input to management training is primarily based on the more general models coming from current management ideology with no or little local management content.

In the management rhetoric or management ideology, participation of researchers from developing countries is the exception rather than rule. There is also little focus on developing countries and their problems in the debate around alternative management ideologies. This was observed already by James Thompson who, in 1956, called on the readers of the *Administrative Science Quarterly* to contribute to the building of an applied administrative science applicable not only to Western societies but also to other parts of the world. Thompson's motivation for this step was dissatisfaction with existing administrative theories and models, which he found appropriate to one type of cultural setting only (Thompson 1956).

There is a need to understand the inevitability of adapting management principles and techniques to the conditions of developing countries in order to increase the probability of their successful integration. For this purpose, comprehension of the local context and the codification of management practice are required. This depends greatly on empirical research, which is indispensable for the pursuit of a more fundamental understanding of local conditions.

A non-Western perspective on management education and training

In countries with traditions of close links between the education system and industry, there is a balance between the two main sources of input for management education and training: the codification of management practice and the prevailing management ideology. In many developing countries, however, the codification of local management practice has in general a low status in universities and among researchers. In such countries, input to management training is primarily based on the more general models coming from current management ideology with no or little reference or links to local management practice. Moore (1980) referred to the Egyptian National Research Centre whose scientists usually considered industry's research enquiries ridiculous and unworthy of their attention.

In the discourse leading to change in management paradigms, participation of researchers from developing countries is the exception rather than rule. There is also little focus on developing countries and their problems in the debate around alternative management ideologies. Although there is a growing awareness and understanding of management theory and techniques as being deeply culture-bound, management education on academic level in developing countries is treated as largely context-free. Indigenously-developed models and theories are largely non-existent, whereas Western theories are readily accepted.

The first source of input is the codification of management practice and organizational behaviour, which contributes to building the base for management and organizational models and theories. Codification assumes participation by analysts (researchers, consultants) with the aim of learning and documenting their findings. Such systematic analysis of enterprises has traditionally had a comparatively low priority in developing countries.

The second source of input is the prevailing management ideology, promoted by technological, scientific, economical, commercial or political events in Western societies. These management ideologies have in the past tended to last for two to three decades, penetrating managerial thinking in most societies. Adopted as generally valid and universally applicable, the ideologies primarily reflect problem formulation and the solutions of Western societies without specifically considering non-Western societies.

Academic institutions in non-western societies need to pay considerably more attention to the development of indigenous management models and theories, possibly based on Western concepts but with necessary adaptations to local needs and conditions. This requires active involvement by indigenous researchers in the analysis and documentation of local industry and business behaviour. Of importance is the codification of current management practice as a base for management training. Western universities and institutions can be highly instrumental due to their long tradition in business and organization research.

Dominant values in management development

Insufficient management competence is perceived by many as one of the major problems contributing to underdevelopment. The statement is mostly repeated with insufficient thought being paid to the business reality of many small business managers in low-income countries. Talking of conditions in developing countries, Robert McNamara, the former head of the World Bank, referred to the limited number of choices as a restricting factor:

> The poor, by the very fact of their poverty, have little margin for error. The very precariousness of their existence habituates them to be cautious. They may be illiterate. They are seldom foolhardy. To survive at all, they are forced to be shrewd.
>
> What we must grasp is that poverty does not make people unreasonable. What it does do is severely reduce their range of choice. They often do what they do because there is little real opportunity of doing otherwise.

The simple truth that goes with all issues related to management behaviour, application of management theories and models and the evaluation managerial efficiency, is the fact that management is not context free but closely linked to the environment where management is carried out. When judging management behaviour, one must therefore take into consideration the underlying conditions that – from the perspective of a Western society – hamper effective management. Such conditions include high degrees of unpredictability, scarcity of resources, political instability and poverty! Under the conditions structural poverty prevailing in developing countries, the management of poverty seems to be as relevant as the management of affluence in the more developed countries.

Management development and training cannot be limited to practical skills at the expense of solid theoretical background and social responsibility. An over-emphasis on practice has led to an anti-intellectual atmosphere in management schools. In particular, the dominant management and organizational theories lack a historical and critical perspective: they tend to be ethnocentric, unilateral and reducing (Davila 1989).

Situation-dependent management training

Tanton and Esterby-Smith (1989) of the centre for the Study of Management Learning at Lancaster University in the UK suggested that management training should follow a structure determined by the stages of development of the country where training takes place. The study was based on data received from 55 management teachers in 21 countries who had been asked to describe what they thought where the main problems for management education in their own countries. As a result of the study, it was recommended that the trainer adapts the following five training stages depending on the development level of the particular country.

Stage one – starting up

The first stage would be the starting up stage. The characteristic of this stage is that the small family business is dominant in the national economy. These family businesses rely on a set of values and ethics based on emotion and family. The need for management education programmes is not recognized by these families. The practical application of rational methods is difficult because the successful business owners are unable to see the necessity of academic training. In this phase there are very few business schools, and those there are are constrained to teach subjects with easily-visible skills, such as accounting and finance. At this stage of development, the institutions rely on the lecture method and the student's role is passive, studying techniques which apply to organizational structure systems rather than considering personal development.

Stage two – growing

As businesses develop, products become more complex and organizational competition increases: more sophistication is required to cope with these growing demands. At this stage, for the first time, an international perspective is introduced, as products are bought and sold in new markets. Administrative systems are recognized as unsatisfactory and the previously-productive short-term goals are seen as inadequate. Similarly, managers who coped with the business needs until this time of expansion begin to reflect the stress of their situation.

At this stage, the demand for management education grows and new institutions open. Many of the institutions are private, non-academic schools which teach skills and subjects necessary for young and in- experienced managers. The courses taught are seen to have immediate application and again the emphasis is on organizational methods and structures.

Stage three – establishing

In the third stage government policy recognizes the need for formal training if businesses are to compete with overseas trade, and industries begin to consider management training for their employees. At this stage, higher priority begins to be given to funding: resources become available in the form of grants awarded both by government and large operations in an effort to improve output.

As government support is given, universities establish management education pro-grammes and the subjects and courses offered increase in scope. Young academics, having obtained training overseas, return with new methods and knowledge and difficulties may arise in institutions as the young, newly-qualified teachers struggle to express their new thoughts and adapt the new techniques within the environment of the older generation of teachers, who may feel threatened by the influx of new 'foreign' information.

As the young, newly-trained academics return to their own countries, they produce relevant academic material, and research develops in their own culture. In this phase, not enough courses are offered in some subjects, although large numbers of courses are offered in general business skills by numerous institutions.

Stage four – consolidation

At this stage, the number of courses offered continues to exceed demand and the competition between course providers leads to greater sophistication and a higher quality of programmes. As the less competent teachers retire and some schools close, others are able to consolidate and focus their resources more efficiently to achieve a higher level of management teaching and academic recognition. In this phase new methods of teaching are sought and traditional methods are rejected. A split becomes apparent between trainers who focus on skills and behaviour and educators who aim to provide a broader understanding of the techniques and processes of management. The latter may become dominant. Thus the demands of abstract analysis and the generation of ideas and concepts may take priority over technical skills trans-ference. The development of the individual becomes an acceptable goal.

Stage five – integrating

In this, the most diverse phase, industries recognize management education, not as an unrea-listic cure-all, but as a collaborator. Conferences and workshops are held with the two forces meeting to exchange and develop ideas. A global approach is accepted and teachers and trai-ners recognize that learning can cross national barriers, in both directions. Consultants pass from nation to nation as methods and techniques are sifted and disseminated.

International networking is dominant in this phase and recognition is given to tailor-made programmes, particularly for senior executives, and post-experience courses become a norm for all competitive companies. The topic of change is tackled as a vital subject of study, as new problems and technological dilemmas are regularly introduced. In this phase the development of the individual is recognised as a necessary element for successful busi-ness, and human skills are given priority using the culture of the nation as a basis for appro-priate exercises.

The 'knowledge-constitutive interests' of Habermas

The structural development of management training outlined above, which goes from less to more sophisticated training and, not least, an increasing emphasis on the individual, cor-responds to a growing insight in and understanding of the interaction between individuals and organizational structures. Jürgen Habermas, the German philosopher of the Frankfurt School, claims there is no single mould into which all knowledge can be compressed. He distinguishes between three types of knowledge which require three types of studies

Table 7.2 Aspects of human activity and teaching focus according to Habermas

Aspects of human activity	Knowledge-constitutive interest	Technical focus
Labour	Prediction/control	Analytical science
Interaction	Understanding of meaning	Hermeneutic
Domination (power)	Emancipation	Critical theory

Source: Giddens (1985).

(or teaching focus). These three 'knowledge-constitutive interests' each correspond to an aspect of human activity.

First, all societies exist in a material environment and engage in interchanges with nature ('labour'). Such interchange promotes an interest in the prediction and control of events. But all societies also involve 'symbolic interaction' – the communication of individuals with one another. The study of symbolic interaction gives rise to an interest in the understanding of meaning. Interpretation of words and signs here become important. Finally, every human society involves forms of power and domination. The third knowledge-constitutive interest, that of emancipation, derives from a concern with achieving rational autonomy of action, free from domination – whether it be the domination of nature over human life, or the domination of some individuals or groups over others. These three aspects are summarized in Table 7.2.

Management training must seek to adapt to the prevailing conditions of each training project. Adaptation mean understanding which of the three knowledge-constitutive interests applies, which type of teaching should stressed and what methods are to be used. This should also apply in different cultural contexts and at different society development levels.

Managing the small firm – practice

The practice of small business management is to be a generalist within the art of management. That is why many management theories and models fit poorly, are inadequate or simply not tried by managers. Bannock (2003) suggests that the biggest constraint any small business owner-manager faces is usually the limitation of their own time and energy, and there are several reasons why multiple business ownership and management is an advantage: the functional load can be split; a broader range of skills can be available; sometimes also more owner capital.

Different factors having a practical impact on management are discussed below. Among the factors are: the setting of business goals and objectives; cultural aspects on management; external and internal uncertainties and their impact on business management; and recent trends and their demand for modified management views and behaviour, such as Corporate Social Responsibility (CSR). To this could be added the application and use of information and communication technology.

The very small business manager with few employees needs to take on many roles for the coordination of production, marketing and sales, as well as for personnel and finance. The medium-size firm has, for necessary reasons of scale, to split responsibility between more than one function and tends with increasing size to come closer to the management structure of the larger firm. But the main issue related to practical management, more or less regardless of company size, is having a clear vision of business goals and objectives.

Business goals and objectives

A small business manager will have identified and defined business goals even if they have not been explicitly articulated. Traditional management theory stresses the importance of setting clear business goals as a precondition for budgeting. Marsden and Forbes (2003) refer to the research on planning in small business and conclude that although planning is often regarded as essential by 'how-to-do writers' and business advisors, the research does not provide clear evidence about its effectiveness. They refer to Hannon and Atherton (1998) who concluded after an extensive review of the literature that there was 'no clear consensus that plans and planning, particularly as a formal activity, have a positive impact on small firms' performance'. They also cast doubt on the usefulness of business plans, arguing that these are often produced solely as a means of obtaining external funding from banks and other organizations and are rarely referred to once the necessary funding is obtained.

In the changing business world it is mostly impossible to predict future revenues and costs, and the budget exercise in the small business therefore becomes a play with figures that gives an illusory feeling of confidence. Real confidence rather comes from the ability to adapt to market changes. Keeping to the budget may be counter-productive – perhaps even dangerous – since it gives a feeling of security, of knowing for certainty that the company is on the right track as long as it sticks to the budget. An alternative to the formal budget for a small firm is to have efficient cost accounting routines and simple diagnosis tools as well as early-warning methods. This is discussed further in Chapter 9.

Firms may need to borrow money from banks, private institutions or individuals and therefore need to provide evidence about their business situation. This requires an adequate presentation of business ideas and the business situation, as well as a financial account (though not necessarily though a formal budget, the adequacy of which is difficult to judge). Hannon and Atherton (ibid.) argue that it is the planning *process* rather than the *plan* that is important, and that in the small firm informal planning makes more sense than formal planning. The following examples shows some of the main headings to be included in the planning process, regardless of whether the aim is to obtain external finance or just for internal consolidation of the business idea.

Formulating or consolidating the business idea

The object is to develop a plan of action for the business and to create a basis for decision-making by prospective investors or other external interested parties. The plan will become an important planning tool for the business to predict problems in advance. This makes it possible to assess the future potential, level of risk and feasibility of the business idea.

For investors, the plan comprises an essential and necessary foundation for decision-making. What is written (or not written) in the plan not only shows how good or bad the business idea is, but it is also a measure of the owner-manager's ability to define and analyse business possibilities and problems, and to identify and plan actions to deal with them. Because the plan can act as document in negotiations between the company and investors, the demands on the quality and scope of the plan increase with the amount of capital or size of loan being negotiated.

A short summary gives the investor a quick understanding of what the business is about. The summary should include information about vital items such as the company and its founders, what the company is doing and what is special about its products or services. Also of importance are the particular skills the founder(s) has/have which make them suitable for the task of commercializing the business idea. Other important aspects are size and rate of growth of the market for the product or service, as well as what share of the market can be achieved and anticipated trends within the market sector.

Sales and profit forecasts for the first and second year should be given and estimates of any finance needed.

About products and services

A detailed description of the product or service and its application is needed that emphasizes its unique characteristics and highlights how it is different from what is currently offered in the marketplace. The current state of the development of new product or service is essential for the potential investor to judge.

Market research and analysis

The aim of this is to provide a sufficient body of facts to convince the investor that the product or service has a significant market within a growing sector and can achieve a satisfactory sales volume despite competition. This is an important issue. The sales forecast developed here will affect the size of the manufacturing process, the distribution plan and the need for capital. Identifying the customers for the expected product and service areas, market size and trends is important, as well is an evaluation of the strengths and weaknesses of rival products and services of potential competitors.

Marketing plan, marketing strategy and pricing

The marketing plan describes how the estimated sales volume will be achieved. It describes what will be done, how it will be done and who will do it. Which characteristics of the product/service should be emphasized, e.g. quality, price, delivery, service?

Pricing policy is one of the most important decisions to make. The price must be right in order to penetrate the market, maintain a position in the market and create profits. Generally speaking, a superior product or service commands a higher price than the competitors. Costs tend to be underestimated.

Timetable

The timetable shows the order and connections between important events in the establishment of the company. It is of assistance when planning and shows critical milestones and deadlines. In addition, the timetable facilitates the acquisition of finance and demonstrates the ability of the company to plan its growth in a way that recognizes obstacles and minimizes the risk to the investor.

Critical risks, problems and assumptions

Every new business has risks and problems as well as possibilities. It is important that these are identified as soon as possible. If the investor discovers them first then the credibility of the manager as well as of the business plan will suffer. On the other hand, discussion of risks and problems demonstrate business competence, thereby increasing credibility.

Financial plans

This part of the plan constitutes the basis for the evaluation of the company as vehicle for investment. The aim is to prove the company's potential and its ability to survive. The financial plans can also be used as the basis for economic structuring. These plans should comprise an income forecast, profit and loss forecast and cash-flow analysis.

Cultural aspects

By their nature, SMEs are predominantly local, and their attitudes and views are therefore coloured by local cultural characteristics: these can be both a strength and a weakness. It is strength because local market behaviour (language, buying patterns and consumer preferences) is well-known to the local enterprise; it is weakness because lack of familiarity with market behaviour in areas remote from the business becomes an obstacle to expansion beyond the home market. Lack of confidence with other cultures and their behaviour and values is a hindering factor for most small business managers, and contributes to the preference of small firms to remain local.

However, the word 'culture' has also been given a metaphorical meaning when used in organizational contexts, and refers to sub-societies with own rules, traditions and behaviour. Kathleen Gregory (1983) suggested that the notion of 'culture' is often associated with exotic, distant peoples and places, with myths, rites, foreign languages and practices. Researchers have pointed out that within our own society, organization members similarly engage in rituals, pass along corporate myths and stories and use arcane jargon, and that these 'informal' practices may foster or hinder management goals for the organization. The study of organizational culture thus becomes translated into the study of the informal or 'merely' social or symbolic sides of corporate life.

The culture concept

There are two basic reasons for the interest in cultural aspects of management. First, the present management or organizational paradigm regards organizations as units with basic values, ideologies and assumptions which guide and fashion individual and business behaviour. These values are evident in more tangible factors such as stories, rituals, language and jargon, office decoration and dress code among individuals. Many of the basic ideas behind this management paradigm, often referred to as organizational culture, originate from cultural anthropology.

But culture is also a sociogeographic concept, and as such it has significance in the globalization process with widespread effects on organizations and business. Not only is there a growing exposure to different nationalities and national traits as firms enter into new markets, creating the need to correctly interpret market behaviour, there is also a growing demand for an understanding of diverse cultural behaviour as the workforce becomes increasingly mobile.

'Culture' is thus a concept that has received more and more attention in organization and management literature. Hofstede (1980, 1991) studied management behaviour in a transnational company. Trompenars (1993) and Hickson and Pugh (1995) have all contributed to our deeper understanding of how the cultural web has impacted on management behaviour. Schwarz (1992), Galtey, Lessem and Altman (1996) have all contributed, and Bjerke (1999) describes five national management styles (Chinese, Arabic, Scandinavian, Japanese and

American). Lawrence studied management styles in some European countries and the United States which resulted in *Management in Sweden* (1986), *Management in Germany* (1980), *Management in the Netherlands* (1991) as well as *Management in the USA* (1996).

What is culture?

In literature one finds various definitions of culture such as:

* culture is a mental programming;
* culture is the man-made part of the environment;
* culture is a projection of mind's universal unconscious infrastructure;
* culture is a system of shared symbols and meanings;
* culture is mirrored through language; or
* culture is learned, not inherited.

Regardless of definition, cultural differences seem to manifest themselves in several ways. From the many terms used to describe manifestations of culture, the following seem to cover the total concept rather neatly: symbols, heroes, myths and stories, rituals and ceremonies and jargon and values. In national as well as organizational cultures, these factors are easily observed.

* Symbols are words, gestures, pictures or objects that carry a particular meaning which is only recognized by those who share the culture. New symbols are easily developed and old ones disappear, and symbols from one cultural group are regularly copied by others. Levi's jeans and Coca Cola have become symbols for American culture. A lavishly fitted out management office may signal a successful and profitable company.
* Heroes are persons, alive or dead, real or imaginary, who possess characteristics that are highly prized in a culture, and who thus serve as models for behaviour. A society or a country may be associated with a hero, for example South Africa with Nelson Mandela and India with Mahatma Ghandi (for his role in the liberalisation process of the twentieth century). In a firm, the founder is sometimes looked upon as a hero. Even fantasy or cartoon characters like Snoopy can serve as cultural heroes.
* Myths and stories exist about shrewd Chinese businessmen negotiating with Europeans or other Westerners who fail to understand Chinese business negotiating style! Or about organizations cultivating stories about spectacular achievements in the past, where a successful salesman or woman closed a vital customer deal.
* Rituals are collective activities, technically superfluous in reaching a desired end, but which, within a culture, are considered as socially essential. Ways of greeting and paying respect to others, social and religious ceremonies are other examples. We know about national rituals and ceremonies when it comes to weddings, celebrations of New Year and the baptism of a child. Also organizations may have their own rituals and ceremonies for rewarding employees.
* Jargon may be special words or linguistic usage that contributes to defining cultural behaviour, mostly within organizations. Throughout its history all desks in IBM offices have had a little sign saying THINK that was introduced by its founder, Thomas J. Watson.

All these terms can be subsumed under the common term of 'practices', which may be specific for different national and organizational cultures. However, we know that many of them are exchangeable between cultures. Levi's jeans, for example, can be found in practically all the corners of the world, even where American culture is by no means predominant or influential. Rituals and ceremonies, on the other hand, are more difficult to transfer from one cultural setting to another: an Arab wedding taking place in Sweden would look exotic and strange to Swedes. In today's global environment, however, cultural practice can be seen as something that is possible to change, but with one important exception: basic values! The value pattern that distinguishes between what we consider as beautiful and ugly, good and evil, dirty and clean, polite and impolite, irrational and rational is something we as individuals carry with us from childhood, and which does not easily change. Psychologists even claim that the average person, regardless of nation, race or cultural group normally does not change his or her basic value pattern beyond their teens.

Management and organizational culture

The attribution of a 'culture' to an organization is a relatively recent phenomenon. The term organizational culture first appeared casually in English-language literature in the 1960s as a synonym for 'climate'. Organizational culture as a management paradigm emerged in reaction to the predominant view from the 1950s to the 1970s of organizations as systems, where individuals were merely treated as system components. A growing interest in anthropological research led many organizational theorists to regard organizations as units of internal value systems where symbols, heroes and rituals thrived. Books and reports by consultants who had been studying highly-successful businesses became instrumental in the change from the systems paradigm to that of organizational culture. In 1985, Peters and Waterman published *In Search of Excellence*, which became a trend-setter for a number of years in organizations around the world. They wrote:

> Without exception, the dominance and coherence of culture proved to be an essential quality of the excellent companies. Moreover, the stronger the culture and the more it was directed toward the marketplace, the less need there was for policy manuals, organization charts, or detailed procedures and rules. In these companies, people way down the line know what they are supposed to do in most situations because the handful of guiding values is crystal.
>
> (Peters and Waterman 1985)

Management and national culture

Although modern culture-free technologies and lifestyles are reshaping much of the global landscape (we use the same Microsoft operating system, wear the same type of jeans, drink Coca-Cola and eat the same hamburgers at McDonald's), this does not imply that all of us are, for example, becoming Americans. Still, the fundamental national cultural values that underpin social behaviours do not change easily. National culture's relevance to international management has been widely recognized in recent years, partly as a result of growing internationalization among enterprises, and thereby through the identification of new organizational and managerial problem areas.

In recent years the work by Geert Hofstede, a Dutch cross-cultural researcher, has had considerable influence on the discussion of culture and its impact on organizational behaviour. Hofstede's contribution to management studies lies primarily in the fact that his works have alerted management to differences in national cultures and their impact on management behaviours across borders (Hofstede 1980, 1991). Amidst the praise for Hofstede's contribution in creating this awareness, his underlying research has been criticized by many for showing considerable flaws with regard to sample size, conclusions drawn and his attempts at quantifying data which are basically unquantifiable. For example, McSweeney (2002) points out that:

- A closer examination of the number of questionnaires used by Hofstede reveals that the average number per country was small, and for some countries it was minuscule.
- Although management literature includes works as good as the best in other disciplines, the continuing unquestioning acceptance of Hofstede's national culture research by his evangelizing entourage suggests that in some management disciplines the criteria for acceptable evidence are far too loose.
- The limited characterization of culture in Hofstede's work, its confinement within the territory of states, and its methodological flaws mean that it is inhibits rather than enhances understanding of particularities.

Although we tend to accept that value systems are culturally rooted and therefore difficult to judge or even understand from another culture, a comparison between cultural behaviours must assume that there are certain issues that transcend cultures borders. According to Hofstede, the following issues qualify as common basic problems world-wide, with consequences for individual and group behaviour:

1 relation to authority;
2 conception of self, in particular the relationship between the individual and society, and the individual's concept of masculinity and femininity; and
3 ways of dealing with conflicts, including the control of aggression and the expression of feelings.

The following section presents a brief overview of management behaviour in some major geographical regions.

Management in Latin America

From the end of the fifteenth century, adventurers from Spain and Portugal carried Latin rule to Central and South America. Overwhelming the inhabitants – the richer civilisations of Central America and the west, and sparser tribes in the south – they turned to the Church to settle which of them should rule what. The Pope drew a line on the map which confirmed present-day Brazil as Portuguese-speaking and the rest as Spanish-speaking (quoted from Hickson and Pugh 1995).

The fact that there is in principle one language (Spanish and Portuguese are grammatically and linguistically close) for all Latin American countries means that the typical SME manager has little incentive to learn another language, since there are no language obstacles to business with other countries in the region. However, insufficient language proficiency becomes a barrier when expansion into other language regions (e.g. Europe, United States) is contemplated. Latin American SME managers are therefore more isolated from the global scene than SME managers in many other countries. This creates difficulties in market outside Latin America and in getting access to information that has not been translated into Spanish (e.g. Internet).

Some of the business principles pertaining to organizational culture with its emphasis on relationships (employee empowerment, listen to the customer) have met with resistance from many SME managers in Latin America. Asking the customer if he (or she) is satisfied with the service of the supplier is a straight-forward way of communicating between supplier and customer in many countries, for example Europe. It is a simple way of telling the client that, as a supplier, I am prepared to listen to your requirements. It describes in essence the Customer's Customer Concept. Thanks to their 'macho' approach, many Latin American SME managers would find it repulsive to ask this type of question, as it could reveal uncertainty about the own performance.

Enterprises in Latin America, SMEs as well as larger firms, have hierarchical organization structures with distance between managers and employees. Management styles are mostly autocratic and the degree of empowerment is mostly rather small. As one SME manager said:

> There is no point in sending employees away for training: when they return they will request a higher salary and, if I do not agree, they will start looking for a new job.
>
> (Personal interview)

It goes without saying that attempting to describe the management behaviour of a whole region such as Latin America can be nothing other than rather superficial. According to Hofstede's four dimensions, a majority of the Latin American countries show high power distance values, a high degree of collectivism, a high degree of masculinity and high scores for uncertainty avoidance.

Management in Africa

Kauda (1994) has a critical view of African management as seen from a Western management perspective: African managers seem to consistently defy all the canons of good management. Their organizations are highly centralized and bureaucratic: intuition rather than formal and objective data analysis guides their decisions; subordinates are closely supervised and lack motivation and opportunities for self-fulfilment due lack of delegation and dependence of their supervisor's favour for career advancement; loyalty to the organization and organizational goals are down-played; and strict adherence to protocol and procedures is common. Activities directed towards upgrading staff capabilities, introducing improved management tools, imposing greater discipline within an organization and improving organizational structure etc., take up an insignificant proportion of an African manager's time. Instead, much time is spent on internal wrangling, jostling with each other to assert authority and in protecting the interest of favourites.

The importance of culture for effective management has become increasingly obvious in recent years, as many of the expectations of African organizations and institutions created and managed along the lines of Western textbooks and models have failed to achieve expected results of economic growth and sustainable development. In nearly all projections of economic development, sub-Saharan African countries score poorly. Africa is seen as the poor relation in the world family of nations, and seems to be condemned to remain so for the foreseeable future. In official statistical data, sub-Saharan African countries nearly always show up the negative end. This situation has therefore resulted in the management of most countries in sub-Saharan Africa being severely criticized for poor performance. In Africa, there are yet few if any examples of very successful (Western-type) indigenous organizations (Iguisi 2005).

What distinguishes African social attitudes from that of other regions is the strong emphasis on family ties and kinship. While, for example, the drive to become an entrepreneur in many Western countries is derived from a wish for self-fulfilment, increasing income and not wanting to be employed or from a desire to exploit a technical innovation, becoming an entrepreneur in Africa may be justified as a way of supporting family members. African solidarity has even a name, Ubuntu ('I am because you are'), which stands for the collective solidarity of the poor on survival issues (Mbigi and Maree 1995).

Management in Asia

Our knowledge – and to some extent also understanding – of management behaviour in the big Asian countries of China, India and Japan has increased lately as a consequence of the growing number of books, research reports and conference proceedings that have focused on practically all aspects of organizations and management in these countries. The almost exclusive focus on these countries may seem to be motivated by obvious reasons, such as Japan's role in the world economy, because China and India are on their way to challenging today's highly-industrialized nations and because China provides the common value system used in many of the East Asian countries. A group of countries that have also been scrutinized with respect to their economic development – albeit not primarily from a management perspective – are the so-called *Asian tigers*.

However, what all these management reports lack is attention to some of the other Asian countries, including Vietnam, Sri Lanka, Indonesia, the Philippines, Laos and Cambodia. These countries are rapidly making their presence felt on the international stage and, even if their business importance cannot be compared in value and volume with the three big Asian countries, there is a need to learn about their management styles and organizational cultures, not least because many of them have their own specific political and socioeconomic backgrounds. Vietnam, for example, is on its way from a state-controlled to a partly-market economy, which requires that management becomes adapted to different ways of marketing, accounting, human management, business planning and so forth.

Management in Arab countries

We may identify four primary influences over Arabs in general and over Arab management, namely the Bedouin heritage, Islam, earlier foreign rule and the demand for oil from the West. The Bedouin tradition, which still carries a romantic image of the camel-mounted tribesman, impregnates Arab culture everywhere, although it is strongest in and around the deserts. This is most visibly symbolized by the traditional costume worn by many city-dwelling politicians and businessmen. The tradition centres on a patriarchal family in which authority runs from father to eldest son and downwards (Hickson and Pugh 1995).

Uncertainty

The concept of uncertainty

A basic feature of uncertainty is the blurred cause–effect relationship. Even if one knows that a certain event is going to happen, the range of possible effects caused by the event creates uncertainty. However, the understanding about cause and effect may vary as illustrated in Table 7.3.

Table 7.3 Four degrees of uncertainty

Degree of uncertainty	Cause–effect understanding	Possibility of prediction
Low	Single	Future can be predicted relatively well
Moderate	Multiple	Future can be predicted as one of several alternatives
Relatively high	Range	Future can be predicted within a range of scenarios of equal weight
Genuine uncertainty	None	Future cannot be predicted

Coping with uncertainty tends to be more successful at lower degrees of uncertainty. Conversely, the higher the degree of uncertainty, the more difficult it is to link cause and effect between the variables of any organization model. In organizations exposed to genuine uncertainty (which occasionally happens in the more-developed countries but more often in less-developed countries), the use of information systems to cope with uncertainty is mostly unsuccessful due to the limited or non-existent ability to predict future events. In such situations uncertainty can only be dealt with in an *ad hoc* manner, i.e. no particular rules apply, but situations have to be treated on a case-by-case basis.

Uncertainty in organizational contexts emanates from interdependence with the environment and from interdependence between different functions within the organization itself. Interdependence between the organization and its environment means that organizational behaviour is based on the assumption that the organization can be described as an open system and thus subject to environmental constraints which the organization must accept. Behaviour is furthermore subject to environmental contingencies that may vary in an unpredictable ways outside the organization' control.

Thompson (1967) classified environment systems: the more heterogeneous they are the more constraints they present to the organization; the more dynamic they are the more contingency the organization has to face. Low- and middle-income countries may be characterized as heterogeneous with regard to infrastructure systems, rules and regulations and skills, which makes strategic and operational planning in organizations and firms difficult, sometimes even hazardous. Unpredictable lead times due to inefficient transport systems, unreliable power supplies and unanticipated bureaucratic hurdles create insurmountable planning difficulties for production firms. Thompson (ibid.) was of the opinion that our Western culture does not contain concepts for simultaneously thinking about rationality and indeterminateness, and the impact this has on how Western organization models and theories are formulated and developed; it is only when organizations are regarded as closed systems that conventional Western theories can be applied in non-Western contexts, which is unrealistic in practice.

The question of rational behaviour when addressing issues of uncertainty can be seen in a wider context involving the confrontation between Western and other cultures – something that has been observed by many scholars. Von Wright (1986) asked if each culture has its own conception of reasonableness and therefore whether comparison between different forms of rationality is possible at all. In a similar remark, Bärmark (1984) claimed that criteria for rationality cannot be formulated unless they are tied to the social and historical context.

Managing uncertainty

Handling uncertainty has always been a management task regardless of whether it relates to long-term strategy or the short-term uncertainties of daily operation. Managing uncertainty

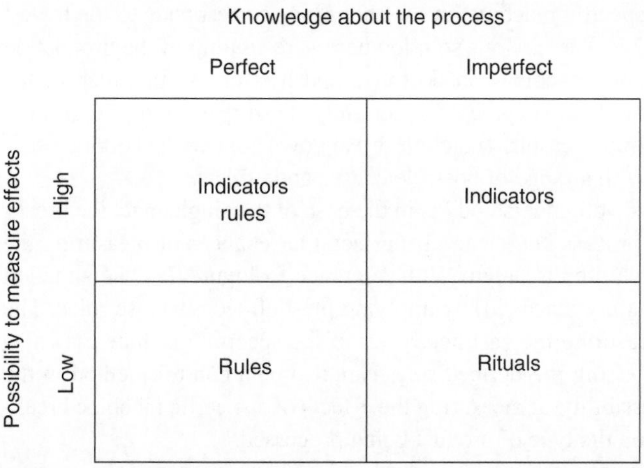

Knowledge about the process

Perfect   Imperfect

	Perfect	Imperfect
High	Indicators rules	Indicators
Low	Rules	Rituals

Possibility to measure effects

Figure 7.3 The two modes of control.

Source: Ouchi (1979).

is here regarded as synonymous with attempts to control an unexpected event that has an impact on the processes of the organization. Early warning analysis is a systematic activity that attempts to identify beforehand all events or situations that could have a negative impact on the organization's ability to achieve its goals, and deals with externally- as well as internally-caused uncertainties; it is further discussed in Chapter 9. We now discuss the management of uncertainty that affects daily operations.

From Table 7.3, we note that the possibility of predicting an event depends not only on the degree of uncertainty but also the extent to which the cause–effect relationship is comprehensible. In a model presented by Ouchi and Maguire (1975), it is suggested that a distinction needs to be drawn between two modes of organizational control: behaviour control (based on personal surveillance) and output control (based on the measurement of outputs). Ouchi (1979) later suggested that when there is sufficient knowledge about a process, rules can be developed and applied as tools in behavioural control. Such rules are in reality a codification of organizational and management behaviour. However, it was also noted that such rules may mostly be both too general and too static to be applicable in more dynamic situations.

A pre-condition for *output control* is the identification of measures that correspond adequately with the actual processes of the enterprise. Such after-the-fact measures only make business control possible if the factors measured are sufficiently well-known and capable of being influenced. If the underlying mechanisms influencing these factors have been identified, it is possible to construct indicators or other simple measures that may be well suited to monitor trends.

To summarise, *output control* measures effects, *behaviour control* uses rules and the choice which to apply depends on knowledge of the process and the extent to which the effects and performance of the process can be measured. If there is insufficient knowledge or no relevant measures can be identified, then the scope for controlling the business process is limited. In such situations, the enterprise has to resort to rituals and ceremonies. The different control alternatives are illustrated in Figure 7.3.

The following scenario from a production process serves as an illustration. The high probability of breakdown of a specific machine on the shop floor corresponds to the lowest degree of uncertainty in Table 7.3. The obvious solution here is re-routing of the production flow for higher reliability. If more machines break down, and it is uncertain which of the machines will stop, there is a moderate degree of uncertainty. Disturbances in the production process can occur for various reasons (machine breakdown, material shortage etc.), resulting in higher uncertainty with a range of possible causes and effects.

If cause–effect relationship is well understood (as in the case of the single machine breakdown), we may claim that our process knowledge is perfect. Our chances of measuring the effect of the machine breakdown are also high. With reference to Figure 7.3, the situation could be controlled (and uncertainty managed) by applying pre-defined response rules. The construction of an indicator measuring the past behaviour of the specific machine may also offer guidance to the manager. Using pre-defined rules can also be a control method in the case where there is only low possibility of measuring the effects of a specific machine breakdown, for example, depending on the type of product being processed.

In the case of genuine uncertainty, for example, production interruption due to an external power cut, our understanding of the cause–effect relationship is low, since information may be lacking about the duration and cause of the electricity failure. Our knowledge of the unfolding situation is incomplete, and the only way the manager can act is to resort to *ad hoc* rituals or ceremonies, such as introducing temporary maintenance work or organizing on-the-job training, while waiting for electrical power to return.

Causes of interruptions to production flows differ between countries in the same way that technology levels and organizational structures differ. Various sources show that around half of all production problems in low- and middle-income countries are externally-caused (e.g. delays in material supply, power failures). Corresponding data from industrialized and high-income countries indicates that externally-caused production interruptions are nearly negligible compared with internally-caused interruptions. For the same reason as in the example above, it can be assumed that organizational control in firms in developing countries is predominantly of an *ad hoc* nature and the application of more advanced control mechanisms such as indicators less useful.

The use of information systems to assist decision-makers in situations involving uncertainty has met with varying success. Simple applications such as the processing of transactions like invoicing and payroll are widely used by small firms, whereas more advanced applications for the analysis of data are less common among small firms. As early as 1988 Shoshana Zubhoff claimed that companies do not derive the full benefit from computers until they are applied to analysis applications. The next section is a brief overview of the use of information systems in small business.

Information and communication technology as management tools

The computer as a management tool means extracting information from raw data to support analysis decisions. Figure 7.4 illustrates an information flow in which various types of signal are emitted by operations and activities.

A variety of signals are emitted continuously as data from operations and activities. The signals may convey messages that material is missing for production, or deliveries to a customer have been delayed. Signals are detected provided there is a suitable interface, e.g. a reporting procedure. After computer processing of the signals by means of a suitable

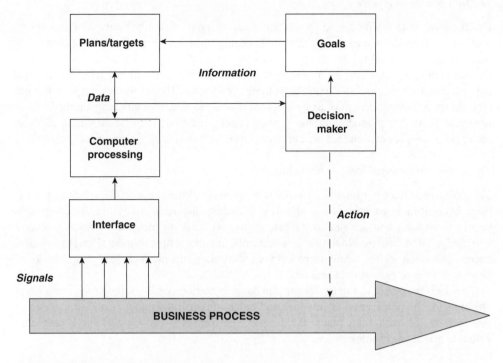

Figure 7.4 Information flow and management control.

application model, the output data are compared with pre-defined plans and reference values. Under the assumption that the interface is adequate for detecting and retrieving the signals, and provided that the computer's application programme is capable of making relevant comparison with the target values of the plan, the information is ready to be used for decision making. The distinction in Figure 7.4 between data and information should be noted!

In this context, it is important that the goals and plans are not only consistent and realistic but also integrated with the information flow. This means that the interface arrangement in Figure 7.4 must be designed in such a way that among all the signals being emitted from the business process, the only ones being captured are those related to the goals and plans. Often, goals and plans are formulated in accordance with what is measurable or which signals it is possible to retrieve. Certain signals may not be possible to detect, even less to retrieve, for example about poor working conditions, about a hostile or unfriendly work atmosphere or about lack of trust between employees and managers etc. These are types of signal that would be important to collect, as they are significant for business and operational efficiency.

Three levels of computer support for business operations

It is possible to discern three levels of computer support for small business operations. The first level, which is also the most common, is characterized by traditional routines for invoicing, payroll etc. This level is seldom controversial as it can be adapted easily to existing practices and routines. The second level uses data as the first level but combines them in order to extract more information. The third level uses more advanced models for analysis. The three levels are discussed next.

The first operational level – processing

On this level, data are processed by the computer as input to administrative and accounting routines, such as invoicing, payroll and bookkeeping. Information is obtained by comparing planned data and actual results. Simple processing applications do not generally make use of the full computing capacity. As an example, a small business in Namibia regularly collects data on customer purchases in terms of volumes and values. However, the company has not realized the additional benefit of using this data to analyse sale, for marketing, on the basis of the most profitable products, on the most valuable customers etc. Such simple analysis requires no complex models, but is easily performed with data used for very basic processing.

The second operational level – simple analysis

Simple analysis does not require an explicit articulation of the cause–effect relationship, i.e. there is no need to go beyond and ask why something happens. Analysing the company's customer profile (who are the customers, when and what do they buy) does not require knowledge of which psychological mechanisms are dictating customers' buying preferences. The cause–effect relationship between customer and product does not need to be known in order to perform the analysis.

The decision-maker in Figure 7.4 utilizes the information coming through the established channels for the preparation of invoices and other administrative documents. In comparing this information with sales plans, the business performance can be evaluated, providing valuable management information.

Box 7.2 Mini-case: SOCA

SOCA is a dairy and fruit farm outside Dakar in Senegal. The farm has its own dairy herds and produces diary products (milk and yoghurt) which represent 65 per cent of turnover. Fruit juices represent the remaining 35 per cent. Products are transported and sold within the Greater Dakar area.

Because distribution costs were high, the company decided to concentrate the sale of its products through five major supermarkets in Dakar. However, after some time the company realised that only a fraction of potential customers ever visited supermarkets for shopping. It was therefore decided to go back to the previous but very costly distribution system through 650 outlets in the Dakar area. It thus became crucial to analyse the business situation to try to reduce distribution costs.

SOCA's general manager had been using a computerized accounting package for some years for financial reporting and control. But the accounting system had no functions for budget follow-up and for sales analysis regarding customers and products. It could therefore not serve as the business operating tool the company needed to help reduce its increasing distribution costs.

The general manager therefore took the initiative to develop an additional computer programme that analysed the daily sales figures per product for each of the 650 outlets. Indicators and trends gave information about profitable and less profitable sales outlets. As a result, the company managed to reduce its 650 outlets to 150 with the goal of a further ultimate reduction to 100 outlets. The savings in cost and time have been significant, thanks to an efficient business analysis application.

The third operational level – advanced analysis

The third operational level for management support is also the most advanced and may sometimes require more skills and information literacy than can be expected in many small businesses. The more complex the computer model, usually the more sophisticated the input data required.

Output from a computer, e.g. analysis results with diagrams and tables, is often accorded considerable credibility, even if the reliability of input data cannot be guaranteed. In advanced analysis, this should be questioned as long as the underlying computer model may be of general nature but applied in a specific context. As such, analysis involves a multitude of parameters and relationships, and it is a complicated task to identify essential signals from the operations, to capture these signals and to measure them by quantitative methods.

A pre-condition for such analysis is therefore that the analysis model is articulated and developed close to the user, that the application is well known to the developer of the model and that the data available really do support the model. The correspondence between reality and model is sometimes very weak, limiting the usefulness of the results.

Box 7.3 Mini-case: Village Industry Services of Lusaka, Zambia

VIS is a non-governmental organization with the mission of promoting business development among microfirms in the informal rural industry sector. The hammer-mill project was such a project, where hammer-mills are lent to small local producers of maize meal. In addition to the 260 hammer-mills lent to small rural enterprises, VIS has assisted in the setting up local repair shops for the maintenance of the mills. Substantial local business opportunities have been provided through the project.

In association with the project, VIS has developed a computer-based performance measuring system to evaluate the project from different aspects. Six variables have been identified as being particularly important to track, for example management performance and transport facilities. Using the system VIS project management can assess and compare the effective use of all 260 hammer mills and measure the extent to which they create local jobs and contribute to business development in the rural areas. The model used was developed by those who know the problem thoroughly and could align the computer model with the local situation.

Information needs

An important discussion about the information needed to run a small business enterprise efficiently has gradually emerged during recent years. Significant criticism has been levelled at the traditional view of accounting data as the basis for management information, and firms have even been urged to remove accounting information from their operational control systems (Johnson and Kaplan 1987; Johnson 1992).

There are several reasons behind this discussion; two are mentioned here. Growing globalization leading to growing competition has resulted in new business practices with an increasing focus on customers and service. It has become obvious that the accounting systems used by most businesses do not have the proper functions to measure customer satisfaction. With a new management ideology that puts increased emphasis on responsiveness to customers and quality, there is a radical shift from treating financial figures as the foundation for performance monitoring to treating them as one among a broader set of measures. This implies that traditional tools need to be complemented by non-financial measures where monitoring of a company's business operations comes to the foreground.

The mental shift in attitudes in favour of a broader set of performance measures among SMEs has been rather slow if measured by the use of innovative new management tools. This is a typical Catch-22 situation: as long as there is no real demand for more adequate management tools, the vendors – often ignorant of the problem – have no real incentives to develop new software products. And as long as the vendors stick to their rather traditional software tools with a relatively low innovation level, there is limited possibility of SME users acquiring more adequate software to assist managers in managing business operations. From the supply side (vendors, consultants etc.) the reason is entrenched habit of associating performance management control with financial control. And as long as there is enough demand for merely traditional accounting systems, vendors have few incentives to develop new concepts. On the demand side, there is a slowly-growing awareness that performance measurement is more than just accounting. In SMEs, this awareness is primarily concentrated in the high-performers.

SMEs and corporate social responsibility

One of the effects that globalization has had on business management is a growing opinion among management theorists that the role of companies should extend beyond pure economic and business dimensions to also include social responsibility. Theories which attempt to define the company's responsibility to society are generally grouped together as theories of corporate social responsibility (CSR). In organizational literature, concepts such as corporate responsibility, business responsibility, corporate citizenship, corporate responsibility and corporate sustainability are also in use.

Over the last decade, CSR has become an important issue for multi-national companies, as non-governmental organizations (NGOs) have increasingly made it their mission to ensue companies to comply with rules like not using child labour or violating environmental laws (Kemp 2001). The concept of CSR has not been without controversy. Milton Friedman claimed that the only responsibility a company has to its stakeholders is profit maximization (1970), whereas many others believes CSR to be a crucial factor for long-term survival and an important management strategy for satisfying stakeholders (Porter and Kramer 2006).

Carroll (2004) argues that four responsibilities (economic, legal, ethical and philanthropic) cover the whole CSR perspective of what society can expect from a company, both economically as well as socially. The use and implementation of the different responsibilities depends of the size of the firm, the field of industry and economic conditions. Carroll also suggests that ethical responsibility has a major impact on a company, and that ethical standard and norms – especially in developing countries – can be very hard to identify. A company has to operate in such manner that the company follows its moral as well as its ethical beliefs and be aware that ethical behaviour can affect the company as much or even more than legal responsibility.

CSR is gradually becoming part of the business strategy in many small firms in high-income countries, whereas implementing CSR strategies among SMEs in developing countries seem to be lagging behind. In July 2007, Indonesia was the first country to announce a mandatory law regarding CSR, which applied to companies active in fields using natural resources. The public debate in Indonesia regarding CSR has increased, and the Indonesian business community promotes the concept of CSR to the local SME sector as a way of reaching US and European markets (Rosser and Leong 2008).

CSR in Indonesia

The 2007 Indonesia CSR law requires companies using natural resources to pay 3–5 per cent of their profit to the government, but the law is in great need of improvement due to misperceptions and lack of a clear definition. Hendeberg and Lindgren (2009) reported that CSR guidelines in Indonesia were hard to follow, since local and central government regard the law differently, and it was claimed that CSR in Indonesia would function better if they were voluntary. Carroll (1998) notes that companies sometimes see regulations differently from law makers, claiming that laws and regulations often hinder rather than help the economic performance of small business.

Empirical data shows that CSR in Indonesia has its foundation in culture and ethical norms. Hendeberg and Lindgren (ibid.) observed that the somewhat vague and complex agenda of CSR easily comes into conflict with cultural and religious differences, which are of crucial importance in a developing country like Indonesia.

Note

1   Examples presented during the General Assembly meeting of UNCTAD, Bangkok February 2000.

References

Bannock, G. (2005) *The Economics and Management of Small Business*. London: Routledge.
Barley, S. and Kunda, G. (1992) 'Design and Devotion: Surges of Rational and Normative Ideologies of Control in Managerial Discourse'. *Administrative Science Quarterly*, 37.
Bärmark, J. (1984) *Kultur, Medvetande, Paradigm* (in Swedish). Gothenburg, Sweden: University of Gothenburg, Department of Theory of Science.
Bjerke, B. (1995) *Business, Leadership and Culture*. Cheltenham, UK: Edward Edgar Publishing.
Björkegren, D. (1989) 'Some Limitations in the Western Model of Executive Training', in Davis, J. (ed.) *The Challenge to Western Management Development*. London: Routledge.
Carroll A. B. (1998) 'The Four Faces of Corporate Citizenship'. *Business and Society Review*, 100/101.
Carroll A. B. (2004) 'Managing Ethically with Global Stakeholders – A Present and Future Challenge'. *Academy of Management Executive*, 18: 2.
Davila, C. (1989) 'Grounding Management Education in Local Research – A Latin American Experience', in Davis, J. (ed.) *The Challenge to Western Management Development*. London: Routledge.
Friedman, M. (1970) 'The Social Responsibility of Business is to Increase Its Profit'. *New York Times Magazine*, September 13.
Gatley, S., Lessem, R. and Altman, Y. (1996) *Comparative Management: A Transcultural Odyssey*. Maidenhead, Berkshire: McGraw-Hill.
Giddens, A. (1985) 'Jürgen Habermas', in Skinner, Q. (ed.) *The Return of Grand Theories in the Human Sciences*. Cambridge: Cambridge University Press.
Gregory, K. (1983) 'Native-View Paradigms: Multiple Cultures and Culture Conflicts in Organisations'. *Administrative Science Quarterly* (Cornell University), 28: 3.
Hannon, P. D. and Atherton, A. (1998) 'Small Firm Success and the Art of Orienteering: The Value of Plans, Planning and Strategic Awareness in the Competitive Small Firm'. *Journal of Small Business and Enterprise Development*, 15: 2.

Hendeberg, S. and Lindgren, F. (2009) *CSR in Indonesia: A Qualitative Study from a Managerial Perspective Regarding Views and Other Important Aspects Concerning CSR in Indonesia*. Visby: Gotland University.

Hickson, D. and Pugh, D. (1995) *Management Worldwide*. London: Penguin.

Hofstede, G. (1980) *Culture's Consequences: International Differences in Work-Related Values*. London: Sage.

Hofstede, G. (1991) *Cultures and Organisations*. New York: McGraw-Hill.

Iguisi, O. (1997) 'The Role of Culture for Appropriate Management and Indigenous Development in Africa'. Paper delivered at the African seminar on *Culture Dimensions to Appropriate Management and Sustainable Development in Africa*. Kampala: Makerere University.

Iguisi, O. (2005) *Management and Indigenous Knowledge Systems: An Analysis of Motivational Values Across Cultures*. Maastricht: Euro-African Management Research Centre.

Johnson, T. (1992) *Relevance Regained – From Top-Down Control to Bottom-Up Empowerment*. New York: Free Press.

Johnson, T. and Kaplan, R. (1987) *Relevance Lost: The Rise and Fall of Management Accounting*. Boston: Harvard Business School Press.

Kauda, J. (1994) *Management Behaviour in Ghana and Kenya: A Cultural Perspective*. Aalborg, Denmark: Aalborg University Press.

Kemp, M. (2001) *Corporate Social Responsibility in Indonesia: Quixotic Dream or Confident Expectation?* Washington, DC: United Nations Research Institute for Social Development. Technology, Business and Society Programme Paper 6.

Lawrence, P. (1980) *Managers and Management in West Germany*. London: Croom Helm.

Lawrence, P. (1991) *Management in the Netherlands*. Oxford: Oxford University Press.

Lawrence, P. (1996) *Management in the USA*. London: Sage Publications.

Lawrence, P. and Spybey, T. (1986) *Management and Society in Sweden*. London: Routledge.

McSweeney, B. (2002) 'Hofstede's Model of National Cultural Differences and their Consequences: A Triumph of Faith – A Failure of Analysis'. *Human Relations* (Tavistock Institute), 55.

Marsden, A. and Forbes, C. (2003) 'Strategic Management for Small and Medium-Sized Enterprises', in Oswald, J. and Tilley, F. (eds) *Competitive Advantage in SMEs*. London: Wiley.

Mbigi, L. and Maree, J. (1995) Ubuntu – *The Spirit of African Transformation Management*. Randburg, South Africa: Knowledge Resources.

Moore, C. (1980) *Images of Development: Egyptian Engineers in Search of Industry*. Cambridge, MA: MIT Press.

Peters, T. and Waterman, R. (1985) *In Search of Excellence*. New York: Grand Central Publishing.

Porter, M. E. and Kramer, M. R. (2006) 'Strategy and Society – The Link between Competitive Advantage and Corporate Social Responsibility'. *Harvard Business Review*, December.

Ouchi, W. (1979) 'A Conceptual Framework for the Design of Organisational Control Mechanisms'. *Management Science*, 25: 9.

Ouchi, W. and Maguire, M. A. (1975) 'Organisational Control: Two Functions'. *Administrative Science Quarterly*, December.

Robbins, S. (1990) *Organisation Theory: Structure, Design and Applications*. Englewood Cliffs, NJ: Prentice Hall.

Rosser, A. and Leong, H. K. (2008) *The Political Economy of Corporate Governance in Indonesia in Reforming Corporate Governance in Southeast Asia: Economics, Politics, and Regulations*. Singapore: Institute of Southeast Asian Studies.

Schwarz, S. (1992) 'Universals in the Content and Structure of Values: Theoretical Advances and Empirical Tests in 20 Countries'. *Advances in Experimental Social Psychology*, 25.

Tanton, M. and Esterby-Smith, M. (1989) 'Is the Western View Inevitable? A Model of the Development of Management Education', in Davis, J. (ed.) *The Challenge to Western Management Development*. London: Routledge.

Thompson, J. (1956) 'On Building an Administrative Science'. *Administrative Science Quarterly* (Cornell University), 1/1956.

Thompson, J. (1967) *Organisations in Action*. New York: McGraw-Hill.

Von Wright, G. H. (1986) *Vetenskapen och Förnuftet* (in Swedish). Stockholm: Bonnier.

8 The SME manager's roles

Strategist, operator and mentor

The owner-manager of a one-person company has no opportunity to delegate tasks. He or she is forced to take on the roles of sales manager, production manager, financial manager and general manager; the only task that he or she escapes is personnel management. However, this task is restored as soon as the first employee arrives. With a growing legal framework specifying terms and conditions of employment, personnel management becomes a high priority task. The step from the one-person company to a micro company with only one or a few employees is a significant one, due to the sudden increase in administrative burdens. This can be observed in the statistics of the growth of firms: in most high-income countries with employment legislation in place, firms with no employees represent around 70 per cent of the total. Despite of numerous support programmes to make small firms grow, this growth is hampered by high administrative burdens, which mangers react to by staying small.

As small firms grow in terms of employment, the owner-manager can generally maintain control of vital business functions until the number of employees reaches a certain limit. This limit has not been confirmed by studies, but as a rule of thumb seems to be around 20 employees. When the firm reaches this size, the complexity and degree of differentiation tends to make overview and control by one person unsatisfactory. For a firm with 20 employees or more, there is therefore a need to delegate responsibility for certain vital functions to dedicated individuals or middle managers. As firms grow in size, the degree of structural differentiation tends to increase rapidly, albeit at a decreasing rate (Blau and Schoenherr 1971). The organizational structure of a medium-size firm will therefore not differ significantly from that of the large firm.

Traditionally it was common to distinguish between leadership and management in the context of the large firm. Leadership was coping with change, whereas management was dealing with day-to-day operational issues. Leadership was primarily outward-looking: understanding and assessing changes in the environment and their potential impact on the organization. Management was primarily inward-looking: watching over internal operations and adjusting operations for increased efficiency. In small businesses, such division between functions is not obvious for various reasons. Lack of internal skills and the high costs of external recruitment is a reason why the general manager, who may also be the owner, prefers to take responsibility both for strategic decisions and for overall internal operational control. Hierarchies in society are reflected in firms as the power distance between manager and employees, whereby lack of trust between manager and employee prevents the manager delegating overall responsibility. In such situations, the monitoring of daily operations may be delegated to individuals but with limited and restricted areas of responsibility.

It is therefore characteristic of small firms, including for those that have exceeded the 20-employee level, that the general manager retains the functional responsibility for making strategic decisions, for monitoring internal operations and for acting as mentor to key personnel.

The SME manager as strategist

Small business managers are often accused of having a short-term strategic perspective which can mostly be explained by the fact that business realities the present has a higher priority than the future. Investments for the future can only be considered if today's business generates sufficient surplus. Long-term strategic thinking therefore gives way to short-term strategic planning, which is primarily programmatic and analytical. This short-term strategic planning is associated with the so-called Deming Wheel.[1] This begins with a plan to design or revise business process components to improve results, and is followed by a step in which the plan is implemented and performance measured. The third step involves assessing the measurements and reporting the results to the decision-makers, which may lead to a further cycle of change.

The process described is also referred to as single-loop learning, where the learning element results in a change leading to improvements. The single-loop process is analytical and carried out according to a scheme, the plan-do-check-act sequence, which is part of strategic planning, and a programmatic approach to strategic management. It has been stressed by several authors (e.g. Argyris 1977; Heracleous 2003) that strategic planning differs from strategic thinking which involves creativity. According to Heracleous (ibid.), the real purpose of strategic planning is to improve strategic thinking. Single-loop learning occurs when there is a mismatch between plan and results and corrections are required. However, the weakness of single-loop learning is that a mismatch can occur either because performance is poor, or because either or both the variables used to make comparisons or the predetermined reference values are not relevant.

Strategic thinking is the creative questioning about the reference values or the current norms guiding the comparison between what is and what should be, between result and plan, and what should be the ground for action. Questions can include:

- How did the current norms develop?
- Are current norms relevant and consistent with present business objectives?
- Do the current norms support change?
- Are the current norms 'set in stone'?
- How often are current norms being questioned?

Psychologically, questioning ruling norms is generally uncomfortable, and small businesses are not exempt from this. If fact, Osborne (1992) noted that managers in small and medium enterprises (SMEs) often make decisions with a minimum of information. In analysing the usage of information in SMEs, Pleitner (1989) likewise found that they mostly work with a general lack of information, but also that they have inadequate information channels and, in particular, that they have inadequate or insufficient information about long-term goals. Other studies (e.g. Rice and Hamilton 1979) show that decisions in SMEs are based on principles that are not generally regarded rational. Decisions thus tend to be oriented towards the most immediate and practical solutions to problems where only a very small number of parameters are considered.

In a discussion about critical reconsideration of governing variables and existing business systems, Heracleous (ibid.) sees the possibility of this developing into a market-driving strategy. Such a ground-breaking strategy is enabled by double-loop learning, since an organization's set of potential action alternatives and mental models expand to include new responses and new ways of thinking about problems faced, leading to radically different strategic actions from what was done in the past.

While high-performance companies tend to respond quickly to new ideas, low-performance companies tend to consider their level of competence satisfactory, as shown in a Swedish study conducted by Gustavsson and Svanfeldt (1994). The study also showed that SMEs have their most influential and important collaborators in local networks, where the SME manager picks up information and important messages on how the manager develops his or her managerial understanding and abilities. However, other studies show that this management influence may look different in other cultural environments.

Sources of management influence

In the studies referred to above, the potential actors and organizations influencing and contributing to the manager's view of conducting business were reported as being:

- research institutes
- chambers of commerce
- suppliers
- customers
- branch organizations
- training institutes
- banks
- local municipalities
- local collaborators
- consultants
- trade fares
- technology parks
- larger enterprises
- universities
- export promoters.

The actors are grouped according to their importance to the manager. *Level one* actors are in practically daily contact with the company, such as customers and suppliers. This group is important and common to nearly all firms. Though not in daily contact, the actors of *level two* still play an important role communicating advances in research, changes in the market, international development etc. New views and ideas can be picked up at trade fares and branch organizations communicating sector-specific matters through journals and websites. *Level three* is in many ways dissociated from the average SME. Due to lack of time, interest, knowledge and a variety of other reasons, small firms do not use the information provided on this level because is not perceived as being relevant.

Cultural differences influence how managers perceive the relevance and importance of ideas and views coming from others. Interaction with actors on different levels may be facilitated or hindered, depending on the power distance between hierarchical levels or on the degree of trust between organizations and individuals. Study results from Chile and Sweden provide an example.

Table 8.1 Sources of influence on management in Chile and Sweden

	Chile	Sweden
Level One	Customers	Customers
		Banks
		Suppliers
		Local collaborators
Level Two	Trade fairs	Branch organizations
	Suppliers	Training institutes
		Municipalities
		Consultants
		Large enterprises
		Trade fairs
Level Three	Research institutions	Research institutions
	Universities	Universities
	Chambers of commerce	Chambers of commerce
	Technology parks	Technology parks
	Export promoters	Export promoters
	Banks	
	Local collaborators	
	Consultants	
	Branch organisations	
	Training institutes	
	Municipalities	
	Large enterprises	

Sources: Gustavsson and Svanfeldt (1994); Ekman and Gronlund (1997).

Sweden and Chile – a comparison

Table 8.1 shows the result from studies of a mixture of technology passive and active enterprises in Sweden and the wood manufacturing sectors of Chile.

Looking at Chile, the actors having the most influence on managers are those closest in level to the SME which, in the Chilean case, is only one category, namely customers. On level two are suppliers who have a weaker and more formal relation to their customers. Also trade fairs play an important role, as the firms pick up new trends in marketing and products and get a chance to demonstrate their own products. Contacts with actors on level three, the level most distant to the firm, are exceptional and Chilean managers often manifest a distinct suspicion towards authorities. In many cases there is a tendency among small business managers to work independently of government institutions whose activities are generally incoherent in that they all have difficulties in reaching the enterprises. Communication is often poor, not least from the SME side which often tend to ignore the support offered by these institutions (Ekman and Gronlund 1997).

In the Swedish case the most important actors are found on level one. Customers and suppliers are often the only actors who provide ideas for technological development. Banks not only handle financing, but also give advice on economic issues with corresponding influence on investments and development. Local collaborators are associations like clubs in close proximity to the company and are mostly informal contacts, but important as sources of information. Decisions about new products and production process development are often based on information gained from local collaboration, especially in areas of similar types of production. Actors of level two are not in daily contact with the company and the technology passive companies are mostly not fully capable of making creative use of information pro-vided by actors on this level. Important actors on this level are retailers of machinery and production equipment. They often know about the latest technical achievements within the industry and have a close relationship with their customers.

These study results show differences as well as similarities between the two countries. It is important to remember that the study refers to the wood manufacturing sector in Chile making generalization hazardous. The striking difference is that the small business manager in the Chilean company is lonely as regards external influence that might convey new ideas and visions. The contact network of the Swedish small business manager is significantly larger and exposes the manager more to ideas and views. It is interesting to note that in both countries there is a mental distance between formal institutions such as universities and small business.

Close links with customers and suppliers contain recipes for success if treated properly and professionally in management strategies. The importance of managing customer–supplier relationships have been shown to be especially relevant for small manufacturing businesses in developing countries (Paulray *et al.* 2008). In the recent past, many small businesses have been operating in relatively protected environments; however globali-zation has increased competition and requires small businesses to adapt in order to survive (Hadjimanolis 1999). Small manufacturing businesses, operating in business-to-business (B2B) markets are being forced to become more competitive and find a way to differentiate themselves from rivals or close their doors (Lind and Scheepers 2009).

The B2B markets differ from consumer markets, since suppliers and customers have closer relationships, compared to manufacturers marketing direct to the consumer. In B2B markets, suppliers manufacture on demand, B2B products and their applications being complex. Industrial products are sold on exact specifications, often have to be integrated into existing systems, and require expert examination and modification. Increased globalization and reports from industry of shorter cycle times, fewer quality defects, reduced costs and streamlined processes have compelled SME suppliers and customers to improve their relationships and have suggested a clearer understanding of reciprocal needs and capabilities among the buying and supplying firms (Forker and Stannack 2000).

Cheverton (2004) argues that a customer's choice of supplier is not just the result the value added by the supplier's products, technologies and service. Being a supplier also involves developing relationships with customers. Value also comes from activities that involve building trust, building customer knowledge and using that knowledge to deliver value and also jointly manage the future.

In a study of SMEs in South Africa, Ecuador and Sweden focusing on customer–supplier relationships the results showed quite significant differences among the managers inter-viewed with respect to what they considered more or less important in the relations (Lind and Scheepers 2009). Managers in purchasing companies ('the customers') were asked about five factors they would consider important in selecting a supplier and when building a business relationship with them. The five factors were: quality in products, in service, price, and active assistance by the supplier in case of trouble and supplier's interest in build-ing a long-term relationship with the customer. Separately, managers in supplying compa-nies ('the suppliers') were asked about the same factors but were asked to respond with what they *assumed* customers would prioritize when selecting and working with suppliers. In both cases, the degree of importance was measured on a scale from 1 (low importance) to 5 (high importance). Figure 8.1 shows the results for the customer in the three countries;

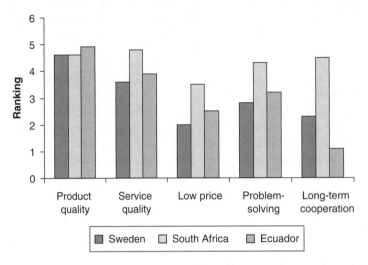

Figure 8.1 Managers as customers: ranking of important factors when selecting suppliers.
Source: Lind and Scheepers (2009).

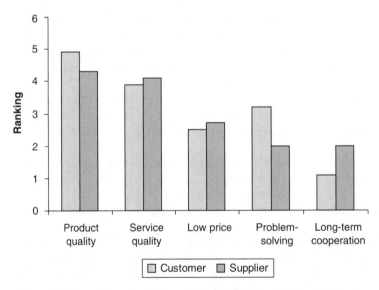

Figure 8.2a Customer and supplier rankings of important factors in Ecuador.
Source: Lind and Scheepers (2009).

Figures 8.2a and 8.2b (discussed below) compare the responses of customers and suppliers in the same country.

The study shows that product quality has the highest priority of the countries represented in the study. The South African part of the study had a high representation of B2B firms in

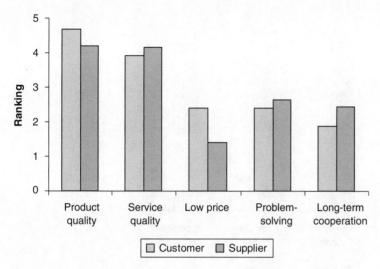

Figure 8.2b Customer and supplier rankings of important factors in Sweden.
Source: Lind and Scheepers (2009).

the manufacturing sector, which may explain the high importance ranking for most factors. Of the five factors, price has the lowest relative ranking. This finding may mark a trend about to be broken, as small business has traditionally been considered to use price as the number one competitive factor. From the study we note that a supplier with a positive attitude to trouble shooting is more important than a lower price, whereas building long-term supplier relations for joint product development and the like does not seem to have a high priority. This is definitely the case in Ecuador.

The view represented by suppliers in what they assume to be the priority order when customers seek suppliers differ somewhat from the customer views of Figure 8.1. Figures 8.2a and 8.2b compare customer and supplier views in Ecuador and Sweden. The study shows that quality in products and service score highest in both countries. Suppliers in the Ecuadorian study tend to assume that price is more important for customers than in Sweden. Suppliers in both countries seem to assume that customers are more in favour of long-term relationships than is actually the case. However, Swedish customers are more in favour of long-term relationships than their Ecuadorian colleagues. The customers value supplier support in case of problems much higher than the suppliers assume about their Ecuadorian customers. The most relevant finding is that price is not considered the most important factor in customer–supplier relationships in either Ecuador or Sweden, despite the behaviour sometimes observed by SME owner-managers, who seemingly compete on price. The results indicate that enterprises can differentiate themselves from competitors by focusing on a bundle of relationship attributes, and not only by focusing on price.

Another significant finding that holds strategic implications for SME owner-managers is whether customers view their products as core or peripheral. In the case of core products, relationship aspects such as long-term commitment, trust, after-sales support, timely deliveries, high quality and support in the case of disruption are worth a higher price. Small business managers need to realize that the core product market requires trustworthy and reliable

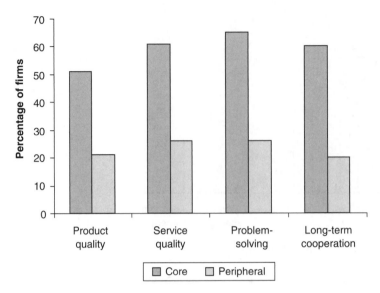

Figure 8.3 Customer rankings of core and peripheral products and services in South Africa.
Source: Lind and Scheepers (2009).

business relations. However, if a product is viewed as peripheral, a different strategy requiring fewer resources from SME owner-managers is required. In the case of peripheral products, customers do not necessarily require after sales service, since products are less complex and less sophisticated. If one supplier fails, it is easier to find an alternative supplier than is the case with core products.

Figure 8.3 shows the percentage of customers interviewed in South Africa prepared to pay significantly more for good service and quality in core as opposed to peripheral products or services. The same results were found also in the Swedish and Ecuadorian segments of the study.

The manager as operations executive

As stated by Jennings and Beaver (1997), the management process in small firms bears little or no resemblance to management processes found in larger firms, and small business managers will be performing a range of functions which in large firms are carried out by dedicated managers with substantial organizational support. Operations management therefore means different things depending on the size of the firm. A large enterprise can allocate specific tasks to mangers trained for those tasks. The small business manager must be more flexible in making optimal use of available expertise and knowledge within the company. In what follows, we focus on two areas where many SME managers spend considerable time and effort: managing the technical system and managing personnel.

Managing the technical system

The technical system refers not only to the collection of production equipment in a manufacturing company but also to the increasing amount of technology crucial to the functioning of the business, not least its administration. Computer breakdown may have an even more serious effect on the business than failures in the production system.

Managing the information system

The term information system generally refers to the combination of information technology (computers, communication facilities) and the people using that technology. Despite differing definitions of information, communication technology and information systems we do not distinguish them here. The development of information technology (IT) has resulted in a steadily-improving performance–price ratio, making computer investments an almost negligible cost in most firms. At the same time, the total costs involved in the processing of information is significant taking into account the indirect costs necessary to keep the information flow updated and efficient. The financial values handled by the information systems have also become less transparent as transactions flows are considerably faster compared to earlier manual systems. Managing the information system is therefore less about monitoring direct investments in computers and more about monitoring its vulnerability, efficiency and overall cost.

An effect of increasing Internet usage is the threat to information systems from external infringement. Viruses are one form which mostly dealt with by data protection software. However, vulnerabilites also arise from the connections between the computers of business partners. The benefits of accuracy, speed and reduction in costs derived from sending customer orders directly to the supplier's production or delivery schedule can be jeopardized by unauthorized tapping of the information flow.

Are information systems and IT unique in comparison with other types of technology, such as production or transport? The following observations suggest this is the case.

- It is difficult to distinguish if perceived effects come from the information system alone, from indirect effects, or from a combination of the two.
- There is a special psychology of expectations around IT.
- Integration with the organization is often complex, and this makes it difficult to distinguish costs and benefits both in time and in space.
- Training in IT has no clear boundaries: how much is application and how much is technology?
- The costs of an information systems application are primarily the costs of the software and its implementation (customization, training etc). While the price for a software package is often well known, implementation costs are mostly difficult to estimate, or even determine *ex post*!

The uniqueness of IT and information systems is probably its duality: it is shaped by organizational needs, but it also creates new forms of organizational structures and behaviour. This makes investment in IT very complicated, particularly as traditional investment analysis models are intended for well-defined and less integrated investments. Traditional methods such as cost–benefit analysis therefore have limited value as assessment tools for IT investments.

Costs–benefit analysis applied to information systems

A general aspect on the problem related to cost–benefit analysis was formulated by Land as follows:

Everybody does cost–benefit analysis on projects. Most of them are fictional. The saddest part is that it is not just the benefits that are fictional, but the costs as well. [Users] don't begin to assess what the real costs of the system are. They do cost–benefit analysis to get money.

We have trouble convincing ourselves of value of business terms. We cost justify new systems on the basis of lies and overstatements, we don't measure the true business value.

(Land 1998)

Land goes on mentions several problems and difficulties in estimating costs and benefits for information system projects:

- A significant proportion of costs are fixed and independent of utilization. Allocating costs to specific information systems projects may therefore be arbitrary.
- Life-time costs are difficult to estimate because the life of new systems is uncertain – technological obsolescence and changing requirements make it increasingly hazardous to provide a reliable estimate of the system's life.
- The project champions tend to have a strong attachment to and belief in the ultimate worth of the system under review. Hence champions have a tendency to underestimate costs – or fail to add contingencies – in order to increase the chance of the project being accepted.
- Many applications are targeted at second order effects – such as better information.
- In many cases, the change which has to be evaluated is a major reorganization in which IT plays an important role – but it is the investment in the reorganization as a whole which adds value and has to be evaluated.

A common tool for cost–benefit analysis is Net Present Value (NPV) and its variants. NPV compares the value of the investment with the net cash flow discounted to present value expected to arise in each year during the projected lifetime of the machine. If the NPV value is greater than zero then the investment can be considered economically justified.

Investments in information systems are seldom exposed to formal investment analysis like the NPV method. The reason for this is twofold: it is difficult to estimate the benefits, particularly within a given time frame; it is also difficult to estimate costs for the process of adapting the software to the organization, or *vice-versa*. Investments are therefore often justified by referring to more intangible returns such as 'the importance of keeping pace with technological development' or 'to stay competitive'. It is obvious that this approach to justifying an investment differs significantly from other more 'conventional' investments, such as in a lathe or a truck.

In the NPV method, a significant parameter is the internal interest rate that defines the cost of capital. This rate is related to how fast the investment should be depreciated. The longer the depreciation time, the lower is the interest rate and the easier it is to justify the investment. In today's IT race, where a new product becomes obsolete within a very short period of time, depreciation time is short (a few years only), which results in a relatively high interest rate. Most managers know that using the NPV method to analyse IT investments is likely to result in a negative value that would not justify the investment. As there may be a variety of reasons behind a decision to invest in IT (business strategy, psychology, prestige etc.), managers may be tempted to skimp on more structured analysis.

Managing the production system

All enterprise activities involve different kinds of production varying from the generation of ideas, problem solutions and concepts in a consulting firm or services in hotels and transport organizations, to the production of goods in manufacturing firms. From this we must conclude there is a wide range of production systems, each having its specific characteristics based on the types of products and services and on the cultural and socioeconomic context of the production site. In spite of the vast variation in production systems, one can identify some common aspects important to the performance and efficiency of the production system. These aspects include the reliability of the system, the ability to manage and plan production against varying lead-times, and the quality of products and services produced by the system. These aspects are all the responsibility of the manager as operations executive.

Reliability of the production system – maintenance

Interruptions in the production system can be costly. Late deliveries to customers can contribute to reducing the supplier's credibility in the market. This can be particularly serious in business-to-business situations where the output from one firm is the input to another and, through this demand and supply sequence, the effects of a problem can spread throughout the entire relationship chain. It is therefore important that the production system undergoes proper maintenance to minimize production interruptions. Maintenance is generally divided into three categories where each can be planned or unplanned and repetitive or not repetitive, as follows:

Preventive maintenance	is	repetitive and planned
Planned repair	is	non-repetitive but planned
Emergency repair	is	non-repetitive and unplanned

Preventive maintenance includes minor operations such as adjusting, lubrication and cleaning, but also major jobs such as overhauling. Emergency repair involves repair of a machine that has already broken down or is malfunctioning, whereas planned repair involves maintenance related to, for instance, the installation of new machines.

The prevention of failures has a high potential for saving value and is therefore more satisfactory, so long as the expense of preventive maintenance and planned (in hours and cost) is less than the cost of emergency repair. However, in many developing countries with a high proportion of externally-caused production interruptions, non-planned disturbances cannot always be controlled within the enterprise itself. Whereas in many industrialized countries internally-caused failures represent significantly more of the total quality cost, the figure for developing countries is almost half of that. On the other hand, the proportion of externally-caused failures is significantly higher in developing countries. These differences are illustrated in Tables 8.2 and 8.3 below. A report from an Egyptian steel company states that:

> It was difficult to implement production plans and schedules to meet the market demands because no one knew when the machines would break down or stop. Emergency repairs were 80 to 90 per cent of maintenance work. The sudden stoppage of one machine may result in the stoppage of a complete production line or even the whole factory.

> (Quoted in Lind 1988)

Table 8.2 Average quality costs in developing countries due to interruptions

	External interruptions (50%)	*Internal interruptions (50%)*
Planned maintenance (20%)	10%	10%
Unplanned repairs (80%)	40%	40%

Source: Author, based on UNIDO reports.

Table 8.3 Average quality costs in industrialized countries due to interruptions

	External interruptions (< 5%)	*Internal interruptions (> 95%)*
Planned maintenance (20%)	< 1%	> 19%
Unplanned repairs (80%)	< 4%	> 76%

Source: Author, based on UNIDO reports.

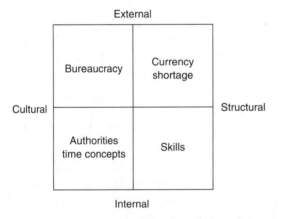

Figure 8.4 Reasons for uncertainty: a categorization of maintenance problems.

The reference to *external* and *internal* as sources of interruptions and the complicating effect this has management control need to be supplemented by two more factors to create a fuller picture. These two factors can be categorized as structure- and culture-based. It is possible to relate uncertainty to the organizational structure (shortage of currency) or to cultural phenomena, for example, the bureaucracy present in several countries. It is admittedly not obvious that bureaucracy is always a cultural phenomenon, but it is nevertheless a plausible assumption as concluded by Issawi (1982). Figure 8.4 attempts to categorize the different forms of uncertainty.

Bureaucracy hampers infrastructure development, such as power supply systems, leading to uncertainty in power supply and reliability. Shortage of currency refers to access to convertible currency for the purchase and import from abroad of equipment to stabilize the production system, such as spare parts. Shortage is not necessarily real but can be due to the banking structure when dealing with small businesses. Authorities and time concepts are

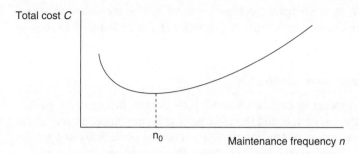

Figure 8.5 Cost of maintenance related to maintenance frequency.

cultural and may hamper or delay decisions about improvements and changes that could have a positive impact in the maintenance system.

Table 8.2 illustrates how costs incurred by production interruptions are distributed between external and internal causes and planned and non-planned maintenance.

Table 8.2 shows there are two main components for maintenance: costs for planned maintenance and for unscheduled (unplanned) repairs. A common expression for the costs is given by the following relationship between total costs (C) and related parameters:

$$C = k_1 \times n + k_2 \times (r/n - m), \text{ if } m < r/n$$

In this, k_1 and k_2 are the respective costs of planned unplanned maintenance, n is the frequency of planned maintenance per machine, r is the total annual machine hours per machine and m is the time interval within which no machine maintenance is required. The interval m is usually specified by the machine supplier and assumes the use of approved spare parts, regular service and trained service staff. In many firms a variety of factors such as aging machinery and lack of standard spare parts reduce the time interval m. From this expression and Figure 8.5, it can be seen that total maintenance costs increase with decreasing interval m, but they will also increase after a certain maintenance frequency due to an over-organized maintenance organization.

According to our formula, minimum maintenance costs occur at a maintenance frequency n_0 given by the following expression after differentiating the expression for total costs C:

$$n_0 = \sqrt{(r \times k_2/k_1)}$$

The cost factor k_1 is basically labour cost and therefore relatively easy to assess. Being costs involved in *ad hoc* repair, cost factor k_2 is assumed to be significantly higher than k_1. The expression for n_0 above therefore supports a recommendation for a maintenance frequency that is optimal with respect to quality and costs. For various reasons, such as lack of internal skills, shortage of spare parts and externally-caused production interrupts beyond management control, this is not always easy to achieve. This situation found in the production environment in many low- and middle-income countries is contrasted with the corresponding situation in many industrialized countries where these and other hindering factors have been eliminated or reduced. This is illustrated in Table 8.3.

In developing enterprise, eight out of ten disruptions (40 per cent + 40 per cent) are unplanned and around half of those are externally-caused, and therefore cannot be considered as internal maintenance problems as they are outside of company control. To reduce the impact of this type of disruption, companies needs to find individual solutions, e.g. certain types of planned maintenance work is pending and can be initiated as soon as external disruptions occur.

Reliability of the production system – lead-times

Lead-time denotes the non-productive time between two activities that belong to the production process. Lead-times are cost drivers and therefore need to be minimized in production process. However, every production system needs to have a certain slack between activities in order not to be too tight. Where too tight, it is inevitable that disturbances will occur.

Fluctuations in lead-times make production planning difficult, sometimes even hazardous. In less-developed countries, besides unreliable machinery, poor transport infrastructure makes lead-times in the materials acquisition system difficult to predict. Modern computer-based planning systems may assist in situations where lead-times can be statistically estimated. However, in many situations lead-times cannot be determined due to genuine uncertainty, and hence cannot be estimated, even with advanced statistical methods.

Reliability of the production system – quality

Total Quality Management (TQM) can be defined as an approach to managing an organization that centres on quality, is based on the participation of all its members and seeks long-term success through continuous customer satisfaction and benefits to members of the organization and society.

Quality is now seen as a critical variable influencing competitiveness and the performance of enterprises. However, in most competitive firms, increased quality is merely one by-product of an approach that stresses continuous improvement in all aspects of the production process. Increased product quality, together with a simultaneous flow of advances in productivity, flexibility and cost performance, occur as a result of dynamic, continuous improvement of the overall organization.

TQM requires management of the process, not just its outputs, and every person within the organization contributes to and operates within such a process. This understanding is fundamental to improving quality and productivity in manufacturing enterprises.

The only partitioning which is ultimately valid is that between the cost of conformance to requirements and the cost of non-conformance. Both are usually capable of improvement. The 'process' may be considered at any level in the organization, e.g. the process may be a particular work stage or it may be the overall process of operating the business. In all cases, there must be facilities to monitor the costs of the process and take action to ensure these costs are minimized.

Failure costs tend to dominate among quality-related costs, followed by costs for inspections and evaluation of quality. The following is a common, but unverified estimate of how costs are distributed for the cost types in the Table 8.4.

The cost factors that dominate in most manufacturing companies are scrap and rework, representing on average between 40 per cent and 50 per cent of quality related costs. (These figures also unverified.)

The multiple components of technical systems require managers to carefully identify those with the greatest potential impact on the organization. Irrespective of product type, the production system always has a high priority, as it is the primary contributor to added value

Table 8.4 Process costs

Type of cost	Cause of cost
Prevention	The costs of any action taken to investigate, prevent or reduce the risk of non-compliance or defects
Appraisal or evaluation	The costs of verifying that quality requirements have been achieved, including the costs of verification and control performed at any stage of the quality loop
Internal failures or anomalies	The costs arising within an organization due to non-compliance or defects at any stage of the quality loop, including the costs of scrap, rework, re-test, re-inspection and redesign
External failures or anomalies	The costs arising after delivery to a customer due to non-compliance or defects, including the costs of claims against warranty, replacement and consequential losses and evaluation of penalties incurred

Source: Author, based on UNIDO reports.

and revenue. Managers in low- and middle-income countries must struggle with uncertain production capacity due to unreliable machinery and other infrastructure constraints. Great fluctuations in lead-times make prediction about future availability of materials difficult.

Managing the human resources

The small business manager can be assumed to have a relatively relaxed relationship with employees even if the relationship between managers and employees is more hierarchical in some cultural contexts. Hofstede (1997) introduced the concept of *power distance* to indicate the extent to which the less powerful members of an organization expect and accept the unequal distribution of power. In countries with a high power distance, subordinates feel dependent on their superiors and are afraid to express disagreement, whereas in low-scoring countries there is less dependence and more of a contractual relationship between subordinates and superiors.

In very small firms with only few employees the relationship is mostly informal and close, whereas in the much larger medium-size firms relations become more formal and the organization structure more hierarchical. With increasing company size, it becomes difficult for a manager to be acquainted with each individual, but if it is not possible for a manager to know each individual, the manger needs to know the capabilities of the human resources in the firm. In a situation where a company needs to reverse a declining trend or when a radical change is necessary for survival, it becomes important to know who among the employees can be mobilized in support and who will not contribute. Hirschman (1970) suggested a typology which groups employees into four categories with respect to two dimensions: degree of creativity and attitude towards the company. This typology is illustrated in Figure 8.6.

The four categories can be described as follows. The *engaged* employee is creative, positive towards the company and its employer and motivated to participate in change processes and contribute his or her best. The *critical* employee can also be described as *devil's advocate*: creative and competent but critical of the state of affairs and dominated by a negative attitude to the firm. The *loyal* employee has perhaps worked in the firm for a long time and,

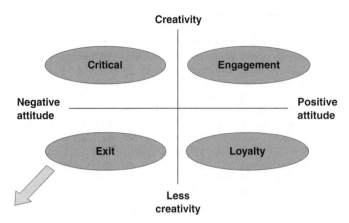

Figure 8.6 Hirschman's typology.

due to age or reduced capacity, has lost creativity and ambition. *Exit* refers to an employee who is uncomfortable in the company for a variety of reasons, making him or her less creative and not positive towards the company. Another environment or company might transform an *exit* person into an *engaged* person.

Based on this typology, a manager should be able to establish a working relation with each employee depending on which of the four categories he or she belongs. This matters in a change process.

Change and the employee – management approach

From the Hirschman typology above it is possible to identify management attitudes towards the four categories of employees in the case of a change process in the company. The two dimensions are basically the same as in the Hirschman model but formulated slightly differently. As Figure 8.7 shows, employees are either less enthusiastic about the change process or enthusiastic and engaged in the process. In addition they are competent and experienced or less experienced.

The manager's attitude towards the employee depends on which of the four categories the employee belongs. A plus sign suggests that this is the attitude the manager should take to ensure employee involvement. The minus sign warns the manager about negative effects: too much control and too little delegation in the case of the competent and experienced employee engaged in the change process; risk of failure and too much involvement in the case of the less enthusiastic and less experienced employee.

Changes in any organization always have the potential to create conflict. Employees may feel left out in the change process or disregarded or neglected by bosses and superiors. Conflicts were previously seen as mainly negative and problematic as they tended to create imbalance in the organizations. However, later views tend to regard conflicts as inevitable occurrences in an organization, having the potential to spur creativity and healthy competition. It is the manager's responsibility to ensure these conflicts do not escalate to the extent that they cease to be creative and become destructive. Figure 8.8 describes what can be seen as the optimal level of conflict in an organization.

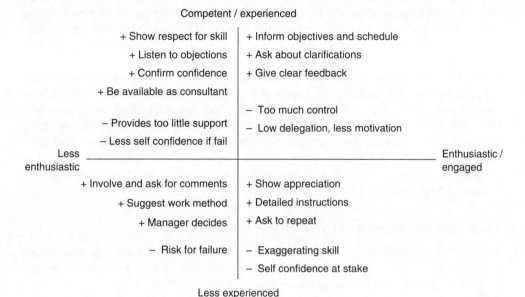

Figure 8.7 Change and the employee – management approach.

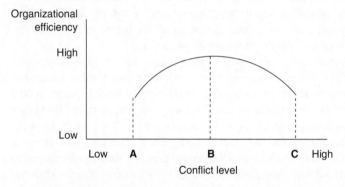

Figure 8.8 Optimal conflict level for organizational efficiency.

A low level of conflict in an organization (A in the figure) may result in a low level of organizational efficiency due to lack of dynamism and initiatives, since there is no internal competition among employees. The result can be stagnation and inability to respond to change. Lack of new ideas may lead to a vicious circle where lack of conflict becomes the status quo and leads to a false sense of security.

At C in the figure, the conflict level is high. The organization is disrupted by groups and individuals being in conflict and unwilling to cooperate. From the organization's perspective the situation may be close to chaotic, as everybody is waiting for a solution. At both levels A and C the conflict is dysfunctional.

Is not possible to specify explicitly where the optimal conflict level B lies. It reflects today's generally-accepted view that a certain level of conflict is more functional, occurring when the working atmosphere supports individual initiatives and innovative thinking. Promoting learning and creativity leads to individual opportunities for career advancement, which in turn can result in competition and increased conflict levels. Managers must continually assess the conflict level to ensure it remains close to optimal and does not escalate out of control.

Conflict as a result of competition between members of an organization is present in all cultures, but the way conflicts are managed may differ depending on the view of how humans interact in groups and between individuals. The discussion above about organizational efficiency and conflict level is based on a Western rational view and assumes a high degree of individualism among employees. In other less individualistic cultures with higher levels of uncertainty and greater power distance, cooperation and competition can have a different significance. Examples include Buddhist management and African management influenced by the spirit of Ubunto.

Competition and cooperation in Buddhist management

Modern management theory is based on the assumption that it is human nature to compete. Buddhism shares this view but stresses the fruitful co-existence between competition and cooperation, and that human beings are capable of striving for both.

> Competition is natural: when they are striving to satisfy the desire for pleasure – when they are motivated by *tanha* (Buddhism for greed as the root of all suffering) – people will compete fiercely. At such times they want to get as much as possible for themselves and feel no sense of sufficiency or satisfaction. If they can obtain the desired object without having to share it with anyone else, so much the better. Inevitably, competition is intense; this is natural for the mind driven by *tanha*.
>
> This competitive instinct can be redirected to induce cooperation. One might unite the members of a particular group by inciting them to compete with another group. For example, corporate managers sometimes rally their employees to work together to beat their competitors. But this cooperation is based entirely on competition. Buddhism would call this 'artificial cooperation'. True cooperation arises with the desire for well-being – with *chanda* (Buddhism for the sincere wish, wholesome desire or zeal – a mental factor that does not involve unwholesome greed). Human development demands that we understand how *tanha* and *chanda* motivate us and that we shift our energies from competition towards cooperative efforts to solve the problems facing the world and to realize a nobler goal.
>
> (Payutto 1994)

Competition and cooperation in the Ubunto perspective

Ubunto is a metaphor that describes the significance of group solidarity on survival issues that is so central to the survival of African communities who, as a result of their poverty and deprivation, have to survive through brotherly group care and not individual self-reliance.

> *Ubuntu* may mark the departure from the current confrontational approach in our industrial relations to a more cooperative and competitive approach of managing survival issues. We are not suggesting a romantic relationship between management and employees. We are suggesting a new way of forming a creative and competitive

dialogue aimed at finding joint solutions. There is no suggestion that conflict will disappear. The collective solidarity of the various groups in the company should be respected and enhanced. The rights of these solidarity groups should be respected. Then the solidarity spirit of Ubunto will have found expressions in the management practices of our companies.

(Mbigi and Maree 1995)

Learning

Closely related to success in the change process is the question of adapting to continuous change in the environment, which requires continuous learning by every member of the organization. This learning implies that every person in every process must have the freedom to observe and to identify changes and have the power to recommend opportunities for improvement. That freedom and power requires that employees have command of all the information from their own processes. This is the key to organizational learning.

Having command of information means that the work process must be observed in such a way that actual performance can be easily measured and that trends in performance can be assessed. To make the information meaningful, the individual employee must be able to associate himself or his group with the observations.

Non-learning organizations learn and change in big steps often initiated by external consultants or from external knowledge. Information generated in this way stays with top management, who plan, decide and then pass down instructions to subordinates and workers. There is no genuine learning in this approach. The consequence is that next time the company needs to adapt to changes in the environment, knowledge must again be brought in from outside, since there is no tradition of making use of knowledge accumulated within the company.

A most important element in continuous learning is an understanding of improvement as a continuous *process of discovery*, not as a series of solutions to overwhelming problems. The latter view implies that things must be fixed once they are broken. The former approach implies a never-ending search for better ways to do the job! In the new business practices, improvements are viewed as opportunities created by a process, designed to increase customer loyalty and to improve the abilities of the employees. One of the methods used to encourage employees to become involved is the reward programme.

Reward programmes

Motivated employees committed to the company's quality and performance standards are of vital importance for continuous improvement. A programme that rewards improvements achieved may contribute considerably to increased motivation. Performance targets should be identified in those areas that are considered important for the company. Such targets may be used to continuously monitor performance in, for example, customer order service and production quality. An example of introducing a reward programme in the company is discussed in the following chapter.

The manager as mentor

Ever since the Hawthorne studies in the 1930s (see Box 8.1), it has been clear that social relations in the workplace are important for the productivity of the firm. With the open system approach that began to influence organization research in the 1960s, it was even more obvious that social relations also include employees' relations within the firm as well as outside in his or her free time. Concepts such as Corporate Social Responsibility have reinforced the awareness that organizations and the surrounding community closely interact.

The concept of *mentorship* has its roots in the Greek mythology, as Odysseus appointed his good friend Mentor as foster parent for his son while Odysseus was travelling at sea.

Mentorship is one of the corner-stones in leadership and in learning organizations. In this context learning is reflecting what one has learned and reflecting on the journey one undertook during the learning process. Reflection about the present situation takes place together with an experienced person, the mentor.

The mentor uses his/her own experience as a lens for critical reflection about his/her own experience and learning from that. The mentor provides support, and provides challenges and visions adapted to the learning ability of the mentoree (the person undergoing mentoring). The mentoree must be active and responsible for his/her own learning. Mentorship is a goal-oriented interaction that is characterized by mutual openness, confidence and familiarity and clear role definitions and mutual expectations are preconditions for good mentorship. It is also important to agree when the mentoring process should finish.

Not all leaders are good mentors. The desire to be a mentor must be there, and the mentor must understand and accept certain important aspects of being a mentor:

- mentoring is not about controlling or taking the lead;
- mentoring is not about manipulating, to 'sell' or to cheat;
- mentoring is not about providing the answers to complicated questions;
- mentoring is not about being decent or good and solving the problem for the mentoree; and
- mentoring is not therapy.

Regarding the last point, mentoring focuses on now and the future, while therapy focuses on then (history) and now. The therapist asks: What are your problems? The mentor asks: How do you intend to reach your goals?

A manager needs to realize that high-performing organizations require high-performing people, and the manager can contribute towards high-performing employees by adopting the mentor role. The mentor role presumes that people have endless resources and capabilities, but they must be mobilized and activated. Furthermore, it is expected that people want to do a good job and to be appreciated, but management attitudes and traditions in many organizations do not live up to such norms. People are social creatures who are geared by their feelings which may be difficult to tackle by managers who have a predominantly rational approach to life. Regardless of all this, dealing with people is one of managers' principal tasks!

Figure 8.8 illustrates the two manager roles – as boss and mentor. As a boss, the manager makes use of resources to achieve the objectives or goals of the firm. The manager's role is here to plan, schedule, execute and evaluate operational activities which requires different resources, for example the human resources. This is the traditional manager role. The additional role of a mentor was not previously identified, but is now considered essential to successful organizations. As a mentor, the manager is assumed to have a dialogue with each employee under the manager's direct supervision. Being aware of the employee's ambitions and wishes, the manager tries to determine if the firm is a resource from which the goals or objectives of the employee can be facilitated. The firm can, for example, invest in language

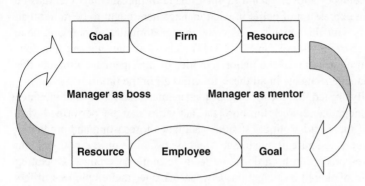

Figure 8.9 The manager's two roles: boss and mentor.

training for the employee that will qualify him or her to negotiate with overseas suppliers or customers. This is a win–win situation both for the firm and the employee.

Box 8.1 Mini-encyclopaedia: the Hawthorne studies

In 1927 the organization researcher Elton Mayo started a five-year research project at the Hawthorne factory of the US company Western Electric. The research objectives were to find out the effects on productivity of factors such as light, fresh air, rest breaks and fatigue. Initially no correlation could be discovered between productivity and these factors.

The first of three phases was conducted in a department assembling electrical components, staffed by female workers who were informed about the project. As the research factors were improved, the researchers observed increased productivity. Surprisingly, productivity was maintained when the factors were reduced to their original levels! The conclusion was that the high importance previously attributed to physical and material working conditions only did not hold.

In the later research phases, this finding confirmed through more detailed research at the Hawthorne factory. A conclusion was that conflicts between managers and employees have their roots in different thinking patterns. On management levels the thinking is predominantly economic and rational, whereas thoughts among workers and employees are dominated by emotional logic.

Conclusion

Ackoff (1979) argued once that managers do not so much spend their time solving problems in a well-ordered world as much as managing a mess. In a similar fashion, Mintzberg noted that:

> If you ask a manager what he does, he will most likely tell you that he plans, organizes, co-ordinates, controls. Then watch what he does. Don't be surprised if you can't relate what you see to those four words.
>
> (Mintzberg (1973)

The view presented in this chapter, that management can be structured into the three activities of strategy, operation and mentorship, seems unrealistically simplified and rational in the light of the two references above. Such a rational image of management can thus be seen as an idealization: an expression of belief in what management ought to be rather than a description of what it is. But this stereotypical view, though formally incomplete, none the less does have a degree of validity (Thomas 1993). The classical management functions do stand out as a meaningful account of the major activities of management, although this does not imply that all managers engage in all these activities all of the time.

It may thus be generally argued that the essence of management centres around the three activities described, although conditions for how the activities can be performed vary between different parts of the world. Political stability facilitates forecasting and prediction about the future and hence also strategic planning, whereas instability in the political and economical systems makes prediction hazardous and leads to more uncertainty. Operating the firm in an atmosphere of shared participation between manager and employees differs from a firm in which responsibility is formal and closely related to the hierarchical level. In an attempt to relate these aspects to a cultural framework, Hofstede (1991) suggests the use of the concepts of *uncertainty avoidance* and *power distance*, and identifies countries where these two 'dimensions' dominate.

Power distance in Hofstede's sense refers to dependence relations between manager and subordinates. In countries with high power distance, subordinates feel dependent on their superiors and are afraid to express disagreement. In low power distance countries, there is less dependence and more of a contractual relationship between subordinates and superiors, resulting in a preference for a consultative rather than autocratic style of leadership. Power distance is thus defined as the extent to which the less powerful members of institutions and organizations within a country expect and accept that power is distributed unequally.

Uncertainty avoidance concerns the extent to which the members of a culture feel threatened by uncertain or unknown features and situations. This feeling is, amongst other things, expressed through nervous stress and in a need for predictability in the shape of written and unwritten rules. In countries with high scores there is a great willingness on the part of employees to remain with a company, reflecting a cautious approach to risk and a high degree of angst in the face of uncertain futures. In low scoring countries there is less anxiety about the future.

The study by Hofstede has been criticized on various grounds such as varying sample sizes from different countries, the meaning of questions exposed to translation difficulties, the quantization of qualitative questions and presentation of scoring lists. Considerable concern has been expressed about the use of IBM as the vehicle for the study. Detailed criticism has been delivered, among others by McSweeney (2002).

Note

1   After William Edwards Deming (1900–1993), an American professor of statistics famous for introducing statistical methods in quality testing in, for example, the Japanese car industry.

References

Ackoff, J. C. (1979) 'The Future of Operational Research is Past'. *Journal of the Operational Research Society*, 30: 2.
Argyris, C. (1977) 'Double-Loop Learning in Organizations'. *Harvard Business Review*, 55: 5.
Blau, P. and Schoenherr, R. (1971) *The Structure of Organisations*. New York: Basic Books.
Cheverton P. (2004) *Key Account Management*. London: Kogan Page.

Ekman, C. and Gronlund, J. (1997) *Collaboration Within Networks: A Multiple Case Study of Companies in the Swedish and Chilean Wood Manufacturing Industry*. Linkoping, Sweden: Linkoping University.

Forker, L. B. and Stannack, P. (2000) 'Cooperation versus Competition: Do Buyers and Suppliers Really See Eye-to-Eye?'. *European Journal of Purchasing and Supply Chain Management*, 6.

Gustavsson, L and Svanfeld, C. (1994) *Smaller Companies' Competence and Technology Support*. Stockholm: NUTEK.

Hadjimanolis A. (1999) 'Innovation Strategies of SMEs in Cyprus, a Small Developing Country'. *International Small Business Journal*, 18(4): 62.

Heracleous, L. (2003) *Strategy and Organization*. Cambridge: Cambridge University Press.

Hirschman, A. O. (1970) *Exit, Voice, and Loyalty: Responses to Decline in Firms, Organizations, and States*. Cambridge, MA: Harvard University Press.

Hofstede, G. (1991) *Culture and Organisations*. London: McGraw-Hill.

Hofstede, G. (1997) *Cultures and Organizations: Software of the Mind*. New York, NY: McGraw-Hill.

Issawi, C. (1982) *An Economic History of the Middle East and North Africa*. London: Methuen & Co.

Jennings, P. and Beaver, G. (1997) 'The Performance and Competitive Advantage of Small Firms: A Management Perspective'. *International Small Business Journal*, 15: 1.

Land, F. (1998) 'Examining the Appropriateness of Information Technology', in Bhatnagar, S. and Odedra-Straub, M. (eds) *Social Implications of Computers in Developing Countries*. New Delhi: Tata McGraw-Hill.

Lind, P. (1988) *On the Applicability of a Computerised Production Control System in an Egyptian Industry*. Stockholm: Royal Institute of Technology.

Lind, P. and Scheepers, M. J. (2009) *Managing Customer–Supplier Relationships in Small Manufacturing Businesses*. Stellenbosch, South Africa: Stellenbosch University.

McSweeney, B. (2002) 'Hofstede's Model of National Cultural Differences and their Consequences: A Triumph of Faith – A Failure of Analysis'. *Human Relations* (Tavistock Institute), 55: 89.

Mbigi, L. and Maree, J. (1995) Ubuntu – *The Spirit of African Transformation Management*. Randburg, South Africa: Knowledge Resources.

Mintzberg, H. (1973) *The Nature of Managerial Work*. New York: Harper & Row.

Osborne, R. (1992) 'Information Power in the Private Company'. *Journal of General Management*, 17: 4.

Paulray, A., Lado, A. A. and Chen, I. J. (2008) 'Inter-Organizational Communication as a Relational Competency: Antecedents and Performance Outcomes in Collaborative Buyer–Supplier Relationships'. *Journal of Operations Management*, 26(2): March.

Payutto, P. A. (1994) *Buddhist Economics – A Middle Way for the Market Place*. Bangkok: Buddhadhamma Foundation.

Pleitner, H. (1989) 'Small firms and the Information Problem'. *European Management Journal*, 7: 4.

Rice, G. H. and Hamilton, R. E. (1979) 'Decision Theory and the Small Businessman'. *American Journal of Small Business*, 4: 1.

Thomas, A. (1993) *Controversies in Management*. London: Routledge.

9 Strategic and operational tools for SME management

Introduction

'The Future belongs to those who can work in an unpredictable environment' and 'Good managers don't make policy decisions' are two quotations that could be read in international management journals a few years ago. They reveal a mistrust of forecasting and concern for the difficulties that may arise if a decision taken now is based on guesswork about what will happen in the future. At the same time, managers have overwhelming desire to find tools for strategic planning. Some of the tools that have been developed are based on sophisticated computer models and information technology. Others are simpler models aimed at strategic thinking and designed as guidance for strategic planning. The simplest tools are found in business journals and other public sources disseminating information, which is interpreted to form the basis for a strategic decision. What all the tools have in common is speculation about the future: how the market will develop, how competition will act and how government rules will change.

The usefulness of tools can only be assessed if the degree of uncertainty can be assessed. Sophisticated tools are based on computer software where statistical models are applied to input data and generate output in the form of statistical information. The more uncertainty in the input data, the more sophisticated the models need to be to generate any usable information. If the variation in input data (standard deviation) is too wide, it may be impossible to determine the mean value of the statistical sample with any confidence, and the uncertainty is referred to as *genuine*. In this case, not even sophisticated statistical models can generate any useful information.

Strategic tools are therefore situation and context dependent. Small firms can seldom afford sophisticated tools for strategic planning, but they may make use of the less sophisticated models discussed below. In environments where political and economic uncertainty runs high, rather that relying on formal tools, small firms should focus less on control to maintain stability, and more on adaptation and creativity.

Tools for the operation of businesses are of a different nature compared to strategic tools, since the present is given much greater weight than the future. Operational tools for assessing performance in the form of indicators are simple to use and require simple input data readily available in most small businesses. Since performance assessment is about summarizing historic data up to the present, the uncertainty characterizing future predictions has less relevance, the exception being early warning analysis.

Strategic tools for SME management

Throughout history man has been obsessed with looking into the future to find out what lies ahead, and early on tools and methods were devised for this purpose. The Delphic Oracle, the Pythia, was widely credited for her prophecies, and was the most prestigious and authoritative oracle in the Greek world.

Forecasting the future is thus a very ancient human activity and is of obvious relevance to managing a business. But evaluations of modern statistical forecasting techniques show them to be no better than 'commonsense' methods. Thomas (1993) even claims that the difference between modern economic forecasters and the shaman predicting and inducing rain may be more in their appearance than their substance. Similarly, long-range strategic planning, which aims to mitigate future uncertainties, is long on analysis and prediction but short on implementation and evaluation. It serves less as a basis for action and decision than as a comforting ritual whereby managers convince themselves and others that they are behaving rationally and that 'everything is under control'.

In his book *Images of Organization*, Morgan (1997) makes a similar comment on forecasting and rational assumptions by referring to an essay by Ely Devons[1] on the use of statistics as a basis for public policy. Devons drew parallels between decision-making processes in formal organizations, and magic and divination in tribal societies. He noted that, although organizational decision-makers would not normally think of examining the entrails of a chicken or of consulting an oracle about the fortunes of the organization or the state of the economy, many uses of statistics have much in common with primitive magic. In primitive societies, magic was used to decide whether hunting should proceed in one direction or another, whether the tribe should go to war, or who should marry whom, giving clear-cut decisions in situations that might otherwise be open to endless wrangling.

Morgan (ibid.) goes to suggest that in formal organizations, the techniques of quantitative analysis seem to perform a similar role. They are used to forecast the future and analyse the consequences of different courses of action in a way that lends decision making a semblance of rationality and substance. The use of such techniques does not, of course, reduce risk. The uncertainties surrounding a situation still exist, hidden in the assumptions underlying the technical analysis, hence Devon's point. The function of such analysis is to increase the credibility of action in situations that would otherwise have to be managed through guesswork and hunch. Like the magician who consults entrails, many organizational decision-makers insist that the facts and figures be examined before a policy decision is made, even though the statistics provide unreliable guides as to what is likely to happen in the future. And, as with the magician, they or their magic is not discredited when events prove them wrong. Just as the magician may attribute failure to imperfect execution or the unanticipated intervention of some hostile force, the technical expert is allowed to blame the model used, or the turn of events, as a means of explaining why forecasts are inaccurate. The analysis is never discredited. The appearance of rationality is preserved.

Modern organizations are sustained by belief systems that emphasize the importance of rationality, and their legitimacy in the public eye usually depends on their ability to demonstrate rationality and objectivity in action. It is for this reason that anthropologists often refer to rationality as the myth of modern society, for, like primitive myth, it provides us with a comprehensive frame of reference, or structure of belief, through which we can negotiate day-to-day experience and help to make it intelligible. The myth of rationality helps us see certain patterns of action as legitimate, credible and normal. It helps us avoid the wrangling and debate that would arise if we were to recognize the basic uncertainty and ambiguity underlying many of our values and the situations with which we have to deal (Morgan 1997).

With the introduction of computers and new forecasting models, a new step was taken in the development of strategic tools for business. The 1970s saw the advent of many knowledge-based systems that fostered the development of applications for business operations and strategic planning. A typical characteristic of knowledge-based management information systems was its focus on the future. The forward-looking systems emphasized the integration of future and current operations that constituted the base for management decisions. This was fundamental not only as a characterization of knowledge-based Management Information Systems (MIS), but it also revealed their weakness: the presumption that the future is predictable!

Kraus (1974)[2] gave three reasons why prediction of even a relatively trivial kind is very complicated and, in practice, impossible:

1   There is never complete knowledge of the present.
2   It is not possible to make error-free deductions from what is known.
3   Our limited imaginations prevent us from asking the right questions about the future.

The three reasons reveal a significant weakness of the forward-focusing MIS. Limited knowledge about the present, due in part to the inability of language to correctly describe complex conditions, means the MIS model may misinterpret reality. Limited fantasy about the future prevents us asking the right questions. For example, what question should an expert be asked about an event that has yet to happen and which may even be unknown?

To make error-free conclusions from what we know is difficult, not only in practice but even in theory. In situations where humans interfere with the socioeconomic system, for example in economics and business, linear systems hardly exist. Mathematics does not provide us with any general tools for solving non-linear problems, and in most cases we can only derive approximate qualitative solutions. Chaos theory has shown that even a simple growth process can turn chaotic. A system exhibiting chaotic dynamics may evolve in a deterministic way, but measurements of the system do not allow the prediction of the state of the system even moderately far into the future. Stock markets exhibit such behaviour.

Knowledge-based MIS arrive at intelligent solutions to queries by developing answers using the rules encoded in the system's knowledge base (Thierau 1987). The knowledge base consists of 'if–then' rules and mathematical rules and formulae. Knowledge is submitted by knowledge engineers, who obtain their data from so-called domain experts. The role of the knowledge engineer is vital to the MIS, and a number of crucial issues can be asked about this role. Are the knowledge engineer and domain expert using terminology in the same way? What is the domain expert's understanding of problems that have yet to be articulated? Does the domain expert always know more about the problem than the user? Can the knowledge engineer always capture the domain expert's knowledge, or are there limitations in the MIS that prevent his or her from doing so? These issues can be summarized as follows:

•   How does the user formulate the problem?
•   How are the cause–effect relations established inside the MIS?
•   What effect do pre-defined models and rules have on the results?

Unpublished Swedish studies reveal that in small and medium Swedish enterprises, knowledge-based business information systems are practically non-existent. This begs the question as to whether SME managers have yet to grasp the capabilities and potential of these systems or whether knowledge-based systems are viewed as irrelevant and at odds with the real needs of managers.

By way of conclusion, we may note that knowledge-based MIS constitute a very strong rationalistic approach. This approach is characteristic of Western rationality and dates back to the early Renaissance views of Francis Bacon and Isaac Newton that, with knowledge about an initial state of affairs and knowing the rules that describe the transition from one stage to another, any future state can be determined. The concept of knowledge-based information systems must therefore be seen as conveying a world-view that has predominated in Western thought for the last 300 years. This view is now being challenged in the wake of a new awareness about the fundamental limitations of technical systems that point to the fact that information processing by humans and machines do not involve the same elementary processes. Not all knowledge can be formalized; not everything that be understood can be expressed in terms of logical relations. Vital facts cannot be abstracted, stored and used independently of their original contexts.

Expressed in practical terms, the following conditions restrict the usability of knowledge-based MIS:

- due to lack of reliable statistics, data about competitors prices and products are not readily available;
- due to financial, political and other factors, markets cannot always be predicted (e.g. inflation);
- due to insufficient or unreliable infrastructure systems, lead-times for acquisition (materials, spare-parts etc.) cannot always be given, even statistically;
- due to insufficient training facilities, the availability of highly-skilled labour is limited; and
- due to cultural traits, such as different time concepts and different organization hierarchies, not all management queries can be foreseen or articulated beforehand.

While knowledge-based MIS are justified on the ground of their broad focus on management information needs, they also highlight the fact that managers need more formal knowledge than can be articulated and stored in a database. Experience, insight and intuition are concepts that are equally important in managerial work. The crucial question is then: How can a computer-based system be designed to assist managers in their daily work, taking into account and utilizing the experience and skill of the individual manager himself? The starting point must be the manager and his competence level, and to build on this. A knowledge-based MIS does not erode the knowledge, experience and skill of individual managers, but rather the knowledge engineer's interpretation of domain experts' knowledge. To some extent, human knowledge may be accumulated in knowledge databases. However, individual experience and skill cannot be captured in general algorithms

MIS make the implicit assumptions that managers are familiar with the use of information as a business asset and with the intrinsic terminology and concepts used by such systems. However, in reality, the very low usage of business analysis applications by managers reveals that they find it difficult to integrate the computer in the strategic and operational activities of their management work. Instead, they relegate computers to simpler processing applications in the administrative domain of their companies (Lind 1995).

Analysis frameworks

Different analysis frameworks have been suggested and developed to identify a firm's position in the market with its current range of products. By comparing different potential alternatives, the manager can make a strategic decision about which alternative to chose, for

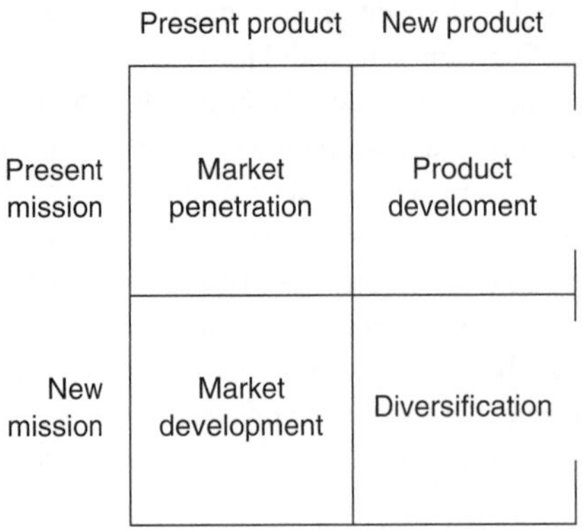

	Present product	New product
Present mission	Market penetration	Product develoment
New mission	Market development	Diversification

Figure 9.1 Ansoff's product/mission matrix.

example, to promote one type of product for a growing market sector. Another type of framework helps the manager analyse different steps in a growth process. Three analysis frameworks are presented below. Ansoff's product/mission matrix and the Boston matrix were developed as marketing models and are presented here as examples of management tools that have been widely used, even if their usage in small firms has been limited.

The Ansoff product/mission matrix[3]

In his book *Corporate Strategy*, Ansoff (1965) presented his Growth Matrix as a tool to assist product and market growth strategy. The assumption was that firms have the ambition to grow in conditions where new or existing products of the firm can be sold in new or existing markets. This product/mission matrix is presented in Figure 9.1.

Market penetration is the strategy whereby a company attempts to grow by improving the position of its existing products and in its existing markets. *Market development* is the strategy of selling the company's current products in a new market. *Product development* involves developing new products for its existing markets, and may involve more effort and higher due to the additional skills and innovation capacity may be required. *Diversification* is the most advanced – and risky – business strategy, namely developing and introducing new products to new markets.

Market penetration includes expansion of market share, promotion of products and services by reinforcing selling and advertising, and by focusing on priority customers. Market development requires knowledge and understanding of customer patterns and behaviour, particularly when the new markets are overseas. Often there is a need for new marketing and sales channels.

The Boston matrix[4]

This analysis framework is described as a growth/share matrix, which means that the market growth for certain product categories is compared with the company's existing market share. As in other strategic discussions, there is uncertainty regarding market development. A wrong assumption about market development for a particular product or product category can result in very misleading strategy decisions based on the Boston matrix.

The Boston matrix identifies business groups (so called Strategic Business Units, SBUs) with respect to their position in the market and how the market develops. A product with a high market share in an expanding market is regarded as a *star* in the Boston matrix terminology, indicating a strong strategic business unit. When the market share is low in spite of an expanding market the SBU is referred to as a *question mark*, which implies that the strategic future is uncertain or undecided for the particular product. For a product with high market share in a non-expanding market it is assumed that development costs have been written off and the revenue from the product has a high profit content. Remaining life cycle time may not be long, but the SBU is described as a *cash cow* as long as the product generates an income. A product with a low market share in a market that is not growing should be considered obsolete in the product mix. The SBU is referred to as a *dog*.

Heracleous (2003) points out that companies that followed these recommendations blindly made important strategic errors. One reason is that it is too simplistic to take important investment decisions based on just two, historically-oriented dimensions. The historical performance of a business or the historical growth patterns of markets are not guaranteed to continue along the same trajectory in future. Second, the relationship between market share and cost savings is not as straightforward as assumed by the growth/share matrix, for example in industries using low-share technologies, such as mini-mills or micro-breweries, and in industries benefiting from computer-assisted manufacturing. Third, even cash cows may require substantial investment to remain competitive, for example, the motor vehicle industry is low-growth and relatively consolidated, but it is also characterized by cut-throat competition. If the leading competitors reduce their investment in new vehicle designs, and product or process innovations in general, they are likely to be quickly overtaken by other more capable competitors.

The Sandcone analysis framework

The Sandcone model was introduced in the 1990s by Ferdows and De Meyer (1990). It suggests that a lasting gain in performance develops only if service attitudes to customers are implemented in a logical sequence, layer-on-layer – hence the analogy of building a sandcone. For stability, the base of the Sandcone must be both wide enough and sound enough to support additional 'layers', i.e. the further business improvements.

The Sandcone model has four layers: quality, dependency or reliability, speed and costs. The foundation is quality. There is enough evidence today that a basic requirement of business is quality in products and services. The model therefore underlines that reducing production or delivery times to customers has limited value unless quality is satisfactory. Even more unsuccessful is any attempt at reducing costs in the company if quality cannot be guaranteed. Service organizations, including hotels and restaurants in industrialized countries with high salary costs, tend to reduce costs by reducing service staff. The consequence of lower customer or guest service is immediately apparent with the Sandcone model.

In summary, they indicated that it is impossible to reduce costs effectively without first considering quality improvements, reliability and speed in that order. Therefore the creation of value requires that quality improvements be made prior to the hunt for speed, reliability or cost reductions. The base of the cone is built with quality. Without the base, the sandcone cannot support the next step of reliability because the interior cone, quality, is missing. By the same token, the development of speed in an organization cannot take place without the supporting cones of quality and reliability, and once speed is has been achieved, the final step of cost reduction is made possible.

Are the models applicable for small businesses?

The three models described above have all been developed with the large firm in mind. The first two in particular have a rational bias by assuming the availability of the necessary skills

```
            High share      Low share

  High         Star      Question mark
  growth

  Low       Cash cow         Dog
  growth
```

Figure 9.2 Boston Consulting Group growth/share matrix.

and funding. In general, this is not the case for smaller firms and even less true for small businesses in low- and middle-income countries where skilled employees are scarce. Knowledge about markets and technological developments is another rational assumption that cannot be taken for granted in all places. Stewart (1978) pointed out that all known techniques are not necessarily available to a particular country and, of the techniques available to a particular country, they are not necessarily in use (e.g. for want of skills or money).

Small firms are close to the local market and have the advantages of being familiar with local consumer behaviour and consumption patterns. In the growing global business environment, local knowledge is a competitive asset that not all small business managers fully capitalize on and hence do not utilize effectively. Since most firms participating in global business have their roots in the Western world, they need to gain an understanding of cultural impact on consumer behaviour in remote markets. Such efforts are costly, take time and are not always successful, as can be gathered from many accounts of international business (see, for example, Hickson and Pugh 1995). Local firms possess this cultural understanding free of charge and can benefit from it. Market penetration and product development strategies of the Ansoff product/mission matrix (Figure 9.1) should be viable strategies for small and medium firms anywhere, so long as the strategy is combined with a focus on added value leading to increased customer value.

The Boston matrix (Figure 9.2) can be used to guide a high-tech firm in a dynamic market in its ambition to upgrade its service or product from a 'question mark' to 'star'. A small firm in a low- or medium-income economy may find it difficult to take this step! The Boston matrix is of little use to the small business manager in markets characterized by low dynamism and shortage of buying power. The Sandcone model on the other hand should be relevant to most firms independent of market potential and cultural context. In spite of this, many small business managers prioritize cost because they believe customers do so. However, several studies show that quality remains the primary competitive factor.

Early warning analysis

By early warning we mean the capacity to recognize that unfavourable or threatening events can seriously jeopardize or even render impossible the current process to achieve a predefined and specific goal. By *early warning analysis* we thus refer to the systematic activity

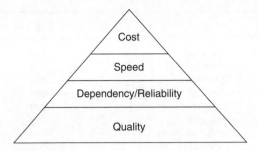

Figure 9.3 The Sandcone model.

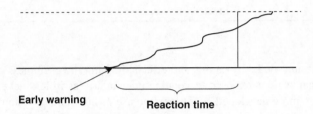

Figure 9.4 Early warning concept.

of identifying beforehand events or situations that would have a negative impact on the organization. Examining early warning signals and designing early warning analysis for business survival and growth is an area that is attracting increasing interest, as a company's ability to *recognise, acknowledge and react* to these signs is key to improved performance and competitiveness.

The crucial idea of an early warning is to have enough time between 'warning' and impending 'disaster' to react to the warning and thereby avert the disaster. The early warning concept can be illustrated as in Figure 9.4.

Intuitively, we can assume that the 'value' of the early warning is somehow related to the length of the reaction time and the importance or seriousness of the disaster. The more serious the potential disaster, the longer the reaction time desirable. In practice, this is not always the case; indeed, quite often the opposite applies. Signals about inadequate customer service are always a serious threat to a firm's business. It should be a top priority issue among managers to identify the most serious real and potential 'disasters' that can happen.

Table 9.1 presents some examples of 'disasters', their origin (external or internal) and whether the time to react is long or short.

Tools that can be developed to pick up signals about future 'disasters' are of course subject to a stipulation that the future is predictable to some degree. This is not always possible since a basic feature of uncertainty is the blurring of cause and effect. Even if one knows that a certain event is going to happen, the range of possible consequences creates uncertainty. If the future is relatively clear, there is basically only one likely future scenario, and hence just one possible outcome. But if the future is likely to be one of several alternatives, statistical methods may be required to determine the most likely scenario.

The success of information systems in coping with uncertainty increases as the future becomes more predictable. Conversely, the greater the uncertainty the more difficult it is to

Table 9.1 Examples of events in early warning analysis

Event	Origin	Reaction time
Unhappy customer	External	Short
New competition	External	Long
Change in government policy	External	Long
Machine breakdown	Internal	Short
Material missing	Internal	Short
Increase in oil price	External	Long
Power cut	External/internal	Short
Increase in administration costs	Internal	Long
Productivity drop	Internal	Long
Quality drop	Internal	Long
Discontented employees	Internal	Long
Wrong strategy	Internal	Long

link the variables of the description model by causes and effects, limiting the usefulness of information technology. In organizations exposed to genuine uncertainty (as in less developed countries, but occasionally more developed countries), the use of information systems is mostly unsuccessful due to the inability to predict future events. In such situations uncertainty can only be dealt with in an *ad hoc* manner, i.e., no particular rules apply and situations have to be dealt with on a case-by-case basis.

Depending on the type of the 'disaster', different types of measures and tools can be used to pick up the early warning signals. These indicators include ratios between actual and expected costs, and ratios between total production and scrapped parts. Such ratios are easily plotted in diagrams which can be extrapolated into the future. Similarly, an organization's cash flow can be monitored to avoid a sudden lack of liquid capital.

Formal information through the media and other channels are sources that can provide useful and important early warning signals, but formal methods are not the only ones used in early warning analysis. Informal methods are also important, for example, experienced managers' intuition, and gossip and small talk between colleagues often contain useful signals that can be further analysed and used to assess important situations.

Early warning tools

Tools that can be used to pick up warnings about future situations and events are:

- indicators for monitoring trends;
- cash flow analysis for the specific monitoring of floating assets; and
- strategy development methods.

From the illustration of the early warning concept above it is obvious that, by monitoring trends, it is possible to extrapolate into the future and predict (with a degree of uncertainty) when an unfavourable situation is expected to occur. Cash flow analysis is one example. However, the use of indicators to measure non-financial trends assumes that results can be measured and that there is sufficient knowledge about operations (production, marketing, etc.). Limited knowledge about operations implies limited knowledge about the resulting effects of an unfavourable event ('disaster'). And if operational goals have not been

Figure 9.5 Categorization of events.

explicitly formulated and used as reference parameters for planning performance, results cannot be adequately measured because of lack of reference values (goals). Common planning tools such as work scheduling, maintenance schemes and budgeting all require that operational goals have been articulated and specified. Figure 9.5 summarizes the discussion thus far.

Probably one of the most important early warning methods is direct communication with clients, suppliers and other crucial stakeholders. Staying in touch with customers is a quick and effective method to determine what is happening in the marketplace, especially if the internal control systems do not provide that communications channel. Changes in customer buying habits are key indicators that something is wrong. Whatever that *something* is, it will be reflected in future profits when it may be too late for corrective action! Nobody wants to hear negative criticism or how good the competition is; but taking customers to lunch, visiting their places of business, undertaking plant tours, trying to understand their business and concerns and staying plugged into their thoughts and perceptions provide the most important early warning information. It is important to ask the hard questions; it is even more important to *listen* is to the answers! Too often salesmen and business owners spend time with the customers they are comfortable with: those who only have good things to say about the company. This situation needs to be reversed: every manager should force him- or herself to find out why people are not buying their products or services. This is the most valuable information!

Operational tools for SME management

While strategic tools assist the manager in strategic thinking and formulating strategic plans, operational tools assist the manager to deal with problems in real time. Measuring and comparing is the same as managing operational performance to meet expectations, such as controlling costs within budget frames or maintaining customer service at high levels.

To assess the operational performance of the enterprise, one needs to measure those output parameters that give the most complete picture of the enterprise from a performance point of view. Such parameters typically include production, finance and customer–market relations.

Performance measurement can take different forms, and different types of parameters may be involved in the measurement. Furthermore, the parameters may be measured in different ways, such as actual value, trend and accumulated value. Basically, the methodology behind combining parameters into simple measures comes from industrial process theory, where the flow of continuous processes (gas, oil, water) need to be continuously monitored and kept under control in, for example, a chemical plant. In principle, there are three kinds of monitoring, the first being where actual value (e.g., volume flowing through a pipe) is measured at a given time; the second is change per unit time (e.g., increase or decrease of fluid flowing through a pipe), and the third is the total volume per time period (e.g. the amount of that fluid flowing through a pipe in a given period). The use of numbers ('indicators') to measure performance has a long tradition in accounting (e.g., liquidity and solidity) whereas their use as control parameters like in industrial situations is more recent.

Performance indicators

Indicators with an industrial background were initially derived from mathematical theory and referred to as proportional, derivative and integrated (P, D, I) types.

P-type indicators often take the form of ratios for which the reference value can be a number. P-type indicators are typically formulated as

$$(all - some)/all$$

which should be as close to unity as possible. An example is production efficiency where *all* is total production and *some* is the number with defects. Another P-type indicator takes the form

$$actual/estimated$$

which may be greater or less than one, depending on the situation. An example is actual revenue compared to forecasted revenue (which should preferably be greater than one). A further P-type indicator takes the form

$$actualX/actualY$$

which again may be greater or less than one. An example is total enterprise performance, where *actualX* is sales and *actualY* is cost, a ratio which should always be greater than one.

For these indicators it may also be of interest to monitor their trend (D-type indicators) to assess how performance is developing for the enterprise. This comparison is often more useful than comparing one and the same parameter with another enterprise since the underlying conditions in different enterprises can often be very different. Financial reporting is mostly of the integrated I-type, for example, accumulated sales. The parameter is here integrated with time; as such, time is required for the data to gain sufficient significant to be used as the basis for follow-up activity.

Indicator example: Customer Service Index

The following indicator measures one aspect of the customer relationship, namely service-ability. The Customer Service Index (CSX) indicator measures the ratio between good and

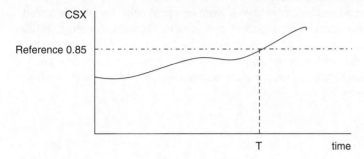

Figure 9.6 Customer service indicator CSX.

bad shipments in a period and is thus of the P-type. The indicator is constructed in the following way:

$$CSX = (s_t - s_d)/s_t$$

where s_t is the total number of shipments and s_d is the number of shipments with defects.

CSX is based on the idea that customers expect orders to be delivered on time, in the right quantity and according to specification; any that do not are regarded as defective. It is the number of shipments rather than their value that is of interest. The total shipments number in a period (e.g., a month) is counted, and the number of defective shipments recorded. The resulting value of CSX can never be less than zero (the number of defective shipments can never be greater than total number of shipments!) and should ideally be as close to 1.0 as possible, a figure of 1.0 being the ultimate goal for good customer service. CSX may vary with time, as shown in Figure 9.6.

The reference value in the diagram is set as a quality goal, for example, a value of 0.85 means that at least 85 per cent of all shipments in the time period should not count as defective. In the diagram this first happens at point T. Now the service level should be further improved, by raising the reference value to 0.88, then 0.90, etc. The ultimate goal is, of course, 1.0.

This indicator serves both as a quality measure and an incentive tool: the employees responsible for shipments may receive a reward when the CSX value reaches the reference line!

It can be argued that the CSX indicator is too simple a tool to be used as a proper service quality measure. On the contrary: most SMEs do not use any structured methods to follow up on shipment quality, yet it is one of the most important aspects of responding to customer needs. In fact, most SMEs do not even know if they have a good or a bad record when it comes to customer shipments! Starting to record shipments is a very important first step towards better customer service.

The Customer Service Indicator is one of a family of indicators with similar function. For example, the Production Quality Index (PQX) compares the number of defective produced parts against total production; it constructed in the same way as the CSX.

Diagnosing the firm

Making a diagnosis of an organization means that certain parameters are selected for observation or analysis to draw certain conclusions about its status. Quite often, however, we do not have the proper measuring instruments, nor do we always know what exactly to mea-sure. Studying symptoms and reaching conclusions from observed behaviour can be a work-ing method to indicate what needs to be done for improvement. Formal accounting routines provide measuring tools which are used for diagnosing the financial condition of the firm. Other aspects, such as social working conditions or customer relations, require different and complementary instruments. This implies the organization must be seen in its environment and its context, as defined by its:

- customers and clients;
- products and services;
- employees;
- management style;
- history; and
- readiness to change and adapt to a changing environment.

All these aspects are necessary considerations for diagnosing an organization. Together they provide an impression of the organization based on its internal culture, the managers' vision for the company, and the customers and client's impressions. Identifying how these three aspects are aligned is an important basis for diagnosis.

Aligning the essential organization elements

The three organization elements are:

Vision:	Top management's aspirations for the company/organization.
Culture:	The organization's values, behaviour, history and attitudes, i.e. the way the employees at all levels feel about the company they are working for.
Image:	The outside world's overall impression of the company. This includes stakeholders (customers, shareholders/owners), the media, the general public and so on.

Misalignment of these elements will give rise to a number of gaps: the *vision–culture gap*, the *image–culture gap* and the *image–vision gap*. Each of these gaps will have a nega-tive impact on the performance of the organization.

The vision–culture gap

This misalignment develops when management moves the organization in a strategic direc-tion that employees don't understand or support. The gap usually emerges when manage-ment establishes a vision that is too ambitious for the organization to implement. The main symptom is a breach between rhetoric and reality. Disappointed managers often blame employees for resisting change; frustrated employees react with suspicion. Such scapegoat-ing is extremely dangerous for companies. To uncover possible gaps between vision and culture, managers should ask the following questions of themselves and their employees:

- Does the company practice the values it promotes?
- Does the company's vision inspire all its subcultures?
- Is the vision and culture of the company sufficiently different from those of its competitors?

The image–culture gap

Misalignment between a company's image and organizational culture leads to confusion among customers and clients about what the company stands for. This usually means that the company does not practice what it preaches. To identify image–culture gaps, the company needs to compare what the employees are saying with what the customers and clients as well as other stakeholders are saying:

- What images do stakeholders associate with the company?
- In what ways do employees and stakeholders interact?
- Do the employees care what stakeholders think of the company?

The image–vision gap

The third misalignment is the conflict between outsiders' images and management's strategic visions. Companies cannot afford to ignore their stakeholders: indeed, the most carefully-crafted strategic visions will fail if they are not aligned with what customers want from the company. Having sounded out employees and stakeholders, managers need to find out whether they are out of sync themselves:

- Who are the company's stakeholders?
- What do the stakeholders want from the company?
- Is the company effectively communicating its vision to the stakeholders?

The 'effective organization'

From these different perspectives one can ask what is meant by an 'effective organization'. The question requires that the perspective is clear: in assessing the first, the owners' criteria may differ from those of the employees. The following list gives some alternatives perspectives for judgement:

- Shareholders are happy with the financial return of their investments.
- The owner-entrepreneur is happy, as he/she sees the company flourish.
- Customers are happy because they receive high quality products and services.
- Employees are happy because the company provides security, status, career opportunities, good salaries, etc.
- Governments are happy because the company is a good tax payer.
- Managers are happy because results are better than expected.
- Researchers are happy because the company/organization is a good example/reference.
- Consultants are happy because the company responds positively to their analysis and improvement programmes.

So the question of effectiveness depends partly on the perspective we take. As customers we tend to appreciate good product quality and good customer service and the customer talks about the supplier as 'an effective organization'. On the other hand, employees may measure the organization's effectiveness by its administrative efficiency, the competence of managers, attitudes to career planning, etc. Quite often, the items above are mixed, and there are even more items to be added to the list!

Academics and practitioners alike have tried to come up with criteria that define *organizational effectiveness*. The list gets longer and longer for every year, although it seems that the following shortlist encompasses what most people agree on.

Effective companies:

- have a bias for action and getting things done;
- stay close to their customers and clients in order to fully understand their customers' needs ('Customer's Customer Concept');
- allow employees a high degree of autonomy and foster entrepreneurial spirit;
- seek to increase productivity through employee participation;
- stay close to the business the employees understand and know;
- have organization structures that are simple, with a minimal number of people in staff support activities;
- tend to blend tight centralized control for protecting core values with loose control in other areas to encourage risk-taking and innovation; and
- make employees know what the company stands for.

Traditional methods of setting business targets (e.g., Standard Cost Analysis) have failed many companies and blindsided their managers to competition. Only the approach of establishing operating targets and productivity programmes based on industry best practices leads to superior and competitive performance. The process being increasingly used for this purpose is called 'benchmarking'.

Benchmarking

Two ancient oriental truths convincingly illustrate the essence of benchmarking. In the year 500 BC, the Chinese general Sun Tzu wrote, 'If you know your enemy and know yourself, you need not fear the result of a hundred battles'. Solving ordinary business problems, conducting management battles and surviving in the marketplace are all forms of war, fought by the same rules – the Sun Tzu rules! The other truth is a simple Japanese word, *dantotsu*, meaning striving to 'be the best of the best'. This is the very essence of benchmarking!

Benchmarking is a positive, proactive process to change operations in a structured fashion to achieve superior performance. The benefits of using benchmarking are that firms are forced to investigate external industry best practices and incorporate those practices into their operations. This leads to profitable businesses that meet customer needs and have a competitive advantage.

Thus, the four steps of the benchmarking process are:

1   Know your operation by assessing internal weakness and strengths. Your competitors will know your weaknesses. By knowing your strengths, you can defend yourself.
2   Know the business leaders and competitors so you can differentiate your capabilities in the marketplace.
3   Incorporate the best. Learn from business leaders and competitors. Why are they the best in their competitive areas?
4   Gain superiority by investigating, understanding and implementing best practice.

Each step in the benchmarking process can be quite comprehensive, requiring the contribution of both time and effort. In the first step the SWOT method can be a useful tool to further

Table 9.2 Part of questionnaire

A. My Manager's ability to foster individual development	Very satisfied (a)	Satisfied (b)	Indifferent (c)	Unsatisfied (d)	Very unsatisfied (e)
Assists me in preparing myself for future responsibilities					
Assists me in competence development in my present job					
Ensures I get proper training for my present job					
Is attentive to my carer plans					
Helps me to improve job performance					
Encourages the planning for my future career					

improve knowledge about the strong and weak parts of the organization, for example the way it is organized, in the way it operates in the market and in the way it manages its resources. *Strengths* and *weaknesses* may be modified, and it is an important part of a manager's job to reinforce the strengths and to diminish the weaknesses. Too often, however, not all the critical strengths and weaknesses applying to an organization have been properly identified.

Internal factors are important for achieving operational goals, but they are not unique in terms of influence and, while internal factors can be influenced by the organization itself, this is normally not the case for *external factors* that originate outside of the organization. External factors may be referred to as *opportunities* and *threats* in that they may create both opportunities as well as threaten the organization and its prospects of reaching its operational goals.

Taken together, strengths and opportunities constitute *driving forces* in the sense that they facilitate achieving operational goals. Threats and weaknesses are *hindering forces*, making it more difficult to achieve operational goals. In a collective context, driving and hindering forces are the critical success factors of the organization. Identifying these factors and responding to them proactively is therefore a high priority management task.

In the following section two more diagnosis methods are presented. The first method can be used by employees to assess their manager with regard to aspects that are considered important in management: employee relations. The second method is an instrument to analyse costs and identify those cost types that contribute to the creation of value.

Diagnosis: assessing management capability

The method is based on a questionnaire divided into ten sections, each of which relates to a crucial quality of management behaviour. The ten qualities refer to abilities such as individual development, motivating others, delegation, planning and communication. For each of these qualities, a number of specific questions are raised that reflect managers' attitudes and behaviour as well as general management capability. The employees are asked to use a five-point Lickert scale[5] when responding to the questions, choosing between 'very satisfied', 'satisfied', 'indifferent', 'unsatisfied' and 'very unsatisfied'. For example, Section A *My manager's ability to foster individual development* is shown in Table 9.2 above.

The other nine sections are listed over page. The same five-point scale is used throughout.

B My manager's ability to motivate others

1	Creates an inspiring working climate
2	Encourages and inspires in tough job situations
3	Is a good example himself
4	Stresses the importance of achieving work goals
5	Gives continuous feedback

C My manager's ability to show appreciation

1	Is honest in work evaluation
2	Pays attention to work achievements
3	Pays attention to good work performance
4	Is prepared to discuss achievements
5	Pays attention to initiatives and creativity

D My manager's ability to show empathy and compassion

1	Displays an interest in and devotion to others
2	Is keen to regard issues also from others' points of view
3	Is trustful and shows confidence
4	Is supportive and backs up
5	Is interested in others' ideas and views

E My manager's ability to communicate and create contact

1	Informs and explains views and rules of the company/organization
2	Is keen to present the background to decisions
3	Is generous with his/her personal time
4	Explains the reasons and background for actions
5	Creates opportunities for talk
6	Informs those concerned

F My manager's ability to make decisions

1	Is good at analysing problems
2	Weighs the consequences of decisions
3	Has a sound judgement in decision making
4	Makes good decisions in pressing situations
5	Takes responsibility for their personal decisions
6	Makes decisions without unnecessary delays

G My manger's planning ability

1	Plans the work in advance
2	Presents clear goals when issuing plans
3	Sets proper goals for the unit
4	Locates competent personnel for the unit
5	Discusses individual goals for personnel in the unit

H My manager's ability to organize and control

1	Is well informed about work in the unit
2	Is good at organizing work
3	Encourages and creates group work
4	Efficient in conducting meetings
5	A fair distribution of job tasks
6	Monitors work achievements
7	Concerned about poor performance

I My manager's ability to delegate

1	Delegates responsibility
2	Gives a free hand in making my own decisions
3	Delegates authority for making decisions and carry out tasks
4	Delegates authority to decide how to carry out tasks

**J My manager's ability to facilitate
  work for others**

1	Assists in finding necessary resources to do the job
2	Assists in removing obstacles to do the job
3	Is supportive in resolving work problems
4	Makes use of employee competence and experience to assist in problem situations
5	Assists in explaining the company's/organization's policies

The procedure is now as follows: each employee to be interviewed receives the questionnaire and is asked to give their answers to the questions raised. When all questionnaires have been completed, the accumulated scores are calculated and entered a table like Table 9.3.

The five responses in the questionnaire in Figure 9.2 are referred to by the letters a, b, c, d and e. By adding the first two columns ($a + b$) and dividing this sum by the total score of the quality, i.e. ($a + b + c + d + e$) the method gives the final score for each quality. The scores thus arrived at give a picture of how the manager is assessed by the employees. This is the final result of the method.

An Excel spreadsheet can be used to illustrate the result in the form of a radar-type diagram. Table 9.3 shows the strengths and weaknesses in the manager's profile as assessed by the employees. The manager in the example gets high scores in individual development, in appreciation, in empathy/compassion, facilitating work. Entering the results into a spreadsheet gives an easily-interpreted picture of the assessment exercise.

Solidarity – feeling related to and in harmony with colleagues in the same organization – is considered a token of a good work environment and a prerequisite for achieving goals of performance for the individual employee as well as for the organization. A good feeling of belonging to the organization and to colleagues may arise if the employee can reach his or her personal goals at the same time as the organization is achieving its business objectives. This puts a demand on managers to balance the two professional roles: focus on the employee and focus on the organizational needs. Letting employees assess the manager in his or her managerial roles as discussed above creates opportunities for the manager to gain a better personal understanding of themselves and their ability to improve organizational quality.

Continuous quality improvement in the organization presupposes a mutual feeling of belonging between employee and organization. The employee's ambition and ability to be

Table 9.3 Calculation of scores

Quality	Score = $(a+b)/(a+b+c+d+e)$
A. Individual development	0.64
B. Motivating others	0.47
C. Appreciation	0.80
D. Empathy, compassion	0.77
E. Communication	0.22
F. Decision-making	0.28
G. Planning	0.43
H. Organizing	0.31
I. Delegation	0.46
J. Facilitating work	0.80

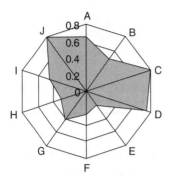

Figure 9.7 Results of a management assessment exercise.

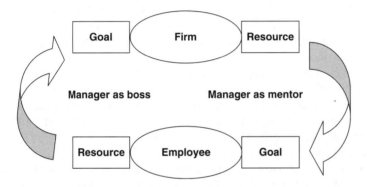

Figure 9.8 The two manager roles: boss and mentor.

an important resource in the organization is reinforced if the organization supports the individual employee in his or her professional and personal development. This is the background to the concept of mentoring discussed in Chapter 8. (See Figure 9.8.)

Each one of the ten management qualities A through J can be attributed to the two roles of boss and manager and also to the two aspects of resource and goal. The allocation is suggested in Figure 9.9.

	Goal	Resource
Mentor	A, D	G, H, J
Boss	B, C, F	E, I

Figure 9.9 The ten management qualities in the boss/mentor perspective.

Diagnosis: analysing costs

Costs in a firm are generally presented in accordance with accounting principles. These principles, and the structure used to monitor the financial situation in a firm, are not necessarily the best to characterize the different types of costs, especially when it comes to distinguishing 'good', 'bad' and 'necessary' costs. Porter (1985) emphasized the importance of adding value in the different production steps towards the end product. Costs related to different activities in the firm may therefore be classified with respect to how much value the activity contributes to the end product. The method presented here is a measure of *cost effectiveness* in a firm.

A method to analyse costs

The costs are classified into four classes depending on their contribution to added value. The four classes are:

Class 1:	Contribute directly to the creation of added value
Class 2:	Contribute indirectly (but definitely) to the creation of added value
Class 3:	Contribute partly to the creation of added value
Class 4:	Do not contribute to the creation of added value

Contribution to added value can be immediate or delayed. Each of the four classes above is therefore divided into two subclasses: one with short-term effect (less than a year) and one with a more long-term effect (more than a year). In this way, the short-term perspective on costs is highlighted in the increase of added value. For each class and subclass, the different types of costs are summarized and each sum is multiplied by a weighting factor. Table 9.4 demonstrates how.

Comparing the sum of the weighted short- and long-term costs in the four classes ($P = A + B + C + D$) with the sum of costs without weighting factors (denoted S) we can define the indicator $I = P/S$, which measures how effective the costs are in contributing to creating added value.

Here are some examples of costs in the different classes and subclasses:

Class 1 (direct contribution)	
Primary material	(short term)
Transport of materials	(short term)
Production salaries	(short term)
Machinery and spare parts	(long term)
Class 2 (indirect contribution)	
Some administrative fixed costs	(short term)
Some administrative fixed costs	(long term)
Research and development	(long term)
Management salaries	(long term)
Class 3 (partial contribution)	
Some administrative fixed costs	(long term)
Finance	(long term)
Class 4 (no contribution)	
Production scrap and re-work	(short and long term)
Customer complaints	(short and long term)

Table 9.4 Cost classes

Class	Weights		Result
	Short term	Long term	
1	× 1.0	× 0.8	A
2	× 0.7	× 0.5	B
3	× 0.4	× 0.2	C
4	× 0.0	× 0.0	D

Table 9.5 Cost types

Class	Short term	Long term
1	Primary material Transport Quality control Sales costs Production salaries	Machinery and spare parts
2	Advertising Administration (40%) Administration salaries (50%) Energy (60%)	Administration (30%) Research and development Maintenance Management salaries
3	Administration (30%) Administration salaries (50%)	General costs Energy (20%)
4	Certain financial costs Energy (20%)	

Table 9.6 Unweighted and weighted costs

Class	Un-weighted sum (000s)			Weighted sum (000s)		
	Short term	Long term	Total	Short term	Long term	Total
1	3,227	160	3,387	3,227	128	3,355
2	567	599	1,166	397	300	697
3	199	80	279	80	16	96
4			320	0	0	0
Totals			S = 5,152			P = 4,148

The classification of costs into the four classes and respective subclass can be done with the help of the cost accounting system, and an example cost distribution is presented in Table 9.5.

We can now summarize the total costs for the different cost types and assign the weighting factors. Table 9.6 shows the results.

Having calculated the sum of weighted costs P and the sum of unweighted costs S, in this example, the cost effectiveness of the firm is:

$$I = P/S = 4,148/5,152 = 0.81$$

The interpretation of this is that 81 per cent of costs contribute directly or indirectly to adding value to the input material. But the implication of this is that there is also a potential for reducing costs 19 per cent without negatively impacting added value creation.

After the diagnosis exercise has been performed and results collected, the next step should be to evaluate the results and to embark on an improvement programme. Several methods have been developed and suggested to assist company management in implementing such programmes. Two are considered below.

The Balanced Scorecard method

The Balanced Scorecard is probably the best known implementation method. Developed in the 1990s, it starts from a set of performance indicators focusing on customer service, internal-business processes and growth, the firm's ability to learn and financial performance. Results from measuring and analysing the indicators are used to set the organization's strategic goals. However, the complexity of the method and the time and effort required to implement it suggests that the method is less attractive to small firms. An alternative is the Goal Matrix method.

The Goal Matrix method

After having identified the improvements required (for example, better delivery service to customers or reduced scrap rates in production), a goal matrix is created where all improvement goals are specified. The goals identified should be limited in number, typically between three and five. Goals might include:

- increasing the number of customers;
- improving service and product quality;
- improving delivery times;
- reducing production scrap rates;
- increasing revenue from sales;
- improving production throughput by reducing lead times;
- reducing energy consumption; and
- improving compliance with environmental regulations.

Since some goals are likely to be more important than others, their relative importance is indicated by assigning a weight to each. The most important goal gets the highest weight; the second-most important gets the second highest weight, and so on. The total sum of the weights is 1.0.

Having identified the goals and assigned weights, an initial matrix is constructed with three alternative achievement levels for each goal, these levels being ultimate goal, present status and minimum acceptable (or 'floor'). It can be assumed there is some linkage between some or all of the goals and their achievement.

Suppose the following four goals were selected:

1   improve delivery to 100 per cent;
2   increase sales of product 'A' to 115 (perhaps determined by production capacity);
3   reduce scrappage by 100 per cent (which corresponds to no scrap at all); and
4   increase monthly revenue to 20,000 (perhaps based on historic achievements and realistic assessments).

Table 9.7 Initial goal matrix

Level	Deliveries	Product 'A' sales	Scrap	Revenue
Ultimate goal	100%	115	100%	20,000
Present status	65%	67	80%	10,000
Floor	50%	35	70%	3,000

Establishing these goals may be challenging, but it should be possible to determine them within a reasonable time frame. The three levels for the four goals are entered into the initial matrix as shown in Table 9.7.

The next step in the method is to construct the main goal matrix, which comprises 11 levels of achievement. The achievement levels used in the initial matrix map to the levels of the main matrix as follows:

- Ultimate goal = level 10.
- Present status = level 3.
- Floor = level 0.

As with the initial matrix, the columns of the main matrix are the goals selected. The rows of this matrix are as follows:

- Row 1 – Initially blank, for the actual performance figures (the *period achievements*) when they are known.
- Rows 2 to 12 – The 11 achievement levels. Levels 10, 3 and 0 are copied from the initial matrix. The other levels are filled in by interpolation – it is not necessary that each increment is exactly equal.
- Row 13 – For the number of the level (0 to 10) achieved for that goal during the period.
- Row 14 – The goal weighting factors.
- Row 15 – For the products of the numbers in the previous two rows.
- Row 16 – For the sum of the numbers in the previous row (the *goal matrix sum*). This is always in the range 0 to 10.

Table 9.8 shows a completed goal matrix. In the period considered, deliveries were 80 per cent, sales of product 'A' were 73 units, scrap was 80 per cent (no improvement) and revenue was 12,800. Bold is used to highlight the data entered and calculated for this period; the levels matching the results are boxed.

The benefit of the goal matrix as an instrument for monitoring and measuring improvements lies in the way it allows incremental improvements to be observed over short periods. Figure 9.11 shows how achievements towards the four goals in the example might change over four months. Such charts may be used as the basis for reward programmes.

A reward system based on the goal matrix

Motivated employees committed to the company's quality and performance standards are of vital importance for continuous improvement. A reward programme that acknowledges improvements achieved may contribute considerably to increasing this motivation. Performance targets are selected on the basis of their importance to the company.

Table 9.8 The complete goal matrix

Parameter		Deliveries	Product 'A' Sales	Scrap	Revenue
This period		80	73	80	12,800
Levels	10 (Ultimate)	100	115	100	20,000
	9	95	109	98	19,000
	8	90	102	95	17,500
	7	85	95	92	16,000
	6	80	88	89	14,500
	5	75	81	86	13,000
	4	70	74	83	11,500
	3 (Present)	65	67	80	10,000
	2	60	55	76	8,000
	1	55	44	73	5,500
	0 (Floor)	50	35	70	3,000
Level achieved		6	4	3	5
Weights		0.3	0.2	0.2	0.3
Values		1.8	0.8	0.6	1.5
Total value		4.7	–	–	–

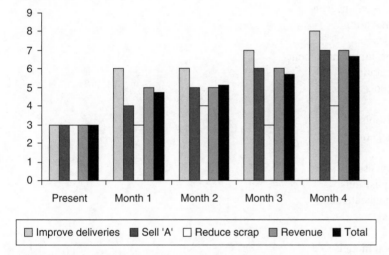

Figure 9.10 The goal results for the first four months.

Table 9.9 Reward system

Total value	Reward
0.0–3.0	0%
3.1–3.5	2%
3.6–4.0	5%
4.1–5.0	7%
5.1–6.0	9%
6.1–7.0	10%
7.1–8.0	12%
8.1–9.0	14%
9.1–9.4	16%
9.5–9.9	18%
10.0	20%

The relevance of the goal matrix should be clear: it enables a system to be formulated that rewards employees involved in and responsible for progress towards the goals in the matrix. The reward might be based on goal matrix sum. Table 9.8 gives an example.

Incentive reward systems such as this are common in firms around the world.

Reward systems should be adjusted to individual firms and to the specific goals of the firm. Furthermore, it is important to make goals achievable, so employees accept them and become motivated by the reward system. A badly-designed reward system (e.g. one based on impossible goals) can be counter-productive, as it can make employees feel stressed or manipulated by the system.

Conclusion

The range of management tools is comprehensive and includes a variety of methods and models, some of which are listed below:

- Balanced Scorecard
- benchmarking
- business process reengineering
- collaborative innovation
- core competencies
- customer relationship management
- customer segmentation
- decision rights tools
- downsizing
- growth strategy tools
- knowledge management
- lean six sigma
- loyalty management
- mergers and acquisitions
- mission and vision statements
- online communities
- outsourcing
- price optimization models
- scenario and contingency planning
- shared service centres
- strategic alliances
- strategic planning
- supply chain management
- Total Quality Management
- voice of the customer innovation.

For SMEs some of these tools are either too complex (for example the Balanced Scorecard) or not suitable due to limited financial resources, information or skills (for example Mergers and Acquisitions). Others, such as Strategic Alliances and Core Competencies, may be applicable to smaller firms.

Notes

1 Ely Devons (1913–1967) was an English economist.
2 Eric Kraus (1912–2003) was Professor of Meteorology and Oceanography at Miami University.
3 Igor Ansoff (1918–2002) was a Russian-American applied mathematician and business manager, who became known as the 'Father of Strategic Management'.
4 Named after the Boston Consulting Group founded in 1963.
5 A way of generating quantitative responses to qualitative questions.

References

Ansoff, H. (1965) *Corporate Strategy*. New York: McGraw-Hill.
Ferdows, K. and De Meyer, A. (1990) 'Lasting Improvements in Manufacturing Performance: In Search of a New Theory', *Journal of Operations Management*, 9: 2, pp. 168–184.
Heracleous, L. (2003) *Strategy and Organisation*. Cambridge: Cambridge University Press.
Hickson, D. and Pugh, D. (1995) *Management Worldwide: The Impact of Societal Culture on Organisations Around the Globe*. London: Penguin.
Lind, P. (1995) 'Good Use and Misuse of Analysis Applications for Decision Support in Enterprises', in Odedra-Staub, M. (ed.) *Global Information Technology and Socio-Economic Development*. Marietta, GA: Ivy-League Publishing.
Kraus, E. (1974) 'The Unpredictable Environment'. *New Scientist*, 63.
Morgan, G. (1997) *Images of Organization*. London: Sage.
Porter, M. (1985) *Competitive Advantage: Creating and Sustaining Superior Performance*. New York: Free Press.
Stewart, F. (1978) *Technology and Underdevelopment*. London: Macmillan.
Thierau, R. (1987) *Effective Management Information Systems*. Columbus, OH: Merrill Publishers.
Thomas, A. (1993) *Controversies in Management*. London: Routledge.

10 Networking and other forms of SME collaboration

Introduction

In Chapter 8, a comparison was made between sources of influence over small business managers in the wood manufacturing industry in Chile and Sweden. The comparison suggested that the Chilean managers tend to have a less dense contact structure whereas the corresponding managers in the Swedish firms had more variety and closeness in their networks. The difference may be attributed to a variety of factors ranging from sheer chance to culture. A high score of uncertainty avoidance for Chile and other Latin American countries, which Hofstede defined as the extent to which the members of a culture feel threatened by unknown or uncertain situations, may reduce the degree of trust between business actors.

Trust has been identified as a vital component which enhances business performance and makes partnerships, strategic alliances and networks of small firms successful (Smitka 1991). The competitive advantage derived from consistently high quality in products and service is important for business success, and Sako (1992) found that achieving competitiveness is easier in a high-trust production system than in a low-trust one. According to Fukuyama (1995), people's capacity to institutionalize trust in the realm of work and business accounts for the industrial success of countries like Japan and Germany. By contrast, the 'missing middle' – the absence of intermediate social groups linking the family with large, centralised organizations like the church or the state – accounts for the relative economic backwardness of Latin Catholic countries. In Fukuyama's view the link between trust and business performance is plausible but not proven. Nevertheless, the idea is so appealing that an increasing number of studies exhort business to create trust as an essential component in making partnerships between firms successful (Sako 1997).

Networking, specifically the contribution of personal contact networks to small business success, has been increasingly emphasized by researchers. Networks provide managers with access to complementary experiences and expertise of other business managers which contributes to additional business knowledge. Szarka (1990) claims that these networks are not restricted by organizational boundaries but rather emerge out of the many interactions that each owner-manager has with other people. The limited nature of any network is a function of quality and productivity: of the network resources and the capability of the manager to use, manage and develop the network. It is this proactive and directed networking capability, and the uniqueness of the relationships developed, that helps differentiate a small firm from its competitors, thus creating potential for competitive advantage. While networking is viewed as an important requirement in enterprises of all sizes, the learning opportunities are argued to be of particular importance to smaller firms.

Networking is the simplest and most common way of inter-organizational collaboration. When firms decide to collaborate on the basis of mutually-agreed strategic considerations, like joint product development or joint marketing, it is more appropriate to refer to partnerships. Partnerships between small and medium enterprises (SMEs) with the aim of becoming more competitive and jointly striving towards higher business performance have increased significantly in recent years.

While the antecedents of partnership formation and the characteristics of the resulting cooperative working relationship have been explored in the literature, there is a lack of understanding of the characteristics of partnership success (Heracleous 2003). Such an understanding is important in reconciling the prescriptions to form partnerships with the reality that a majority of such partnerships do not succeed. High failure rates have different explanations and can be traced back to the situation before the parties entered into the partnership, or to what happened during the partnership. Insufficient, unclear or misleading communication during the planning phase creates an unsteady platform for the partnership. During the partnership, these aspects can easily cause the partnership to derail for reasons that are related to primary characteristics such as commitment, coordination and trust. Partners belonging to different cultures with other value systems may have different views on conflict resolution, on attitudes to time keeping and on communication.

Networks and networking

Networks

The network organization model is a flat alternative to the organization hierarchy and is gradually coming to be seen as *the* organizational model best suited to today's society characterised by changing social structures in large parts of the world. Most network studies thus advocate what organizations must become if they are to compete in today's competitive environment. Two major types of networks are represented in the network literature, the inter-organizational network and the internal network. However, it is not just in their flat structure that that they differ from the traditional hierarchy. Hierarchical organizations have the attributes of a system: components are easily identified and related to each other in an ordered way; it is obvious whether a component belongs to the system or to its environment; and all components strive towards a common goal.

Are network and hierarchical structure mutually exclusive? IKEA, one of the world's leading furniture companies, delivers most of its products in knocked-down form, leaving customers to assemble the parts into a finished product. It is obvious that IKEA is not a traditional systems organization since one of the key production steps (assembly) takes place outside the company's premises by non-company staff, namely the customer. In fact, many of today's organizations are best described as hybrids between hierarchy and network.

Adler discusses attempts made by different observers to explain the trend towards the hybrid organizational type (Adler 2005). He notes the considerable attention paid recently to data suggesting the secular trend toward larger firms has stalled and may even be reversing. This has led some observers to argue that the underlying new trend is toward the disintegration of large hierarchical firms and their replacement by small entrepreneurial firms coordinated by markets. In Adler's view, this argument understates the persistence of large firms, ignores transformations underway within these firms and masks the growth of network relations between them. The underlying trend is a progressive swelling of the zone between hierarchy and market, and a proliferation of hybrid organizational forms that introduce high-powered market incentives into firms and hierarchical controls into markets.

Is it possible to assess the network organization as superior to the hierarchical form? Many would answer 'yes' to this question by referring to the conditions prevailing in the globalized market. This is characterized by rapid technology growth (particularly communications technology) and by the emergence of new market sectors related to environmental protection and climate change. Uncertainty about business potential and customer preferences together with the new market sectors now taking shape is leading to new and changing business clusters. The network is highly suitable for inter-business collaboration since firms can step in and out of the network at short notice and enter into another network that may be more suitable and appropriate to immediate requirements. This is a significant advantage over the hierarchical organizational form, but the network organization also has a weakness – absence of responsibility.

Adler (2005) argues that neither market nor hierarchy, nor any combination of the two, is particularly well suited to the challenges of the knowledge economy. Markets and firms have been observed to embody varying mixes of three ideal-typical organizational forms and their corresponding coordination mechanisms: (a) the hierarchy form relies on the authority mechanism, (b) the market form relies on price and (c) the network form relies on trust. Inter-firm relations embody and rely on varying degrees of trust and hierarchical authority even if their primary mechanism is price. Similarly, firms' internal operations typically rely to some extent on both trust and price signals, even if their primary coordination mechanism is authority.

Types of networks

Features and structures vary in different types of networks depending on context and the reasons for their creation. Reasons can include increasing innovation capacity by sharing resources, gaining access to new markets, decreasing transaction costs by better utilization of resources and working together in lobbying processes. Networks can be seen as creating synergy effects through the joint contribution of efforts and resources, which together create capacities and capabilities that are beyond the ability of each participant.

Heracleous (2003) suggests a network typology based on two dimensions: interdependence and durability. Interdependence refers to the extent to which firms involved in the network utilize each others' outputs (e.g., raw materials) and resources (e.g., market-related information) in their own operations. A high degree of utilization reflects the operational and strategic importance of inter-organizational relationships and constitutes a high level of dependence. It is likely to be associated with dense, redundant ties and the potential for high levels of trust to operate. This type of network is typically found in partnerships. Network durability, the second dimension of the typology, refers to the extent to which these networks persist in the longer term – and with broadly similar participants – in terms of both structure and content. Networks are constituted through inter-organizational linkages, and durability allows the development of dense redundant ties supporting the creation of trust and generative learning.

An example of a network type with a high degree of durability but very limited interdependence is an industry association formed for the purpose of regulatory lobbying, of pre-empting the creation of state regulation through the institution of self-regulation or promoting professional or craft education and regulating a specialist labour supply. Such networks are usually characterized by long-term persistence and relatively stable membership.

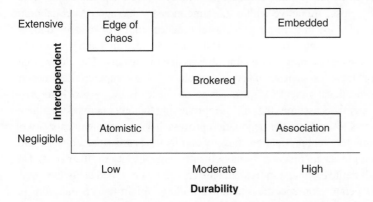

Figure 10.1 Network typology based on organizational interdependence and network durability.
Source: Heracleous (2003).

But even though they have high durability, they typically have a low degree of organizational interdependence.

Heracleous (ibid.) goes on to suggest five types of network collaboration, positioned within two-dimensional interdependence–durability space as shown in Figure 10.1.

1   The *atomistic* network has negligible interdependence other than through independent transactions and no durability of relationships beyond individual transactions

2   The *edge of chaos* network is the other extreme of this axis where extensive operational and strategic interdependence can exist between organizations but not necessarily persist for very long period Such situations can occur in the case of emerging firms not yet having established technical competence or market segments. Even though the structure of the network may be relatively stable in the short to medium term, the participants change continually and the external forces at work may shift in due course to a less turbulent and uncertain state.

3   The *embedded* network is characterized by a high degree of durability as well as an extensive level of inter-organizational dependence Such networks can involve cross shareholdings, personnel exchange, information exchange and significant inter-trading. High interdependence and extended durability are likely to be accompanied by dense redundant ties, high levels of trust and coherent cliques that define membership. The Japanese *Keiretsu* type of organization is an example that is presented below.

4   The *brokered* network is characterized by intermediate inter-dependence and moderate durability It often involves a strategic centre which acts as leader and co-ordinator of the network. The nurturing of social capital and building of trust are limited features of this type of network, as they rely on governance mechanisms to maintain membership and on the self-interest of members to uphold compliance, as long as the cost of opportunism exceeds the benefits of non-compliance.

5   The *association* network is usually characterized by long-term persistence and a relatively stable membership But even though it has high durability, it typically has a low degree of organizational interdependence. Examples are small business organizations formed for the purpose of regulatory lobbying.

A further kind of inter-firm collaboration is a business cluster where the participating firms are mostly geographically close, are active within the same industry and agree to collaborate in product development and marketing. Firms in a cluster produce similar or related goods or services and are supported by a range of dedicated institutions located in spatial proximity, such as business associations or training and technical assistance providers. The cluster may jointly invest in common facilities such as expensive machinery for computer-aided design used in product design and development. A special type of cluster is the *virtual enterprise* where one of the cluster members assumes the role of representing the other network members in dialogues with customers to facilitate the negotiation process. The accumulated capacity of the virtual enterprise guarantees that production capacity and facilities are satisfactory in spite of the fact that individual cluster members may have insufficient capacity on their own. The cluster concept is not well defined, though individual clusters can be described using the typology suggested above. Depending on specific situations, a cluster of firms can therefore be characterized as an edge of chaos network, a brokered network or an embedded network.

India provides an example of a country where clusters have played a significant role in the development of industry regions known as cluster regions. The city of Ludhiana in Punjab is known as the 'Manchester of India'. The Ludhiana region has become a concentration of small to medium-sized manufacturing firms working together in clusters. Cluster firms here contribute 95 per cent of the country's woollen knitwear, 85 per cent of the country's sewing machines and 60 per cent of the nation's bicycles and bicycle parts. Other well known Indian cluster regions are Agra with 800 registered and 6,000 unregistered small-scale units making approximately 150,000 pairs of shoes per day with a daily production value of 1.3 million USD. Bangalore and Pune are likewise important cluster regions in the electronic and computer sectors. Despite considerable achievements in production volumes and sales, the majority of the Indian small firm clusters share significant constraints like technological obsolescence, relatively poor product quality, information deficiencies, poor market linkages and inadequate management systems. Moreover, with the integration of the Indian economy in the international business community, clusters (even the best performing ones) are increasingly feeling the competitive pressures coming from international markets.

Examples of networks types

The association network

Township and Village Enterprise (TVE) is a Chinese-specific term used to identify those firms that are either collectively established by – or initially based on and closely associated with – rural communities such as townships and villages (Sun 2003). TVEs became an interesting large-scale experiment in association networks between small firms and the local government of townships and villages. Problems inherent in the TVE structure, such as diverging priorities between local authorities and business managers, has led to a degeneration of the TVE mechanism and its transformation to a similar network type, where household industrial and commercial firms attach themselves to an established collectively-owned or state-owned enterprise. The household firm pays a fee for the use of the established firm's name (and thus its licence and commercial reputation), stationery, letters of introduction and – most importantly – its bank account numbers and receipt books. Taxes were collected from the established public enterprises rather than from the attached households. Such business affiliations give more autonomy and flexibility to household firms than subcontracting. Interdependence between the household firm and the larger counterpart is formally close but operationally more limited. However, durability is, high.

The atomistic network

Although in modern economies, SMEs may not have a clear advantage in technical flexibility over large firms and may pay broadly the same factor prices, they are organizationally more flexible, which is an important advantage in rapidly changing markets (Dallago and McIntyre 2003). Dallago (2003) reports that during the economic and political transition in Eastern Europe, some SMEs began to develop new patterns of inter-relationships, and an increasing number of small enterprises pursued greater specialization by narrowing their production spectrum. They also increasingly relied on negotiating 'friendly' market division and other forms of inter-enterprise cooperation, mostly based on personal relationships of trust and cooperation developed before the transition.

Other small enterprises have entered contractual agreements with large enterprises, either as producers of components or suppliers of maintenance, repair and after-sale services, to diversify risk in an uncertain and depressed economic environment. These enterprises have thus given their markets autonomy in exchange for greater safety and lucrative business. Due to the nature of an economy in economic and political transition, durability and interdependence between collaborating firms can be assumed to be at the lower end for a majority.

The embedded network – SEWA

The Self Employed Women's Association (SEWA) is a trade union registered in 1972 and located in the province of Gujarat in India. It is an organization of poor, self-employed women workers who earn a living through their own labour or small business. Not in regular salaried employment, they do not receive the welfare benefits of workers in the organized sector. They are the unprotected labour force of the country. Of the female labour force in India, more than 94 per cent are in the unorganized sector. However their work is not counted and hence remains invisible. In fact, women workers themselves remain uncounted, undercounted and invisible.

At SEWA, workers are organized to achieve their goals of full employment and self-reliance through the strategy of struggle and development. The struggle is against the many constraints and limitations imposed on them by society and the economy, while development activities strengthen women's bargaining power and offer them new alternatives. Practically, the strategy is carried out through the joint action of union and cooperatives.

There is also much to be done in terms of strengthening women's leadership, their confidence, their bargaining power within and outside their homes and their representation in policy-making and decision-making. It is their issues, their priorities and needs which should guide and mould the development process and, toward this end, SEWA has been supporting its members in capacity-building and in developing their own economic organizations.

SEWA is both an organization and a movement. The mutual dependence between the small businesses on the one hand and between the businesses and the organization on the other is very strong. Also durability is high, for many women even lifelong.

The embedded network – Value Stars

The Value Stars network describes a situation where a small number of suppliers jointly contribute to delivering a service or a product to a common customer.

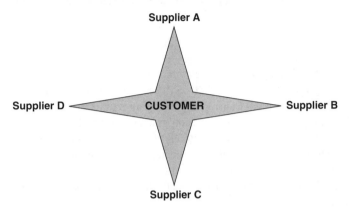

Figure 10.2 A Value Star.

As the name suggests, the network is intended to create value for all members through an active customer dialogue which aims to understand the customer's vision and goals while becoming aware of how their own product or service fits with customer's business situation. Each supplier must understand their role in the eyes of the customer and have an on-going dialogue in order to continually adjust to changes in customer requirements and to have continuous feedback about their performance. The active and fair dialogue between supplier and customer should result in mutual understanding and resolution of problems that might otherwise jeopardize collaboration.

Demand-driven improvements in service and product quality should guide the supplier on requirements to guarantee proper quality levels. Demand-driven development in products and service minimize risks and costs by eliminating developments that may not be required. Long-term commitments and close customer collaboration are the characteristics of the embedded network.

Box 10.1 Mini-case: the Volvo Company

Volvo is a vehicle manufacturer with production in many countries. In the Gothenburg plant in Sweden, the workforce is around 15,000, the majority comprising blue collar workers in production. The cleaning of work clothes was outsourced to a local laundry who processed large quantities of overalls and other work clothes each week. When delivered to the laundry, many of the items had defects such as missing buttons or rips, and were returned to Volvo in the same condition after cleaning. The cleaned but defective items were mostly put in storage and later discarded. The annual budget for discarded working clothes at Volvo was significant!

The laundry firm (say Supplier A in Figure 10.2) suggested to Volvo that defective working clothes should be repaired when handed in for cleaning. A tailor shop became attached to the network as sub-supplier (say Supplier B) and performed the necessary repairs. Since then the volume of working clothes scrapped by Volvo has been reduced to zero, resulting in a substantial annual cost reduction.

The laundry firm learnt that interest in its customer's business pays and it also pays to be prepared to take the first initiative. Openness with customer and co-supplier is important: a readiness to share knowledge and experience with *selected* others. Once the network is established it is important to show trust!

The brokered network

A business incubator is designed to accelerate the growth and success of entrepreneurial companies through an array of business support resources and services. A business incubator's main goal is to produce successful firms that will leave the programme financially viable and freestanding. The relationship between the incubator and the incubatee is a network where durability and interdependence depends on both parties. The incubation process should be long enough for the incubatee to take in, learn and reflect upon what is required for the business to develop. On the other hand the incubation period must have a well-defined time frame to make performance assessment possible. The degree of interdependence must be well defined and the roles in the incubation process clarified and agreed by the parties. The incubator process can be seen as a network close to the brokered network typology.

Networking in Asia

The economic development of Asia and the rapid advance of Asian companies have created a growing interest in business styles and organization forms. Despite the region's inherent diversities and associated contradictions, it is generally accepted that the countries comprising the Asian region have sufficiently similar geographic, historic and cultural characteristics for them to be considered as parts of a cohesive geopolitical entity differentiated from their Western counterparts. Consequently, it is possible to build a case that these similarities have led to the development of differences and particularities in Asian management systems and processes in comparison with of the West. In the major traditional societies of Asia, it is the extended family system that not only preserves social cohesion and solidarity, but in many cases provides the backbone of business and industry. The host of Chinese and Indian family-owned and operated companies in all Asian countries – the infamous Korean Chaebols and Japanese cartels, and the indigenous family businesses in Indonesia and Malaysia – are all examples of this characteristic. It can be argued that the historic internal migration of Chinese and Indian family entrepreneurs throughout the region, coupled with the effects of and reactions to European colonization, have contributed significantly to the economic resurgence of Asia in the post-Second World War era (Chatterjee and Nankervis 2007).

The importance of the highly-personal, particularistic and diffuse ties between family firms in Taiwan, Hong Kong and other Chinese business communities, as well as the long-term alliances between Japanese companies, demonstrate the variable nature of market relationships and the limited generality of the Anglo-Saxon model of firms and markets (Whitley 1992).

There are three dominant types of business systems in East Asia: the Japanese *Keiretsu*, the South Korean *Chaebol*, and the networks of Overseas Chinese business. The development of each of these systems has been historically influenced by several dimensions of their institutional context, particularly political and financial factors. All three systems constitute embedded networks as described above, as they involve significant interdependencies and ties among the organizations involved, and they persist over the longer term with broadly similar participants (except in the case of Chinese business networks, which exhibit high interdependence and persist in the longer term, but with a relatively lower degree of stability in participants) (Heracleous 2003).

Japanese Keiretsu

Japanese corporations exhibit a relatively high degree of specialization and more extensive use of relational contracting within wider business systems (*Keiretsu*) that are vertically or horizontally oriented and characterized by high degrees of interdependence. These interdependencies include equity ties, interlocking directorates, inter-trading and information and personnel exchange. *Keiretsu* also exhibit significant ties with state agencies. Strategic decision-making is relatively decentralized, and consensus-based. It is driven more by existing competencies and strategic commitments than by unrelated opportunities that present themselves opportunistically. Management has a high degree of autonomy from shareholders and exhibits a relatively high stakeholder orientation, illustrated in implicit lifetime employment systems and long-term, seniority-based advancement. The main source of authority is the holding of office; formal rules and procedures are more important in the *Keiretsu* than particularistic, personal ties. Thus, in terms of the embedded network typology above, the Japanese *Keiretsu* exhibit multiple, dense formalized ties, and extended scope based on extensive inter-firm networking (Whitley 1990, 1992).

South Korean Chaebol

The *Chaebol* incorporate a wider variety of activities than either the *Keiretsu* or Overseas Chinese businesses within their authority structures and organizational scope. The degree of relational contracting and other cooperative activities is therefore much lower in these network types. In marked contrast with the *Keiretsu*, there is a strong connection between ownership and control, with the *Chaebol* being tightly controlled by owner-founders and their families. Strategic decision-making is highly centralized to founders and family members, where personal, particularistic connections are more important than formal rules and procedures. In a similar fashion to the *Keiretsu*, employment is still long-term and advancement is seniority-based, but within a much more centralized climate that may stifle innovation and self-initiative. The *Chaebol* are highly geared and dependent on state-owned banks for funding; their strategic direction has often been influenced by state policies and objectives. The *Chaebol* thus exhibit a mixture of formalized, equity ties with informal, personal ties and a low level of inter-firm relational contracting since they incorporate a higher variety of activities within their organizational scope (Biggart 1991; Whitley 1990).

Chinese family business networks

Chinese business networks are based on personal, kinship or ethnic ties, rather than denser, formalized ties. As with the *Chaebol*, the patriarchs of Chinese firms are almost worshipped and their beliefs permeate the organization's culture. There is a high level of specialization in individual firms owned by Overseas Chinese (but a significant level of diversification within families). The stability of actors is lower in Chinese family business networks than in both the *Chaebol* and the *Keiretsu*. The participants in different deals change depending on its nature and what they can offer to its successful execution. Thus, strategic decision-making is relatively more opportunistic than planned. As in the *Chaebol*, control is strongly centralized and associated with ownership; but the personal element features much more prominently. The holding of office is less important than relationship to the founder-owner; role and task definitions are much less formal and more protean than in either the *Chaebol* or the *Keiretsu*. The potential longevity and successful internationalization of Chinese family businesses are matters of considerable debate. Chinese business networks tend to depend more on finance from savings, relatives and business contacts than banks or state-controlled agencies. Individual firm specialization means that the extent of sub-contracting and relational contracting is high within a web of informal, personal connections. Thus Chinese business networks consist largely of informal, personalized ties with low formalization, and exhibit extended scope through a relatively high degree of inter-firm interactions (Whitley 1990).

Partnerships

Partnerships between firms can be characterized using the network typology of Figure 10.1, most belonging to the embedded type. However, the different aspects of partnerships justify their separate discussion.

Entering into a partnership

The motivation for entering into a partnership with another company, in the local market or overseas, can be ascribed to various factors such, as the wish to expand business and to increase profit. The path to these goals may be strewn with unexpected or unforeseen obstacles. However, some problems are well-known and have been documented, and a selection is discussed below.

Behind the formation of every business partnership are the partners' expectation that value will be created. However, it is not always obvious how value should be defined, created and shared; indeed, the potential alliance partner may have a value-creation perspective that does not respect or support his counterpart's collaborative objectives. Since business collaborators rarely have the same strategic objectives, the partners' views of value creation may be different, but they have to be compatible.

How a firm benefits from a business partnership is highly dependent on what each partner is committed to do and actually does over an extended period of time. While not all contingencies can be identified during the formation process, there are ways to sort out many of the problems that plague business collaborations. These are areas that business partners have to deal with, especially in the initial stage of a partnership. Problems areas of concern include identifying the areas of interests in the alliance (its *strategic scope*); each partner's benefits and contributions to the alliance (its *economic scope*); and who is actually to do what in the alliance (its *operational scope*). How each individual partner acts will be affected by previous experiences and by initial expectations.

Referring to the network typology in Figure 10.1, business partnerships can take a variety of forms, from business contacts (where partners act as agents) to more sustainable commitments that may ultimately lead to the establishment of joint companies. Partnerships can come into being between suppliers and customers that ultimately results in a take-over.

General motives for a business partnership

When is cooperation of interest to a firm? Three basic requirements must be fulfilled:

1   future must be at least as important as the present;
2   common goals must be articulated; and
3   the profit or benefits must be sufficient.

One more factor that must not be omitted – *trust*! Partners must be able to trust each other and strive for win–win situations.

The motivation for a partnership may be based on a firm's market position. A satisfactory market position motivates cooperation to defend the present situation or to catch up with a stronger market leader, while a weak market position may motivate restructuring of products or business approach in cooperation with other firms. The following four criteria distinguish a partnership or an alliance from mere traditional cooperation between enterprises:

1   the participating enterprises striving towards a common goal must be independent when the cooperation starts;
2   the participating enterprises share benefits coming from the cooperation and control of activities;
3   the participating enterprises contribute continually with strategically important inputs such as products, technology and training; and
4   the participating enterprises need a contract or joint venture agreement in case of future disputes (not generally necessary in an alliance)

By entering into a business partnership, the enterprise expects to increase its added value in current activities as well as adopting strategic know-how by learning from the business partner. However, if an enterprise depends too much on the know-how and skill of the other partner, the result may be reduced competitiveness and weaker business strength.

Experience shows that, in spite of careful preparatory discussions between tentative partners, opinions about the long-term strategic role of the partnership and what can be expected from a more short term perspective differ between partners. The problem goes back to the generic motives for partnerships, which are closely related to the two basic questions: what is the relative importance of the business partnership, and what is the company's present position in the market. The four situations are illustrated in Figure 10.3.

One partner may have a leading market position but feel threatened by the superior technology of competitors or its own inadequate product development. Entering into a partnership with a suitable partner can be a way of defending and securing the leading position. In case of a follower, the partnership may be seen as an opportunity of catching up with the market leader by joint product development or outstanding joint marketing.

A market leader with no particular reason to feel threatened by competition may still want to consider entering into a partnership with a suitable partner, if only to make sure that the leading position remains strong through collaboration with the partner. In such situations, the importance of entering into the partnership may have more strategic value than urgency. When the firm is a follower in the market, it may have a strategic reason to enter into a partnership with a suitable firm, to restructure its product base or even the organization. This may not be of immediate importance but a way of surviving in the long run.

Position in the market

Leader   Follower

		Leader	Follower
	Urgent	Defend	Catch up
Relative importance			
	Peripheral	Remain	Restructure

Figure 10.3 General motives for partnerships.

Box 10.2 Mini-case: Seasafe Marine Software and Inde-Dutch Systems

Seasafe Marine used to be a market leader in propeller simulation software for the ship-building industry, an application based on sophisticated models and software design. As computer technology shifted from 32 to 64 bits processors, the company was forced to convert all software to the new processor type. As a Swedish company, Seasafe Marine realised that costs of converting the software would be overwhelming due to high salary levels. After surveying the Indian software market, contacts were established with Inde-Dutch Systems, an Indian software firm based in the Northern part of India. With reference to Figure 10.3, Seasafe Marine was a market leader with an urgent need to solve a problem. Inde-Dutch Systems followed the computer industry trend in the Indian market and saw the opportunity of taking on the software conversion task together with Seasafe Marine as a way of catching up with more advanced compa-nies. For Seasafe Marine the strategy was to defend its position in the market through the partnership with Inde-Dutch Systems.

A few years later, the success of this partnership led to the formation of a joint company based in India.

How many resources to be invested in the partnership?

Another fundamental issue is the amount of resources that should be put into and taken out of the partnership. The input dimension is of course determined by whether the allocated resources are intended for specific short-term operations or if they are seen as a basis for a more sustainable and long-term partnership. The output dimension is also determined by the time frame: whether resources generated through the partnership should be retrieved by the partners, or retained as a financial platform within the partnership itself. Combining these two dimensions gives rise to Figure 10.4.

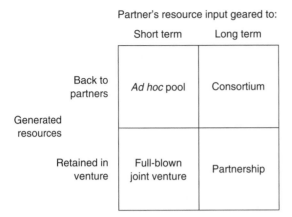

Figure 10.4 Invested resources in partnerships.

What should characterize the partnership?

A partnership in which an existing product is to be introduced into an existing market places different demands on the partners than the situation in which a new product is to be introduced into a new market. Here too we can identify four different situations as to what will be required of the partners.

The least demand on a partner occurs when, for strategic market (or political) reasons, it contributes nothing more than a name. When both partners have current products to be marketed and sold in an existing market, the aim of the partnership should be to expand the present market by striving towards jointly-increased volumes and revenues. When products are under development and the market potential exists the, joint activities should concentrate on marketing and preparing the market for the launch of the product. In the case of a new market, an existing product may need modifying, upgrading with new functions or re-packaging to attract potential customers. Products still at the idea stage or in design and intended for a market whose potential is uncertain require analysis regarding the potential size of the market, customer preferences, distribution channels etc.

The supplier–customer partnership

It may sometimes be difficult to distinguish between a partnership and a more traditional relationship between customer and supplier, not least because it may also vary with time. The purpose of a supplier business is to create and maintain customer relations, and the greater the dependency between customer and supplier, the more likely that the relationship will deepen.

Partnerships with customers can be complex. Customers will be concerned about a supplier's performance in areas that extend beyond the supplier's price or the quality of its product or service. This has been confirmed in several reports (Lind and Scheepers 2009). Customers tend to assess suppliers' willingness to develop or adapt its standard offering to their requirements. Such requirements may be based on demands on the customer from *their* customers, on what the customer can learn from the supplier and on the long-term benefits and ease of working with the supplier. Entering into partnership with a customer can be a way for a supplier to defend its business position by becoming a preferred supplier to

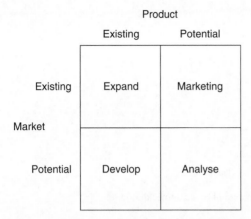

Figure 10.5 Partnership characteristics.

one or a few customers. Such development may follow from closer interaction between customer and supplier in a win–win situation.

The supply side of companies has become increasingly important during the last few decades. One reason is that the costs of purchased goods and services represent the major part of total costs in certain sectors. In the car industry, purchased items account for 50 to 70 per cent of total product costs, while for main contractors in the construction industry material costs can be even more. Even if these figures are on the extreme side and not representative of the average SME, they mark the trend to semi-finished parts in the material input in these sectors.

It is not only how much companies buy that is changing, but also the relationship between customer and supplier. Both parties have an interest in building a business relationship that goes beyond just selling and buying, such as solving shared problems from a win–win perspective. Rather than just having suppliers that manufacture items that they previously produced for themselves, many companies now rely on their suppliers to design and develop semi-finished parts that are installed in their own final products. Similarly, many companies that previously outsourced their advertising now enter into partnerships with companies to manage their total marketing activities, such as operating call centres or a sales force, or even rely on their accountants to operate their entire financial control systems. Increasingly, suppliers contribute to the technical development of their customers and are the source of much of the knowledge and skills on which customers depend. This change has been accentuated in the wake of new and costly technologies that are required but not necessarily within the company's own premises or ownership.

Figure 10.6 illustrates how the beginning of a down-turn in a product's life cycle can be diverted as the product is re-designed and improved, a result from a close supplier–customer dialogue.

The growing importance of the supply side has considerably affected companies' views of suppliers and the roles they should play. A reliance on outsourcing would imply an extension of the supplier base of a company, but generally companies seem to have reduced the number of their suppliers considerably. The main reason for this is that collaboration in technical development and greater dependence on suppliers requires close, long-term cooperation between customer and supplier. Collaboration is resource-hungry and firms therefore have to

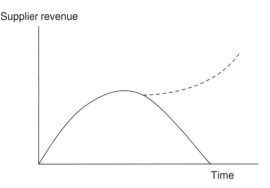

Figure 10.6 Product development based on supplier–customer dialogue.

restrict the number of companies with which they become deeply involved. Developments on the supply side of companies have made individual suppliers more significant, and relationships with them are important assets for customers. The main issue facing managers is no longer about 'buying the right products at the right time and the right price', but of handling and developing relationships and partnerships with key suppliers over long periods.

Partnerships in a nutshell

The following points summarize the above discussion:

* Business partnerships are effective when moving into related business sectors or new geographical markets.
* Business partnerships between strong and weak companies rarely work.
* Successful business partnerships are distinguished by their ability to evolve beyond initial expectations and objectives.
* Business partnerships with an even split of financial ownership are more likely to succeed than those in which one partner holds a majority interest. What matters is clear management control, not financial ownership.
* A business partnership must be based on mutual cooperation between the parties involved. There is a need to create a climate of trust and a mutual understanding of why the partners entered the partnership.
* The point of departure for a successful partnership is when the future is at least as important as the present, when each partner has clearly expressed and articulated their own goals – and correctly perceived those of the other – and when potential benefits and profits are satisfied.
* A jointly-developed business plan, reflecting potential obstacles as well as benefits, is a necessary precondition for any business partnership.

Assessing partnerships

The method presented below has been developed to assist managers and consultants in analysing the degree of fit between prospective partners. Eight characteristics of varying degrees of importance have been identified for a partnership to have a chance of becoming

Table 10.1 Characteristics in the *Partnership Assessment Guide* are presented below

Characteristic	Definition	Weight
1. Turnover	Annual income of the company	0.10
2. Employment	Average number of permanent employees	0.05
3. Technology level	Type of production equipment in use	0.15
4. Management capability	Management structure and capability	0.20
5. International orientation	Foreign customers and/or business partners	0.05
6. Market penetration	Market activities of the company	0.15
7. Corporate culture	General maturity of the company	0.10
8. Financial strength	Solidity, cash-flow and banking contacts	0.20

successful. It should be emphasized that no formal method can fully identify all possible parameters that determine the route to failure or success. The method below should therefore be seen as guidance: the first test of whether a potential partnership has a fair chance of succeeding. The eight characteristics of this *Partnership Assessment Guide* are listed in Table 10.1 along with their respective weights.

The weights given are an example; they are not fixed but depend on the relative importance of the characteristics to the partnership as a whole. The sum of all weights is equal to 1.

Each partner assesses their business against a five-point scale for each characteristic, yielding eight each in the range 0 to 4, where 0 means low and 4 means high. These choice numbers are multiplied by the weight for the characteristic and added together. The total score gives an indication of the viability of the proposed partnership, which prospective members can then use to decide whether to proceed.

Tables 10.2 and 10.3 present a complete questionnaire based on the weights in Table 10.1.

This *Partnership Assessment Guide* was designed for a manufacturing firm but can be adapted to any type of company by re-defining some of the characteristics to reflect the specific situation.

Table 10.2 Example partnership assessment questionnaire

Characteristic	Choices	Score
1. Turnover	> 2.5 million USD	4
	1.1 – 2.5 million USD	3
	0.5 – 1.1 million USD	2
	0.1 – 0.5 million USD	1
	< 0.1 million USD	0
2. Employment	> 200 employees	4
	100 – 200 employees	3
	50 – 100 employees	2
	10 – 50 employees	1
	< 10 employees	0

(continued)

Table 10.2 Continued

Characteristic	Choices	Score
3. Technology level	Latest (e.g. CAD, NC machines, robots)	4
	Modern (e.g. multi-operation machines)	3
	Machine production with traditional equipment (automatic production with operator control)	2
	Semi-manual production (manual production with machine support)	1
	Manual production only	0
4. Management capability	Internally effective (e.g. cost control), externally efficient (e.g. business analysis, business control)	4
	Based on modern management and business principles (e.g. strategic business planning, operations planning and monitoring, customer orientation, employee empowerment)	3
	Based on goal-setting and business planning	2
	Based on rudimentary business planning	1
	Primarily *ad hoc*	0
5. International orientation	Extensive experience (e.g. established partnerships with overseas companies)	4
	Earlier experience of overseas partnerships (successful or less successful)	3
	International trade (export/import of products/services)	2
	No international experience but preparatory activities undertaken (e.g. information collection, training)	1
	No international experience and no preparations	0
6. Market penetration	Market leader in home country for product/service	4
	Substantial market share in home country for product/service; market penetration in neighbouring countries	3
	Company has active sales force for its products	2
	Dedicated marketing activities planned for product/service (e.g. advertising, sales campaign)	1
	Market potential uncertain	0
7. Corporate culture	Strong commitment to company vision, values and goals; continuous feedback on business performance; information flows freely; various forms of reward; flat organization structure; openness encouraged	4
	Absence of common goals; management style is modern and open; information flows freely; rewards are mostly money; strong emphasis on rules and discipline; no real empowerment	3
	Management more regulating than facilitating; no dialogue on company performance; certain information flows controlled; rewards are rare; company loyalty is salary-based	2
	Autocratic atmosphere centrally controlled by a single individual; controlled information flows; no rewards; stable organization	1
	A closed organization; no creative atmosphere; strong hierarchy	0
8. Financial strength	Own capital / total capital > 0.5 own capital / total assets > 1.0	4
	Own capital / total capital > 0.3 and < 0.5 own capital / total assets > 0.5 and < 1.0	3
	Own capital / total capital > 0.1 and < 0.3 own capital / total assets > 0.2 and < 0.5	2
	Own capital / total capital < 0.1 own capital / total assets < 0.2	1
	No financial figures available	0

Table 10.3 Example partnership assessment response grid

Characteristic	Choice (0 – 4)	× Weight	= Score
1. Turnover		0.10	
2. Employment		0.05	
3. Technology level		0.15	
4. Management capability		0.20	
5. International orientation		0.05	
6. Market penetration		0.15	
7. Corporate culture		0.10	
8. Financial strength		0.20	
		Sum of scores =	

SME networking: the JAPP model

Entrepreneurs and small business managers are individuals who may be characterized by their attitudes to risk taking, uncertainty and business opportunities. Seeking business contacts for joint projects and partnerships may seem attractive for certain manager types but dismissed by others as too uncertain or risky. This may not only stem from the traditional fear of revealing business secrets but also from a lack of initiative and ability to seek partners. In the wake of new business principles that highlight openness and networking as a more successful approach to business than 'the lone wolf' syndrome, the JAPP model was developed as a structured method to assist small business mangers to establish contacts.[1]

JAPP from a cultural perspective

Following the notion about individual management characteristics above, it has been suggested that management type can be described *inter alia* as dynamic, problem-oriented or opportunity-minded. These three attitudes are defined as follows (Lind 2009):

1   Dynamic: Proactive and eager to take initiatives.
2   Problem-oriented: A feeling of being exposed to and threatened by uncontrollable external factors.
3   Opportunity-minded: Sensitive and open to current trends in business and society.

The findings of a study of SME management behaviour with respect to these characteristics carried out in four North European and fifteen Asian countries were correlated with the Hofstede dimensions of *power distance* (PDI) and *uncertainty avoidance* (UAI) (Hofstede 1984, 1991).

The strongest negative correlation observed was between power distance and dynamism, which would indicate that in countries characterized by high power distance, dynamism is hindered by cultural factors, such as subordinates expecting to be told what to do (Hofstede ibid.). High PDI countries are hierarchical both in organizations and in society, with higher concentrations of authority. These and other characteristics of high PDI countries are likely to limit managers' ability to be proactive and their eagerness to take business initiatives.

The reverse situation occurs in low PDI countries, where organization structures tend to be flatter, the concentration of authority much lower and management capability often measured by the degree to which it is proactive in business.

Table 10.4 Correlation between cultural and management factors

Correlated variables	Correlation factor	Degree of correlation
Dynamism – UAI	−0.72	Strong
Problem – UAI	−0.18	Weak/none
Opportunity – UAI	−0.84	Very strong
Dynamism – PDI	−0.98	Very strong
Problem – PDI	0.45	Moderate
Opportunity – PDI	−0.66	Strong

Source: Lind (2009).

The second strongest correlation in Table 10.4 appears between uncertainty avoidance and opportunity orientation. In countries with high UAI, opportunity orientation among managers can be expected to be lower. Managers are also less willing to make individual and risky decisions, there is an increased fear of failure and achievements are mostly measured in terms of security (Hofstede ibid.). This is likely to have a hindering effect on managers' ability to be sensitive and open to current trends in business and society. In low scoring UAI countries, on the other hand, managers are more willing to make individual and risky decisions.

The other two situations where correlation is strong are between uncertainty avoidance and dynamism, and between power distance and opportunity orientation. When uncertainty avoidance is high, willingness to take initiatives may be reduced. When power distance is high, the take up and exploitation of business opportunities may be limited.

It appears from Table 10.4 that there is no clear correlation between problem orientation and uncertainty avoidance, which might have been expected. There is moderate correlation between problem orientation and power distance: management may feel threatened by higher concentrations of authority in society.

JAPP – a description

JAPP – Joint Activities for Profit and Progress – is a programme to assist entrepreneurs and small business managers needing the mental encouragement to regain creativity by entering into a dialogue with other managers, from which new and attractive business ideas and concepts may develop. The programme helps participants in a pre-selected group to identify new business partners, to find attractive combinations of products and service offerings and to identify new customers and markets. A JAPP group will have typically fifteen participants from up to fifteen enterprises.

The JAPP model can be applied in a variety of ways. The structure is simple and is built on a local interest to influence and improve the situation for entrepreneurs and small enterprises. The basic idea is that small enterprise managers have the power and will to assist each other in developing joint business scenarios if there is a sufficiently strong win–win possibility. The JAPP process is preferably carried out with the assistance of an outside facilitator (consultant) who has the role of a catalyst rather than problem solver. The programme is achievement-oriented and strives towards realistic and immediate results. JAPP has the following structure:

- The JAPP process spans a time period whose length varies with the ambition of the participants. Several months should be allocated, though not for consecutive process sessions.

- The initiative to form a JAPP group is taken by an organization working for SME development. The organization is assumed to have an overall view of local individual SMEs and can therefore make a preliminary list of potential participants.
- A JAPP group is formed with the selected SMEs and with other interested parties, such as a local bank, a chamber of commerce or an export organization, as appropriate.
- A facilitator is appointed. The facilitator will actively participate in the group's work, not only with each of the participating SMEs, but also as a catalyst in group meetings to catch and elaborate new ideas coming up and to contribute to their realization. The facilitator is supposed to make use of his/her contact network in order to help marketing the services of the group. The facilitator will also decide when training is necessary for continued group work. In such situations, he or she will be responsible for delivering the required training.

The objective of JAPP is to create a common forum where the SMEs will find counterparts with whom to jointly develop new business ideas and concepts. This also implies identifying market and customer opportunities for quick business results. The programme has been designed to last for four months, but should be adapted to local conditions.

JAPP working procedure

Month 1

The facilitator spends one day with each participating SME. Once a week there is a group meeting where issues such as potential synergy between products are discussed as well as joint marketing activities and joint business calls.

The first month requires the facilitator to be very active and take the leading role, as the participants may still be wary of the whole idea. It is the facilitator's responsibility to create confidence in the programme as quickly as possible. After the first month, the group decides if the working routines are appropriate or whether they should be modified to better suit the participants.

The process begins with a brief analysis of each enterprise by the facilitator who also produces a preliminary action plan for each enterprise. The facilitator leads the first joint sessions where the first attempts are made to find joint interests between participants. The first subgroups should emerge.

Month 2

Work continues from the first month. All new ideas and concepts that emerge are taken care of and treated accordingly. Meetings are arranged with subgroups and local banks to discuss the financing of new projects etc. The facilitator should be instrumental in these discussions.

Month 3

Work continues from the second month. The facilitator participates in selected projects only, as group activities are delegated to individual groups. The facilitator is available for consultation.

Month 4

Final session with summing up and result reporting.

Results

There are three levels of possible outcome from the programme:

1   One or a few of the participating SMEs are in the position to further develop ideas that have emerged during the programme. For a majority of the SMEs, however, no notable progress can be observed.
2   A significant number of the SMEs have identified possibilities for cooperating or have decided to continue cooperating after the programme to implement new ideas.
3   New ideas about joint project developments and joint marketing activities result in significant progress for a number of the participating SMEs.

The hope is that at least the second of these outcomes is achieved in the programme. There are three major reasons why this may not happen:

1   Psychology: Small enterprises in crisis (economically, commercially) loose their creative ability and, therefore, face difficulties in breaking the viscous cycle whereby lack of creativity leads to reduced business performance that in turn reduces creativity. The JAPP project creates opportunities to establish contacts with other small enterprises in similar situations and to help break the creative block.
2   Network: Each small enterprise has a network of colleagues, friends, customers, suppliers and other potential business contacts. Ten or more small enterprises have at least ten times as many potential customers, which represents substantial market potential! By generously sharing their networks with the group members, suddenly, each participating enterprise has a much bigger potential market to work with. See Table 10.3 below.
3   Knowledge: As each enterprise represents a specific knowledge base, significant synergy can emerge within the project group. The combination of a product and a service can create new added values; the experience of one enterprise from a particular market sector and its specific demands can benefit another enterprise in the group; the facilitators' knowledge and experience of export markets can lead to export projects etc.

Table 10.5 summarizes the reasons why different stakeholder groups might get involved in a JAPP programme and the benefits they might expect as a result.

A JAPP process does not need many participants before the opportunities created become substantial. For example, if two firms have two customers each, each firm has the potential of doubling its customer base: besides its own two customers, firm A approaches the two customers of firm B, and vice-versa. Fifteen JAPP participants with ten customers each have the potential of creating 2,250 customer–supplier relationships, a situation shown in Table 10.6. (Customers in common will reduce this figure.)

Conclusion

Networking among small businesses is increasingly emphasized by researchers because networks provide managers with access to complementary experiences and expertise thereby contributing to additional business knowledge. While networking is viewed as an important requirement in enterprises of all sizes, the learning opportunities are argued to be of particular importance to smaller firms.

Table 10.5 Stakeholders' interests in the JAPP programme

Stakeholder group	Reasons for involvement	Benefits of involvement
Local government	Create employment Prevent bankruptcies Prevent job losses	Contact with SMEs SME support programmes Export schemes Identification of JAPP participants
Banks/financial institutions	Support to customers Less credit losses Public relations	Identification of JAPP participants Venture capital
SME organizations	Expand the SME sector Create job opportunities A new model for enterprise support	Recruitment of JAPP facilitator Help with financing
Individual SMEs	Find new business partners Identify new market segment Increase own customer base Help out of circle of decline	

Table 10.6 The potential 2,250 sales opportunities afforded by 15 firms with 10 customers each

Firms	1	2	3	4	5	6	7	8	9	10	11	12	13	14	15
1	10	10	10	10	10	10	10	10	10	10	10	10	10	10	10
2	10	10	10	10	10	10	10	10	10	10	10	10	10	10	10
3	10	10	10	10	10	10	10	10	10	10	10	10	10	10	10
4	10	10	10	10	10	10	10	10	10	10	10	10	10	10	10
5	10	10	10	10	10	10	10	10	10	10	10	10	10	10	10
6	10	10	10	10	10	10	10	10	10	10	10	10	10	10	10
7	10	10	10	10	10	10	10	10	10	10	10	10	10	10	10
8	10	10	10	10	10	10	10	10	10	10	10	10	10	10	10
9	10	10	10	10	10	10	10	10	10	10	10	10	10	10	10
10	10	10	10	10	10	10	10	10	10	10	10	10	10	10	10
11	10	10	10	10	10	10	10	10	10	10	10	10	10	10	10
12	10	10	10	10	10	10	10	10	10	10	10	10	10	10	10
13	10	10	10	10	10	10	10	10	10	10	10	10	10	10	10
14	10	10	10	10	10	10	10	10	10	10	10	10	10	10	10
15	10	10	10	10	10	10	10	10	10	10	10	10	10	10	10

Networking is the simplest and most common means of inter-organizational collaboration; more advanced and mutually-committed forms of collaboration are generally referred to as partnerships. Partnerships between small and medium firms have increased significantly during recent years in attempts to find and maintain competitive advantage.

The network organization model is a flat alternative to the hierarchical model and is becoming a normative approach. The claim is made that this is what organizations must become if they are to be competitive in today's competitive environment! Two major types of networks have been discussed: the inter-organizational network and the internal network, both having the flat organization structure.

In addition a network typology based on two dimensions has been discussed. In this model *interdependence* refers to the extent to which firms involved in the network utilize each others' outputs and resources. This type of network is typically found in partnerships. *Durability* is the second dimension of the network typology, and refers to the extent to which these networks persist in the longer term, and that broadly lead to the creation of trust and generative learning.

Partnerships are mostly intended to last. With high levels of durability and interaction, they can be classified as embedded networks. For a partnership to be successful, prospective partners need to have well-considered ambitions and motives for entering into the partnership. In addition, both partners need to have clear views about what will be invested and how the surplus generated is distributed.

Entering into a partnership with another company requires that certain basic conditions apply, for example, the difference in size must not be too great. A partnership assessment grid was presented as an instrument to be used to analyse the degree to which the potential partners match. If there is no real match, or the match is insufficient, partnership is less likely to succeed.

The JAPP method was developed as a structured method to assist small business managers establish contacts. The background for this method was the understanding that certain types of managers do not easily get into contact with other managers to discuss potential business collaborations. The aim of the method is to facilitate the first contacts between mangers and firms.

Note

1   The JAPP model was developed by the author in a SME management development programme for African and Asian countries, funded by Sida (Swedish International Development Cooperation Agency).

References

Adler, P. (2005) 'Market, Hierarchy and Trust: The Knowledge Economy and the Future of Capitalism', in Grey, C. and Willmott, H. (eds) *Critical Management Studies*. London: Oxford University Press.

Biggart, N. (1991) 'Explaining Asian Economic Organisation: Toward a Weberian Institutional Perspective'. *Theory and Science*, 20.

Chatterjee, S. and Nankervis, A. (2007) *Asian Management in Transition*. London: Palgrave.

Dallago, B. (2003) 'SME Development in Hungary', in Dallago, B. and McIntyre, R. (eds) *Small and Medium Enterprises in Transitional Economies*. London: Palgrave.

Dallago, B. and McIntyre, R. (2003) 'Public Policy in SME Development', in Dallago, B. and McIntyre, R. (eds) *Small and Medium Enterprises in Transitional Economies*. London: Palgrave.

Fukuyama, F. (1995) *Trust: The Social Virtues and the Creation of Prosperity*. New York: Free Press.

Heracleous, L. (2003) *Strategy and Organization*. Cambridge: Cambridge University Press.

Hofstede, G. (1984) *Culture's Consequences*. Beverly Hills, CA: Sage.

Hofstede, G. (1991) *Culture and Organisations*. London: McGraw-Hill.

Lind, P. (2009) 'SME Managers' Views on SME Management – A Comparative Study'. Paper presented at the *4th International Conference on Management, Theory and Practice*. Tartu University, Estonia.

Lind, P. and Scheepers, M. J. (2009) *Managing Customer–Supplier Relationships in Small Manufacturing Businesses*. Stellenbosch, South Africa: Stellenbosch University.

Sako, M. (1992) *Price, Quality and Trust – Inter-Firm Relations in Britain and Japan*. Cambridge: Cambridge University Press.

Sako, M. (1997) 'Does Trust Improve Business Performance?', in Lane, C. and Backmann, R. (eds.) *Trust within and between Organisations*. Oxford: Oxford University Press.

Smitka, M. J. (1991) *Competitive Ties: Subcontracting in the Japanese Automotive Industry*. New York: Columbia University Press.

Sun, L. (2003) 'Ownership Reform in the Absence of Crisis: China's Township, Village and Private Enterprises', in Dallago, B. and McIntyre, R. (eds) *Small and Medium Enterprises in Transitional Economies*. London: Palgrave.

Szarka, J. (1990) 'Networks and Small Firms'. *International Small Business Journal*, 8: 2.

Whitley, R. (1990) 'Eastern Asian Enterprise Structures and the Comparative Analysis of Forms of Business Organisations'. *Organisation Studies*, 11: 1047–1074.

Whitley, R. (1992) *Business Systems in East Asia: Firms, Markets and Societies*. London: Sage.

11   The small firm in a global context

Opportunities and threats

Introduction

Global, globalization, global world and *global context* are all concepts that add further dimensions to the more traditional terms *international* and *internationalisation*. 'Global' and 'international' are semantically very close but not the same: global implies *one world*, whereas international refers to a political and cultural complex of countries. While 'international' has retained its meaning, 'global' has expanded into a semantically more varied concept with sociocultural implications.

The global village was a metaphor coined in the 1960s by Marshall McLuhan, a Canadian media professor. He suggested that the world could be likened to a village where people have come closer through communication and information technology. The metaphor conveyed a picture of opportunities and possibilities for everybody to come together and jointly work for a better world. The rhetoric also created the 'global traveller' living in the global village. However, the overwhelming majority of the inhabitants of the global village have very limited opportunities to travel the world from their homes in, say, African villages or South American small towns. Most are not in possession of the benefits offered in the global village, with possible exception of mobile phones and television. In fact, the global traveller represents a tiny fraction of the world's population. The often euphoric views and expectations of globalization are in contrast to the centre–periphery discussions in development theory in the 1960s and 70s that saw the world divided between those who had and those who had not (Frank 1978; Prebisch 1950).

Small and medium enterprises (SMEs) in low- and middle-income countries are affected by globalization in different ways, with a much more limited scope for benefiting from global trade, technological development or strong capital markets. According to the globalization rhetoric, business opportunities should be open to all firms, but in reality they are hindered by trade regulations imposed by developed nations in the rounds of trade negotiations, which in recent years have sought to lower trade barriers around the world, allowing countries to increase trade globally. However, since 2008 these talks have stalled over a divide on major issues such as agriculture, industrial tariffs and import quotas.

Critics of globalization argue that the notion of free trade based on comparative advantage works primarily to the benefit of industrialized countries that can take advantage of cheap labour and goods produced in developing countries. Where free trade does not deliver such advantages to developing countries, they employ protectionist policies to support globally non-viable but industries important to domestic politics (Kingsbury 2004). The International Monetary Fund (IMF) has recognized that economic globalization has not been an unmitigated success, stating that:

A large part of the world's population – especially in sub-Saharan Africa – has been left behind by economic progress. As a result, the disparities between the world's richest and poorest countries are now wider than ever, with increasing incidences of poverty within countries.

(IMF 2002)

Many proponents and critics of economic globalization also argue that the world remains a long way from an idealized free-trade model. Some even suggest that pro-free traders are less interested in free trade as such but rather the untrammelled pursuit of profit, which can be achieved by free trade where that suits, but by government intervention or protection where that suits (Kingsbury ibid.).

Globalization and the globalization process have supporters and critics. Many writers view globalization as the transformation of societies and their institutions towards a new individualism and more democratic societies (e.g. Giddens 1998). Others fear Western cultural colonialism of the Third World (Iyer 1988), where Western value systems and lifestyles gradually infiltrate and take over original behaviour and views. Writers on economic and political development in Africa are predominantly critical of what the globalization process has produced (e.g. Padayachee 2010), including the growing gap between rich and poor, contrary to initial expectations (e.g. Isaak 2005). In what follows, the small and medium business sector is discussed from these varying viewpoints, focusing both on the opportunities that globalization may hold, and the different types of threats to which small businesses are exposed.

Globalization and the small and medium business sector

Changes in the global business environment can be attributed largely to the processes of technological innovation, increasing foreign direct investments (FDIs), and expanding trade and financial networks. Indeed, the advent of new techniques, not least in the transport and communications sectors, has been of determining and crucial importance for this development. They are the underlying reasons for the flows of money, goods and information that characterize modern society. The countries whose people have benefited most from this development live in the advanced economies of the world which have been at the forefront in both technological innovations and their commercial exploitation. This development has owed much to the liberalization of ideas, which have opened economies to market forces and have had a broad impact across the whole spectrum of the business environment, including cultural and social environments, and legal and political systems. For many countries, mainly the advanced Western economies, individualist cultures fostered capitalist enterprises, along with legal systems to protect property and democratic national political systems responsive to their citizens. The defining characteristics of the market economy, inherited from the early industrializing Western economies, have come to be identified with liberal market reforms in the context of nation-states (Morrison 2006).

The opportunities and benefits of globalization have had varying effects on countries depending on their position on the development scale. While the most affluent high-income countries (who are also the ones directing the globalization process) benefit most, several middle-income countries have also reached an economic development level where foreign investments bring in advanced technology and create dynamic markets. On the other hand, in recent years, low-income countries have fallen further behind the technological leader and are therefore unable to exploit technologies exploited elsewhere, resulting in an emerging poverty trap (Fiaschi and Lavezzi 2005).

Small firms and globalization in low-income countries

One aspect of globalization that creates benefits for small and medium firms in both middle- and high-income countries comes from technology. Communication technology, as well as new techniques which improve production processes, have had direct as well as indirect effects by facilitating the manufacture of better products, by developing more efficient organizations and in the upgrading of management skills. For small firms in the majority of low-income countries, the impact of globalization is often masked by local factors of more significance. In fact, measures of economic development and technology usage in low-income countries come into conflict with general economic growth models, and would therefore need to be measured by dedicated and modified yardsticks.

Francis Stewart (1978) concludes from her excellent research on technology and under-development that the huge gulf between the organizational form to which advanced-country technology in designed and suited, and the forms of organization indigenous to most Third World economies has meant that the use of advanced-country technology also generally requires the use of advanced-country organizations. These organizations are directly imported in the case of foreign investment; in other areas they are imported indirectly via management contracts and/or managers training overseas. Advanced-country technology thus leads to advanced-country techniques of management. The shortage of these techniques is the result of the import of a technology which requires managerial techniques completely out of step with local possibilities. Managerial dependence follows from technological dependence. And of course technological dependence is reinforced by managerial dependence, since the imported managers/managerial techniques are designed to manage the imported advanced-country techniques, and therefore when the managers make a technical choice they do so in directions in which their specialized advantage lies – in the further importation of advanced-country technology.

An alternative to advanced-country technology has been discussed within the concept of *appropriate technology*, described as a technology designed with special consideration to resource limitations, and local environmental and economic conditions. Appropriate technology is closely linked to the name of E. F. Schumacher who studied village-based economies and suggested using technology in a way that takes account of both human needs and limitations (Schumacher 1973).

Appropriate technology normally has the following characteristics (Stewart 1985):

- more labour-intensive than a less-appropriate technology;
- less capital-intensive;
- less skill-intensive;
- makes more use of local materials/resources;
- is smaller scale; and
- produces a more appropriate product designed for lower-income consumers.

Appropriate technology is not geared to large-scale production and therefore does not benefit from economy of scale. But economy of scale is in itself formed by the history of technological development in which particular organizational forms have favoured the development of large-scale survival. This has in turn resulted in various forms of organizational overhead, such as marketing and administration, with the aim of increasing market power, requiring more marketing and administration and so on. A low-income country with an economy that is predominantly based on appropriate technology may find different forms of competitive strategies in which growth is not necessarily a survival factor. Small firms operating in this context can survive without access to advanced-country technology.

Imbalance in world trade

The imbalance in world trade – the way high added-value commodities flow from North to South and primary products, such as agriculture and raw material, flow in the opposite direction – is partly explained by the small role manufacturing industry plays in most developing countries. Chile is the leading copper exporter in the world: when world prices are high the revenue of the country is high; conversely, when there is a slump in prices it is low. The Chilean economy is therefore highly dependent on external factors beyond its own control. By creating a domestic added-value manufacturing industry to refine basic copper into high-value products, the country would not only reduce its external dependence significantly, but also increase export value and its revenue.

The present world trade environment thus provides opportunities for developing countries to derive tangible benefits if they produce competitive value-added manufactured goods for global markets. Nevertheless, most developing countries remain marginalized. The 'Doha Development Agenda' was aimed at assisting developing countries to become more effective partners in the global trading environment, and initiatives such as the EU European Banking Authority (EBA) or the US African Growth and Opportunity Act (AGOA) have opened potential markets by reducing duties and quotas. The EBA acts as a hub and spoke network of EU and national bodies, safeguarding public values such as the stability of the financial system, the transparency of markets and financial products and the protection of depositors and investors. The intention behind the AGOA was to assist the economies of sub-Saharan Africa and to improve economic relations between the United States and the region. But the lack of competitive productive supply capacity and the lack of compliance with technical market specifications (standards and technical regulations) continue to be difficult obstacles for developing countries that often effectively prevent them from entering international markets.

As a result, international trade continues to be dominated by the industrialized countries whose share is around the 80 per cent (by value), which should be compared to developing regions, such as Latin America and Africa, whose share amounted to 6 and 2 per cent respectively in 2000, Africa's rising to around 2.5 per cent in 2006 (O'Brien and Williams 2004). In contrast, the world's 48 poorest countries have seen their share of world trade decline by more than 40 per cent since 1980, to a mere 0.4 per cent in 2000. Reasons for this include policy decisions in the negotiation rounds and poor compliance with international rules and regulations intended to protect humans and the environment from toxic and poisonous materials. Regarding the latter, the World Trade Organization (WTO), together with United Nations, has issued two recommendations which have been ratified and agreed to by a majority of countries. These agreements define the international rights and obligations of member countries to set standard-related measures that affect trade. The recommendations are known as the Technical Barriers to Trade (TBT) Agreement and the Agreement on Sanitary and Phyto-Sanitary (SPS). (Phyto-sanitary refers to health and safety measures for animals and plants.)

The agreements can have a significant impact on a country's trade and exports. Divergent and higher standards can become a serious barrier to trade for enterprises in general, and especially SMEs in developing countries, due to the high costs incurred in manufacturing to foreign standards proving compliance in an internationally-recognized manner. A further challenge is posed by some of the TBT/SPS proposals submitted by member countries (and reviewed and examined by the WTO and other member countries), which may result in more stringent standards in the fields of technical notification and conformity assessment requirements.

To overcome these challenges and to gain greater access to export markets, developing countries not only need to comply with international standards and follow the WTO recommendations, but also actively participate and contribute to the international debate on safety rules and standards. To achieve this, enterprises will need to deal with the increasing use of TBT and SPS measures on two fronts simultaneously. Not only will enterprises need to initiate steps to upgrade their production systems and enhance their competitiveness to conform to the requirements, but also improve their awareness of the TBT/SPS measures, so they can use them to challenge other's attempts to restrict of trade. Consequently, there is a significant need to create awareness among all concerned stakeholders in a country on how their interests could be safeguarded and how they can make use of the TBT and SPS Agreements and other provisions, proposals and strategies under the WTO umbrella.

It should be noted in this context that not only are international organizations like the WTO involved, but that national country governments are responsible for implementing the provisions of the TBT and SPS among local producers. Large firms in the industrialized world, who outsource production to low- and middle-income countries to reduce the costs of material and production, also have a responsibility to establish standards and control their suppliers and partner firms to ensure compliance with quality rules. Examples from the pharmaceutical industry show that many advanced firms in high-income countries fail to take this responsibility seriously.

For developing countries, turning standards from barriers into trade opportunities will demand the proactive participation of a broad range of stakeholders in the development of new international standards. More active participation should create the necessary conditions for organizations like the International Standards Organization (ISO) to develop a standard which would also consider the unique and varying needs pertaining to developing countries. Here, consideration must be given to the realities and priorities of developing countries, which can be different from of the developed world, to meet the stakeholder needs in those countries.

In low- and middle-income countries, there has been limited understanding of the WTO recommendations among the manufacturers/exporters affected due to the complex and bureaucratic use of words and concepts. As a result, there is generally little response or comment to the TBT/SPS regulations from the industry side. The limited access of manufacturers and exporters – mainly SMEs – to this type of information hinders developing countries' ability to retaliate against provisions or proposals considered detrimental. Other reasons are lack of experience in drafting proposals, lack of procedures for the dissemination of proposals to organizations in industry, services and trade, an inability to respond to TBT and SPS proposals issued by other countries within the stipulated period of time, and lack of active participation in the TBT and SPS committee meetings, etc. The competitiveness the industries needs to be increased and procedures for strengthening SME management skills must be developed in order to infuse management with a working awareness of the importance of compliance with WTO, TBT and SPS requirements for trade, so they comprehend and better comply with these requirements, while at the same time increasing their influence and participation in the development of international standards for export products of interest. Drawing on current research into SME performance in developing countries, there is a need for:

- enterprise managers to understand the importance of product and service quality for trade;
- enterprise managers to realize that trade is an opportunity and not a guarantee; and that utilizing an opportunity requires skills, understanding and context awareness;
- stakeholders need to influence the creation of standards to ensure they create trading opportunities, doing so through early involvement in the standard-setting process at national, regional and international levels; and
- governments to establish a method to monitor enterprises' compliance with the provisions of the TBT and SPS Agreements, respond to proposals and to participate in the standards development process.

The introduction of these WTO recommendations will not remove all hurdles to trade between developing and developed countries but, if complied with by a significant number of small and medium-sized manufacturing firms in low- and middle-income countries, they will facilitate the firms' integration in the international market. Trade is not a guarantee for a company but an opportunity, and reducing the technical barriers to trade by complying with the emerging international standards for the selection of appropriate materials and in producing environmentaly-friendly products is a real opportunity for many small businesses in the developing world.

Opportunities for small business in the global context

The global market provides challenging opportunities for small and medium firms in both developed and developing countries. However, these opportunities also result in growing competition from high added-value and high customer-value products and services. Since prices must be compatible, this has led to an emphasis on cost control. Cost reduction strategies have resulted in outsourcing of part or all production to low-salary countries as a means of maintaining profit levels. Small and primarily middle-sized enterprises in middle-income countries are the primary targets for this outsourcing strategy.

However, success in the global market is no more guaranteed than success in the home market. Being familiar with traditions and rules of the local market, understanding consumer preferences and buying patterns, as well as being part of local customer and supplier networks, is a business asset of high competitive value that few foreign companies can share. If, despite that, a local firm does not manage to be competitive in the local market, it would be naïve to believe that doing business in the global market could be a success.

The way small business managers can prepare for an entry into the global market is by meeting the requirements for efficient management. This includes awareness and understanding of new rules and agreements regulating international trade, such as the TBT Agreement discussed above. Complying with these rules in the home market prepares the ground for international trade. The purpose of participating in global business is not only to export, but may also be to enter into a business collaboration or partnership with a foreign firm in one's home market. High management competence and a proven track record in the local market are necessary aspects of becoming an attractive partner.

The following list summarizes some of the professional qualities that managers need to acquire to be competitive in a global context. This involves not just knowing what to do, but understanding why it is important and getting it done right. Meeting these requirements is still no guarantee for success, but failing to meet them is a guarantee of failure!

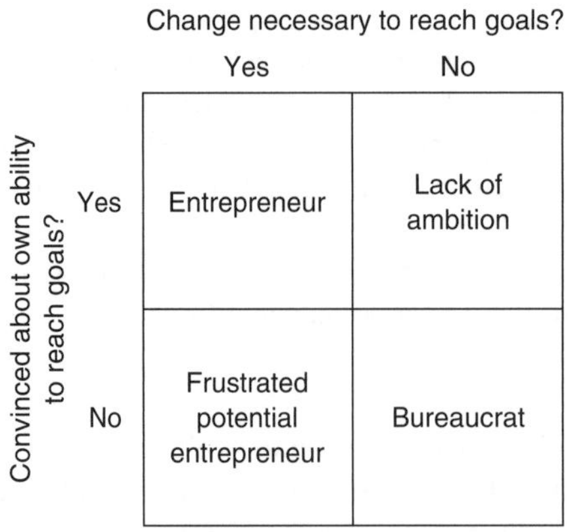

Change necessary to reach goals?

	Yes	No
Yes	Entrepreneur	Lack of ambition
No	Frustrated potential entrepreneur	Bureaucrat

Convinced about own ability to reach goals?

Figure 11.1 Different attitudes towards necessary change.

Source: Modified from Hammer and Champy (1998).

- A clear understanding (vision) of what needs to be done: Managers must have a clear understanding of the professional qualities and business conditions needed to operate in the global context and what results should be expected. When implementing organizational changes that may be considered necessary for the global market, the expected end results are generally articulated in the form of a vision. The clearer the picture presented by this vision and the stronger the buy-in to it, the higher the probability of success.
- A strong awareness of current reality: The commitment to participate in global business requires awareness of the current reality. The manager must acquire all necessary and relevant information and shatter individual perceptions and self-imposed distortions of reality.
- The conviction that the manager can shape the future of the firm: A vision becomes a living force only when people truly believe they can shape their future.

One type of manager does not, in fact, feel they are contributing to creating current reality of the firm, and they do not see how they can contribute towards changing that reality. Another type of manager welcomes the opportunity of shaping their own and the company's future. In fact, it is possible to discern four different management attitudes towards the change necessary to enter a global market. These are illustrated in Figure 11.1.

Being convinced of one's ability and seeing the need for change as precursor to entering a global market makes the manager an entrepreneurial type. The 'frustrated potential entrepreneur' sees the need for change but is less sure of his or her ability – either because the current business situation in the home market is enough to deal with, or the manager find the idea of entering a global market too perplexing at present. Managers convinced of their ability but unwilling to accept the need for change is characteristic of the satisfied manager suffering from 'lack of ambition'. Finally, managers doubtful about his or her ability and unwilling to understand the need to become a global actor is the bureaucratic type, who mistrusts the benefits of expanding the market.

Threats to small business in the global context

The foremost threat to a small, local business entering the global scene comes from lack of management awareness and understanding of important principles related to international business, such as culture, language and international relations.

Principles related to international business

A small firm wanting to enter the global market needs to understand the major factors shaping the international or global business community. A firm that is used to operating in a highly price-sensitive home market, where competition is primarily based on price, may find that quality in products and services are the primary competitive factors in the global market. Firms in fierce global competition furthermore learn that high quality combined with a competitive price requires tough and continuous cost control. Those firms which do not manage to comply with these rules will not last long in the global competition.

Small firms need to catch up with larger firms' concern for the environment by realizing environmental awareness has become a business asset in the global economy. Openness about the strategies a firm follows to avoid causing environmental damage and to prevent pollution (in the case of hazardous production) is about to become a formal requirement for export permits to certain countries. The TBT Agreement discussed above is a step in that direction. At present, these measures are regarded as threats by many small firms, particularly in low- and middle-income countries, as they exclude the firms from potential export markets.

Efficient financial transactions between countries are a precondition for a firm to close a business deal across boundaries. Global financial flows can today generally be trusted for accuracy, even if delays in transactions cannot be excluded. A more immediate problem is the national money transfer system that delays payment between suppliers and customers. For a small business supplier, this may be further aggravated by a customer's poor payment record, caused either by lack of money or negligence in fulfilling business agreements. Claims on an overseas customer that are delayed both through the international and the home country's banking procedures can have highly-negative effects on the small business economy. A supplier's claim of 1,000 USD that is delayed for six months is reduced in value by an amount that depends on inflation. With an annual inflation of 10 per cent (not unusual in low-income countries) the value of the claim after six months is around 950 USD. The difference may be of the same magnitude as the calculated profit, which is then lost. Financial uncertainty and lack of knowledge about the international payment system is regarded by many small business managers as a potential threat to marketing and selling overseas.

In addition, doing business across borders may involve other costs that can hit the small firm hard. Custom duties for import and export, as well as various kinds of bribes paid to ensure smooth handling of goods at ports and in transit are not unusual. Ghana's Minister of Ports, Harbours and Railways has expressed grave concern at alarming rate of bribery, corruption and pilfering in the nation's shipping industry. For example, vehicles imported into the country have a nasty habit of disappearing even under the watch of security personnel. He promised to tackle this problem, but said it simply would not go away (*The Statement* 2001).

Principles related to culture

Timeliness – being on time and accepting that time is an important factor in organizational efficiency – is central to certain cultures but more peripheral to others. Many Western countries, such as the northern parts of Europe, tend to be obsessed with time, and being on time for appointments and meetings is generally considered highly important. This creates efficient organizations but is also a stress factor in private as well as in business lives. In cultures in southern parts of the world, the attitude to time and being on time is more relaxed. This may create a less stressful life but at the same time reduces organizational efficiency, giving rise not only to difficulties in planning but also increased costs due to unnecessary long lead times between activities in administration and production.

Participating in global business means that firms become exposed to different cultural attitudes, of which different attitudes to time tend to be most common. Lind (1991) reported how a computer-based materials control system an Egyptian industry about to implement would give immediate notice in case there were disruptions in the material flow. If such a situation occurred the problem could immediately be attended to. However, the time element in this situation was subordinated to the question at whether there was a higher-ranking manager available to approve the decision needed to solve the problem. Using the typology suggested by Hofstede it can be assumed that other countries scoring high in power distance (like Egypt) would exhibit a similar attitude to time (Hofstede 1991).

Principles related to language

Information technology has facilitated business communication between partners, and the simplified English of the Internet communication permits the transmission of basic messages. However, the communication of sensitive business strategies and plans, as well as dialogue between business partners (such as potential suppliers and customers) in different cultural environments requires adequate language proficiency and the ability to express sensitive views and thoughts. Many small business managers lack the ability to express themselves accurately in English, which is also the most common language in global business. Relying on external consultants and other advisors to negotiate business deals with foreign business partners is a solution, but not without risks. Improving language competence is therefore a must for small business managers wishing to participate in global business.

Principles related to international relations

The global business community is a complex system with many actors and limited transparency. A small business manager may not always have all the necessary information to make proper judgements about market development, competitors' strategies and the political situation in different regions. In a global context, there are many kinds of actors on different levels whose decisions have impact on business. Certain decisions taking place on global levels can become public information through channels available to all. Changes in oil prices and in other raw materials traded on stock markets can be followed everywhere, and with the help of early warning analysis business managers may in some situations be ready to take appropriate measures.

A more difficult planning situation for the small business manager occurs when decisions are taken which are not openly accounted for but will have impact the conditions of doing business in a country or a region. Political unrest may be one such situation, but also non-political situations are common. For example, it is not unknown for multi-national company with local suppliers to find alternative suppliers with lower labour costs levels in another country and relocate production to that country. Such decisions are usually announced just before closure to avoid protest action by workers that might jeopardise production.

In today's economic world order, the liberalization of trade and financial flows has created new business opportunities and less bureaucracy. At the same time, certain control mechanisms have become obsolete or simply disappeared. Large companies involved in international operations have been able to benefit considerably by researching, analysing and adapting to the new rules of the game. Small firms with limited management capabilities and time resources have been unable to do this to the same extent. The following Mini-case from Senegal describes how a small firm depending on material supply outside of its own control became a victim of decisions taken elsewhere.

Box 11.1 Mini-case: Société Nationale des Conserveries du Sénégal (SNCDS)

SNCDS is a fish cannery in Senegal, a country with one of the largest and most-developed fishing industries in West Africa. Fisheries represent one of the most important sectors in Senegal's economy. The fishing industry supplies food for domestic consumption and is a significant source of foreign exchange.

SNCDS has a highly modern and efficient canning factory located in Dakar harbour, where it has facilities for loading a trawler's catch into the factory where the canning process begins. Work is manual and provides employment for a great number of women. The domestic fleet of large fishing boats and trawlers is small, and European trawlers fishing off the West African coast are therefore SNCDS' main source of tuna. The company is entirely dependent on these deliveries and interruption means the factory cannot produce.

The foreign trawlers fish under bilateral agreements, but when the price of fish goes up elsewhere in the Atlantic, they leave the West African waters for more lucrative catches elsewhere. SNCDS and similar small and medium firms in the Senegalese fish industry are very vulnerable because of the uncertainty of fish input. Participating in this global business is therefore both an opportunity and a threat as long as no alternative exist.

While fishing continues under this bilateral agreement between the European Union and West Africa, the EU is annually paying considerable sums (200 million USD in 2010) to selected West African countries for the right to allow fishing trawlers from EU countries to fish in West African waters. The payments are intended as compensation to the local fishing population, since they are not any longer in the position to catch their own fish. However, it is uncertain how much of the EU subsidy have reached the local population.

Doing business across borders: business communication

Business communication across borders takes place on three hierarchical levels. On the higher level, a company negotiates with government officials or a ministry about licenses, possible sites for production or business premises or import/export quotas. Large firms are mostly the major actors here. Companies may also negotiate with trade unions about employment rules, salary levels, working conditions etc. This is typical of situations when production is transferred between countries.

The most common level of cross-border business communication happens when company A negotiates with company B about joint ventures, local representation, partnerships, or simply about normal business deals. A common factor of crucial importance on all three levels is to be aware of and understand how much the outcome of a business negotiation process depends on the way we communicate and understand the essence of cross-cultural communication.

Cross-cultural communication

Communication is the exchange of messages between a *sender* and a *receiver*. Uncertainty in the communication occurs when the message is either distorted or its meaning is not clear to the receiver. Sometimes uncertainty may be caused by cultural differences in values or behaviour.

Words referring to model concepts or words referring to 'touchable things' can have different connotations when used in different cultural contexts. *Democracy* is such a model concept whose meaning depends on the polity of a country. Communication based on model concepts is therefore more open to misunderstandings.

The language philosopher Ludwig Wittgenstein claimed that 'we make to ourselves pictures of facts; the picture becomes a model of reality' and 'the logical picture of the fact is the thought'. The meaning of this is that we create a picture of what we see or experience and this picture becomes a model by which we understand reality. This is also the basis for converting our thoughts into words for communication. Communication problems occur if the thoughts of the sender and receiver are based on different models. Figure 11.2 describes the communication process.

The sender in the figure has a thought based on the picture that has been created of a specific fact in the sender's reality. However, the thought is also coloured by the cultural context and its value system, language, socio-economic and technological context. The thought is concerted into a word by which communication takes place with a receiver in a different cultural context. The receiver is familiar with the word. However, the word creates a somewhat different thought and thus also a different picture and fact in the receiver's reality.

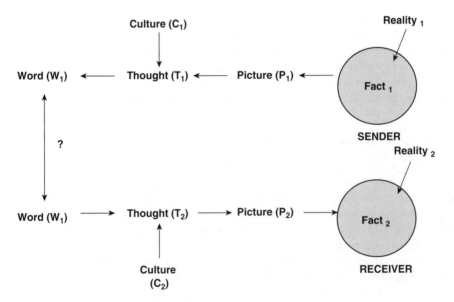

Figure 11.2 Communication between sender and receiver.

Lind (1991) describes in an example from Egypt concerning the relationship between production failures and the age of machinery. In the Egyptian sender's view, the fact that more than 80 per cent of the machines were ten years old or more had no bearing on machine reliability and the negative effects this might have on the production flow. (The Egyptian production environment was such that machinery of similar age was common in the industry and therefore not of particular concern.) From a cultural point of view the very high power distance characteristic of Egyptian management (in Hofstede's typology) meant it was inappropriate to question the adequacy and capacity of the production facilities. However, from the European receiver's perspective, the age of the machines suggest a possible scarcity of spare parts, worn out machine components and other facts resulting in increasing the risk of failure. Even if the common word *reliability* is used in the communication, it creates different thoughts and pictures of reality between sender and receiver.

Communication uses language but language sometimes puts limits on what can be communicated. Language has two main functions: to convey messages and to regulate their meaning. However, a language's capacity to regulate meaning is limited. The building blocks of messages (words, grammar) define the language's maximum capacity, and it may be insufficient to express and convey all the feelings, reactions and memories desired. It may therefore be necessary to supplement messages with alternative means of expressions, such as gestures and body-language. For communication between cultures these non-language alternative are sometimes crucial for correctly understanding a message. In many cross-cultural business discussions, English is not the mother tongue of any of the participants which often restricts their ability to communicate vital matters. This puts an extra emphasis on correctly interpreting and deciphering what is being said in a conversation. The more diverse the context to be explained, discussed and conveyed from sender to receiver, the more diverse and versatile must be the means of communication. Ashby (1956) expressed this in The Law of Requisite Variety as *only variety can absorb variety.*[1]

Figure 11.3 identifies some of the more common barriers to communication, where interpretation by the receiver is distorted due to reasons not obvious to the sender.

By filtering information, the sender may omit or hide (either consciously or unconsciously) certain elements which are required to make the message intelligible to the receiver. A business proposal may seem clear enough to the sender, but requires additional items of information to create a clear picture for the receiver. The sender may be insensitive to the receiver's need for clarity and explanations, due to lack of experience, skills or cultural

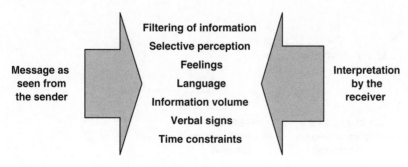

Figure 11.3 Barriers in the communication process.

understanding on both sides. Likewise, being insensitive to feelings may hinder smooth communication. Not understanding the values of another culture can result in the use of improper language or expressions, or references to heroes or symbols in the other culture that are interpreted as inappropriate. The volume of information delivered by the sender may be too large, thereby obscuring the essence of the message. Too much information may also tire or weary the receiver. In preparing a communication, the amount of information should be adapted to the situation (time, receiver's capacity, language etc.). Being sensitive to non-verbal signs of the receiver and less occupied by personal performance are fundamental skills in all communication processes. Many business communications have gone awry due to time constraints. Careful planning is required to allow the messages to be delivered in a sequence and order that is not jeopardized by sudden time constraint.

How to prevent communication barriers

Actively listening and trying to understand the contents of the message is the key in communication. Some aspects of active listening are suggested in Figure 11.4. Although it should be obvious that efficient communication requires mutual listening, it often happens that, as the speaker talks, while seemingly concentrating on what is being said, the listener is preoccupied with preparing his or her next contribution to the communication.

Strong feelings like aggression and strong emotions need to be controlled, since the other party may be made to feel uncomfortable or uneasy by an outburst of uncontrolled feelings. Non-verbal signs often convey important and useful information about the status of a communication. Correctly interpreting such signs can mean the difference between a successful and less successful outcome of a negotiation!

Language should be simple, but not too simple! Unnecessarily complicated and complex words and expressions are sometimes used to convey the speaker's competence and expertise. This is seldom of benefit to the communication, since it may increase the risk of misunderstanding and reduce the clarity of the message for the receiver. In addition, it may create a feeling of inferiority in the receiver, which does not benefit the communication. To confirm that the communication is flowing without barriers, continuous feedback should be obtained by periodically asking the other party to confirm what is being discussed.

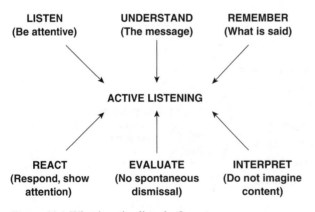

Figure 11.4 What is active listening?

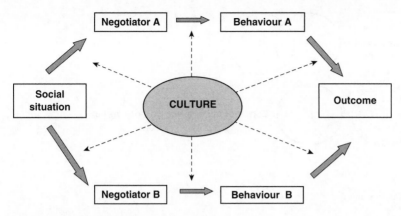

Figure 11.5 Cultural influence on negotiation.

Negotiation

Negotiation takes place between two or more parties, either individuals or groups of individuals. In what follows, we assume two parties representing different cultures – a common situation in cross-cultural business situations. The underlying social situation of both parties determines the negotiators' behaviour during the negotiation. This has been described in numerous publications, ranging from the more anecdotal to serious attempts at understanding and explaining cultural impact on negotiation styles (Hickson and Pugh 1995; Bjerke 1999; Trompenaars 1993).

Several authors have attempted to utilize the typology suggested by Hofstede to illustrate different negotiating styles (Hofstede 1991). For example, in countries characterised by large power distance (e.g. Arab countries and countries in Latin America), the key negotiator comes from top management and the negotiators play an important role. In countries characterized by high collectivism (East Asia, Latin America) face-saving is important for the negotiating partners. Face-saving has two meanings in Chinese culture: *li-an* concerns a person's moral character and honour, *mian-zi* connotes reputation and prestige. Both are important in social interactions considering the importance of recognition by others in Chinese culture. The Chinese fear of losing face is the fear of having their ego and prestige deflated (Bjerke 1999). In countries with strong masculine cultures it is considered important to 'win the negotiation'. In Scandinavian countries (having relatively weak masculine cultures), Hofstede's typology predicts that the preference is for negotiations to be brought to a successful conclusion by consensus and agreements, rather than by 'winning a battle'.

The negotiation situation may be described by reference to Figure 11.5. It illustrates how the underlying social situations influence the negotiators. Such situations are described by cultural characteristics like the ones briefly discussed above. The social situation determines more or less the negotiator's view of the situation and behaviour during the negotiation. The outcome of the negotiation is therefore a result of negotiating skills and practices which are in turn influenced by each negotiator's cultural background.

Negotiation outcome

A negotiation can result in either outcome or no outcome. When there is no overlap of acceptance zones, as shown in Figure 11.6, a positive outcome is not possible. A positive

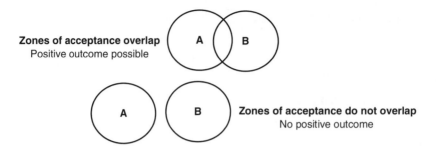

Zones of acceptance overlap
Positive outcome possible

A   B

A   B   Zones of acceptance do not overlap
No positive outcome

Figure 11.6 Negotiation outcome.

outcome depends on negotiation skills, not only an understanding of cultural differences, but also on the prior availability of adequate and relevant information. Surroundings and circumstances (like physical facilities and practical arrangements) are important for contributing to a creative and stimulating atmosphere.

Conclusion

In his book, *Images of the Organization*, Gareth Morgan (1997) reflected on the future and the negative aspects of capitalism, and asks whether the decline in Western markets is going to be reversed by some new value-added service economy that finds a new way of creating and distributing wealth. Is the expansion into massive new markets – China, Eastern Europe, India and South America – going to provide a breath of new life? Will Third World countries become the new economic superpowers, following the path already charted by the Pacific Rim 'Asian tigers'? Is their economic power going to be undermined by a new Third World unionism that creates similar constraints to development as those experienced in the West? What is going to happen to the social fabric of Western and Eastern societies given that the 'invisible hand' conceived by Adam Smith is no longer doing its job in guiding the system for the good of all? We are in the midst of a dialectical unfolding, the future of which cannot be seen. Who knows whether the crisis currently being experienced by Western capitalism will prove to be a point of complete transformation of the system, or just another stage in its evolution?

Future changes in society may be dramatic, creating new political and economic rules and conditions: new management attitudes will be required to cope with new situations. Or changes into the future may follow the same trajectory we have been following in the past but with incremental changes that we can cope with based on earlier experience. Whatever scenario we chose, it is safe to assume and predict that small firms will always play a vital role in society. Opportunities and threats will always be there and good managers will always be able to distinguish between them and to benefit by the right decisions.

Note

1 Ross Ashby (1903–1972) was a British psychiatrist who contributed to the theory of cybernetics.

References

Ashby, R. (1956) *An Introduction to Cybernetics*. London: Chapman & Hall.

Bjerke, B. (1999) *Business, Leadership and Culture*. Cheltenham, UK: Edward Elgar.

Fiaschi, D. and Lavezzi, A. (2005) 'Appropriate Technology in a Solovian Nonlinear Growth Model'. *Oxford Review of Economic Policy*, 23.

Frank, A. G. (1978) *Dependent Accumulation and Underdevelopment*. London: Macmillan.

Giddens, A. (1998) *The Third Way*. London: Polity Press.

Hammer, M. and Champy, J. (1998) 'Business Process Analysis (BPA): The Key to Success in a Changing Environment', in *Scoping Study on Business Process Reengineering: Towards Successful IT Application, International Journal of Production Research*, 36(3).

Hickson, D. and Pugh, D. (1995) *Management Worldwide: The Impact of Societal Culture on Organisations around the Globe*. London: Penguin.

Hofstede, G. (1991) *Culture and Organisations*. London: McGraw-Hill.

IMF (2002) *Globalisation: A Framework for IMF Involvement*. Washington, DC: International Monetary Fund.

Isaak, R. (2005) *The Globalisation Gap*. Upper Saddle River, NJ: Prentice Hall.

Iyer, P. (1988) *Video Nights in Kathmandu*. New York: Knopf.

Kingsbury, D. (2004) 'Globalisation and Development', in Kingsbury, D., Remenyi, J., McKay, J. and Hunt, J. (eds) *Key Issues in Development*. New York: Palgrave.

Lind, P. (1991) *Computerisation in Developing Countries – Model and Reality*. London: Routledge.

Morgan, G. (1997) *Images of Organization*. London: Sage.

Morrison, J. (2006) *The International Business Environment*. Basingstoke, Hampshire: Palgrave Macmillan.

O'Brien, R. and Williams, M. (2004) *Global Political Economy – Evolution and Dynamics*. Basingstoke, Hampshire: Palgrave Macmillan.

Padayachee, V. (2010) *The Political Economy of Africa*. London: Routledge.

Prebisch, R. (1950) *The Economic Development of Latin America and Its Principal Problem*. New York: United Nations.

Schumacher, E. F. (1973) *Small is Beautiful: Economics as if People Mattered*. London: Blond and Briggs.

Stewart, F. (1978) *Technology and Underdevelopment*. London: Macmillan.

Stewart, F. (1985) 'Macro Policies for Appropriate Technology', in James, J. and Watanabe, S. (eds) *Technology, Institutions and Government Policies*. London: Macmillan.

The Statement (Ghana) (2011) 'Harbours Minister deplores incidence of bribery at nation's ports', February 27.

Trompenaars, F. (1993) *Riding the Waves of Culture*. London: Economist Books.

Part 3

Case studies

The following case studies are intended to illustrate organizational and management behaviour in small and medium enterprises in different cross-cultural environments. Drawing general conclusions from one study is always a delicate issue: what may be true of one firm is not necessarily valid for all.

The case studies have been collected and documented specifically for this book and do not appear elsewhere. After each case a number of discussion topics have been added in the form of questions. Chapters relevant to particular case studies are noted.

The following table summarizes the main attributes of the case studies.

Study	Company	Country	Focus	Notes
1	Freight Enterprise S.A.	Argentina	Leadership	
2	Alstermo Bruk	Sweden	Strategic management	Extended
3	Olympia International	South Africa	HR management	
4	Viettuan Trading	Vietnam	Entrepreneurship	Brief
5	Polmarco	Poland	Strategic management	
6	Lokal Industries	The Philippines	Entrepreneurship	
7	Ningxia	China	Operations management	Brief
8	IE Electronics	Sri Lanka	Leadership	Brief
9	Mandelay Coating	South Africa	Management	Brief
10	Carbex AB	Sweden	Operations management	
11	Kun Mining	China	Business development	
12	Doradca Consulting	Poland	Service sector	
13	Bernard Botejue Industries	Sri Lanka	Business development	
14	My Anh Garment Mfg.	Vietnam	Operations management	Brief
15	Sterisol AB	Sweden	Innovation	

12   Freight Enterprise SA

*Alicia B. Giacchero, Nora Donnin and
Fanny Martín*

DEPARTAMENTO DE ECONOMÍA, UNIVERSIDAD NACIONAL DEL SUR, BAHIA BLANCA, ARGENTINA

COUNTRY: ARGENTINA

Background

This family transport company was formed in 2005 as a Society of Limited Responsibility (SRL), as successor to a sole venture founded in 1990 and owned by the father.

The company is based in the same location as the original firm in Bahía Blanca city, about 700km south of Buenos Aires. It has a warehouse located in a one hectare plot comprising 2,000m^2 of covered space and one loading bay of 500m^2. The company operates to ISO 9000 standard and was approved by the local authority. It is provided with electronic security and surveillance personnel. There is a storage annex of 300m^2 that serves as a depot for goods.

Vision, mission, strategy

The long-term *vision* of the firm is to achieve the highest possible welfare level for its employees, customers and suppliers to obtain a good reputation within the sector, and steady growth and improvement in service.

Its *mission* is to capture as large a share of the shipping business as possible by serving customers efficiently within the region through speedy and cost-effective transport to various destinations. The firm wants to serve as a bridge between freight demand and supply, so contributing to the development and prosperity of the regions in which it operates.

The *strategy* of the firm is to ensure high standards within all responsibility areas; to increase the number of customers; and to stay on good terms with nationwide logistics operators. The strategy in relation to the internal process goals is to maintain the quality of services and to reduce costs without detriment to the first objective.

Business relations with the customers in the shipping business begin with demand for a small amount of goods, which increases over time, contributing to more and more of the company's revenue. At this point problems tend to arise, since big enterprises do not want to lose their bargaining power in tariff negotiations and hence become more competitive.

Finally, the firm has not defined any goals related to personnel education and growth rates.

Company data

Sales development since 2005 is shown in Table 12.1.

A report from March 2009 shows that the company's consignments represent around 2 per cent of total number of units leaving Bahía Blanca city. The company serves

Table 12.1 Sales development

Year	Sales (USD)
2005	605,150
2006	813,133
2007	1,039,701
2008	1,514,226
2009	1,358,365
2010	1,207,074[a]

Note
a Forecast.

Table 12.2 Employees

Year	Average	Maximum	In month(s)
2005	20	26	November
2006	21	24	April
2007	29	34	November
2008	31	33	February
2009	29	31	February, March, May
2010	23	25	January, February, March

Table 12.3 Transport fleet

Type of vehicle/equipment	Number of units[a]	Age
Chassis for local and regional distribution	1 (4)	2001
Trailers	0	
Trucks	8 (2)	2005
Semi-trailers	8 (2)	
Freight elevators	3	2000
Small cars	(1)	2004

Note
a Numbers in brackets are additional vehicles provided by other enterprises.

customers who are primarily located within the province of Buenos Aires, and to some extent in the city of Buenos Aires and the Provinces of Río Negro and San Luis.

Employment

Today, the firm has 23 employees, varying during the year due to variation in business. The split between employees engaged in transport of goods and in administrative and management activities is in the approximate ratio of 70:30. Employment during recent years is presented in the Table 12.2.

Between 2005 and 2010, a total of 158 persons have been employed by the company, 73 per cent staying less than one year. Out of this group 26 per cent broke their employment contract and stayed less than one month. This personnel turnover is particularly high among trucks drivers but lower among warehouses employees. However, employment turnover is not unique to this company.

Economic indicators

Figure 12.1 shows revenue, costs and profit before tax in millions of Argentinean Pesos (ARS). (In 2010, the exchange rate was approximately 1 USD = 4.1 ARS.) As can be seen, profit before tax increased steadily to 2008 but declined thereafter. Figure 12.2

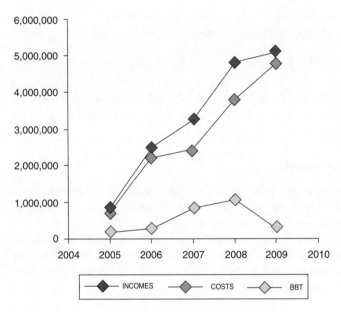

Figure 12.1 Revenue, costs and profit before tax (ARS).

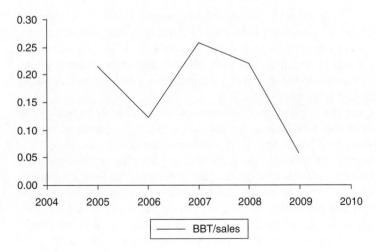

Figure 12.2 Profit margin.

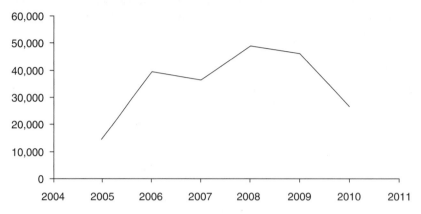

Figure 12.3 Income per employee (ARS).

shows the ratio between profit before tax and sales income (profit margin); this peaked in 2007. Finally, Figure 12.3 shows the income per employee: this also increased annually to 2008, but declined subsequently.

Products and/or services provided

The freight services provided by the enterprise break down as follows: 70 per cent food; 20 per cent cleaning articles and 10 per cent paints and house electronics products. The firm has a fleet of trucks which an average age of less than 10 years.

The company has warehouses with one refrigerated chamber of 150m^2 and freight elevators in order to provide one integrated logistic service for stock-building and the distribution of products. The logistic services are called *multicustomer* and are kept in the warehouses and can be set up outside of the customer locations.

Market–customer orientation

Half of the sales income is generated by five of the 1,200 company's customers. The most important customer is Unilever[1] (cleaning products), representing 20 per cent of income, followed by Garbarino (house electronic products) and Exologística (12 and 11 per cent of income respectively). Unilever of Argentina has been the most important customer during the company's existence, accounting for an annual average 32 per cent of sales and 40 per cent of labour costs of Freight Enterprise S.A.

The demand for transport services is more or less the same as for all other transport companies, and the company is therefore looking for alternative goods (for example, boxes). The company is also looking for new customers[2] who will not demand an exclusive business relationship, so avoiding price monopoly. Customers should preferably neither claim for compensation in case of service delays nor for quality standards during the freight operation.

Competition is characterized by more or less similar service levels among firms in the sector, but in comparison Freight Enterprise S.A. is among the more important ones. However, the sector is also characterized by firms of different sizes and one network of subcontracts among them, which make it possible to supply transport services under more attractive conditions.

Organization and management

Management style: leadership and power

Leadership and power are in the hands of one family member (a son). The relationship between the leader and the members in the group is good and characterized by a high grade of reliability, security and consideration among the leader, the employees and the others family members in the company.

The leader has an important position within the firm, having the power to hire and fire employees. Leadership is individualistic and oriented towards reaching ambitious goals. The leader is satisfied with his role, having been selected by the other family members after a crisis that was solved with the help of an external consultant. Others characteristics of the leader are his honesty, business knowledge and sometimes explosive character. The structure of the work routine has been formalized through a software application called *Transoft*.

Corporate and organizational culture

Corporate and organizational culture is transmitted to the employees through the concept of customer orientation and the organization chart. Externally, the firm's culture is communicated by various means, including its retention of the original firm's logo, symbolizing the new firm's intention of maintaining the family's business values.

The employees consider that the work culture is characterized by fast work within a wide range workspace. Teams appear well-organized, enjoying the changing work rhythm and contact with customers. The workers assume that promotion does not depend on working more but on the quality of their work. They prefer to work at a moderate distance from the leader, and they feel themselves part of one family.

Within the organizational culture, the employees' values are salary increase, employment stability, better working conditions and less stress at the workplace, in this order. The recognition of values at the workplace and those of self-recognition represents the meaning of work and is the basis for a career.

Many aspects of paternalistic organizational culture can be recognized immediately, including loyalty; few horizontal communication channels (e-mails); one familiar context, but with one strict control system to achieve goals; and lack of opportunities for communication between hierarchies and sectors.

Present situation: opportunities and challenges

Today's level of business activity (in terms of revenue, profit and employment) could be increased in case of growing market demand, since the company has ample resources for expansion. The possibilities could be greater if other alternatives within the enterprise were analysed, such as consulting or employee training, but would require the leader were to change his ideas about the usefulness of these activities.

Problems and problem areas: how problems have been addressed and solved

The company uses some external consulting in accountability and legal questions to improve its competitiveness. The enterprise manager himself compiles basic short- and medium-term economic indicators from basic data on production and costs. However, the firm has no contacts with consultants or other supporting organizations for assistance in training of human resources, finance and economics or marketing. The manager and some of the employees have participated in training courses at the Chamber of Commerce and the unions related to security in driving and in the loading and unloading of goods. The employees in the latter category are highly-motivated to study these subjects which they consider important for building their expertise. Meanwhile, the impact of the shortage of training cannot be assessed, as neither the union nor the company has useful statistics for comparing the impact of training.

Notes

1 There exists today a business conflict between both enterprises because of contract disputes.
2 'New customers' are customers new in the last three months.

Questions

1 How can the leadership of the company be characterized?
2 What could be the reason for the high turnover of truck drivers?
3 How can Figure 12.3 (income per employees) be interpreted?

13 Alstermo Bruk AB

Per Lind

DEPARTMENT OF MANAGEMENT, LINKOPING UNIVERSITY, SWEDEN

COUNTRY: SWEDEN

Exposing management control: the closure of Alstermo Bruk

Introduction

Organizational capital (financial and non-financial assets) and organizational core activity domains (product, technology and market) are corner stone concepts of management control. Chandler comments in his concluding remarks to his historical exposé of American enterprises that the success or failure of American industrial executives in the allocation of funds, facilities and skills provides a useful test of their performance and ability (Chandler 1962).

It is generally accepted (Rumelt 1984; Levinthal 1991) that an organization ceases to exist when its stock of organizational capital reaches zero. This may be a *sufficient condition* for liquidation. But is it also a *necessary condition?* There are studies (e.g. Haveman 1992) that claim organizations may fail to survive even with a residual stock of organizational capital. This may happen if changes in the environment lead to – or require – extensive modifications in a majority of the organization's domains.

Assuming such modifications are initiated by management, they are subject to how managers perceive and interpret the immediate future. But regardless of interpretation, the manager's range of choices is conditioned by the company's culture and history. Strategic decisions in response to external changes should therefore not be made without consideration of the company's history. This requires that significant events in its past be identified, enabling the characteristics of the company to be mapped out. In such analysis, focus needs to shift between management and leadership with regard to the company's activities (Danielsson 1986).

The rise and fall of Alstermo Bruk, a 120-year-old Swedish company, that is presented below is used to illustrate how strategic decisions can become counterproductive if they are not based on an understanding of what is the essence and nature of the company. For Alstermo Bruk, the 'cure' adopted to restore the slump in business performance was expansion in new directions. Market signals were interpreted and strategic decisions were made accordingly. However, the anticipated market opportunities could not be utilized because they did not match the particular strengths of Alstermo Bruk. Increased management control was of little use, as there was uncertainty about what to control and how to do it!

Organizational change, age and mortality

In the ecological theory of organization suggested by Hannan and Freeman (1989), organizations tend to resist change due to high inertia. In attempting at identifying the power of this inertia, Haveman (1992) proposed a number of constraints which organizations can mobilize to resist internal and external changes. An example is the investment already made in equipment or production and in marketing personnel specific to a particular type of product. Organizational history can also have a constraining effect on changes. It has been noted that changes in organizations are much less frequent than changes in their environment. However, when changes do occur, they tend to divert resources from operating to reorganizing, thereby reducing the efficiency of operations (Haveman 1992).

The question of age in organizational mortality is the aspect of organizational ecology that has been subject to the greatest empirical examination. What this reveals is that the risk of mortality tends to decline with the age of the organization (Levinthal 1991). Different reasons have been suggested as explanations, for example that organizations tend to become more effective with age (cf. the learning curve) as they accumulate skills and knowledge (Nelson and Winter 1982). On the other hand, Hannan and Freeman (1989) argue that selection processes eliminate organizations with low reliability. Such reliability can be improved through the development of highly standardized routines, forming the basis of continuity in organizations' behaviour over time (Nelson and Winter 1982).

Also Thompson argued that standardization is a way of coping with uncertainty in organizations whose internal functional interdependence is not too complex. However, when organizations become more complex, for example through more advanced production systems, interdependence assumes new patterns. As interdependence becomes sequential and reciprocal, rather than standardization, planning and mutual adjustments (feedback) becomes a better way of reducing uncertainty (Thompson 1967). The question of standardization as a means of preserving continuity and retaining organizational capital for improved reliability is therefore related to the organization's level of complexity in Thompson's sense.

Organizational capital and organizational domains

The term *organizational capital* (Prescott and Visscher 1980) which stands for both financial and non-financial assets, has been used by Levinthal (1991) to define when an organization ceases to exist: a business fails to survive when it can no longer meet its financial obligations to debt holders, employees or suppliers, and is forced into bankruptcy or liquidation. Conversely, a firm may be buffered from failure if it has a strong market position, a vast manufacturing infrastructure, technological capabilities and good management. But, as suggested by Hambrick and d'Aveni (1988), a firm's failure in a given year is not due solely to poor performance in that year, but is likely to be associated with an erosion of its competitive position over a period of time. Therefore, time-related changes in a firm's organizational capital reflect a variety of organizational decisions and environmental factors (Levinthal 1991).

Organizational capital is a somewhat loosely-defined concept. Its original meaning (i.e. capital as financial assets) has been broadened to include a variety of non-financial assets. The basic idea is that the organization together with its capital adds up to more than the sum of the two – a total company resource that cannot be easily imitated, counteracting competition and contributing to the uniqueness of the company. The non-financial part of organizational capital is a form of collective knowledge, i.e. the sum of individual cognition accumulated over time as experience and reflections which can be shared by a group.

The organizational capital resides in the organization's original domains. Thompson (1967) suggests that these domains have three dimensions, namely products sold, clients served and technology employed. Changes in domains involve changes in the organization's formal structure, in patterns of activity and normative order, as well as in stated goals and forms of authority (Hannan and Freeman 1977, 1984). Change that affects two or three dimensions may require such substantial modifications that the company may find itself in new fields of activity which require different competencies and profiles.

In the following analysis of Alstermo Bruk, we note that the company had accumulated considerable organizational capital in its original organizational domains. As the company's response to change in its environment affected all three dimensions, significant parts of its organizational capital were rendered obsolete.

Alstermo Bruk – a brief history

Alstermo Bruk, located in the county of Smaaland in Sweden, started production in 1871. The company's range of products was initially bookbinding and cardboard boxes of various types, made from wood pulp derived from spruce and pine which grew in abundance practically outside the factory.

Product quality was competitive and marketing and sales were successful as evidenced the many awards gained around the turn of the century: silver medals in Sweden and France and at the Trans-Mississippi and International Exhibition in Omaha, United States, for high quality artificial leather.

Periods of stagnation alternated with more dynamic periods as the company grew in market share and developed new products. In 1922, Alstermo Bruk introduced a new range of products with which it would be identified for almost half a century: luggage manufactured from the company's own artificial leather. The Great Depression in the 1930s did not leave Alstermo Bruk untouched and the sales situation worsened when the factory was destroyed by fire in 1936. When production was resumed a year later, the factory had been re-equipped with modem machinery. The increased production capacity was most useful in the following years when, due to the war, the domestic market was closed to imports.

The first paper machine had been installed in 1906, which thus marks the beginning of in-house production of fibre board materials. Because of excess production capacity, material which was not used for in-house manufacture of boxes and suitcases was sold as semi-finished product to the shoe industry, to the paper industry and to producers of binders and office products. Production was diversified into a fibre board division and a products division. Although only a minor part of the total fibre board production was used as input material in the products division, the annual turnover of the latter was around 50 per cent of the total.

In spite of significant changes in the company's environment during the first half of the century – and in spite of changes in the company's internal organization in the same period due to new technologies and markets – there was continuous growth in its financial results. This internal stability of the organizational structure – not unusual in the old iron, glass and paper Swedish factories in the first half of the century – can possibly be explained by strong structural inertia (a loyal and skilled work force, real financial assets such as land etc.) which acted a buffer against undesired change, regardless of what happened in the company's environment. In Alstermo Bruk's case, this relative stability lasted until the end of the 1960s, at which point a long period of decline set in, that would lead to the liquidation of the company 20 years later.

The period from 1945 to 1970 represents the Golden Age for Swedish industry. Alstermo Bruk also had its most profitable period in these years. New markets developed, both in Europe and overseas, in Australia, Africa and in the United States. New products were developed and introduced with the help of creative marketing activities, such as specially-designed suitcases for the Swedish Olympic team in Melbourne in 1956. Revenue from the products division significantly exceeded fibre board production in relative terms. For example, in 1945, revenue from finished products (boxes, etc.) was 50 per cent of total revenue. In volume, however, this production used only 15 per cent of the total output from the fibre board division.

Competition increased in the 1960s, particularly from the emerging low-cost countries of the Far East, where new plastic materials began to displace fibre board for the manufacturing of travel bags and suitcases. The first signs of decline in profit were noted towards the end of the 1960s. At the same time, new technology in the printing industry, based on offset printing, rendered the use of matrix paper obsolete which further reduced the company's market sector. Towards 1970, the outlook was rather gloomy due to changes in the company's traditional markets. Diversification away from the company's original field of activity was considered necessary.

Turnover, which had been relatively stable during the Second World War, rose sharply during the 1950s and 1960s as a result of conscious and committed efforts in the marketing and sales of suitcases and boxes. When the market suddenly shifted from fibre to plastic materials, the effect on Alstermo Bruk was immediate. From the early 1970s, turnover sank by an average yearly rate of six per cent and was halved over a ten-year period.

To compensate for diminishing demand for the company's traditional luggage products, efforts concentrated on the modernization of fibre board production in particular and company's efficiency in general. Decisions were taken to renew production facilities and to computerize production planning and inventory control routines to meet an expected growth in demand for fibre board. However, the change-over to the new machines and installation of the new computer system were problematic. Difficulties in adapting the new equipment to the company's production structure (workers' skill, raw material, logistics, etc.) and differences between the computer-generated schedules and the company's production planning practices resulted in delayed customer deliveries and significant deterioration in quality.

Production and planning problems occurred frequently over a very long period, and it was not until the middle of the 1980s that the new production facilities reached full production capacity. In the meantime, the market had changed significantly, both through new plastic-based materials and from increased competition, not least from East European producers of fibreboard flooding the market with low-priced products. The company was therefore forced to withdraw from certain markets due to price competition. However, the new technology employed in the fibre board division had resulted in a significant increase in labour productivity, as shown in Table 13.1.

It should be noted that the strong increase in labour productivity in the period 1970–1990 happened at the same time as the company was experienced a sharp decline in turnover. This increase in productivity is explained through increased automation in production and through a substantial reduction of the work force. As wages and social costs rose sharply during the same period, production costs were not reduced in pace with declining turnover.

Table 13.1 Turnover and turnover per employee in the period 1945–1990 (SEK)

Year	Turnover	Turnover per employee
1945	39,000,000	173,000
1955	40,000,000	190,000
1965	46,500,000	210,000
1970	61,500,000	258,000
1990	32,000,000	371,000

Table 13.2 Changes in ownership and of the general manager, 1900–1990

Period	New owner	New general manager
1900–09	1	1
1910–19	1	2
1920–29	0	2
1930–39	0	1
1940–49	1	1
1950–59	0	0
1960–69	2	2
1970–79	1	2
1980–89	3	3
1990–92	1	2

From the end of the 1960s, profits thus began to slump, and changes in ownership as well as in general management became more frequent. Table 13.2 shows changes in ownership and of the general manager between 1900 and 1990.

As new owners took over, new approaches were attempted to manage the emerging problems. To compensate for financial losses, the company assets, including land and buildings, were sold in 1964 and 1986. This resulted in a gradual loss of own capital and a decline in the company's stability, something that would hinder negotiations with potential financiers in the coming years.

During the 1970s, Alstermo Bruk decline became more or less permanent, even if there were shorter periods in the first years of temporary rises in operating results. The new management teams, which arrived at an accelerating rate, sometimes instituted organizational changes which deviated significantly from the paths of their predecessors. To some extent, this resulted in highly-qualified and experienced personnel being replaced by new and inexperienced workers.

The company was put into liquidation in 1989 for the first time. After financial reconstruction with the help of a financial contribution from new owners and a new bank loan, the company was able to continue production after a short while. However, in less than two years, the company was in bankruptcy again. After further reconstruction with new owners, Alstermo Bruk continued in operation for another one year and a half before being wound up in August 1992.

The decline of Alstermo Bruk: causes and effects

In attempting to explain the causes and effects that led to the fall of Alstermo Bruk, some of the tenets of ecological organization theory have been advanced. Ecological theory states that stable organizational forms will be selected over those that are changeable. Structural inertia is therefore a property of all organizational forms and stable organizational forms will therefore exhibit lower failure rates (Haveman 1992). A consequence of this would be that less stable organizations have higher failure rates. (Ecological theory accepts flexibility and adaptation, as long as changes do not affect the core of the organization. Stability refers here to core stability.)

Why do organizations change if there is a risk of failure? Tushman and Romanelli (1985) suggest that a company tends to risk an organizational change when changes in its environment renders previous organizational strategies and orientations obsolete, so that the organization in its form is faced with extinction. Such extinction can be the result of gradual environmental change or caused by sudden, dramatic changes.

Given the change from fibreboard to new plastic-based materials for luggage manufacture followed the typical S-shaped curve, impact on Alstermo Bruk could have been foreseen. But in view of the company's age and stability, this change in the marketing environment was seen as sudden and dramatic. The company's answer to the change was to sacrifice its reputation as a luggage manufacturer and to concentrate on becoming a supplier of capital goods, i.e. semi-finished fibreboard materials.

What made the changes in the late 1960s and 1970s, so crucial for Alstermo Bruk? And why could not this period of decline, lasting for more than 20 years, be halted? Many organizational changes had occurred before the 1970s as new markets were opened, as new ranges of luggage products were developed and as new production skills were adopted. Haveman (1992) suggests an answer: under conditions of sudden environmental change, the impact of diversifying away from an organization's original domain(s) depends on the degree to which new activities are related to existing competence. The more closely-related the new activities are to the original domain(s), the better an organization's subsequent performance and survival chances. Previous changes, such as offering new products to old customers with similar production and distribution technology, had required adjustments to only one dimension of the domains. However, the new situation, in which new types of products were offered to different customers, and made and sold with different technology, required substantial modifications to all three dimensions.

What were then the original domains of Alstermo Bruk? As already noted, Thompson (1967) suggested three dimensions in an organization's domain, namely products sold, clients served and technology employed. From this we can identify Alstermo Bruk's original domains to be luggage and boxes (products), international markets for luggage with a loyal dealer network (clients) and a highly-skilled workforce based on proven technology and craftsmanship (technology).

For the first time in the history of Alstermo Bruk, major external changes affecting all three dimensions occurred during the 1960s and at the beginning of the 1970s. The company came to a crossroads, where the two options were either to continue and grow in the production of luggage products, which meant changing to plastics (technology), or to concentrate on the fibreboard division (material), which meant new types of customers, products and technology. The choice was, in other words, to stick to the existing market but shift to new materials or to seek new customers in different application areas based on fibreboard material. The latter course was chosen and significant investments made in new production equipment and facilities.

In retrospect, it is reasonable to ask if the management decision could be justified, particularly as the thorough-going changes to organizational domains would divert resources away from operation to reorganization, thereby reducing efficiency. And in view of the company's expertise in luggage production and distribution, accumulated over a long period of time, its position on the learning curve was probably at its height. By adapting to the new plastic material, the company could have remained within its original domain.

Changes in organizational capital and organizational domain

Levinthal (1991) uses the word organizational capital as a variable to describe what happens when an organization fails to survive. When the organizational capital, consisting of financial and non-financial assets (strength in market positions, know-how, experience, etc.) can no longer be mobilized to generate sufficient cash flow, then the company is forced into bankruptcy.

For Alstermo Bruk, its organizational capital was gradually eroded in a long-drawn-out process that had already started in the late 1960s as the market first turned away from its fibreboard material towards plastic materials. Many firms facing similar situations may endure lengthy periods of this kind, but are protected from immediate extinction by periods of success in the past, during which their organizational capital was replenished (Levinthal 1991). Alstermo Bruk had, in fact, successfully accumulated organizational capital ever since the 1930s, when the factory was rebuilt after the fire, laying down the capacity and technology base for the expansion of the following 20 years. Land and other assets constituted a significant part of the company's financial reserve, and a loyal and skilled workforce produced high quality products with proven technology to satisfied customers in international markets.

Alstermo Bruk was thus shielded from immediate problems, but started to spend its organizational capital at an accelerating pace during the 1960s. The transition from a consumer goods to a capital goods supplier required changes to the distribution system and sales force. In order to meet expected market demand, additional production capacity was installed in the form of new rolling machines with a technology that was partly new and untried for Alstermo Bruk. For a variety of reasons, this change of production technology caused severe production disruptions with effects that lasted for almost ten years. In this period, a substantial part of the company's customer base was lost as the focus was on solving internal production problems. The costs involved in the transition of the company into a capital goods supplier led to a strained economy and, as the periods of liquidity shortage became more frequent, all assets of value (land, buildings) were gradually sold. Table 13.3 summarizes the company's capital situation before and after the radical changes in original domains initiated around 1970.

Examples of non-financial assets before 1970 include: the company's extensive knowledge of luggage production (quality, materials, mountings) as well as applications (fashion, etc.); extensive skill and experience in the manufacture of such products, based on semi-automated production and craftsmanship; and a solid reputation on the international market for high quality, timely deliveries and competitive prices. Well-known designers, including a member of the royal family, contributed to the company's image as a major luggage manufacturer.

In the period after 1970, knowledge and experience of luggage production and marketing became secondary as focus shifted to fibreboard materials. The well-established international distribution system became largely obsolete as fibreboard required other channels to the market. Long customer relations based on quality and reliability, hence less exposure to

Table 13.3 The company's capital situation before and after the changes of *circa* 1970

Period	Organizational domains	Financial assets	Nonfinancial assets
Before 1970	Loyal customers	Land	Ample and relevant
	Efficient retailer system	Buildings	Partly obsolete
	Well-known products		
After 1970	New customers	(none)	Partly obsolete
	No retailer system		
	Less compatible products		

price competition, were terminated, partly because fibreboard as luggage material became obsolete and partly because Alstermo Bruk, promoting the fibreboard material as its major product range, approached new customers with other types of applications.

The erosion of the company's organizational capital was thus a fact towards the end of the 1980s: financial assets were liquidated and market strength was drastically reduced due to a persistent focus on the technology of making fibreboard materials without paying due attention to customer needs and market demand. When, in the second half of the 1980s, the market signalled a growing interest in more environmentally-friendly materials such as fibreboard, the company's financial resources were so depleted that new and aggressive initiatives were difficult to mobilize.

Exercising management control

Boeker (1992) has shown that poorly-performing organizations tend to replace chief executives more frequently than those organizations that perform well. This is well illustrated by Alstermo Bruk where owners and/or executive management was changed in 1970, 1973, 1978, 1982, 1985, 1988, 1990, 1992 (see Table 13.2). A direct consequence of this was that competence and experience as well as a well-developed *Fingerspitzgefühl* for material and production (important for quality) was gradually lost as new management teams were installed. The earlier management practice – autocratic and with informal rules of the thumb to measure performance and productivity – gradually changed to more informal relations between managers and employees at the same time as new and formal routines developed for planning and control. This was both a consequence of – and a prerequisite for – the appointment of managers with no previous branch experience.

The standardized way of organizing production for luggage products had led to stability in structure and work. With the shift from primarily semi-automatic luggage production to mixed semi-automatic and automated production of fibreboard, where output from one production step became the input to the next, a new type of internal interdependence developed which required improved planning. Formal accounting models were therefore introduced and gradually computerised during the 1970s.

The accounting principles which were adopted for the fibreboard division, and which dominated throughout the remaining years of the company, were based on the contribution method. In this method, costs designated as variables are summed along the path of the production process to arrive at a direct cost. This direct cost is subtracted from the selling price to generate a contribution to cover the fixed costs. This accounting principle prevailed in manufacturing industry for a long period, and was justified as long as direct costs dominated. As the share of overhead costs increased, rough methods for the allocation of these costs become inadequate. Accounting procedures based on contribution have therefore become increasingly criticized by academics as well as by reflective practitioners (Johnson and Kaplan 1987).

At Alstermo Bruk, the use of the contribution model resulted in genuine misinterpretation of real financial results. As a consequence, long-term customer contracts were in fact unprofitable from the very beginning, a fact that escaped notice due to the lack of transparency of the accounting model.

The introduction of new and formal routines for management planning and control led to the development of new role patterns at Alstermo Bruk. Like many other Swedish works in the glass, steel and paper industry with roots in the early phase of industrialization, Alstermo Bruk represented a relatively closed form of organization. For example, marketing and sales had been separated from the rest of the organization and taken care of either by agents or dedicated sales persons who were only remotely attached to the company. Roles had been well settled and conflicts because of shared or competing roles were unusual.

As distributors and agents were reduced – a consequence of the company's new orientation and strained economy – responsibility for marketing and sales came to rest more closely with other functions in the company. Actors who felt the need to contribute to reinforce sales activities took their own initiatives, acting both in production and marketing/sales roles. This caused conflicts with customers due to incompatible customer commitments in price and quality. One consequence of this role conflict was that necessary price adjustments could not be made for long-term contracts, which had very serious impact on the company's financial situation.

Other types of role conflict also appeared as a result of the changes in the company's organizational domain: as the financial situation worsened, the employees called for management attention and action. A classical observation in this context (Slater 1955), which had clear parallels with the situation at Alstermo Bruk, is that a person considered to have 'the best ideas' in a group is generally not the same person who is rated as 'the most liked'. The 'ideas' person, by focusing on task activities, thus helps the group to adapt to its external environment. The 'most-liked' person, on the other hand, by focusing on socio-emotional activities, helps the group to become internally integrated. The crucial situation forces the executive managers to try to lead both types of tasks. As they require opposite types of personalities, thus rendering a combined attitude impossible (Slater 1955), the executives at Alstermo Bruk in reality tended to choose the socio-emotional roles, which did bring some comfort to the employees but did not save the company.

The end of Alstermo Bruk: retrospective view

In the two periods of reconstruction which followed after the company went bankrupt in 1988 and 1990, efforts were made to rebuild market share by finding new application areas for the company's traditional fibreboard material. By adding new ingredients to the original fibre mix, the material was endowed with radically different properties (fire retardant, electrically insulated, etc.). From the short-term perspective, these strategies were understandable in the light of the immediate need to improve the cash flow.

In a longer perspective, however, the outlook for the survival of Alstermo Bruk was very limited as long as its organizational strength was not restored. Without sufficient financial capital, any attempt to develop and market new products (materials) through costly and time-consuming activities became hazardous. And the company's stock of customers in its traditional market for boxes and suitcases could not be mobilized for the newly-developed materials.

When the environment undergoes a sudden transformation, firms affected may seek radical new directions in terms of technology, markets or products. The more the activities involved in this change differ from the firm's original competence, and the more of the firm's original domains are transformed, the more significant is the risk for failure and erosion of organizational capital. This type of change hurt Alstermo Bruk badly in the 1960s and 1970s, as the company was transformed from a producer of suitcases and boxes in a homogenous market to producer of semi-finished products (materials) in a highly diversified and less homogenous market. The changes affected vital dimensions of the firm's domain such as technology, products and customers.

Major changes can therefore not be performed without eroding organizational capital, for example, certain competences becomes obsolete and need to be replaced, customer loyalties are sacrificed as market sectors are abandoned, etc. Owners and executive managers must therefore have a good understanding of the effects of changes and of strategies which may be needed to restore organizational capital. A sufficiently long-term perspective is therefore necessary as organizational capital has been accumulated over a long period. Identification and evaluation of this capital and its impact on the company's future strategy becomes an important task for the company's management. Top management's failure to take this long-term perspective may lead to false strategies.

The frequent changes in ownership and the variations in management focus and attitudes did not allow sufficient consistency in the management control of Alstermo Bruk. Strategies were frequently interrupted and modified as new leaders took office, each time spending part of the organizational capital. In seeking an explanation for the long and unbroken period of decline at Alstermo Bruk, it is inevitable that management control of Alstermo Bruk, for the period in question, becomes seriously exposed.

Epilogue

As a member of the board of Alstermo Bruk during its last period from 1990 up to 1992, the author had opportunities to reflect on the reasons for the decline of the company from the 1960s onwards. Questions such as what went wrong, and why, came into the foreground. Most of the questions and the explanations offered have been reported here.

A more speculative but none-the-less interesting issue is the extent to which deeper understanding and knowledge of organizational behaviour could have suggested a more adequate strategy in the late 1960s and early 1970s, one could have secured a more positive outcome. If so, what form would it have taken?

It should be evident from this brief account of Alstermo Bruk and its history that the company *is* its history. The concept of sediment as used by Danielsson (1983) is quite relevant and useful in this context. Danielsson writes:

> Solutions developed for a company's financial and organizational problems tend to remain more or less intact for a very long period. Such solutions settle in layers and become sediments.
>
> The one who makes himself acquainted, from a financial perspective, with how companies function will find great difficulties. One may expect to find a logical chain of arguments and assessments, starting from a well defined point of reference. When this logical chain cannot be found, one may try to build such a chain. The main issue is that there are no such standard solutions that are related by logical chains.

It seems to be exactly these standard solutions that managers were looking for during the 1960s. It started with the shift in management ideology during the 1950s that marked the advent of what has been called systems rationalism. The rhetoric of the systems rationalism intimated that management was simply a general skill of systems analysis. Accordingly, managers who understood the organizational system could apply their skills to any organization. Details were considered irrelevant and the workforce was mostly absent from systems models (Barley and Kunda 1992).

This was also the era when formal accounting system was introduced at Alstermo Bruk:

> In the 1950s there was a change in focus, from people, customers and process to costs, profits and accounting relationships. But accounting systems provide almost no

information about customers, other than revenue data. Revenue data simply tell what customers paid for items received. They say nothing about whether customers wanted or liked what they received.

(Johnson 1992)

Table 13.2 above shows the increasing number of changes in management after 1960. It can be assumed that the managers who took office were influenced by the new management ideology. Planning, forecasting and control were the watchwords. Craftsmanship and responsiveness to demands from customers and retail dealers were not seen as rational in this new context.

All this paved the way for the transformation of Alstermo Bruk from a semi-automated manufacturer, with substantial elements of handicraft, into a process industry equipped with fully-automated paper machines. This reduced the relative importance of the fabrication of luggage, the flagship of Alstermo Bruk. But it facilitated the management objective to have a more controllable and modern factory.

Could there have been an alternative strategic direction for Alstermo Bruk?

Greater appreciation of the accumulated skills in the fabrication of luggage products, better understanding of the potential value of customer goodwill and the very well established retailer network should have resulted in more focus on the fabrication of products and less focus on – or even discontinuation of – fibreboard production. As the market was flooded with cheap board from Eastern Europe, it might have been more economical to buy the material needed from outside. That would also have offered the possibility of switching to new materials.

Brief discussion indicates that the new managers of Alstermo Bruk after 1960, facing the emerging problems of the company, were inclined to adopt and apply the new managerial theories that had just emerged and which were generally accepted at that time. However, this meant that the historical 'sediments' of the company were not considered important by the new managers. Customers, retailers and employees, representing the accumulated skill of the company, were considered secondary to the more immediate needs of management control.

References

Barley, S. and Kunda, G. (1992) 'Design and Devotion: Surges of Rational and Normative Ideologies of Control in Managerial Discourse'. *Administrative Science Quarterly*, 37: September, pp. 363–399.

Boeker, W. (1992) 'Power and Managerial Dismissal: Scapegoating at the Top'. *Administrative Science Quarterly*, 37: September, pp. 400–412.

Chandler, A. (1962) *Strategy and Structure*. Cambridge, MA: AM Press.

Danielsson, A. (1983) *Företagsekonomi – en översikt*. Lund: Studentlitteratur.

Danielsson, A. (1986) *Ledarsknets Villkor in Samtal om Ledarskap, Ledning & Ledare*. Stockholm: Svenska Dagbladet.

Hambrick, D. and D'Aveni, R. (1988) 'Large Corporate Failures as Downward Spirals'. *Administrative Science Quarterly*, 33: March, pp. 1–23.

Hannan, M. and Freeman, J. (1977) 'The Population Ecology of Organisations'. *American Journal of Sociology*, 82: March, pp. 929–964.

Hannan, M. and Freeman, J. (1984) 'Structural Inertia and Organisational Change'. *American Sociological Review*, 49, pp. 149–164.

Hannan, M. and Freeman, J. (1989) *Organisational Ecology*. Cambridge, MA: Harvard University Press.

Haveman, H. (1992) 'Between a Rock and a Hard Place: Organisational Change and Performance under Conditions of Fundamental Environmental Transformation'. *Administrative Science Quarterly*, 37: March, pp. 48–78.

Johnson, T. (1992) *Relevance Regained*. New York: Free Press.

Johnson, T. and Kaplan, R. (1987) *Relevance Lost: The Rise and Fall of Management Accounting*. Boston: Harvard Business School Press.

Levinthal, D. (1991) 'Random Walks and Organisational Mortality'. *Administrative Science Quarterly*, 36: September, pp. 397–420.

Nelson, R. and Winter, S. (1982) *An Evolutionary Theory of the Firm*. Cambridge, MA: Harvard University Press.

Prescott, E. and Visscher, M. (1980) 'Organisational Capital'. *Journal of Political Economy*, 88: June, pp. 446–461.

Rumelt, R. (1974) *Strategy, Structure and Economic Performance*. Boston: Harvard Business School Press.

Slater, P. (1955) 'Role Differentiation in Small Groups'. *American Sociological Review*, 20, pp. 300–310.

Thompson, J. (1967) *Organisation in Action*. New York: McGraw-Hill.

Tushman, M. and Romanelli, E. (1985) 'Organisational Evolution: A Metamorphosis Model of Convergence and Reorientation'. *Research in Organisational Behaviour*, 7: 17, pp. 1–222.

Questions

1   The company management took a number of strategic decisions with significant impact on the company. What were these decisions?
2   What could have been done to rescue the company from bankruptcy?
3   What impact did the frequent changes in management and ownership have?

14 Olympia International

Eslyn Isaacs

DEPARTMENT OF MANAGEMENT, UNIVERSITY OF THE WESTERN CAPE, CAPE TOWN, SOUTH AFRICA

COUNTRY: SOUTH AFRICA

South Africa

In 2010 South Africa was known for hosting the very successful FIFA Soccer World cup and the visitors were amazed with the quality of service delivery from the transportation, food and accommodation sectors.

South Africa is regarded as the economic hub of Africa with a purchasing power parity of 10,100 USD. The population has grown to 49.5 million, of whom 17.38 million are actively part of the labour force. Despite its relative economic position, it has an unemployment rate of approximately 24 per cent (2009 estimate). The services sector contributes 65.8 per cent, agriculture 3 per cent and industry 31.2 per cent to the GDP of the country. The major industries are mining (world's largest producer of platinum, gold and chromium), automobile assembly, metalworking, machinery, textiles, iron and steel, chemicals, fertilizer, foodstuffs and commercial ship repair.

The small, medium and micro enterprise (SMME) sector plays an important role in the economy of South Africa and currently contributes 39 per cent to GDP and comprises 55 per cent of the labour force.

Olympia International

Olympia International, a manufacturer of high quality paints, was established in 1985 as a small paint contracting business from a 200m^2; premises in the suburb of Bellville, Western Cape. The business has a Greek owner. The Greek culture of hard work, knowledge of the building industry and paint was prevalent. The owner was an extremely knowledgeable building contractor and was well connected. The business was very successful. The family soon realised that it could gain a competitive advantage by producing their own brand of paint.

Mr Palesh Moodley, of Indian origin and with a degree in chemistry, was appointed as the first production manager. Within a short time the paint manufacturing division became very successful. With the assistance of the owner, Mr Moodley used the opportunity to improve his managerial competence. After the owner's untimely death, the owner's son took over the business, but with his limited managerial experience and knowledge of the paint and construction industry, he did not perform that well and decided to sell the business. In 1998 Mr Moodley bought the paint manufacturing business when it was a small industry, today it is a 7 billion Rand industry.

Over the past 12 years the business has shown significant growth and the owner was forced to seek larger premises. The business is currently situated in the Parow Industria, approximately 10km from the airport. It currently employs 56 people: 50 in production and transport and six in management and administration. As the business is related to the building industry, it is often forced to change its workforce to take account of the changing environment.

The South African paint industry consists of at least 13 players with the older businesses focusing on producing traditional paints for the industrial and household markets, whilst a number of smaller businesses focus on specialist paints for industrial and household purposes. Olympia is a specialist paint producer and markets directly to building contractors.

The key success factors of Olympia International are honesty, straightforwardness, good value for money, high quality, fast delivery service, innovative coating solutions through complementary products/services, managerial and technical expertise, good networking systems, employee empowerment and access to financial resources.

Olympia has a sales office in the Province of Gauteng. The company has managed a few export orders.

Continued growth has necessitated the owner changing the business from a sole proprietorship to registering it as a Close Corporation. The Close Corporation has three members: Mr Palesh Moodley, his wife and a financial investor. The financial investor is not directly involved in day-to-day decisions.

Statutory requirements for operating a business in South Africa

Businesses operating in South Africa must meet various statutory requirements, including taxation (business and personal taxation, unemployment insurance fund and skills levies). Businesses are required to register with a particular Sector Education and Training Authority (SETA) and under the terms of the Broad-based Black Economic Empowerment (BBEE) Act. The purpose of the SETA is to ensure businesses identify employees who have the potential to advance in the business but currently do not have the skills, and to register them for training. Businesses who send their employees on recognized training courses can then claim part of the training investment back from the SETA. Businesses who partially or fully comply with BBEE requirements are allocated points; a company's BBEE status is normally taken into account when tendering for government contracts.

Small and medium enterprises are no exception, and it is clear from the above that the owners of Olympia International know the 'rules of the game' and ensure they play by those rules.

General administration and human resource management

Research has shown that two areas which are often neglected in SMEs are general administration and human resource management. In Olympia International these two aspects are adequately covered by Mrs Moodley and three additional female employees. The positions they occupy are those of financial administrator, administrative clerk, telephonist and office management assistant.

The administrative clerk and telephonist are computer and bookkeeping literate, and are responsible for taking orders and dealing with general enquiries. The administrative clerk is also responsible for managing the employees' wages and salaries.

Mrs Moodley is the financial director of the company and ensures that all financial documents and reports are updated and reconciled, financial statements are prepared and audited and submitted to the South African Revenue Services and Registrar of Close Corporations.

Mr Moodley is the current Chief Executive Officer but also in charge of marketing and production.

Manufacturing

Mr Moodley, with his science degree, is responsible for the development and testing of all new paints, and their manufacture oversees. He ensures the paints meet the required SABS

(South African Bureau of Standards) and comply with the green environmental requirements.

Mr Moodley is assisted by 50 employees who work as machine operators, packers, drivers and drivers' assistants. The workforce has been stable over the past 25 years. The employees are extremely loyal and staff turnover is only 1 per annum. It is not just a spirit of loyalty and unity that is visible, but the spirit of *Ubuntu*. The workforce has grown from 10 in 1985 to 50 in 2010.

The workforce is drawn from nearby formal and informal settlements. Most of them use public transport to get to work. They have to catch trains and buses at 5:00 am to get to work by 8:00 am, but despite this they are highly motivated and dedicated. The key to this motivation in a sometimes hazardous environment are the benefits they receive from the job. These benefits include profit sharing, bonuses (13th cheque) which are received according to performance appraisals and targets achieved.

Performance bonuses are received after six months. None of the workers belong to a union but, with the benefits the company provides, it is clear to see why employees are so motivated in their jobs.

The basic raw materials are purchased locally, while some of the sophisticated machinery was imported.

Paint manufacturing involves a chemical process, which could be hazardous. Employees are therefore required to be very careful, and receive regular on-the-job training. This is further necessitated due to the fast and continuous technological changes that are taking place, making machinery redundant in a short time period.

Olympia International promises delivery of an order within 24 hours. This promise has given the company a strategic competitive advantage. This was also the primary reason why the contract to supply paint for the Gran West casino was awarded to Olympia International.

Marketing and sales

The business employs four people in the sales division with Mr Moodley also taking responsibility of the marketing and sales department. This type of business requires networking with stakeholders, particularly people in local and national government responsible for housing, architects, building supply retailers and wholesalers.

Knowledge and experience of paint and the paint industry is essential for sales people. This has directly contributed to the success of the company, and turnover has increased at a rate of approximately 15 per cent per annum. Since the World Cup, related projects have had a positive effect on the company's turnover. Hopefully, this will continue, as maintenance will be required at all the stadia and other buildings such as hotels, guest houses and shopping centres.

Products and services

The company produces high quality paints for interior and exterior walls, wooden surfaces, tile and zinc roofing surfaces and all types of flooring.

The products and services extend to the following specialist markets:

- Architectural: Architects advise their clients of the types of paints available and they therefore becomes a source of information.
- Decoration: People who decorate homes or businesses.
- Retail: Selling through hardware stores, specialist paint stores or even traditional retail outlets.

- Shop fitting: Businesses involved in shop fitting but offers turn-key services.
- Light industrial: Businesses in the steel industry who paint their products prior to delivery to their customers.
- Export: To various neighbouring countries, i.e. Namibia, Zambia, Zimbabwe.
- Redecoration: People and businesses redecorating their homes and premises.
- Maintenance: Many businesses and private owners have a policy of painting at least every 7 years. Most paint manufacturers provide a guarantee of about 7 years on high quality paints.

Olympia International produces over 60 different products, from economical household paints to high performance architectural coatings.

Projects

The range of products has been used with exceptional success on the following projects:

- Red Cross Children's Memorial Hospital, Rondebosch, Cape Town;
- retirement village 'Villa Bravo' Uitsig, Durbanville, Cape Town;
- hotels: Le Vendome Hotel, Sea point, Grand West Casino and Entertainment World, Goodwood, Cape Town;
- the International Hotel School, Green Point, Cape Town; and
- the office complexes of the retail clothing giants Edgars, Markhams and RJL.

Financial management

The financial affairs are dealt with by Mrs Moodley, who ensures the books are audited at the end of every year as required by the Close Corporation's Act. The distribution of costs is as follows:

Administrative	10%
Manufacturing	70%
Marketing and sales	15%
Management	5%

The company achieved an average profit of 15 per cent in each of the past three years.

Achievements

In December 2002, Olympia International was voted the WECBOF Business of the year. Olympia International is a quality and environmentally-conscious manufacturer.

Question

1   How has the company managed to have a committed and loyal workforce?

15 Viettuan Trading, Technology and Product Co. Ltd.

Vo Van Huy

UNIVERSITY OF TECHNOLOGY, BUSINESS RESEARCH AND TRAINING CENTRE, HO CHI MINH CITY, VIETNAM

COUNTRY: VIETNAM

Background

The company was founded in 2003 and owned by two friends, Mr Anh Tuan and Ms Minh Hang. Their business concept was to find the way to earn money through their ability and their idea on manufacturing purified drinking water derived from discussions between close friends. Now their company, Viettuan, supplies purified drinking water branded *Morning Dew* to the Hanoi market.

Management

Mr Anh Tuan is the managing director of Viettuan. Until 2002, he worked as legal consultant to a company called Invest & Consult Company. All through his career he had a desire for self-determination, and to create something by his own efforts, no matter what. After discussion with friends, Anh Tuan decided to establish his company with financial support from a friend – Ms Minh Hang. Mr Tuan is also helped by his girlfriend who has the role of chief accountant.

Company

In 2004, Viettuan had a turnover of 600 million Vietnamese Dong (VND), equivalent to 40,000 USD. Net profit was negative because Viettuan was very new and small private company. However, the company continued to look for financial funding to invest in machines and offices, but the owners did not want to borrow money from banks.

The company has a unique product: purified water. Purified water is produced by a technique based on a US water producing assembly line with capacity of 1,000 litres per hour. Last year, the inventory of the company was about 30 million VND (2,000 USD).

Viettuan Trading is facing fierce competition from other private and joint-venture enterprises in the industry. In Hanoi, there are over 100 different trademarks of purified water; therefore, the company is now trying to establish as many agents as possible. Six persons in the delivery section and two persons in the marketing and customer service section now continuously find potential customers. The managing director requires his staff to find customers by legal and respected means that do not involve subjecting his competitors to 'spoiling tactics'. The managing director gives assurances that there are no environmental problems or waste associated with the production of purified drinking water.

Products

Viettuan produces only one mass product: purified drinking water. The company drilled a well more than 100 metres deep. Water is pumped from the well and processed through a water processing line. After purification, water is poured into 500ml bottles or 5 gallon flagons; bottles are packed 24 to a cardboard box. Every month the company supplies 5,000 flagons and 9,000 boxes of 500ml bottles. The quality of the purified drinking water is strictly verified by the Hanoi Medical Office every month.

The materials for producing *Morning Dew* consist of empty plastic flagons and bottles, caps, taps, plastic wrapping to cover flagons and bottles, paper boxes and other things. All are provided by domestic suppliers and the company can order them easily. Suppliers or suppliers' agents will take materials to the company and all transportation costs are included in the price.

To advertise *Morning Dew*, the company tries to create good relationships with current customers, distribute fliers, use outdoor advertising boards in bars and restaurants and advertise in newspapers and magazines. Mr Tuan and Ms Hang expect they can diversify products by supplying different sizes of bottles to meet the different needs of customers and improve the quality and taste of drinking water. They also intend to design bottles with carrying ropes which should be convenient for travellers.

Customers

The majority of customers are around 1,000 individual buyers. The company also has over 200 agents who supply Viettuan products to other enterprises, bars and restaurants within Hanoi and its surroundings. The regular and loyal customers account for 80 per cent of total customers and they contribute 70 per cent of total turnover.

It is very difficult for Viettuan and other purified drinking water producers to introduce their products to customers. In Vietnam, people do not have the habit of drinking purified water because that water is rather expensive compared to normal tap water and people think that the quality of purified water is the same as that of boiled water. Viettuan had to find many different ways of accessing customers, such as personal relationships and the prestige of the managing director, by means of product quality and through the relationships between current customers and their other customers. This experience and the relationships of the managing director help the company in expanding Viettuan's market.

Understanding the consumption behaviour of customers is not only a problem but also an opportunity for the company. The number of drinking water consumers is rising everyday because of the decreasing availability of clean drinking water, and the company estimates that it can expand the number of customers by up to 20 per cent per annum in future years.

Staff

Viettuan has total of 18 employees including four employees in the production section. Now, employees do not work in shift but still have to work eight hours per day, six days per week. The managing director guesses that employees may have to work shifts next year when the company has more orders and customers. Sometimes the company gets trouble with delivery employees: delivery employees have to work hard when delivering heavy packages and many of them will suffer from health problems as a result of this work. In addition, most of these employees have a few qualifications and have inappropriate attitudes towards customers which can force the company to dismiss them. The managing director expects that the company can hire better-skilled employees and train and retrain their employees. The Labour Union is not established in Viettuan but the company provides all legal working conditions and welfare for its employees. All problems between managers and employees are solved by discussion so there are no conflicts in the company.

Questions

1   Purified drinking water has been a big product in Western countries for a number of years. What have been the marketing strategies in these countries, and could the same strategy have been applied in Vietnam?

2   Customer service is important and Viettuan has a problem here when delivering the products. How should the company seek a solution to this problem?

3   Vietnam is a high power distance country according to Hofstede's study. How would this influence management at Viettuan?

16 Polmarco

Veslava Valiucko

UNIVERSITY OF GDANSK, GDANSK, POLAND

COUNTRY: POLAND

Background

Polmarco started its activities in the furniture manufacturing business in January 1981 in Gdynia, Poland. Today it is a company with its head office in Gdynia and a manufacturing plant in Leba, employing about 80 people in total. The Managing Director is the company owner; his son is a Senior Executive with a *procura* (law qualification).

Production was orginally focused on furniture for individual residential clients. In 1989 Polmarco enlarged their customer base by offering commercial and industrial clients furniture made to follow individual the arrangement of their interiors. Since then the company has equipped over 500 bank agencies and 200 other public premises. The Leba production plant was opened in 1995. This new plant is equipped with modern machines which allow the most demanding furniture arrangement projects to be carried out in a wide variety of materials.

Polmarco customers are not only from Poland: for several years the company has been exporting to the Scandinavian market, to Great Britain and other countries. About 50 to 70 per cent of Polmarco products are exported. To lessen the risk of a fall in demand, for the time being the company is willing to keep the share of export sales below 50 per cent. The domestic market is (in the management's opinion) much more stable and demand can be relied on to a greater degree than foreign customers. On the other hand, foreign sales are usually more important orders since they allow higher earnings not only through larger volumes but also by virtue of the exchange rate.

Due to considerable investments in new machinery in 2005, Polmarco is now able to manufacture catalogue furniture on a really large scale. At present they offer a full variety of furniture systems, including desks, shelves, cupboards and containers for regular office spaces and – in special sets – for cabinet offices. Experience gained throughout their 25-years' activities and a highly qualified staff allows the company to make reliable and modern furniture with a two-year warranty. The evidence of the good business record is a wide circle of satisfied clients who appreciate the quality, effectiveness and comprehensive approach to their needs.

Organization design and culture

Authority in the organization is rather centralized: the main decisions are taken by General Director, Senior Executive or Production Manager. The General Director has a consultative leadership style. Once a week he gathers all his managers together to talk about problems that have occurred or new ideas. He is also open to discussion with other employees, often reminding them he is always be ready to talk. The General Director often visits the manu-facturing plants and talks to his employees. This is an important motivational tool: employ-ees (especially machines operators) feel important, appreciated and honoured when asked about their problems by the most important person in the company. They are also allowed to produce some furniture for themselves. With the General Director's permission, an employee may stay after working hours to make themselves some furniture, paying only the cost of the materials. This arrangement was developed after the management realized employees tended to make furniture for themselves regardless of whether they were allowed or not! The company found it better to allow this practice and be informed about it than to be cheated.

Job specialization appears not to be important in this furniture manufacturing company, since the machinery is so innovative and easy to run, the machine operators only press but-tons and remove the finished products. Formalities at Polmarco are moderate. ISO proce-dures require some rules to be followed, especially in the Sales Department but neither in the Marketing and Transport Departments nor in the Warehouse are there any procedures to follow as employees follow oral instructions from colleagues or managers.

Employees are treated in a rather friendly manner. No penalty system exists for being late, making mistakes, etc. This is mostly due to recruitment difficulties. Despite the high unemployment rate (especially in Leba where the manufacturing plant is based) people are not willing to work. There are often situations when a new employee comes to work for three days in a row and then disappears not even asking for the paycheck due. It is consid-ered a very strange situation, especially as no employees complain about working condi-tions or pay levels (which are above the market average). Because of this, it is not possible to regulate some behaviours by penalties or reprimands. These negative motivation tools make employees resign. As the company cannot allow itself to lose precious employees, it does not take into consideration any of these tools.

Organizational change

In 1995 the production plant was moved from Gdynia to Leba. This important change has lowered costs and increased production capacity, but has also complicated the information, documents and materials flows between the different company sites. The company has learned a lesson, and in order to improve the situation there are plans to move all facilities, such as back office, production, warehouse, etc., to Lebork, not far from Leba. The com-pany has acquired large premises to fit all these functions in one place.

In 2004 Polmarco applied for ISO certification. The ISO standards have been implemen-ted by a special company. Despite initial protests restraints, management found many posi-tive features in the adoption of the standards. In 2006 Polmarco invested in modern CNC (computerized numerical control) machinery. This major change has definitely influenced the production process. Now that the machinery is easy to operate, the manufacturing pro-cess is not only faster but also more accurate. It has enabled series production and catalogue sales to replace the traditional manufacturing system, where all furniture was made to order (taking much longer and being more expensive). At the beginning, manual workers did not want training for operating the new machines as they were convinced the previous working methods (taught to them by their fathers and grandfathers) were superior; they also doubted that the machines could be more accurate than a human worker. There was also fear about being replaced by modern machinery making products of higher quality! One year later blue collar workers started to praise the new equipment and the improvements it has brought to their work.

In 2006 a video camera system was installed in the manufacturing plant. It was clearly explained to the employees that its purpose that was to observe possible improvements in the production process. At first employees were very unhappy and complained that they felt observed, uncomfortable, etc. The reason employees stopped complaining is that they noticed they were not being punished more than before and they did not need to worry about negative consequences of the system. There was something that had not been conveyed to the employees although it probably convinced them even more. Improvements were made as a result of being able to monitor on a video screen rather than in the plant itself. The best example of an improvement is that lifts have been installed next to the machines where the operator earlier had to remove heavy parts from a pallet on to the machine. The lifts allowed heavy parts to be raised as high as the machine, enabling the operator to move parts with just one hand. The new solution improved working conditions, decreased the risk of back injuries and proved the effectiveness of the system.

In 2009 another change was made in the production system. A CAD (computer-aided design) program enables furniture parts to be produced based on a picture imported into the CNC program. It means that employees no longer have to draw a component on paper and then cut it from a piece of material; it is now sufficient to draw the component in the CAD program and the CNC machine produces the component according to specification. The new software enables faster production and fewer errors (like the wrong shape) and also saves on material. Concurrently with the new programme, Polmarco started applying bar code labels to manufactured components. It saves trouble in packing the right components when preparing an order. The employee preparing the order scans the component bar code and can easily check if the component fits with the order record. Preparing an order has become much faster and accurate, and customers are happy to receive complete orders.

Motivation

Employee's earnings are in general not based on results, and results between employees are never compared; they do not get any positive incentives for their work. Employees receive an annual bonus if the company's turnover reaches a certain level.

Employees complain that they would like to earn more, even though their earnings are rather high in comparison with competitive companies. They do not complain about the working conditions, probably because the management treats the safety aspects with care and attention. Conflicts can occur in the factory that require management involvement. However, strong loyalty between employees makes it difficult for managers to get involved and to identify those individuals who might be the cause of the problem.

Financial control

The General Manager and Senior Executive regularly check the accounting information. All the other financial activities are under the Chief Accountant's control. The Chief Accountant has been with the Company for a long time and is trusted enough not to be controlled by the General Director.

The Purchase and Supply Department also play a role in the financial control. The employees in this department verify that the invoices received materials purchased have the same prices as were negotiated with the supplier. Their daily duty is also to search for cheaper suppliers providing as a high quality as those used currently. To lower warehousing costs, stock levels are kept to the minimum. The Production Manager is responsible for the quantities purchased and therefore approves every material purchase plan.

Sales

Polmarco does not have its own stores but cooperates with the sales chain. The trading companies that mediate between final customer and Polmarco place orders and receive the products two weeks later. Payment usually takes place a month or even two months later. Polmarco does not have problems with bad debts.

The situation today: opportunities and challenges

A SWOT analysis shows there are both opportunities and threats to be considered. The economic crisis is a problem in the sector even if customer demand for furniture has not dropped much. When the value of the euro goes down it affects export earnings; this is important in view of the high share of exports in the company's sales.

Polmarco is planning to implement ISO 14001. Customers in the Scandinavian market are very aware of environmental problems and prefer ecological furniture, which has prompted Polmarco to work on being even more ecological than it is now. The transfer to a new site in Lebork will definitely lower costs in a longer term. The company is applying to the EU structural funds for investment and is also hoping that the euro exchange rate will change to its benefit and help expand foreign markets further. Management wants to utilize the company's strengths which are: low prices, high quality, accurate packing (very important for shipping), modern technology and ecological products to find clients even on other continents. They also know that to achieve that they need to address their weaknesses which so far are: need for employees and weak or no marketing.

Questions

1   What is the reason behind the company's human resources problems?
2   Management refers to low price and high quality as part of the company's strengths. Is this a viable strategy?
3   According to management, entering the Scandinavian market requires an increased focus on ecological furniture. How can this be defined, and how can it be incorporated in a winning marketing approach?

17 LOKAL Industries, Inc.

Mercedidas Alviar-Esguerra

INSTITUTE FOR SMALL SCALE INDUSTRIES, UNIVERSITY OF THE PHILIPPINES, QUEZON CITY,
THE PHILIPPINES

COUNTRY: THE PHILIPPINES

From small beginnings

Then and now

The year is 1988; the setting, a small rented room; the main character, a young woman with a month-old infant. Bundles of fabric and swatches of cloth provide colour to the otherwise dreary room. They compete for space with infant things and household basics. Keeping an eye on the sleeping baby, the woman works on the fabric with a pair of shears. She trims fabrics for her grandma's baby clothing business.

Today, 16 years later, the same woman now makes toys out of fabric. But she no longer wields the shears. Machines have taken their place. She has 20 employees working for her, which doubles or triples at peak periods. Her workplace is no longer a cramped rented space but a two-storey factory: divided into sections, well-equipped, spacious, well-lighted and ventilated. The one-woman operation is now a full-fledged business. It is known as LOKAL Industries, Inc. LOKAL stands for Lorna Kaiaw, the young mother-entrepreneur in our story. The infant, named Angeia Vida, is now a teenager. She has a brother, Angelo Paolo, 13; and a sister, Angelica Beata, 12. All three go to exclusive schools and are in the top of their class. The Kalaw family lives quite comfortably in a three-storey concrete building in Barangay Longos Malabon City. According to Lorna, their present home is a 'testimony to hard work, nurtured by love – love for each other and for the whole family'.

Classic story with a difference

Lorna Trinidad-Kalaw's story is a classic: a young man or woman puts in a modest capital and, with diligence, creativity and persistence, makes the initial investment grow. What makes her different?

If you ask her, she will credit her achievements to her strong resolve, fortitude and vigour. Possibly, she adds, it may be genetic. She belongs to the third generation of entrepreneurial women who built a business out of needlecraft. She ventured into business neither by force of circumstance nor by chance. She seemed inevitably drawn to it. Who knows, maybe it began even before she turned 10 years old!

The second in a family of seven children, she remembers herself as precocious little girl who grew up in the care of her maternal grandmother. When she turned 10, her grandma's baby dress shop was her playground. The young Lorna was always a welcome sight at the factory. The workers looked forward to her amiable presence every morning for she was a happy, laughing child.

Later on, when she grew older, she helped around by trimming the baby dresses, all the while engaging the sewers in small talk. She carefully observed how they worked. Thus did she discover and develop a talent for needlework. From conversations with the workers, she found that many of them had been with her grandma from the start. From them, she learned about loyalty at an early age.

A family and a business is born

Lorna grew up in Batangas a rather ordinary girl, according to her. She went to a public elementary school in Santo Tomas, Batangas (The Philippines) and moved to the Our Lady of Fatima Academy in Tanauan, Batangas for her high school education. She got her economics degree from St. Paul's College in Quezon City. She tried to be a career woman and worked at STD Overseas Manpower Services, taking up law studies in the evening. Then Ronnie came along. How they met, became friends, lovers and, eventually, a couple is an interesting story by itself. Love grew on the line. She was placing an overseas call and it so happened that the PLDT employees were on strike. The supervisors were manning the boards, Ronnie, among them. He was fascinated with her voice; he asked for her number; they became phone pals. They met in person, became friends and started to go out. Ronnie and Lorna got married in 1987 a few months after Lorna quit her job as Operations Manager of the manpower placement company. She was pregnant and needed bed rest. Moreover, her job was taxing mentally and emotionally, if not physically. She had to interact with many people – from the foreign principals to the creditors and OFW-applicants. Dealing with the applicants was particularly stressful: she sympathized with their troubles especially in raising placement fees. Nevertheless, she was grateful for the work discipline and managerial training she got from the job. 'And it was here that I met Ronnie', she adds laughing.

As a full-time housewife, however, she felt she had too much time on her hands. To stave off some of the boredom, she would cut fabric for baby dresses in a bedroom of the Kalaws' residence (her in-laws) which served as the newly-wedded couple's first home. Trimming the fabrics also became an outlet for her creative energies. And she felt there was much more within her waiting to be released. Eventually, Lorna attended a stuffed toy-making seminar at the Technology and Livelihood Resource Center (TLRC).

The seminar proved to be a piece of cake. She enjoyed the course immensely. The first products of that seminar were stuffed animals. Those were to become the progenitors of the Kalaws' stuffed toy universe. Lorna saw the potential of a stuffed toys business even as the country was facing an economic crisis. In spite of the uncertain business outlook, Lorna was determined to set up her own shop. She sold two of her most beloved pieces of jewellery for a shot at business success. The 50,000 pesos proceeds from the sale allowed her to rent a two-room apartment in Tinajeros, Malabon and buy the initial materials for her dream business. With one sewer, five second-hand sewing machines borrowed from her mom and loads of grit, LOKAL Industries was born and registered in a few months. The year was 1988.

Early setbacks

Ronnie provided for his family by working as a unit supervisor of PLDT. Together with his brother, he sold Lorna's first products to colleagues. It was quite a small undertaking, very young and not yet a *bona fide* business. Lorna allowed instalment payments. As payments came in on the 15th and the 30th of the month, the modest sales provided sustenance to the infant business. Not too long after, however, Ronnie was prohibited from continuing his side business at the telephone company. This was quite a setback for Lorna, but she remained unfazed.

They continued to make toys. Lorna was full-time in the business while Ronnie pitched in after work and during weekends. When she had made a considerable volume of items, Lorna would look around for buyers. She first explored the Malabon town proper hoping to get an order, clinch a contract or simply negotiate a sale. These efforts came to naught. She thought of going back home on foot to comb the shops lining the busy streets of Malabon. She stumbled upon a Philippine Telephone and Telegraph (PT&T) office, which had stuffed toys on display. Informed they were giveaways for the patrons of PT&T's *regalogram* service, she smelled an opportunity.

This was to be her initiation into the formal and complex world of business. She had to deal with the PT&T executives as well as managers from its sister company and procurement arm, Waterous Garden. Lorna finally won a contract for supplying the tele-communications company with 1,000 stuffed toys, but not before she had pulled some strings. She approached a *kumpare*, whose sister Menchy was the company's vice president. After seeing her sample, Menchy recommended her to Waterous Garden. When Lorna dis-covered that the company was paying a good price per unit, she lowered her quotation by five pesos to increase her chances of getting an order.

Lorna felt ecstatic after closing the deal. But when she was preparing to manufacture the order, Lorna realized that she didn't have enough materials to produce the volume required. She decided to use a substitute material instead. Having used a material of better quality, Lorna assumed her first major client would be pleased. She was wrong: PT&T rejected the goods. Instead of sulking, Lorna immediately produced the stuffed toys according to the material specifications with a 50,000 peso loan from a sister-in-law and on borrowed time. The company finally accepted delivery. The deal marked the beginning of a fruitful six-year relationship with the company.

LOKAL gets bigger

After a few years, the Kalaw family moved to a two-storey house in Longos, still in Malabon. They devoted the entire first floor to the shop; one room on the second floor for storage; and another room on the same floor for the Kalaw family quarters. Multi Needles, Inc., Novelty Philippines and a few other exporters eventually became LOKAL Industries' major clients. When Philippine tourism peaked in 1993, the company's growth seemed unstoppable; LOKAL Industries was getting monthly orders ranging from 3,000 to 10,000 items. And as their share in the stuffed toy market grew, competitors started to feel the heat. Lorna would get phone calls informing her that the caller had an exclusive contract with a certain client. In some cases, she would find herself the subject of negative gossip among her rivals. But all their bullying could not stop the Kalaws from expanding. LOKAL Industries' clientele list simply grew longer.

The company's market grew to include companies involved in direct selling, such as Tupperware. LOKAL's product line also became more diverse. Educational toys and kitchen and bedroom coordinates were soon included. Traders also started to approach the Kalaws to apply as agents. Through them, LOKAL Industries was able to reach markets that would have otherwise been inaccessible.

Despite booming sales, Lorna still continued to use the classified ads and Yellow Pages to prospect for more clients. She also went on with her practice of walking into hotels to introduce her products.

'My first products were the result of long and tedious experimentations and an out-and-out desire to learn', reveals Lorna. 'God knows how many stuffed toys I bought in the beginning only to tear them apart and restore them to their original form repeatedly until I achieved perfection', she continues. This is a technique she follows to this day. Soon realizing the importance of innovation, Lorna pored over magazines for design ideas. She also looked at the products already on the market. If Japan was successful in modifying Western technology and making it better, so was Lorna with stuffed toys. She cites quality, delivery and commitment as her business management guideposts.

The new partner

Lorna's husband, Ronnie, eventually quit PLDT. Nine years in the corporate world made him realize he was getting nowhere in his job. He joined LOKAL Industries, full of energy and confident in his ability to contribute to its growth. However, two months as a full-time partner didn't work out as well as they expected. The business was not enough to sustain them and their growing family.

A mechanical engineer by profession, Ronnie eventually got another job as production manager of an exporter of wooden doors. The 25,000 peso monthly salary that was offered – double his previous pay – was just too good to let go. Ronnie was efficient, hardworking and ready to learn. In time, he was given more responsibility. Before long, Ronnie felt he was eating, breathing and dreaming wooden doors! After five gruelling months, he decided to call it quits. For the second time, Ronnie was jobless.

This proved to be auspicious for, by this time, LOKAL's volume of operations was more than Lorna could cope with. She needed an extra hand – more than an extra hand: someone she could fully trust. This time, the couple committed to join their strengths and talents to make the business a more stable source of income for the family. The couple decided to keep separate duties based on their respective skills so they could complement each other. With his managerial experience in his past jobs, Ronnie was tasked with handling production. He lost no time introducing to the LOKAL workplace the system that he used in his previous job.

It didn't work at first. The workers were hard pressed to adapt to Ronnie's rather strict and methodical ways. When workers were slow to comply, Ronnie would lose his temper. Lorna herself could not stand the rigors. After all, she thought, she had managed quite well without the systems he was introducing. This often led to conflicts and shouting matches between the couple.

Eventually, Lorna and Ronnie talked things over and settled their differences. 'We really didn't have a choice but to compromise; at the end of the day, we are still the loving couple', says Ronnie. 'After all, our family roles – that of being husband and wife and being parents to our children – come first and foremost', he stresses.

The couple agreed to sit down to review the set-up. They have since kept separate offices. 'Ronnie oftentimes tells me I talk too much and laugh too loud over the phone. This distracts him from his paperwork', Lorna shares with a laugh. This is what makes her the right person to be in marketing, a position she holds along with product development.

Lorna sees Ronnie as systematic, orderly and organized. Ronnie is an achiever; when he does things, he makes sure that the output isn't only 'good enough' but 'impeccable'. 'He is a perfectionist, quite impatient sometimes, but a big help', Lorna concedes. Thanks to Ronnie, LOKAL Industries became known for its commitment not only to quality and on-time delivery but also to financial obligations. Ronnie is so strict with money that even relatives find it difficult to ask for favours. He uses funds strictly for their intended purpose.

He also sees to it that debts are paid immediately, even before creditors send their statements. All these practices have created a good impression on their creditors, giving LOKAL access to more loans.

On the other hand, Ronnie sees Lorna as someone who has strong faith in herself. She is self-confident, but down to earth when dealing with other people. She is also a friendly, generous and kind boss – one who sees workers as human beings rather than mindless robots. She banters with them and treats them on special occasions such as on Valentine's Day and on the couple's birthday. She gives out incentives during school opening and after every big project.

'We both have strong personalities', says Lorna. And this put them at loggerheads during the early days of their business partnership. Each wanted to call the shots. The couple would quarrel frequently due to their different approaches and ideas, especially when it came to production. Lorna says that Ronnie oftentimes spoke of theories and logic while she argued on the basis of her experience.

In time, the complementary, 'give-and-take' relationship prevailed. In search of more opportunities to expand, with support from PhilToy (a local organization of toy retailers and manufacturers), the couple exhibited at fairs in 1997. LOKAL supplied products to many of the PhilToy member retailers, including a popular gift shop, Blue Magic.

More expansion

In 1998 after seven years in Longos, the company rented premises at Dagatdagatan Village in the industrial hub of Malabon City. The bigger work space accommodated bigger production, as additional orders – including some from a Malaysian firm – began to arrive. In 1997, the Asia Pacific Economic Cooperation Forum was held in Manila and Subic. Since LOKAL Industries had by then carved out a name in the stuffed toy business, the couple was able to cash in on the conference. Their stuffed toys found their way to many of Metro Manila's top hotels. Months later, LOKAL Industries started exporting to Denmark.

After almost 16 years of operating and doing business from one rented place after another, LOKAL Industries moved to its permanent building early this year. The new factory at Dagatdagatan Village in Caloocan City is literally a product of Ronnie's hands, as he had designed it himself. He based his design on the concept of having all business operations (from marketing, administration and finance, to production and warehousing) under one roof for best results.

The present premises of LOKAL Industries comprise two buildings. The couple's offices are located on the second floor of the first building. Production activities are done in the second building. Gone are the borrowed machines. The present machine complement consists of a pneumatic stuffing machine, an electro-mechanical die cutting press, a pneumatic plastic accessories setter, fibre opening machine, several high-speed sewing and embroidery machines and a thermal cutting machine. With this expanded capacity, LOKAL can produce a maximum of 6,000 items a day, which can go up to 16,000 items, if the output of networks is taken into account.

The showroom and reception area – complete with a fully stocked pantry – is in the first building. A comfortable bedroom on the third floor comes in handy when Lorna needs to stay overnight.

The company has an estimated net worth of 20 million pesos, with land and building accounting for 11 million pesos, and the machinery, materials and inventory 9 million pesos.

In 2000, LOKAL opened its retail arm, Angel's Touch Marketing, the Malabon City Square (MCS); another store opened in 2003 at Tangas City. Presently, Angel's Touch has two stores at MCS. Since the couple started in retailing, their client list has continued to expand to include Jollibee, Colgate Palmolive, Purefoods, Avon, Kraft and some pharmaceutical companies for which they produced promotional items.

Organizational setup

The core staff of LOKAL Industries increased from one to 20 in a span of 16 years. The organizational set-up evolved as the business grew. Assisting Lorna in production are a materials preparation supervisor, a sewing supervisor, a finishing supervisor and a warehouse supervisor. LOKAL Industries also employs rectifiers who maintain the quality standards of the company. Lorna also takes on marketing and product development responsibilities, with the help of a pattern-maker, a sample maker and an assembler.

Aside from handling production, Ronnie is also in charge of human resources. He screens and interviews applicants and selects the workers. Angel's Touch Marketing is Ronnie's turf. It is a single proprietorship in his name. Each store has a sales clerk who does roving inventory. During the peak season, Ronnie hires additional sales clerks for each store.

Personal life

The couple's three children are achievers; all of them graduated valedictorian in grade school.

Preoccupied with the business, the Kalaws admit they have no close friends, but without regret. They say they couldn't have successfully balanced business, home and social life. All their free time is spent with their children. The family enjoys vacationing together and hanging out with each other to ease the tension and strengthen their bonds.

Ronnie is more attached to the kids than Lorna. He sees them off to school, attends to their school projects and assignments more often and cooks their breakfast. Lorna does not mind this at all. She is grateful that Ronnie tries to make up for what she does not have the time to do as a mother. It's also his way of letting her get much needed rest and sleep, she adds.

Ronnie doesn't like bringing work home, but sometimes it cannot be helped. Lorna says that she sometimes works at night using the computer in their bedroom.

Lorna acknowledges she has achieved business success at the expense of her duties as wife and mother. She could not explain to the children when they were younger why she was always busy in the factory. 'But the kids have grown up and matured ... they now understand.' When she delivered her valedictory when she graduated, Angela Vida recounted how she acquired asthma by inhaling the very fine, often- invisible fibre of the fabrics when they were still living in a small room. Lorna was deeply touched when she heard this.

In spite of setbacks, God has been good to them, Lorna asserts, and so they try to give back. They help less fortunate relatives and donate regularly to charities such as The Apostleship of Prayer and the Sisters of Charity.

Lorna says she plans to retire from the business in 10 years time and perhaps groom one of her supervisors to eventually take on her role in LOKAL.

She has taken up advocacy as a member of PhilToy. She wants work as a consultant for other enterprises. Even as she states that being in the toy business can be financially rewarding, Lorna feels sad that many of the pioneers in the industry have folded up.

Lorna believes in helping other members of the industry. It is second nature to her to share knowledge and information as well as excess orders and facilities. She finds it strange that others are not as willing to share. Lorna also calls on other successful small entrepreneurs to help young achievers by referring them to the right contacts. She does not want people to grope – not knowing where to go and how to go about it – as she had to when she was starting out.

LOKAL in 2004

By 2004 LOKAL Industries' production was more efficient because it was fully mechanized, thanks to Ronnie. However, Lorna says, that 'even if the company uses machines, I do not want the company to be fully-dependent on technology. I still prefer people over machines'. The company has a permanent labour force of 20. LOKAL Industries controls a wide network of contacts and subcontractors in Nueva Ecija and Pampanga with regular contractors numbering from 120 to 130.

Lessons learned

Fifteen years of doing business has given the couple experiences that money cannot buy, they agree. Their relationship with each other as business partners is better than ever. Without the setbacks they faced earlier, they wouldn't have been able to achieve such fine teamwork, not just with each other, but with their business associates and customers as well.

The company grew from referrals and recommendations from satisfied customers. Today, LOKAL can start a project without spending a peso. It maintains a network of 10 traders who find her terms reasonable and acceptable. It has also come to the point where LOKAL Industries can now choose its clients. Lorna proudly relates getting a big order from Purefoods Company through the company's advertising firm for which she got full payment in advance – way beyond LOKAL's usual 50 per cent down payment term.

Lorna urges small entrepreneurs to treat financial obligations seriously. When banks and other financial institutions realized how well the Kalaws meet their obligations, they became more accommodating to the business. Nowadays, LOKAL has a ready source of funds whenever it needs to buy more materials and supplies.

Excellence has become a cliché in business and industry, with many entrepreneurs paying lip service to it. At LOKAL Industries, excellence is taken seriously. Ronnie and Lorna make sure that the company is able to deliver the products to customers on time. They also take pains to ensure that their products are always of the best quality.

Manufacturing problems have also taught the Kalaws valuable lessons in problem solving. According to Lorna, problems occur in the plant almost every 15 minutes, and the couple responds to these promptly. When problems arise, the couple discuss the solution in real time, in other words, right away. Afterwards, the couple assign each other tasks to address the situation quickly and efficiently before parting ways.

Finally, Lorna advises business hopefuls to start small, for that way one can gradually learn the ropes and take small risks at a time. She knows whereof she speaks! LOKAL Industries after all began in cramped space and modest goals. Could Lorna have imagined, while cutting fabric for her grandmother's business and keeping an eye on her newborn, the growth she would achieve years later?

Questions

1 Has Lorna changed her style and approach from being an entrepreneur to a small business manager?
2 Has the company been exposed to any serious risks during its existence?
3 How can the entrepreneurial and management characteristics of Lorna be described?

18 Ningxia ABC Environmental Equipment Co. Ltd.

Xu Jinlian

MANAGER, NINGXIA ABC ENVIRONMENTAL EQUIPMENT

COUNTRY: CHINA

'The customer is the most important'

Ningxia ABC Environmental Equipment Co. Ltd. is a private company located in Shizushan City, Ningxia. It was founded in 2005 and employees increased from three persons in 2005 to 17 in 2010. The owner had previously been engaged in equipment and spare parts purchasing in a middle-sized state-owned company in Ningxia for more than 20 years. After he left this company he set up his own firm.

The main business of the company is selling equipments, spare parts, PPH pipes and chemicals used in the PVC industry, multi-silicon industry and coal chemical industry in the north-west of China. All the products are bought from overseas suppliers and most of them are of top quality. The company has responsibility for all maintenance of the products; sometimes it processes some welding joints according to customers' requirements. If and when the company cannot fulfil the maintenance it will ask for the help of the overseas offices in China. Meanwhile it has a warehouse prepared for spare parts and those that wear out for urgent customer requirements.

At the very beginning the sales value amounted to about 2 million Chinese Yuan (CNY), equivalent to 300,000 USD. In 2009 the sales value was 38 million CNY (5.84 million USD) and in 2010 turnover was doubled.

In total, the company has four departments, for finance, sales, trade and commercial and after-sales service. The owner is general manager and he has an assistant general manager at his side. Each department has a manager who is responsible for daily operations. The finance department reports directly to the owner; sales and costs are recorded on a daily basis for weekly and monthly reports.

Every Monday a meeting is held to plan the jobs for the coming week, during which the employees report information about and from customers, job status and other things. The owner regularly asks all sides about relevant information. He will himself phone customers on a daily basis if needed.

The owner emphasizes good relationships with customers. Customers are divided into different groups according to products and services, and there is always one employee tasked with direct contact with a customer through discussions and meetings. The employee knows who is in charge of the purchasing plan, the payment periods, job flows and other information about customers. He regards his customers as his friends and helps them not only with business-related issues but also with personal matters if required. Furthermore, he communicates very well with the top management of the customers.

Customer payments are dealt with in the following way:

- Equipment: 30 per cent of the price is paid in advance, 60 per cent is paid before ship-ment. The remaining 10 per cent is paid – usually after 12 to 18 months – provided the equipment functions well and to the customer's satisfaction.
- Spare parts: 100 per cent payment in advance. Spare parts are always urgently required and the value is low compared to equipments. Customers therefore agree with this approach.
- Non-competitive products: The company accepts ordinary invoicing according to cus-tomers' monthly payment schedule. These customers are mostly large state-owned companies of good reputation.

Ningxia ABC Environmental Equipment is a trading company, and sometimes the service is poor because of low employee skills. Customers complain about late shipment, damaged parts and slow maintenance. When a customer complains, an employee will first phone to get the details, explain to the customer and guide the customer in how to settle simple issues himself. After that the employee will visit the customer as soon as possible. If the issue has still not been resolved, an expert will arrive at the customer within 48 hours. The principle is to resolve the issues and problems first before getting together to discuss who should be responsible for the problem and take the costs. Sometimes costs are shared by both or three parties.

In China, especially in north-west China, people prefer to join big companies, especially state-owned ones. Ningxia ABC Environmental Equipment has suffered a lot from staff turnover. To date, only five people have worked for it for more than three years; others do not stay more than a year. The owner has taken action by raising salaries and bonuses. Most of employees are young girls and, after their marriage, most of them choose to leave the company. The owner worries that most of the employees have limited knowledge and can-not communicate smoothly and successfully with the customers. He is too kind to dismiss employees unless they are willing to learn.

Questions

1 In spite of its pronounced customer orientation, the company seems to have problems with customer service. What needs to be done to improve the situation?
2 What should the company do to improve the employment situation?
3 What can be said about the leadership of the company?

19 IE Electronics (Pvt) Ltd.

Per Lind

GOTLAND UNIVERSITY

COUNTRY: SRI LANKA

The company

IE Electronics (IEE) was founded 25 years ago in Sri Lanka by Mr Tisil Cooray. Mr Cooray, an electrical engineer, realized that there was a local market for electrical appliances such as TV antennas for the emerging consumer electronics market. The company grew significantly in its first years and is now a market leader in its sector. In recent years contacts were developed with overseas companies, and the company now has a joint production agreement with overseas firms in Finland and the UK. Component that are not available in Sri Lanka are sourced from Singapore.

The country

Sri Lanka is a South Asian country that was for a decade plagued by ethnic conflicts. These have now been settled, but with serious consequences for the country's economic development. In spite of this, there have been periods with relatively strong growth in industrial development, in which overseas investments have grown. The country benefits from bilateral trade agreements with neighbouring India. The agreement favours the export of the country's tea – the primary export commodity – but at the same time allows Indian manufactured products to enter the market under reduced import restrictions. This has resulted in increased competition among certain locally-produced product.

Company structure

IEE has received substantial consulting assistance from UNIDO (United Nations Industrial Development Organization), and took a significant step as it changed to a distributed factory layout of four autonomous units or divisions. Unit One is the factory for assembly of electrical components, and also houses administration and the head office; Unit Two is the Modarawila Plant for transformer manufacture; Unit Three is the workshop for tools; and Unit Four is Marketing and Sales which also houses a design centre.

In connection with the restructuring of the company, Mr Cooray brought his son into the firm, and the latter is now the acting managing director with primary responsibility for marketing and sales. However, as company chairman, Mr Tisil Cooray is the *de facto* controlling force. He is also daily involved in business strategies. Mr Cooray is very much concerned with costs, and has a firm grip of how costs are controlled. He is very keen to let his son grow and mature, but does not fully trust his son's cost consciousness. His daughter, who was sent to a college in the United States, has now returned and heads part of the company's marketing activities.

The son is very much up-to-date with modern business concepts, at least theoretically, and wishes to introduce modern management principles. Being customer-oriented is part of this, and the company therefore has hired new and dynamic sales staff to cope with market demand and customer requirements. However, the new development has led to increased operating costs (salaries and overheads). Mr Cooray has also advocated cutting the price of key products to meet competition, especially from overseas vendors now entering into the local Sri Lankan market. This has led to loss, which Mr Cooray thinks will be overcome as sales will grow, due to better customer service and lower prices.

Strategy

The company's mission statement is:

- to continuously improve products and services;
- to acquire advanced technology through joint ventures, machinery and tools and employees; and
- to look for new ways of reaching customers and offering customized solutions.

Present weaknesses in the company's activities include serious delays in product development and the improvement of existing products. Also co-ordination among departments is lacking as departments and managers work at their own rate rather than a company as a whole. Mr Cooray has also complained about delays and increasing overhead costs in the process of building a more efficient management team.

On the plus side, IE Electronics has a well-established brand name in Sri Lanka, and is one of very few companies in the business for over twenty years. In addition, up to now, the company has achieved price leadership due to comparatively low overhead costs. And it has the joint ventures established with overseas companies.

Questions

1 What *potential* risk is there in the formal transfer of responsibility from the older to the younger generation of the company's management? Is there a reason to apply cultural aspects to this issue?

2 Profit has decreased as a result of the new strategy. Explain how Mr Coorany might have thought about this. What risk is there in such a strategy? Would the risk be the same in any developed country?

3 If you were a business consultant to IE Electronics, what specific areas would you look into? Explain why.

20 Mandelay Coating

Kobus Visser and Isaacs Eslyn

DEPARTMENT OF MANAGEMENT, UNIVERSITY OF THE WESTERN CAPE, CAPE TOWN, SOUTH AFRICA

COUNTRY: SOUTH AFRICA

Background

Mandelay Coatings is a paint manufacturing business owned by Mr Galliem Jacobs. He came from a poor family and built his business up 'through clear thinking'. He says that the person from whom he purchased his factory from often used to say that Mr Jacobs was fortunate, because he had achieved his present position through ability and not through wealth. Mr Jacobs spoke a lot about the disastrous effect that apartheid had on his confidence and other Blacks. He emphasized the psychological effects and the fact that Black people grew up without confidence. He mentioned a case where he was employed by the third largest paint company in South Africa and, as a paint range, was asked to design the Nova paint range. This was so successful it sold in large quantities all over South Africa. But because he was not White, the company sent down a white Afrikaner to be his manager. This man did not have a passion for the business in the same way that Mr Jacobs did. The manager would spend the day playing golf and return at the end of the day to ask Mr Jacobs if everything was fine, and to sign the supervision register. When satisfied clients came to visit, Mr Jacobs would be thanked, but his manager would go off to lunch with the visitor. This made Mr Jacobs feel this company was not the right place for him to be (they did not value what they had in him). Mr Jacobs became one of the country's foremost paint chemists. Friends urged him to start his own business, and clients – national and international – kept putting in orders. He designed a range of fireproof paints of which he sold the copyright to a larger company (the product was too expensive for him to manufacture). This paint was used to paint the steel framework of Cavendish Square.

Mr Jacobs is a trained paint chemist. He started off as a paint technician at Plascon in 1977. He worked there for a year and moved to Vadek paints and decided to work in a development laboratory where he analysed paints and the paints of their competitors. Then he moved to a small company where he worked for two years before it went bankrupt. His move to the large company for whom he developed the Nova range coincided with the height of apartheid. Developed the Nova range towards the end of his stay, he did not get any recognition for it. He became frustrated: he was a senior person and he had experience, but he felt exploited. He decided to go to a small company that made good products under licence from a British company. He felt that he would be recognised in this company. That was the time when American sanctions began (1984) and the small business was struggling. It did not perform well in the market. It was a bad time for him to switch over to a small company, but he needed a new start. The company was taken over but could not survive. The new management bought out the business. They asked Mr Jacobs to stay on as paint chemist and, within a year, he was made a director of the company. Then he also became a shareholder. He developed products that the market needed. He stayed with this company for ten years before he resigned.

This was the time of the new South Africa and Mr Jacobs saw that there were many opportunities, particularly for people who were disadvantaged before. He investigated the situation carefully and decided to give it a try. The company that he left was also at that stage in difficult times. He saw more potential in starting from scratch. New schemes had been put into place, among which was a measure by which a certain percentage of tenders are awarded to previously disadvantaged people. Mr Jacobs was inspired to try, believing in his own abilities, his strong technical background, his insight into what the market wants and the marketing training that he had received. He also had close contact with clients: he made sure that he got feedback and made the necessary changes when he had developed a product for a client. The managing director of the company he left tried to persuade him to stay, but he has never looked back. In his words:

> It is hard work. You work seven days a week, often 24 hours a day. You must be prepared to be committed. You must have your family behind you. You can't start a business and have domestic problems.

Mandelay Coatings created employment for 10 people.

The competitive edge of small businesses

In his early days as paint chemist, Mr Jacobs analysed the paints of competitor companies. By doing this, the company could compare its own products with those of the competition and judge their position in the market in terms of quality. Sometimes companies have had to match the products clients requested from competitors. By analysing the products of competitors, Mr Jacobs developed a keen understanding of the paint market. This has assisted him in positioning his own small business in a competitive market.

As a small business, one of the advantages that Mandelay Coatings has in a market dominated by large companies is its ability to be more flexible. If a client wants product with certain properties not currently part of their range, Mandelay Coatings designs it according to their needs. That gives them a market. Clients also know that they will make a small quantity of a certain colour. Clients know that Mandelay Coatings is 'hungry for contracts and they will make it happen'. At present they are fulfilling orders for next day delivery, to make sure that they do not fall behind when new clients come in with urgent orders. By delivering on time, they keep their clients happy.

Close contact with clients

Mr Jacobs ensures client satisfaction by keeping in close contact with them. When he has developed a product for a client, he makes sure that he gets feedback and makes the necessary changes. He feels that to have survived in the business for two years is a feather in his cap. 'I think its being connected with the right people, and having the right attitude [made me successful].' He says that, to his surprise, the bulk of his clients are White people. 'They are selective and they know what they want – a good product at a good price.' He has been able to satisfy them. Without their support he would not have survived.

Adaptability

All the product information of Mandelay Coatings is stored on a computer. Products can be scaled up to whatever size required – 100 litres, 300 litres, 500 litres. The company uses the Brilliant accounting package on their computer, and orders are executed through this package. It calculates how much VAT needs to be deducted. It includes an accounting package. They were advised by their auditors to use this programme.

Questions

1   What is the management style of Mr Jacobs?
2   What is the business idea of Mandalay Coatings?
3   What makes Mandalay Coatings a successful firm?

21 Carbex AB

Per Lind

DEPARTMENT OF MANAGEMENT, LINKÖPING UNIVERSITY, SWEDEN

COUNTRY: SWEDEN

Background

According to Mr Ströberg, the Managing Director of Carbex, the company was founded in 1887 and has always been in the business of making carbon brushes. Carbon brushes constitute an essential part of electric motors and generators and are also used for the transmission of electric signals. Carbon brushes are made in all sizes, from those needed by very small motors to the biggest ones in power plants. A patent for the first self-adjusting carbon brush was granted to the founder of Carbex, Mr Loewendahl, in 1909. The patent has since then been under constant improvement. Carbex's other main product is slide rings, a device making it possible to lead electricity and electronic signals through rotating equipment, such as power turbines, car steering wheels and radar to mention a few applications. Both these products are made for new machines as well as replacements for old ones. Carbex is also a wholesale supplier of all kinds of parts for electrical motors and engines. The wholesale business is some ten years old, and is a response to the demand for replacing not only the carbon brushes in a broken machine, but also other parts broken at the same time. Carbex makes the carbon brushes from a sintered mix of carbon and copper and silver respectively. The production is mechanized and automated as well as manual. Much of the machinery for production is made in-house.

Brushes are sold around the world. The wholesale business is restricted to the Nordic countries. Marketing is through participation in industry fairs and by personal calls. These fairs are attended together with the representative in each country, respectively. Some promotion is also made by advertising in magazines. The main form of market promotion is personal calls and visits to current and potential customers. There are about five producers of carbon brushes in Sweden, and in the rest of Europe there are about ten producers. Carbex is one of the smallest producers in the business and has therefore specialized in making brushes for hi-tech applications. International competition is tough, since the Carbex products are easy and relatively cheap to transport. Carbex customers include all kinds of manufacturers, and the company mainly relies on a few big clients such as ABB, Tetra-Pak and Electrolux. The average ratio between big and small customers in regard of sales is 80:20. This may change as a few big customers have shown interest in Carbex which may lead to markets opening up and broadening in Italy, Germany, United States, Japan and China, to mention a few. Trust in Carbex' product and service quality has resulted in long-term business relations with big customers. Although the market for carbon motor brushes is declining, there is increasing demand for slip ring brushes. Carbex is presently negotiating to become a service and maintenance provider for a big international manufacturer of slip rings and to become this company's sales representative in Sweden.

Carbex is also negotiating to take part in the production of packaged solutions for carbon brush and slip ring combinations.

A sudden peak in demand is, of course, putting extra strain on management, but this is not at all negative, according to Mr Ströberg. Investment and recruitment must be undertaken, but this is only done after have orders being secured. Meanwhile, Carbex is relying on neighbouring companies as subcontractors and on casual employees.

The two main competitive advantages that Carbex have are high quality and flexibility. Reporting lines are short, which allow salespersons to communicate directly with the production manager, who can reset machines within a short time, should a customer be in serious need. A single order can be made and delivered within 24 hours. This is partially necessary since Carbex products are often part of complex production systems whose idleness is very expensive, making the delivery of replacement parts very urgent. The organization of Carbex enables employees to make decisions about production changes when Mr Ströberg is absent. Carbex cooperates with its customers as well as with its suppliers. Carbex always participates in discussions with the customer in the design of the component to be produced. Carbex also demands that a prototype be tested in the actual environment of its intended usage. There is no common standard for the kind of products Carbex makes. Hence all the products from Carbex are custom made. However, orders differ in size from a single brush to 20,000 units. Carbex is now gearing up for a higher level of sophistication as it gets into medical technology and other hi-tech areas. In Mr Ströberg's opinion, this is a very interesting development as it puts even higher demands on his business and most likely will lead to a higher profile on the market. Carbex has acquired the Technical ISO 9001 certification and ISO 14001.

Carbex is wholly owned by Addtech, a company quoted on the Swedish stock exchange. Mr Ströberg studied electrical engineering in Stockholm and has worked for ABB. He started at Carbex in 2004 and his introduction to the company was very much facilitated through the assistance of some long-time employees of the company and also by the fact that records of important events had always been kept in order.

Through Carbex, Mr Ströberg is a member of the Association of Swedish Engineering Industries, an employers' association. He is also the chairman of the local employers' association. The production employees are members of the Union of Swedish Metal Workers and the administrative staff are members of the Swedish Industry Employees Association.

Carbex employs 23 people of which 15 are directly involved in production. Cooperation between Mr Ströberg and the unions is running quite smoothly. A tiring thing is all the environmental and safety inspections. All together some ten authorities regularly visit the workplace. He finds these inspections a constant disturbing factor as they take time and the inspectors' verdict must be followed without question. He appreciates the need for safety but complains that the inspections require production to be shut down. In Mr Ströberg's opinion, very little consideration is given to Carbex needs of running a business. On top of that, the inspections have to be paid for by Carbex – a situation not entirely to Mr Ströberg's satisfaction.

Needs for improvements in the workplace are discussed in a monthly meeting. In this forum, the weekly activities are also planned together with the staff. Beside this kind of staff interaction, Mr Ströberg thinks there is a mutual trust between him and the employees. This shows as problems are most often discussed openly and solved, together taking consideration of both sides involved. There is an overall friendly atmosphere at Carbex where the sense of superior-subordinate is rare to find. Mr Ströberg does however recognize the fact that some people – old-timers mainly – see him as more of a boss than a colleague. This, he stresses, is also important to respect and is not to be seen as a failure, but just another way of working together. The employees of Carbex are all on monthly wages.

Mr Ströberg appreciates the responsibility with which his employees work. He can see that all of his staff have a large measure not only of professional skill but also of common sense. This is expressed, for example, in the careful handling of material and the staff's ability to take initiatives of their own. Mr Ströberg always takes advice from his staff on how to fit a separate order into the general flow of production. One thing that Mr Ströberg thinks is good is to take on temporary staff. This makes it easy to meet peaks in demand. Another thing that makes it hard, or rather costly, to run a business is the rule that health insurance is to be covered by the company for a maximum of three weeks, even if injuries occur outside the workplace.

New employees must undergo on-the-job training. At least three month of 'apprenticeship' is required before responsibility can be given for any part of production. Depending on the task, it then can take as long as five years before an employee is considered fully competent for his or her work. Further education is provided depending on type of work. However, this year everyone is supposed to undergo training in computer knowledge and economics. The purpose of this is to provide a general ability to handle all the more computerized equipment. The economics training is to spread economic thinking throughout the staff and, with it, the possibility of delegating even more decisions. Carbex also provides training and education in language and mathematics to those who need these skills in their work situation.

For the last 20 years there has been a trend for salary costs to replace materials costs as the main cost. Nowadays labour is the main expenditure followed by material, machinery and marketing. At Carbex only one person is responsible for economy and administration, but Mr Ströberg also monitors the financial situation. These two people are the only ones involved in financial control. An overall budget is made for a year ahead for each product and for expected customer s respectively. Once per month the overall budget for the company is reviewed and analysed. The cost estimates for every project/order is monitored closely and, if necessary, the estimate is revised. Thanks to good contacts with customers, Mr Ströberg is able to make budget predictions for the year. The stock of confirmed orders runs normally no longer than one month ahead. Some customers declare their intention to purchase, but to put too much trust in that is, according to Mr Ströberg, quite risky.

Carbex's business is growing on all markets. The turnover has increased from 12–14 million SEK ten years ago to 70 million SEK in recent years. This trend is forecast to continue in the years to ahead with an expected annual growth rate of 15 per cent. The number of employees in production as well as in administration has not grown as much; while company turnover has increased, employment has decreased. The increase in turnover has been possible with new machinery.

Questions

1 What is the impact of close union involvement in a firm like Carbex?
2 The company has benefitted by its patent. What happens when the patent runs out?
3 Carbex is located in a small regional town of Sweden. Are there negative and positive aspects of such location compared with a more urban environment?

22 Kun Mining Company Ltd.

Lifeng Shen

MANAGING DIRECTOR, KUN MINING COMPANY LTD

COUNTRY: CHINA

Introduction

The Kun Mining Company is a small business operating on mainland China. The description given here is intended for use as a case study, and some aspects of the company have been disguised to this end. As such, the study reflects the current situation of countless Chinese small and medium-sized enterprises. The description covers the company's establishment and development, its management and performance and the opportunities and challenges it faces.

Establishment and development

Development of the western regions of China is fundamental, according to a strategic principle issued in 2000 by the central government. The goal of this principle is to reduce the differences in social economic development between the western and eastern regions. To advance this principle, the central government has unveiled a series of advantageous policies such as financial support and tax reduction. This greatly inspired the pioneering passion of many investors. I was one of them.

The western regions have 12 provinces and autonomous regions. Among them, Shaanxi is the so-called dragonhead, possessing better geological and traffic conditions in comparison with other regions. Moreover, it is abundant in energy resources, especially oil and coal. Thus the provincial capital of Xi'an has become the first choice of investors.

In 2007, Kun Mining (a limited liability company, hereafter referred to as Kun) was registered in Xi'an. We selected prospecting for mineral resources as the company's main investment direction. The name Kun in Chinese has the opposite meaning of Qian, the former indicates female while the later indicates male, which also well-expresses the nature of the business, in that was funded by women.

Registration was quickly accomplished after the funds were obtained. We scheduled the investment according to the need of prospecting. To date, some 25,000,000 CNY (about 3.75 million USD) has been invested in prospecting projects and spent on routine operations.

Development

When a book is opened, you never know what will happen next. To our pleasant surprise, Kun has been going well and on track to reach its goals. The staff of 28 staff includes a small management group, a finance section, a bigger prospecting engineering section and an affiliate office.

Kun now owns three prospecting claims ranging from valuable metal to coal. According to the authoritative State Mineral Resources Assessment Bureau, the proven reserves prospected by the company have reached 75 million USD. (The real figure is higher giving the company more opportunities to draw investment funds at a favourable rate.)

Management and performance

Organization structure

Kun is registered as a limited liability company. Two shareholders hold 70 per cent and 30 per cent of the company shares respectively. The senior shareholder appoints three directors while the junior shareholder appoints two directors, thus composing the board. The board has at least one meeting each year to discuss development programmes and make decisions. Between meetings, the General Manager takes responsibility as executive director. The General Manager is appointed by the board and is trusted to recruit senior management officials.

Performance model

Step I: get permission to prospect

After the establishment of the company, we started to do research on the geological composition of Shaanxi province and the area in which prospecting was encouraged by the local government. Professionals suggested several districts which the Physical Geological Survey Brigade of the State did little prospecting in the early 1970s. We applied to the local government for them and soon got permission.

Step II: create prospecting design and submit for approval

There are different departments specialized in prospecting design. It is important to get a constructive design for any geological programme. It shows what the prospecting will search for and how the work will be done. Methods and possible results will also be revealed in the design. The design should be submitted to local government for approval before the prospecting starts. Usually a prospecting project comprises three periods: initial prospecting (which proves existence and trend of the ore body), general prospecting (which reveals possible reserves and grade) and extensive prospecting (which describes proved reserves and industrial exploitation).

Step III: organize the prospecting teams

To carry out an intended prospecting project, there would be at least eight teams, each with a specific responsibility:

1   earthquake physical experiment;
2   drilling;
3   geophysical measurement;
4   geological recording;
5   sampling;
6   chemical analysis;
7   on-site supervision; and
8   other methods needed.

Table 22.1 Staff sections

Section	Staff	Functions
GM office	1+2	Work out annual project plan and financial budget Day-to-day running of the company
Finance office	3	Put the financial budget into effect Support core activities through good planning
Engineering office	17	Implement prospecting projects Organize all technical teams needed Recommend valuable resources for prospecting
Support section	5	Drivers Cleaners Security guards

Except for associated works, such as road construction, all the above tasks need to be undertaken by qualified teams. We have to negotiate with each team according to the requirements of prospecting programme.

Step IV: submit prospecting results for authoritative assessment

Prospecting results not only reveal the geological data but also the economic value. Through government assessment, the company will decide whether to draw co-investment funds or transfer to bigger mining company.

Financial control

Prospecting is a systematic process and usually lasts three to four year for overall fulfilment. Thus it is important to have effective financial control. Sometimes you can't advance all programmes at the same time. The following rules have proved to be of benefit to Kun's finance control:

- recruit professionals to make the design;
- work out budget accordingly;
- stick to the budget;
- select experienced and qualified staff;
- appoint a strong engineering supervisor; and
- examine the implementation of each engineering contract.

Network

Kun's network falls into three parts: prospecting teams, material suppliers and government branches. To our satisfaction, Xi'an, the city in which Kun is located, has the best workforce for geological prospecting and government services are also acceptable. In the past four years Kun has been growing quickly and smoothly. However, prices for materials required have been skyrocketing in an unpredictable way, which has given us a great headache. To

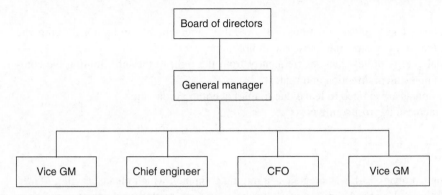

Figure 22.1 Organization structure.

avoid exceeding the budget, we have to adopt packaged engineering contracts, taking price rises into consideration during negotiations and allowing the contractors a price margin.

Culture and ethics

Like many new startups in China, Kun has a short history. Compared with state-owned giants, Kun is very young and small. But that is not to say Kun is fragile. Kun has had a solid foundation from the day of its birth. It is a company that was created by people who have extensive commercial, investment and management experience and who also are familiar with Chinese policies and regulations. Furthermore, managers in Kun have shared ideas with each other throughout its existence. In part, the culture and ethics can be summarized as follows:

- we cooperate and create a difference;
- company and staff grow together;
- respecting technical guidelines will reduce risk for conflicts;
- 'do your own job excellently, support others extensively';
- good faith is worth more than money; and
- investors take the risk, staff share the benefit.

Guided by these ethics, Kun now has a fine team, which is not only professional, but also dedicated.

Opportunities and challenges

Strengths and opportunities

- Experienced team leaders;
- adequate investment capital from shareholders;
- abundant natural resources in the local province;
- highly qualified recruitment base in the region of the company (number of universities and colleges list top three in China); and
- national supporting policy.

Challenges and problems

- Complicated geological situations lead to false judgment by professionals with the result that some prospecting may lead to nothing;
- national energy policy changes frequently from the right to the left, limiting the company's investment direction and scale;
- professionals are enticed to leave due to market competition; and
- rapid increase in prospecting costs.

Conclusion

Kun Mining Company Ltd. was created as a mining company, which means it will go far to reach its final goal of producing minerals in the future, no matter who becomes the final business dealer. To some extent, reserves proven through prospecting assure great opportunities for future investment. Kun Mining should therefore have at least three ways of going further, these include:

1 drawing more prospecting capital by increasing shares, building and operating its own mining factory;
2 listing the company on the stock market; and
3 transferring some of its prospecting assets to other mining companies at a favourable price.

Questions

1 Kun Mining is a company managed by women. Does this show in the above account by the managing director?
2 The eastern coastal region of China is today considered the dynamic region. What are the future chances for the company in the western region?
3 What is the leadership style of the company?

23 Doradca Consultants Ltd.

Piotr Wrobel

UNIVERSITY OF GDANSK, GDANSK, POLAND

COUNTRY: POLAND

History

Doradca Consultants Ltd. is one of the oldest consulting companies in Poland. It has been involved in the processes of privatization and restructuring in Poland, Central Europe and the former Soviet Union republics since the beginning of the cold war thaw. Established in 1985 in Sopot by a group of lawyers, economists and scientists from the University of Gdansk, Doradca Consultants was involved in establishing cooperatives and joint ventures and provided accounting, tax, legal and organizational consultancy services for Poland's emerging private sector throughout the late 1980s. At that time Doradca was supported by the underground Solidarity trade union, as one of the very first independent initiatives and a place where Solidarity activists dismissed from state sector jobs could find work. At the end of this period Doradca commenced rendering services to foreign investors and developed the first full-fledged feasibility studies for the International Finance Corporation. Some people connected with Doradca, known as Gdańsk liberals, played a prominent role in Poland's economic and social life during the transition a few years later.

The change in the political system and the emergence of a market economy brought new challenges for the company. New customers with new needs appeared as compared to the centrally-managed economy. How did the company cope with that? Doradca's key employees included academics that were well acquainted with Western markets and Western companies. There were also several foreign experts working for Doradca. Moreover, the local consultants were given training in modern management techniques. Another strategy to adjust the company's offer to new market needs was licensing. A number of products were created on the basis of licences acquired from Huthwaite International, a UK based company.

In 1991 Doradca was transformed into a limited liability company, with the consultants and Lazard (a renowned French investment bank) as its shareholders. Soon after that, the French investor declared their willingness to acquire a controlling stake in the company. The other shareholders – particularly the consultants – chose independence, refusing the offer. Today most shares belong to four active partner–consultants.

In the following years, step by step the company launched new types of service: quality assurance, environmental management and a wide range of training including e-learning. In line with its strategy, the company established two daughter companies: a joint venture called Doradca East based in Volgograd (Russia) and Doradca Auditors (Gdansk, Poland), dealing with the verification of financial statements.

During the 25 years of its existence Doradca has carried out more than 2,000 consulting assignments. Currently the company ranks among the top 20 management consulting companies in Poland measured by revenue, between 2 and 3 million Euros. It employs some 50 people full time, providing financial, organizational development, marketing, quality management and strategic consulting services in Poland and other European countries.

Strategy, services

The mission of Doradca is:

> ... to render high-value management consulting services, providing clients with practical and concrete benefits, thanks to our consultants' knowledge, expertise and skills. We realize that the most valuable assets of our company are the knowledge and skills of our employees. Therefore, we build an environment for their personal development, improvement of professional qualifications and acquisition of new and unique experiences. On this basis we establish conditions for designing new, client-specific solutions and ideas which reflect external changes and increase our customers' wealth.

The company's offer is focused on three target groups:

1   medium and big companies – domestic and international;
2   government – central and local level; and
3   international organizations, e.g. the World Bank or the International Finance Corporation.

The core business of Doradca is management consulting. The following list of units illustrates the scope of services:

*   Organization Development Department, handling OD services and strategic advice, including strategy elaboration, BPR/BPI, analysis and design of managerial and organizational systems; privatization and restructuring;
*   Corporate Finance Department, dealing with the analysis and design of financial and accounting systems, feasibility studies and business plan preparation, valuation reports, tariff studies, due diligence analyses, ABC;
*   Market Research Department, responsible for the development of strategic marketing plans, market research, benchmarking, preparation and implementation of public relations campaigns;
*   Management Standards Department, dealing with quality management, environmental management systems and standards related to safety (e.g. ISO 9000 and 14000, OHSAS);
*   Project Management Department, responsible also for project management services, including courses licensed by STS and carried out in the formula of so-called blended learning; and
*   Huthwaite Poland, a licensee of Huthwaite International (UK), carrying out training programmes aimed at increasing efficiency of sales, negotiations and teamworking, including SPIN® sales efficiency courses.

In addition to these departments and sections the company collaborates closely with Legal Counsels who provide legal support for Doradca and render legal advisory services. An important role in the company's offer is played by interdisciplinary complex assignments (e.g. restructuring) encompassing numerous skills and specialisms. Most of the services offered are tailor-made solutions, designed to satisfy clients' specific needs.

Obviously, the scope of the offer has evolved in line with the changing market needs. There are services that are losing their significance, e.g. privatization assistance (as a result of the decreasing number of state owned companies being privatized); quality management systems (due to increased competition, especially from freelancers). On the other hand, new services are being implemented and there are old ones that are winning new markets, e.g. e-learning courses in project management, organizational audits focused on cost killing, coaching services and public-private partnership assistance.

Although most of the projects are carried out in Poland, there are also many assignments implemented abroad. One of Doradca's interests is advice regarding business development in Eastern markets. The company has carried out consulting projects in numerous countries including Slovenia, the Czech Republic, Russia, Estonia, Kazakhstan, Kosovo, Lithuania, Belarus and Ukraine. These assignments often take place in cross-cultural environments when consultants bridge two different worlds – Western companies and Eastern companies and markets.

Doradca has built its competitive advantage on:

- experienced consultants;
- references from clients (2,000 consulting projects in the company's history); and
- strategic alliances with partners.

Like its competitors, Doradca has built its position by developing intellectual capital.

Marketing and sales

Marketing activities in the consulting industry are unique. What may be surprising to some is the sector does not perceive advertising as a professional activity. The assumption is that good companies do not have to advertise themselves. This attitude is changing slowly, although many companies still follow the rule.

The marketing of Doradca is focused on building the reputation of professional experts in certain areas lying within core competencies of the company. These activities include:

- participation in business conferences – consultants present the company's experience to potential clients;
- publication of books and articles by the company's employees;
- networking with ex-Doradca consultants who play important roles in business;
- membership in Lewiatan business association;
- membership in strategic alliances (see below); and
- internet website.

The company acquires most projects by taking part in tenders and through active references – satisfied customers recommend the services of Doradca to other clients.

Strategic alliances

Strategic alliances play an important role in the company, especially where this entails:

- responding to sophisticated and complex customer needs; and
- preparing new products.

Apart from typical consulting projects, such as financial analysis or salary system redesign, there are a number of complex, interdisciplinary problems which clients enquire about. Usually these projects require a unique and wide range of skills that are not present in one company. In that case, the customer's enquiry is addressed by forming an alliance. Like another leading consulting companies, Doradca has a number of close domestic and foreign allies representing a wide variety of skills and knowledge: technical consulting, legal advice, banking industry, executive search, human resources management, e-learning courses, IT hardware and software. Some of these allies are big international companies, but there are also a number of highly-specialized freelancers.

New products might be developed within the company or with the aid of other experts' know-how. In many cases it is cheaper and faster to use existing knowledge instead of 'reinventing the wheel'. This kind of alliance is most fruitful if the expert is not Doradca's direct competitor.

Among many alliances, two are particularly worth mentioning. In the mid-1990s, Doradca became a representative of a British consulting company, Huthwaite International, dealing with training programmes aimed at increasing sales effectiveness. The programmes are focused mainly on high-value goods and services. As a result of that cooperation, Doradca got access to high quality services tested in many countries worldwide. Today the company has a strong training department called Huthwaite Poland which generates a substantial part of company's sales.

In 2005 Doradca joined E-I Consulting Group, strengthening its international dimension. The group includes medium-sized consulting companies from the Netherlands, France, Italy, Greece, the Czech Republic and Poland. By being a member of such a club means that the company has access to unique expertise and resources. Members of the group carry out consulting projects together, helping each other in acquiring new clients. They also have an opportunity to exchange knowledge about current trends in different European consulting markets.

Organization

The implementation of nearly every contract is organized on project basis. Some of the assignments are quite short – they last a few weeks – while some last as long as one or two years. This requires flexible management of core assets – i.e. consultants. At Doradca, some departments group employees with similar specializations. At the same time, consultants are members of project teams, often more than one team simultaneously. As a result, management in such an organizational structure resembles a matrix. Many consultants have a few supervisors at the same time. The same people play the roles of project managers and team members.

In addition to the company's in-house staff, Doradca maintains a number of external specialists who are involved in some project teams. In the case of complex projects, as when Doradca is a member of a consortium, the company's consultants take part in a virtual team. Sometimes they are managed by Doradca's representative, sometimes by an external specialist from another company.

The matrix organization requires consultants to be good team players with high interpersonal skills, open to new challenges. The company offers its employees a career path from assistant at the very beginning through consultant, senior consultant, director and finally to a partner as the highest level in consulting. Employees with partner status own some of the company's shares.

The flexible and project-oriented organization produces varying workloads for consultants. There are periods requiring very hard work with long hours spent in the office, travelling or working at the client's office. But there are also times when work is less intensive.

Knowledge management, innovations

Knowledge management is an enormous challenge for every consulting company. In fact, what such companies sell is knowledge. Effective knowledge management means that companies improve existing knowledge and create new knowledge to finally offer valuable services to the market. This requires identifying knowledge gaps, acquiring new knowledge and developing existing knowledge, making employees exchange their knowledge with each other and, finally, protecting key knowledge. How does Doradca cope with that challenge?

- New knowledge and new services are designed both by their own consultants and with the help of strategic allies. One of Doradca's partners – the Development Director – is responsible for innovations. The company constantly manages a portfolio of innovations. That process – mainly developing new services – might be compared to testing. At the beginning, all ideas have to comply with financial requirements set by partners (the business plan stage). Then each of the promising services is given a limited time to prove its profitability. Some of them are successful and some have to be abandoned.
- Consultants are chosen for project teams based on their competences as well as on their career path (future profile).
- Consultants share their knowledge with colleagues while working in teams.
- There is a system of internal trainings (Doradca's Academy) run by consultants. Employees also take part in external trainings.
- IT system supports the storage and retrieval of codified knowledge (analysis, reports, clients' data). There are some problems with access to all the necessary data through the central database as some of the data is only stored on personal laptops.
- An important part of the culture is collaborative problem solving and teamwork.
- To some extent master–pupil mentoring system is used.

Opportunities and threats

The typical threat to consulting companies is the risk of losing their most valuable assets – the consultants. As a rule, some employees make a shift in their career after a few years of work in the consulting industry. In many cases those consultants are hired by companies which are the consulting company's clients. The departure of a consultant is especially harmful if that person is the sole specialist in a certain field. As a result, the company may lose the opportunity to offer certain services. In the history of Doradca there was one such difficult moment when the company lost approximately half of its resources. In 1991, the CEO of the company – Jan Krzysztof Bielecki – was nominated Prime Minister. It came as no surprise that he offered some of his close partners from Doradca positions in the government. As a result, the company lost several key employees. To make matters worse, the promotion of the CEO to the government meant that Doradca was excluded from bidding for public contracts. Simultaneously, the company lost its most valuable assets as well as an important source of orders.

In every business there are many external dangers. The year 2009 was marked by a global financial crisis. It also influenced the Polish market for consulting services as

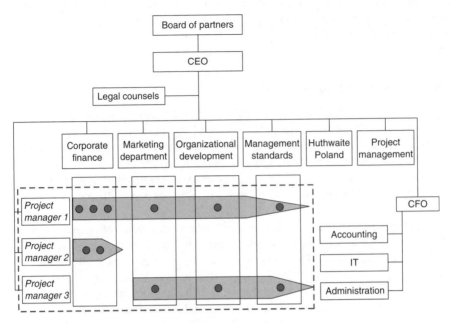

Figure 23.1 Organizational structure of Doradca.

clients – both domestic and international – reduced their spending on consultants and trainers. Most consulting companies were affected, especially big ones with high fixed costs. In order to survive, they had to lower their prices to the level of domestic consulting companies. Obviously, competition became very tough, influencing Doradca's sales level.

There are interesting opportunities in the market connected with the growing demand for some consulting services. Public–private partnership (PPP) is getting more and more popular among local authorities. PPP involves contracts between a public sector authority and a private company, in which the private party provides a public service or project. That partnership is a way to provide citizens with different public goods, e.g. healthcare, transport, culture, recreation, waste management. All these projects require the professional assistance of economists, lawyers and engineers, thus creating demand for consulting services.

Another chance lies in using EU funds to support the consulting and training services of the company. There are many programmes run by state agencies which aim at increasing the competitiveness of Polish companies, especially small and medium enterprises (SME)s. In the past many SMEs could not afford such services. Today, consulting and training companies may obtain some funds for their services offered to SMEs. As a result, the total demand for consulting services has been increasing, creating a huge opportunity for the sector to grow.

Questions

1   How has the transfer from a socialist country to market economy country changed the business climate in Poland?
2   How has Doradca managed to benefit in this new economic environment?
3   How does Doradca ensure that its consulting staff stays with the company?

24 Bernard Botejue Industries

Julian Nanyakkara and Chamli Puskpakuara

KELANIYA UNIVERSITY, COLOMBO, SRI LANKA

COUNTRY: SRI LANKA

Background

Founder Bernard Botejue began his career as an employee of Sri Lanka's pioneering garments manufacturing company. He set up his own business as sole proprietor with a small amount of capital. There was strong involvement from family members in the running of business, but there was no formal structure in the organization. The business was initially established in 1948 mainly for the domestic market, and Bernards became a household name in woven/knitted garments, especially underwear. There were buyers in the capital city, Colombo, who had Indian business connections and they in turn exported the merchandise to India.

Structural developments

The company was incorporated as a limited liability company in 1967. In the 1970s, the export market was entered directly and the plant production was expanded. Bernards made a name for high quality materials and products. Initially only the company's own knitted materials were used for production but after the government's import liberalization policy of 1977, foreign materials started coming in.

There was greater exposure to modem technology in the years that followed. The company's investment in an expensive knitting plant culminated in failure. The plant was an attempt at backward linking of fabric and garments but it failed as the local market could not justify the scale of knitting plant. Moreover, only one type of knitted material could be made using the plant and this did not give sufficient flexibility to supply the different types of fabric required by the garments plant. Outsourcing by importing offered a high degree of variety in the fabric used.

Also in 1977, a sister company called Texafabric was formed to supply gloves to a single buyer in the United States. This was an outcome of a business relationship that developed when Bernard Boteju (senior) visited a trade exhibition organized by the Sri Lanka Export Development Board (EDB). Since then the New York-based buyer has been continuously placing orders for gloves with Texafabric.

Production system

The garments, the total production of which is exported, are made with the designs provided by the buyers. The company operates four production lines at their Colombo factory; each one is complete with separate cutting, sewing, inspection and packing sections. The degree of automation applied in the factory is at a comparatively low level, with manual intervention at all stages. Although a Lectra system is in use for pattern marking, the templates cut using this are employed for manual cutting only. Investment in automated cutting is not considered to be economically justified.

However, recruiting and retaining employees is a crucial problem that the company faces, particularly in Colombo. Decision to locate the new factory at Embilipitiya was partly because of this problem.

Market development

Initially in 1977, even though there was an export drive, only a few buyers came to Sri Lanka. After 1977, orders were allocated to Bernards under a quota system from Hong Kong. The buyer supplied all materials and only cutting and sewing was required to be done by Bernards. The company started taking part in exhibitions organized by the EDB for meeting business partners and developing business. Local buying offices were getting established.

The Bernards company received Board of Investment (BOI) status in 1992 under the provincial factory scheme, and now produces exclusively for the export market. This led to the formation of a sister company, Philknit, purely for supplying the local market. Philknit is at present managed by another of Mr Botejue's sons, and mainly supplies the government security forces, but under Bernards brand name.

The management structure of Bernards has now been properly defined and strengthened compared with the somewhat *ad hoc* structure followed by the family business in earlier days. As a dynamic member of the Sri Lanka Apparel Exporters association, Mr Botejue (junior) has achieved a lot in general at the government policy level and in international trading strategy. The company received ISO 9002 accreditation in 2001. The company recorded a turnover of 6 million USD in 2001.

Products are made to a buyer's design and none of Bernards proprietary designs from the early days are now manufactured. Fabric has to be obtained from vendors approved by the buyers. Among the leading US buyers from Bernards are May Department Stores, Charming Shoppers, Fabu, Perry Allis, Another Time, Gap and JBS. There are few European buyers at present other than German buyer, Quille; and from England, Readmans too place orders.

There has been a strategy to expand by relocating the major production facility in the country town of Embilipitiya. The new factory has around 700 employees. The Colombo factory has around 350 employees now that operations have been transferred to Embilipitiya. Mr Botejue intends to retain the Colombo factory as small-scale showcase for buyers and visitors who mainly come to Colombo for business deals. The relocation gave the company access to a new labour market avoiding the severe competition for labour in the Colombo area. The cost of land is low at Embilipitiya, but transport costs increased as the new location is away from the main export port. The acceptance of Bernards factory by the local community as a newcomer to the locality is growing day by day. Bernards have taken on a number of unemployed graduates at the Embilipitiya factory.

Human resources and productivity

With regard to the availability of labour, Bernards are relatively better off with the relocation away from Colombo area. The unskilled workers recruited are initially given two to three weeks of training. A further week of on-the-job training prepares the worker to work independently on the line. Employees in need receive personal attention from the employer, and mechanisms are in place for finding the needy, often going out of the way to offer help. In the Colombo factory, there is a well-run hostel under a warden, as most female employees come from outstations. Taking on unemployed graduates from the area and training on the job has brought many benefits to the company as well as the local community. Mr Janaka Boteju believes that good labour relations are the key to the productivity and loyalty of employees. There have been *ad hoc* salary rises under political pressure from the government, and incentive schemes have been discontinued by the company.

Bernards use the Lectra CAD system for marking; this cost them 50,000 USD initially and a further 25,000 USD to upgrade. Manual cutting is prohibitive as the technology is costly and there is no need for this technology when considering the level of precision needed in cutting the type of garment they manufacture. As an investment for quality and productivity in cutting, Mr Bernard understands very well the need for new technology but he is concerned about the payback. Bernards use IT and computers at a minimum level for word processing and e-mail.

Strategic considerations

It has been possible to evolve management strategy through experience rather than any formal training. Nevertheless, there is a need to develop an educational system to support the technology transfer process. Currently Bernards faces price-based competition from other local companies and China. There is a need for better productivity, but it is questionable whether this alone can solve the problem. There are low salaries in Vietnam and Madagascar. There are high costs of importing fabric to Sri Lanka from Taiwan, Hong Kong and Singapore. For Bernards the quota-based market is only 25 per cent and other market share is non-quota. As a result of the war in the north, the market there was reduced and this type of industry needs to develop technical and design expertise locally.

Mr Boteju's vision for the future is conditioned by several key concerns. Presently, there is a lack of knitting know-how and design expertise. The industry depends on costly accessories from China. There is a virtual technical/engineering vacuum. In general, the Sri Lankan apparel industry has already developed from basic tailoring to professional tailoring. Where to go next? Shouldn't we project Sri Lanka's product image as a group first rather than as individual producers?

Questions

1   How do the business conditions of Bernards compare with those of a similar company in a high-income country?
2   How has the company managed to adapt to various changes in the market and Sri Lankan society in times of war and peace?
3   The textile sector is of significant importance to small businesses in Asian countries. Will Bernards survive in the long run, and what would be required to do so?

25 My Anh Garment Manufacture and Export Co. Ltd.

Vo Van Huy

UNIVERSITY OF TECHNOLOGY, BUSINESS RESEARCH AND TRAINING CENTRE, HO CHI MINH CITY, VIETNAM

COUNTRY: VIETNAM

Background

In 1990, Ms Tu Thi Bich Loc and her husband opened a small garment workshop with only 15 sewing machines. When government approved the open economy policy, Ms Loc chose garment sector for her business because she knew that many labourers were unemployed but skilful in making clothes, and garment products were exported easily at that time. The workshop had to move to four different places during between 1990 and 1994. In 1994, Ms Loc and her husband decided to start a private company called My Anh.

Ms Tu Thi Bich Loc and the company

Until 1990, Ms Tu Bich Thi Loc worked on the staff of the state postal company. Ms Loc is now the managing director of My Anh and has sole responsibility for all customer contact and marketing. Her husband also works in the company and takes care of technical management. All problems regarding the company are shared within the family, and up to now it has been the biggest advantage of the company.

My Anh is now located in two places. The office and automatic embroidery workshop is located in Hanoi, but the factory is located in the adjoining Hatay province. Ms Loc is in the possession of a rather big area in Hatay with some old houses built during French colonial era in which all the workshops are located. In the factory, the company has three workshops for cutting, making up and packing. The company does not have a marketing department, all marketing activities being undertaken by Ms Loc.

Three years ago, the company was supported by a Danish non-governmental organization in the DANIDA programme. Thanks to that programme, My Anh had established many good relationships with Danish entrepreneurs and some of them are becoming major customers.

In 2004, the company earned approximately 6 billions Vietnamese Dong (VND), equal to 400,000 USD, and had a profit of 10 per cent. The company has to pay 28 per cent revenue tax annually. My Anh owns 130 sewing machines and some other valuable machines, one a patented cutting machine invented by Loc's husband. All sewing machines are made in Japan. Currently the company uses only 60 per cent of its machine capacity because of a labour shortage. The valuation of My Anh assets is about 6 billion VND, but the company has to borrow half of that money.

My Anh has many competitors that are state, joint-venture and private entrepreneurs in Vietnam. They compete by recruiting skilled employees and by getting export quotas from the government as well.

Products

All products of My Anh are manufactured to order. Currently, the company produces European flags for Danish companies and clothes for a South Korea exporting company. Last year, the company produced over 100,000 items of which 90 per cent were exported. For the flag products, the company bought materials such as colour fabrics, thread and hanging accessories from domestic suppliers and, based on the designs ordered, the employees cut, made up and packed the different kinds of flag. Because there are no quotas for the export flags, the company now concentrates on these products.

Another product that My Anh produces is clothes for a South Korean enterprise. This enterprise orders from My Anh to process clothes and then the company exports to European or US markets. Due to the difficulty in getting export quotas from the government, My Anh does not want to process clothes and export them directly to these markets. It has to buy export quotas for very high price from enterprises already in receipt of quotas for these markets. For clothes products, all materials are supplied by customers in order to maintain product quality.

Finished products are delivered to Hai Phong port or Noi Bai airport by transport companies. Ms Loc said that transport companies know a lot about custom formalities, so My Anh can save much money and time when getting deals with them. Ms Loc is proud of My Anh's quality of product: 'Many foreign companies have recognized our quality as the best among garment producers in Vietnam.'

Customers

My Anh has some big foreign customers and domestic ones. Two of the biggest and most regular customers are Danish companies who place orders with My Anh for every kind of European flag. They had the first order to My Anh after Ms Loc visited Denmark in a Danida (Danish International Development Agency) programme and every year they order 70,000 to 80,000 items. The biggest domestic customer is a company named No 40 which was managed by the military ministry in the past but now a joint-stock company. No 40 has many good links to governmental staff, so it easily gets export quotas for garment products. The No 40 company submits orders to My Anh to manufacture garment products as required by foreign customers. Now, the South Korean company for which My Anh is producing clothes is a customer of No 40.

Ms Loc ensures that her company is on good terms with all her old and current customers. She found that all customers have been satisfied with product quality and delivery time. Therefore, she hopes that with the expansion and upgrading of production infrastructure, the company will have more regular and big customers.

Staff

The administration department of My Anh is located in Hanoi and has three accountants and two who deal with exports. In the factory, 100 workers are divided between three workshops and managed by a foreman and a wages clerk. The average wage of workers is about 650,000 VND (approximately 42 USD) per month. The company always takes care of their staff. All staff are served with a cheap lunch or dinner prepared by hired cooks. Many rural workers are accommodated in the company campus with very low rental fee of 20,000 VND per month, including electricity and clean water. The company often informs its staff about social insurance and encourages them to join, but the final decision rests with the staff member. Ms Loc believes that the company can hire many skilled workers when the company completes its house and factory rebuilding programme.

Questions

1   How would you explain the success of My Anh as a small Vietnamese company?
2   What has been the business strategy of Ms Loc?
3   Vietnamese firms are considered relatively dynamic and well managed. Is this the case here and, if so, what could be the reason?

26 Sterisol AB

Per Lind

DEPARTMENT OF MANAGEMENT, LINKOPING UNIVERSITY, SWEDEN

COUNTRY: SWEDEN

Background

According to Mr Rylander, the Managing Director, Sterisol AB is in the business of producing and selling products for personal hygiene at workplaces and public institutions. That is their niche in the non-consumer market. The product range includes liquid soaps as well as a number of other cleansing products, disinfectants, lotions and creams.

Sterisol started in 1974 as a sales company under Barnaengen, a big Swedish soap manufacturer owned by the Nobel group (Kema Nobel at that time). The task was then to sell solid soaps. Initially, the venture was not very successful. The break came with the opportunity to produce liquid soap. At that time there were a lot of discussions about the risks of the preservatives thought necessary. Instead Sterisol set out to make a preservative free soap – unique at the time. Instead of killing the bacteria that got into the soap, the idea was that the bacteria should be kept out of the soap container all together. Sterisol started developing such a container, and the problem of preventing bacteria from getting in was finally solved in 1977. The solution was a bacteria-safe valve. This valve was attached to a self-deflating bag that served as the container. Until 1980 the soap was still produced by Barnaengen, but that year Sterisol bought a company in Vadstena and started production of its own.

When Sterisol started production in Vadstena in 1982, the local authorities were very positive and helpful. It supported the venture by helping to finance the plant and then letting it out for Sterisol to rent. In 1992 Barnaengen/Nobel group sold Sterisol to a German company. That arrangement did not work out very well. Soon after, Mr Rylander and a few others from the management group obtained finance through the Gepe group, following which, by means of a management buy-out, they took over as majority owner of Sterisol (management was part-owners). The Gepe group is in the position of being able to provide the capital needed for Sterisol's investments. Sterisol has an annual turnover of approximately 96 millions and it has about 55 employees. Of these 15 are involved in actual production and another 10 are employed in subsidiaries in Denmark and Finland.

Today, Sterisol has a market share of around 60–70 per cent of its main niche in Sweden (large industries with more than 500 employees): it is the market leader by far. It has a market share of about 35 per cent of the soap market as a whole. In Norway, for example Sterisol, has 80 per cent of all hospitals, and the total market share in Finland is 20 per cent. It considers the Nordic countries as its home and primary market. The rest of Europe is considered to be a secondary market, receiving less marketing input than the home market. Recently, Sterisol began cooperating with a sister company in the Gepe group concerned with export marketing. This means that new resources are going to be activated in the European market.

Sterisol regards the rest of the world as their third market. Their entry into the US, Middle East and Eastern European markets has met with varying degrees of success, and extra effort is going to be made in the latter two in the near future. Projects are also running in India and China.

Marketing and sales promotion is mainly based on personal calls from representatives. Ideally, Sterisol works with personal calls from sales representatives. In the other Nordic countries Sterisol is therefore aiming to establish sales companies. One limit to Sterisol's expansion, though, is the fact that soap will eventually become very expensive to transport. As with many liquids, the point where it would be more cost effective to produce locally is soon reached. Long-range plans are prepared for three years ahead, which offers a good chance of making correct budget estimates. Raw materials are bought from a number of suppliers; other than a demand for high quality there is no formalized cooperation with suppliers and customers. This has worked well since, after a struggle, Sterisol managed to persuade suppliers to make and supply bacteria-free materials.

Sterisol would like to see as many of the staff take part in as many different kind of tasks as possible, and for the staff to take as large a responsibility for the company as is possible. Hence responsibility is delegated throughout the organization. However, some of the tasks at the plant (such as pre-production, involving the setting of the machines) require specialized skills and it is not easy to devise a satisfactory system for job rotation; not so in the packaging department, where job rotation has been successfully implemented. There is some job rotation in production but not to any great extent.

As far as administration and sales go, Sterisol tries to have all the functions covered by at least two persons. This is to limit the effects of absenteeism. Sterisol also manages the organization by a policy 'handbook' (now IT-based). In this handbook the organization is described, along with its goals, strategies and policies.

In management three line functions or departments can be discerned: marketing, research and development and production. These are supported by an economics department and by a department working with quality assurance and to develop new products. In marketing and sales there is one department for Sweden and one for the export market. There is also a support department that provides information about market shifts and other things of general interest. The Production function also reaches down all the way to production, where it cooperates directly with maintenance and storage.

There are some alliances with external – especially medical – experts, for example in the fields of toxicology, bacteriology and dermatology. Otherwise, the company has no regular need for external consultants, apart from auditors to review the accounts.

Sterisol has a Triple A credit rating. The owner's equity is constantly growing; from its original 4 million in 1992; passed 30 million in 2006. Sterisol has a goal for Return of Investment (ROI) of 25 per cent. The annual budget is made every autumn. The budget work is delegated to the heads of the various departments, who then have the responsibility to keep this budget in their respective profit centres. Long-term goals (based on the long-range planning) are set by the management team and distributed with the budget instructions to those responsible at the profit centres. Budget and consequential estimates are reviewed and analysed twice a year. All deviations from the budget are traced and explanations sought. Sterisol works with the Balanced Scorecard technique, with one overall card and individual cards for each function and department.

Sterisol has finished expanding its physical production facilities by extending the building. This allows an increase in production volumes and had become necessary after a few years with under-utilization of production capacity. This investment was financed with help from the owner so that external finance was not needed. The expansion also enabled out-going goods to be kept separate from incoming goods. Previously the two had to meet in one space, which caused some inconvenience.

Annual staff turnover is on average zero. According to Mr Rylander, this could perhaps be too low. He would like now and then to have the opportunity of getting in new and younger ideas. Not the least in marketing and sales, in order to match the demography of the purchasers of Sterisol's products. However, he sees the low turnover as a sign that the company is well run and that the staff are satisfied. There is also a low rate of absenteeism due to illness and related reasons. However, there have been cases of long-term sick leave caused by monotonous work, something that Mr Rylander hopes will disappear once job-rotation is extended.

Support is expressed for getting the staff to take initiatives. As at many workplaces in Sweden, there is a system for rewarding employees' new ideas. Mr Rylander stresses the fact that everybody's ideas are worth considering, since everybody has a unique perspective on things. Mr Rylander also tries to keep salaries competitive for everybody. Mr Rylander sees this as important, since one should bear in mind that no chain is stronger than its weakest link. Hence, everybody should be recognized for her or his contribution to the company.

At Sterisol there are active efforts to make the employees feel part of the company and to get a sense of camaraderie. The personnel strategy is to have as few but as competent employees as possible. All staff should be able to recognize his or here place in the context of the whole production. Further, everybody should have feeling of purposefulness in the task he or she is performing. The relation between managers, supervisors and subordinates are open and built on mutual trust. Further education is supported, whether it is directly connected to the work task or not. Broadening one's span of competence is, in Mr Rylander's view, always to be supported.

Responsibility for everyday decisions is meant to be delegated as far as possible – as long as decisions are made in line with company policy. Economic responsibility is also delegated and deviations from budget and estimates are allowed in so far they are well motivated. There are, though, some differences among middle management in respect of how much they actually delegate. However, delegation of responsibility is constantly promoted by the Managing Director. At Sterisol there is an almost religious relation to the products, to the extent that employees react adversely and strongly in cases where hygiene standards are not respected by everybody. Cleaning the entire production area every morning for an hour and a half guarantees that hygiene standards are maintained.

Production is somewhat restricted by regulation of the amount of toxic waste allowed. Otherwise Mr Rylander has not experienced any difficulties in his contacts with the authorities, even though he wishes for a little more flexibility on occasions. Sterisol has been granted both quality (ISO 9001) and environment (ISO 14001) certificates for their production.

Questions

1 Employment turnover is almost zero, which is too low according to Mr Rylander. What lies behind this view and how much turnover should be optimal?
2 How can the leadership style of Mr Rylander be characterized?
3 A small firm developing a new type of product can be a risky adventure. How did Sterisol cope with this?

Index